Force and Statecraft

FORCE AND STATECRAFT

Diplomatic Problems of Our Time

THIRD EDITION

Gordon A. Craig
Alexander L. George

New York   Oxford
Oxford University Press
1995

Oxford University Press

Oxford   New York
Athens   Auckland   Bangkok   Bombay
Calcutta   Cape Town   Dar es Salaam   Delhi
Florence   Hong Kong   Istanbul   Karachi
Kuala Lumpur   Madras   Madrid   Melbourne
Mexico City   Nairobi   Paris   Singapore
Taipei   Tokyo   Toronto

and associated companies in
Berlin   Ibadan

Copyright © 1983, 1990, 1995 by Oxford University Press, Inc.

Published by Oxford University Press, Inc.
198 Madison Avenue, New York, New York 10016

Oxford is a registered trademark of Oxford University Press

Library of Congress Cataloging-in-Publication Data
Craig, Gordon Alexander, 1913–
Force and statecraft : diplomatic problems of our time /
Gordon A. Craig, Alexander L. George.—3rd ed.
p.   cm.   Includes bibliographical references and index.
ISBN 0–19–509243–0. —ISBN 0–19–509244–9 (pbk.)
1. World politics—20th century.   2. World politics—19th century.
3. World politics—To 1900.   4. International relations.
5. Diplomacy.   I. George, Alexander L.   II. Title.
D443.C73   1995   327'.09'04—dc20   95–3946

1 3 5 7 9 8 6 4 2

Printed in the United States of America
on acid-free paper

Preface to the Third Edition

In this new edition we have endeavored to do justice to the great changes that have taken place in the structure of international relations since 1989 when the second edition was completed. Although the basic organization of the book remains the same, there are extensive changes in its contents. In Part I, additions have been made in chapters 8 and 9, chapter 10 has been expanded into a discussion of the whole period from the inception of détente to the dissolution of the Soviet empire, the unification of Germany, and the breakdown of the Soviet Union, and chapter 11 has been remodeled to discuss the Gulf War and the crises in its wake that have discouraged hopes for a speedy elaboration of a new international order.

In Part II, new chapters have been added on "Knowledge for Statecraft: Lessons of History" and "The Role of Force in Diplomacy: A Continuing Dilemma for U.S. Foreign Policy," and new case studies have replaced older ones in chapter 15 on "Coercive Diplomacy." With great reluctance, the authors have decided, because of considerations of space, to eliminate the former chapter on U.S.–Soviet security cooperation and, in Part III, the former chapter called "The Christian Statesman: Bismarck and Gladstone." The chapter on ethical and moral restraints, somewhat expanded, has been moved to Part II, where it now stands as a companion piece to the new chapter on the role of force in diplomacy.

In place of the original Part III, the authors have written an epilogue, reflecting upon the diplomatic revolution that has taken place since the end of the First World War and upon new developments in the state system since the end of the Cold War.

We would like to thank Paul Gordon Lauren and Bert Patenaude for helpful suggestions for this version. Alexander George also expresses appreciation to the Carnegie Corporation of New York for funds to support research for the book and related projects.

Stanford, Calif.   G.A.C.
December 1994   A.L.G.

Contents

Introduction

Since the emergence of war as a feature of relations between communities, reflective and concerned persons have had apocalyptic visions of its potentiality for destruction and have searched for ways to prevent conflict. In general, they have placed their hopes on five different means: on religious and moral codes forbidding resort to war; on agreements to restrict or abolish the use of certain kinds of weapons; on agreements to limit military operations or to regulate the usages of war; on doctrines designed to make war more efficient, to match the level of violence to the political objective and thus to avoid unnecessary destruction; and, finally, on political systems designed to reduce the friction between groups or nations to the point where wars would be unprofitable or dangerous to the aggressor.

With the first four of these experiments, only modest success has been achieved. Religion has not only failed to discourage war but has often motivated it; attempts at arms control and disarmament have had minor successes that all too often, once achieved, encouraged evasion; the rules of war that alleviated the brutalities of eighteenth-century conflict are clearly ineffective in an age of nuclear weaponry; and recent experience hardly encourages one to believe in the capacity of modern governments to employ war strictly as an instrument of policy, restraining its inherent expansive tendencies. In the history of the West from the Middle Ages to the present, the most effective restraint upon the warlike tendencies of the individual, group, or state has been the pressure exerted by external forces, and the periods least affected by interstate violence have been those in which there existed a viable international community and an accepted body of law and custom to guide and control it.

Such periods were, to be sure, at least before the nineteenth century, brief and far between; the age of the Italian city states before the papacy of Alexander VI and the period sometimes called the age of Walpole in the first half of the eighteenth century are lonely exceptions in a long history of disorder and armed tumult. But after the twenty-five years of warfare caused by the French Revolution and the ambitions of Napoleon Bonaparte, the Congress of Vienna in 1814–1815 created an international system that secured the peace for two generations and then, as modified by Bismarck, for most of the rest of the century. That example has served, if not as a model, at least as an admonition to later statesmen. After World War I, Woodrow Wilson attempted to establish a new system of collective security to replace the one that had finally collapsed so disastrously in 1914, and during World War II Franklin D. Roosevelt tried to set the stage for a postwar system that would extend into peacetime the cooperative working relations that characterized the wartime alliance of the United States with the Soviet Union and Great Britain. In the late 1960s and early 1970s, Richard Nixon and Henry Kissinger attempted to develop a relationship with the Soviet Union that would serve as the foundation for an international system that would overcome the strains of the Cold War; although their success was brief, the end of the 1980s saw a renewal of this effort, the initiative being taken this time by Mikhail S. Gorbachev.

Both the fact that it took until the nineteenth century for the European states to create an effective concert of powers and the failure of recent attempts to achieve the relative success of that earlier experiment can be explained by the requirements of a viable international system. These are threefold: (1) an agreement among the principal states concerning aims and objectives that reflects the dominant values that they are seeking to preserve and enhance in creating and participating in the system; (2) a structure appropriate to the number of states interacting with each other, the geographical boundaries or scope of the system, the distribution of power among member states, and the stratification and status hierarchy among them; and (3) commonly accepted procedures—that is, norms, rules, practices, and institutions for the achievement of the aims and objectives of the system. During the long stretch of time that intervened between the breakdown of the authority of the Holy Roman Empire and the religious wars that followed the Reformation, centuries in which Europe was composed of a welter of political units of indeterminate sovereignty and ill-defined borders, not even the most gifted political leaders could be expected to conceive of, let alone develop, anything so ambitious. As will become apparent, it was only in the seventeenth century, when modern states came into existence that possessed efficient institutions, strong armed forces, and a rational theory of statecraft, that any progress toward effective collaboration became possible, and even then it took a century of intermittent conflict and the threat of domination by a single power before the major European states were able to achieve an agreement with respect to basic objectives and the structural and methodological requirements of a viable system.

The eventual collapse of the nineteenth-century experiment and the twentieth-

century failure to find a substitute for it can be explained by another characteristic of an effective international system, namely, that it must be able to adapt
to environmental developments and to internal changes within its member states
that affect its performance and its ability to maintain itself. The modern period
has been one of profound and continuing changes in socioeconomic organization, military technology, transportation, and communication, to say nothing of
those mutations in the internal political structure of states that have resulted
from the rise of public opinion, the emergence of a large variety of organized
interest groups, and the increasing scope and complexity of governmental organization. It has also been an age of intense nationalism, which has been reflected in the breakup of the old colonial empires and the multiplication of new
sovereign states, and of ideological conflict on a global scale. All of these forces,
singly and in combination, have had an impact upon international politics that
amounts to a diplomatic revolution; and this has made it increasingly difficult
to maintain old structures or to devise new ones. Adaptation to accelerated
change has become the major problem of modern statecraft, testing the ingenuity
and the fortitude of those charged with responsibility both for devising means
of controlling international violence and for maintaining the security of their
own countries.

The first part of this book deals with the emergence of the modern states,
the conflict in the eighteenth century between their desire for order and their
anarchic tendencies, the laborious and painful birth of the nineteenth-century
system, its procedures, and the various changes in its structure before its collapse
in 1914. But its more particular theme is the impact of the diplomatic revolution
just alluded to, and the ways in which this crippled the system-building experiments of Woodrow Wilson, Franklin D. Roosevelt, and their successors.

Because statesmen have not succeeded in inventing the perfect international
system, interstate violence remains a major factor in contemporary world politics, and the period since 1945 has seen three major conflicts in the Far East,
four short but destructive wars in the Middle East between Israel and the Arab
states and another between Iran and Iraq, numerous civil and interstate conflicts
in Latin America, a war in the South Atlantic between Great Britain and Argentina, a protracted struggle in Afghanistan, touched off by the Soviet invasion
of that country in 1979, an irregular war on the frontier between the Union of
South Africa and Angola, in which Cuban troops played a significant role, a
muddled conflict in the western Sahara between Morocco and Algerian-backed
guerrillas, and a short but highly destructive conflict in the Persian Gulf between
Iraq and a United Nations Coalition led by the United States. Nor is this list
exhaustive.

This book will not attempt to deal with the causes or the operational and
strategical aspects of these confrontations or of military conflict in general. Nevertheless, international violence is never remote from the heart of its concern,

and Part II focuses upon the uses of force as an instrument of statecraft. One of the marked characteristics of our time is the frequency with which states employ threats of force to deter or to halt encroachments on their interests, a practice that, in the pages that follow, will require some analysis of the techniques of deterrence and coercive diplomacy.

Again, competition and rivalry between states, abetted sometimes by misperceptions and miscalculations, often plunges them into tense diplomatic confrontations and brings them to the brink of war; and the problem of protecting their essential interests in such situations, without warfare and without escalation of low-level military conflict, poses a difficult dilemma for policy makers. In the age of thermonuclear weapons, the successful management of crises is more critical than ever, and an appropriate theme for special attention, the more so because crises not only pose threats but often offer opportunities for constructive change in interstate relations. Indeed, the potentially constructive role of crises in international relations has led some observers to argue that in the present age crises have become a substitute for war. If so, it is hardly necessary to enjoin policy makers to take seriously the requirements and modalities of crisis management, but it is certainly permissible in a book like this to try to analyze them in such a way as to make it possible to distinguish between effective and faulty procedure.

Finally, because, as we have discovered to our cost, nations do get into wars, it is necessary to consider the best ways of getting out of them. Terminating a conflict by means short of surrender is often much more difficult than starting one, and because the process has received so little analytical attention, it seemed advisable to include here an examination of the forces that prolong wars and of the conditions and processes that seem, on the basis of experience, best designed to lead to cease-fires and peace agreements.

Tensions that arise in interstate relations do not, fortunately, always lead to war. A dangerous crisis may have a sobering effect on both sides and create a mutual desire to relax tensions, and this may be followed by diplomatic efforts to reach a mutually acceptable accommodation or a resolution of conflicting interests. One side may recognize the legitimacy of some of its adversary's grievances and seek to appease it; as the two sides resolve their salient disagreements, they may also recognize interests that they have in common and work out the basis for a cooperative relationship. The reorientation of the relationship from one of initial hostility to cooperation is generally, in our day, called détente, although, as we shall see, it is an imprecise and ambiguous term. For that very reason, however, and because the process has become a point of contention between the United States and its European allies, it requires analysis.

Fundamental to all of these diplomatic procedures—to deterrence and coercive diplomacy, to crisis management and war termination, and to détente—is negotiation, as vital to the relations of contemporary great powers, and as worthy a subject for study and reflection, as it was in the days of Machiavelli and Wicquefort and Callières. Because of its central importance, it is the first of the topics considered in the second part of the book.

Finally, at a time when increasing numbers of citizens have religious or conscientious doubts about the tendencies, the methods, and the dangers of contemporary international relations, it seemed appropriate to include in Part II a chapter on the difficult problem of the role of ethics and morality in world politics.

This book grew out of the authors' long-standing concern over the challenging tasks confronting American foreign policy and their conviction that it would be worthwhile to examine the kinds of problems of force and statecraft that confront policy makers from the combined perspectives of the diplomatic historian and the specialist in strategy. Accordingly, we developed a course with these objectives in mind and taught it together several times at Stanford University. In our course, as in this book, we selected for controlled comparison a wide variety of case studies drawn from the diplomatic history of the nineteenth and twentieth centuries in order to throw some light upon contemporary problems of foreign policy. It was our intention there—and this was the reason for employing the comparative method—to make some tentative generalizations about the diplomatic procedures and techniques that we discussed with our students. In the pages that follow, and particularly in Part II, we have carried our classroom conclusions a bit further and have had the temerity to formulate theories about the requirements of successful employment of the instruments and techniques under discussion, as well as about their appropriate uses and limitations.

It need hardly be added that these formulations are in the nature of working hypotheses that are subject to modification and elaboration. Still, we do not apologize for offering them to our readers. This is a time for serious reflection upon foreign affairs and, if these pages help to provoke it, we shall be satisfied even if our views suffer serious correction.

DISCIPULIS NOSTRIS
QUORUM INDULGENTIA ET SEDULITAS
AUCTORIBUS EXEMPLO
FUERUNT

I

The International System
from the Seventeenth Century
to the Present

1

The Emergence of the Great Powers

I

Although the term *great power* was used in a treaty for the first time only in 1815, it had been part of the general political vocabulary since the middle of the eighteenth century and was generally understood to mean Great Britain, France, Austria, Prussia, and Russia. This would not have been true in the year 1600, when the term itself would have meant nothing and a ranking of the European states in terms of political weight and influence would not have included three of the countries just mentioned. In 1600, Russia, for instance, was a remote and ineffectual land, separated from Europe by the large territory that was called Poland-Lithuania with whose rulers it waged periodic territorial conflicts, as it did with the Ottoman Turks to the south; Prussia did not exist in its later sense but, as the Electorate of Brandenburg, lived a purely German existence, like Bavaria or Württemberg, with no European significance; and Great Britain, a country of some commercial importance, was not accorded primary political inportance, although it had, in 1588, demonstrated its will and its capacity for self-defense in repelling the Spanish Armada. In 1600, it is fair to say that, politically, the strongest center in Europe was the old Holy Roman Empire, with its capital in Vienna and its alliances with Spain (one of the most formidable military powers in Europe) and the Catholic states of southern Germany—an empire inspired by a militant Catholicism that dreamed of restoring Charles V's claims of universal dominion. In comparison with Austria and Spain, France seemed destined to play a minor role in European politics, because of the state of internal anarchy and religious strife that followed the murder of Henri IV in 1610.

Why did this situation not persist? Or, to put it another way, why was the European system transformed so radically that the empire became an insignificant political force and the continent came in the eighteenth century to be dominated by Great Britain, France, Austria, Prussia, and Russia? The answer, of course, is war, or, rather more precisely, wars—a long series of religious and dynastic conflicts which raged intermittently from 1618 until 1721 and changed the rank order of European states by exhausting some and exalting others. As if bent upon supplying materials for the nineteenth-century Darwinians, the states mentioned above proved themselves in the grinding struggle of the seventeenth century to be the fittest, the ones best organized to meet the demands of protracted international competition.

The process of transformation began with the Thirty Years War, which stretched from 1618 to 1648. It is sometimes called the last of the religious wars, a description that is justified by the fact that it was motivated originally by the desire of the House of Habsburg and its Jesuit advisers to restore the Protestant parts of the empire to the true faith and because, in thirty years of fighting, the religious motive gave way to political considerations and, in the spreading of the conflict from its German center to embrace all of Europe, some governments—notably France—waged war against their coreligionists for material reasons. For the states that initiated this wasting conflict, which before it was over had reduced the population of central Europe by at least a third, the war was an unmitigated disaster. The House of Habsburg was so debilitated by it that it lost the control it had formerly possessed over the German states, which meant that they became sovereign in their own right and that the empire now became a mere adjunct of the Austrian crown lands. Austria was, moreover, so weakened by the exertions and losses of that war that in the period after 1648 it had the greatest difficulty in protecting its eastern possessions from the depredations of the Turks and in 1683 was threatened with capture of Vienna by a Turkish army. Until this threat was contained, Austria ceased to be a potent factor in European affairs. At the same time, its strongest ally, Spain, had thrown away an infantry once judged to be the best in Europe in battles like that at Nördlingen in 1634, one of those victories that bleed a nation white. Spain's decline began not with the failure of the Armada, but with the terrible losses suffered in Germany and the Netherlands during the Thirty Years War.

In contrast, the states that profited from the war were the Netherlands, which completed the winning of its independence from Spain in the course of the war and became a commercial and financial center of major importance; the kingdom of Sweden, which under the leadership of Gustavus Adolphus, the Lion of the North, plunged into the conflict in 1630 and emerged as the strongest power in the Baltic region; and France, which entered the war formally in 1635 and came out of it as the most powerful state in western Europe.

It is perhaps no accident that these particular states were so successful, for they were excellent examples of the process that historians have described as the emergence of the modern state, the three principal characteristics of which were effective armed forces, an able bureaucracy, and a theory of state that restrained dynastic exuberance and defined political interest in practical terms. The seventeenth century saw the emergence of what came to be called *raison d'état* or *ragione di stato*—the idea that the state was more than its ruler and more than the expression of his wishes; that it transcended crown and land, prince and people; that it had its particular set of interests and a particular set of necessities based upon them; and that the art of government lay in recognizing those interests and necessities and acting in accordance with them, even if this might violate ordinary religious or ethical standards. The effective state must have the kinds of servants who would interpret *raison d'état* wisely and the kinds of material and physical resources necessary to implement it. In the first part of the seventeenth century, the Dutch, under leaders like Maurice of Nassau and Jan de Witt, the Swedes, under Gustavus Adolphus and Oxenstierna, and the French, under the inspired ministry of Richelieu, developed the administration and the forces and theoretical skills that exemplify this ideal of modern statehood. That they survived the rigors of the Thirty Years War was not an accident, but rather the result of the fact that they never lost sight of their objectives and never sought objectives that were in excess of their capabilities. Gustavus Adolphus doubtless brought his country into the Thirty Years War to save the cause of Protestantism when it was at a low ebb, but he never for a moment forgot the imperatives of national interest that impelled him to see the war also as a means of winning Swedish supremacy along the shore of the Baltic Sea. Cardinal Richelieu has been called the greatest public servant France ever had, but that title, as Sir George Clark has drily remarked, "was not achieved without many acts little fitting the character of a churchman." It was his clear recognition of France's needs and his absolute unconditionality in pursuing them that made him the most respected statesman of his age.

The Thirty Years War, then, brought a sensible change in the balance of forces in Europe, gravely weakening Austria, starting the irreversible decline of Spain, and bringing to the fore the most modern, best organized, and, if you will, most rationally motivated states: the Netherlands, Sweden, and France. This, however, was a somewhat misleading result, and the Netherlands was soon to yield its commercial and naval primacy to Great Britain (which had been paralyzed by civil conflict during the Thirty Years War), while Sweden, under a less rational ruler, was to throw its great gains away.

The gains made by France were more substantial, so much so that in the second half of the century, in the heyday of Louis XIV, they became oppressive. For that ruler was intoxicated by the power that Richelieu and his successor Mazarin had brought to France, and he wished to enhance it. As he wrote in his memoirs:

> The love of glory assuredly takes precedence over all other [passions] in my
> soul. . . . The hot blood of my youth and the violent desire I had to heighten
> my reputation instilled in me a strong passion for action. . . . *La Gloire,* when
> all is said and done, is not a mistress that one can ever neglect; nor can one
> be ever worthy of her slightest favors if one does not constantly long for fresh
> ones.

No one can say that Louis XIV was a man of small ambition. He dreamed
in universal terms and sought to realize those dreams by a combination of diplomatic and military means. He maintained alliances with the Swedes in the
north and the Turks in the south and thus prevented Russian interference while
he placed his own candidate, Jan Sobieski, on the throne of Poland. His Turkish
connection he used also to harry the eastern frontiers of Austria, and if he did
not incite Kara Mustafa's expedition against Vienna in 1683, he knew of it.
Austria's distractions enabled him to dabble freely in German politics. Bavaria
and the Palatinate were bound to the French court by marriage, and almost all
of the other German princes accepted subsidies at one time or another from
France. It did not seem unlikely on one occasion that Louis would put himself
or his son forward as candidate for Holy Roman emperor. The same method of
infiltration was practiced in Italy, Portugal, and Spain, where the young king
married a French princess and French ambassadors exerted so much influence
in internal affairs that they succeeded in discrediting the strongest antagonist to
French influence, Archduke Charles of Austria. In addition to all of this, Louis
sought to undermine the independence of the Netherlands and gave the English
king Charles II a pension in order to reduce the possibility of British interference
as he did so.

French influence was so great in Europe in the second half of the seventeenth
century that it threatened the independent development of other nations. This
was particularly true, the German historian Leopold von Ranke was to write in
the nineteenth century, because it

> was supported by a preeminence in literature. Italian literature had already run
> its course, English literature had not yet risen to general significance, and
> German literature did not exist at that time. French literature, light, brilliant
> and animated, in strictly regulated but charming form, intelligible to everyone
> and yet of individual, national character was beginning to dominate Europe.
> . . . [It] completely corresponded to the state and helped the latter to attain its
> supremacy. Paris was the capital of Europe. She wielded a dominion as did
> no other city, over language, over custom, and particularly over the world of
> fashion and the ruling classes. Here was the center of the community of Eu-
> rope.

The effect upon the cultural independence of other parts of Europe—and one
cannot separate cultural independence from political will—was devastating. In
Germany, the dependence upon French example was almost abject, and the

writer Moscherosch commented bitterly about "our little Germans who trot to the French and have no heart of their own, no speech of their own; but French opinion is their opinion, French speech, food, drink, morals and deportment their speech, food, drink, morals and deportment whether they are good or bad."

But this kind of dominance was bound to invite resistance on the part of others, and out of that resistance combinations and alliances were bound to take place. And this indeed happened. In Ranke's words, "The concept of the European balance of power was developed in order that the union of many other states might resist the pretensions of the 'exorbitant' court, as it was called." This is a statement worth noting. The principle of the balance of power had been practiced in Machiavelli's time in the intermittent warfare between the city states of the Italian peninsula. Now it was being deliberately invoked as an instrument of European statecraft, as a safeguard against universal domination. We shall have occasion to note the evolution and elaboration of this term in the eighteenth century and in the nineteenth, when it became one of the basic principles of the European system.

Opposition to France's universal pretensions centered first upon the Dutch, who were threatened most directly in a territorial sense by the French, and their gifted ruler, William III. But the Dutch needed strong allies if their opposition was to be successful, and they did not get them until the English had severed the connection that had existed between England and France under the later Stuarts and until Austria had modernized its administration and armed forces, contained the threat from the east, and regained the ability to play a role in the politics of central and western Europe. The Glorious Revolution of 1688 and the assumption of the English throne by the Dutch king moved England solidly into the anti-French camp. The repulse of the Turks at the gates of Vienna in 1683 marked the turning point in Austrian fortunes, and the brilliant campaigns of Eugene of Savoy in the subsequent period, which culminated in the smashing victory over the Turks at Zenta and the suppression of the Rakoczi revolt in Hungary, freed Austrian energies for collaboration in the containment of France. The last years of Louis XIV, therefore, were the years of the brilliant partnership of Henry Churchill, Duke of Marlborough, and Eugene of Savoy, a team that defeated a supposedly invulnerable French army at Blenheim in 1704, Ramillies in 1706, Oudenarde in 1708, and the bloody confrontation at Malplaquet in 1709.

These battles laid the basis for the treaties of Utrecht in 1713 and Rastatt in 1714, by which France was forced to recognize the results of the revolution in England, renounce the idea of a union of the French and Spanish thrones, surrender the Spanish Netherlands to Austria, raze the fortifications at Dunkirk, and hand important territories in America over to Great Britain. The broader significance of the settlement was that it restored an equilibrium of forces to western Europe and marked the return of Austria and the emergence of Britain as its supports. Indeed, Utrecht was the first European treaty that specifically mentioned the balance of power. In the letters patent that accompanied Article VI of the treaty between Queen Anne and King Louis XIV, the French ruler noted that the Spanish renunciation of all rights to the throne of France was actuated by the hope of "obtaining a general Peace and securing the Tranquillity of *Europe* by a Ballance of Power," and the king of Spain acknowledged the importance of "the Maxim of securing for ever the universal Good and Quiet of Europe, by an equal Weight of Power, so that many being united in one, the Ballance of the Equality desired might not turn to the Advantage of one, and the Danger and Hazard of the rest."

Meanwhile, in northern Europe, France's ally Sweden was forced to yield its primacy to the rising powers of Russia and Prussia. This was due in part to the drain on Swedish resources caused by its participation in France's wars against the Dutch; but essentially the decline was caused, in the first instance, by the fact that Sweden had too many rivals for the position of supremacy in the Baltic area and, in the second, by the lack of perspective and restraint that characterized the policy of Gustavus Adolphus's most gifted successor, Charles XII. Sweden's most formidable rivals were Denmark, Poland, which in 1699 acquired an ambitious and unscrupulous new king in the person of Augustus the Strong of Saxony, and Russia, ruled since 1683 by a young and vigorous leader who was to gain the name Peter the Great. In 1700, Peter and Augustus made a pact to attack and despoil Sweden and persuaded Frederick of Denmark to join them in this enterprise. The Danes and the Saxons immediately invaded Sweden and to their considerable dismay were routed and driven from the country by armies led by the eighteen-year-old ruler, Charles XII. The Danes capitulated at once, and Charles without pause threw his army across the Baltic, fell upon Russian forces that were advancing on Narva, and, although his own forces were outnumbered five to one, dispersed, captured, or killed an army of forty thousand Russians. But brilliant victories are often the foundation of greater defeats. Charles now resolved to punish Augustus and plunged into the morass of Polish politics. It was his undoing. While he strove to control an intractable situation, an undertaking that occupied him for seven years, Peter was carrying through the reforms that were to bring Russia from its oriental past into the modern world. When his army was reorganized, he began a systematic conquest of the Swedish Baltic possessions. Charles responded, not with an attempt to retake those areas, but with an invasion of Russia—and this, like other later invasions, was defeated by winter and famine and ultimately by a lost battle, that of Pultawa in 1709, which broke the power of Sweden and marked the emergence of Russia as its successor.

Sweden had another rival which was also gathering its forces in these years. This was Prussia. At the beginning of the seventeenth century, it had, as the Electorate of Brandenburg, been a mere collection of territories, mostly centered upon Berlin, but with bits and pieces on the Rhine and in East Prussia, and was rich in neither population nor resources. Its rulers, the Hohenzollerns, found it difficult to administer these lands or, in time of trouble, defend them; and during the Thirty Years War, Brandenburg was overrun with foreign armies and its population and substance depleted by famine and pestilence. Things did not begin to change until 1640, when Frederick William, the so-called Great Elector, assumed the throne. An uncompromising realist, he saw that if he was to have security in a dangerous world, he would have to create what he considered to be the sinews of independence: a centralized state with an efficient bureaucracy and a strong army. The last was the key to the whole. As he wrote in his political testament, "A ruler is treated with no consideration if he does not have troops of his own. It is these, thank God! that have made me *considerabel* since the time I began to have them," and in the course of his reign, after purging his force of unruly and incompetent elements, he rapidly built up a force of thirty thousand men that was so efficient that in 1675, during the Franco-Swedish war against the Dutch, it came to the aid of the Dutch by defeating the Swedes at Fehrbellin and subsequently driving them out of Pomerania. It was to administer this army that Frederick William laid the foundations of the soon famous Prussian bureaucracy; it was to support it that he encouraged the growth of a native textile industry; it was with its aid that he smashed the recalcitrant provincial diets and centralized the state. And finally it was this army that, by its participation after the Great Elector's death in the wars against Louis XIV and its steadiness under fire at Ramillies and Malplaquet, induced the European powers to recognize his successor Frederick I as king of Prussia.

Under Frederick, an extravagant and thoughtless man, the new kingdom threatened to outrun its resources. But the ruler who assumed the throne in 1715, Frederick William I, resumed the work begun by the Great Elector, restored Prussia's financial stability, and completed the centralization and modernization of the state apparatus by elaborating a body of law and statute that clarified rights and responsibilities for all subjects. He nationalized the officer corps of the army, improved its dress and weapons, wrote its first handbook of field regulations, prescribing manual exercises and tactical evolutions, and rapidly increased its size. When Frederick William took the throne after the lax rule of his predecessor, there were rumors of an impending coup by his neighbors, like that attempted against Sweden in 1700. That kind of talk soon died away as the king's work proceeded, and it is easy to see why. In the course of his reign, he increased the size of his military establishment to eighty-three thousand men, a figure that made Prussia's army the fourth largest in Europe, although the state ranked only tenth from the stand-point of territory and thirteenth in population.

Before the eighteenth century was far advanced, then, the threat of French universal dominance had been defeated, a balance of power existed in western Europe, and two new powers had emerged as partners of the older established ones. It was generally recognized that in terms of power and influence, the leading states in Europe were Britain, France, Austria, Russia, and probably Prussia. The doubts on the last score were soon to be removed; and these five powers were to be the ones that dominated European and world politics until 1914.

II

Something should be said at this point about diplomacy, for it was in the seventeenth and eighteenth centuries that it assumed its modern form. The use of envoys and emissaries to convey messages from one ruler to another probably goes back to the beginning of history; there are heralds in the *Iliad* and, in the second letter to the Church of Corinth, the Apostle Paul describes himself as an ambassador. But modern diplomacy as we know it had its origins in the Italian city states of the Renaissance period, and particularly in the republic of Venice and the states of Milan and Tuscany. In the fourteenth and fifteenth centuries, Venice was a great commercial power whose prosperity depended upon shrewd calculation of risks, accurate reports upon conditions in foreign markets, and effective negotiation. Because it did so, Venice developed the first systemized diplomatic service known to history, a network of agents who pursued the interests of the republic with fidelity, with a realistic appraisal of risks, with freedom from sentimentality and illusion.

From Venice the new practice of systematic diplomacy was passed on to the states of central Italy which, because they were situated in a political arena that was characterized by incessant rivalry and coalition warfare, were always vulnerable to external threats and consequently put an even greater premium than the Venetians upon accurate information and skillful negotiation. The mainland cities soon considered diplomacy so useful that they began to establish permanent embassies abroad, a practice instituted by Milan and Mantua in the fifteenth century, while their political thinkers (like the Florentine Machiavelli) reflected upon the principles best calculated to make diplomacy effective and tried to codify rules of procedure and diplomatic immunity. This last development facilitated the transmission of the shared experience of the Italian cities to the rising nation-states of the west that soon dwarfed Florence and Venice in magnitude and strength. Thus, when the great powers emerged in the seventeenth century, they already possessed a highly developed system of diplomacy based upon long experience. The employment of occasional missions to foreign courts had given way to the practice of maintaining permanent missions. While the ambassadors abroad represented their princes and communicated with them directly, their reports were studied in, and they received their instructions from, permanent, organized bureaus which were the first foreign offices. France led the way in this and was followed by most other states, and the establishment of a Foreign Ministry on the French model was one of Peter the Great's important reforms. The emergence of a single individual who was charged with the co-ordination of all foreign business and who represented his sovereign in the conduct of foreign affairs came a bit later, but by the beginning of the eighteenth century, the major powers all had such officials, who came to be known as foreign ministers or secretaries of state for foreign affairs.

From earliest times, an aura of intrigue, conspiracy, and disingenuousness surrounded the person of the diplomat, and we have all heard the famous quip of Sir Henry Wotton, ambassador of James I to the court of Venice, who said that an ambassador was "an honest man sent to lie abroad for the good of his country." Moralists were always worried by this unsavory reputation, which they feared was deserved, and they sought to reform it by exhortation. In the fifteenth century, Bernard du Rosier, provost and later archbishop of Toulouse, wrote a treatise in which he argued that the business of an ambassador is peace, that ambassadors must labor for the common good, and that they should never be sent to stir up wars or internal dissensions; and in the nineteenth century, Sir Robert Peel the younger was to define diplomacy in general as "the great engine used by civilized society for the purpose of maintaining peace."

The realists always opposed this ethical emphasis. In the fifteenth century, in one of the first treatises on ambassadorial functions, Ermalao Barbaro wrote: "The first duty of an ambassador is exactly the same as that of any other servant of government: that is, to do, say, advise and think whatever may best serve the preservation and aggrandizement of his own state."

Seventeenth-century theorists were inclined to Barbaro's view. This was cer-tainly the position of Abram de Wicquefort, who coined the definition of the diplomat as "an honorable spy" and who, in his own life, demonstrated that he did not take the adjectival qualification very seriously. A subject of Holland by birth, Wicquefort at various times in his checkered career performed diplo-matic services for the courts of Brandenburg, Lüneburg, and France as well as for his own country, and he had no scruples about serving as a double agent, a practice that eventually led to his imprisonment in a Dutch jail. It was here that he wrote his treatise *L'Ambassadeur et ses fonctions,* a work that was both an amusing commentary on the political morals of the baroque age and an incisive analysis of the art and practice of diplomacy.

Wicquefort was not abashed by the peccadilloes of his colleagues, which varied from financial peculation and sins of the flesh to crimes of violence. He took the line that in a corrupt age, one could not expect that embassies would be oases of virtue. Morality was, in any case, an irrelevant consideration in diplomacy; a country could afford to be served by bad men, but not by incom-petent ones. Competence began with a clear understanding on the diplomat's part of the nature of his job and a willingness to accept the fact that it had nothing to do with personal gratification or self-aggrandizement. The ambassador's principal function, Wicquefort wrote, "consisted in maintaining effective communication between the two Princes, in delivering letters that his master writes to the Prince at whose court he resides, in soliciting answers to them, . . . in protecting his Master's subjects and conserving his interests." He must have the charm and cultivation that would enable him to ingratiate himself at the court to which he was accredited and the adroitness needed to ferret out information that would reveal threats to his master's interests or opportunities for advancing them. He must possess the ability to gauge the temperament and intelligence of those with whom he had to deal and to use this knowledge profitably in negotiation. "Ministers are but men and as such have their weaknesses, that is to say, their passions and interests, which the ambassador ought to know if he wishes to do honor to himself and his Master."

In pursuing this intelligence, the qualities he should cultivate most assiduously were *prudence* and *modération.* The former Wicquefort equated with caution and reflection, and also with the gifts of silence and indirection, the art of "making it appear that one is not interested in the things one desires the most." The diplomat who possessed prudence did not have to resort to mendacity or deceit or to *tromperies* or *artifices,* which were usually, in any case, counterproductive. *Modération* was the ability to curb one's temper and remain cool and phlegmatic in moments of tension. "Those spirits who are compounded of sulphur and saltpeter, whom the slightest spark can set afire, are easily capable of compromising affairs by their excitability, because it is so easy to put them in a rage or drive them to a fury, so that they don't know what they are doing." Diplomacy is a cold and rational business, in short, not to be practiced by the moralist, or the enthusiast, or the man with a low boiling point.

The same point was made in the most famous of the eighteenth-century essays on diplomacy, François de Callières's *On the Manner of Negotiating with Princes* (1716), in which persons interested in the career of diplomacy were advised to consider whether they were born with "the qualities necessary for success." These, the author wrote, included

> an observant mind, a spirit of application which refuses to be distracted by pleasures or frivolous amusements, a sound judgment which takes the measure of things, as they are, and which goes straight to its goal by the shortest and most neutral paths without wandering into useless refinements and subtleties which as a rule only succeed in repelling those with whom one is dealing.

Important also were the kind of penetration that is useful in discovering the thoughts of men, a fertility in expedients when difficulties arise, an equable humor and a patient temperament, and easy and agreeable manners. Above all, Callières observed, in a probably not unconscious echo of Wicquefort's insistence upon moderation, the diplomat must have sufficient control over himself to resist the longing to speak before he has really thought what he shall say. He should not endeavour to gain the reputation of being able to reply immediately and without premeditation to every proposition which is made, and he should take a special care not to fall into the error of one famous foreign ambassador of our time who so loved an argument that each time he warmed up in controversy he revealed important secrets in order to support his opinion.

In his treatment of the art of negotiation, Callières drew from a wealth of experience to which Wicquefort could not pretend, for he was one of Louis XIV's most gifted diplomats and ended his career as head of the French delegation during the negotiations at Ryswick in 1697. It is interesting, in light of the heavy reliance upon lawyers in contemporary United States diplomacy (one thinks of President Dwight D. Eisenhower's secretary of state, John Foster Dulles) and of the modern practice of negotiating in large gatherings, that Callières had no confidence in either of these preferences. The legal mind, he felt, was at once too narrow, too intent upon hair-splitting, and too contentious to be useful in a field where success, in the last analysis, was best assured by agreements that provided mutuality of advantage. As for large conferences—"vast concourses of ambassadors and envoys"—his view was that they were generally too clumsy to achieve anything very useful. Most successful conferences were the result of careful preliminary work by small groups of negotiators who hammered out the essential bases of agreement and secured approval for them from their governments before handing them over, for formal purposes, to the *omnium-gatherums* that were later celebrated in the history books.

Perhaps the most distinctive feature of Callières's treatise was the passion with which he argued that a nation's foreign relations should be conducted by persons trained for the task.

> Diplomacy is a profession by itself which deserves the same preparation and assiduity of attention that men give to other recognized professions. ... The diplomatic genius is born, not made. But there are many qualities which may be developed with practice, and the greatest part of the necessary knowledge can only be acquired, by constant application to the subject. In this sense, diplomacy is certainly a profession itself capable of occupying a man's whole career, and those who think to embark upon a diplomatic mission as a pleasant diversion from their common task only prepare disappointment for themselves and disaster for the cause which they serve.

These words represented not only a personal view but an acknowledgment of the requirements of the age. The states that emerged as recognizedly great powers in the course of the seventeenth and eighteenth centuries were the states that had modernized their governmental structure, mobilized their economic and other resources in a rational manner, built up effective and disciplined military establishments, and elaborated a professional civil service that administered state business in accordance with the principles of *raison d'état.* An indispensable part of that civil service was the Foreign Office and the diplomatic corps, which had the important task of formulating the foreign policy that protected and advanced the state's vital interests and of seeing that it was carried out.

Bibliographical Essay

For the general state of international relations before the eighteenth century, the following are useful: Marvin R. O'Connell, *The Counter-Reformation, 1559–1610* (New York, 1974); Carl J. Friedrich, *The Age of the Baroque, 1610–1660* (New York, 1952), a splendid volume; C. V. Wedgwood, *The Thirty Years War* (London, 1938, and later editions); Frederick L. Nussbaum, *The Triumph of Science and Reason, 1660–1685* (New York, 1953); John B. Wolf, *The Emergence of the Great Powers, 1685–1715* (New York, 1951); and the excellent survey by D. McKay and H. M. Scott, *The Rise of the Great Powers, 1648–1815* (London, 1983). For the fluid state of international relations in this period, see the brilliant studies by J. H. Elliott, *Imperial Spain, 1469–1716* (Harmondsworth, 1970) and *Richelieu and Olivares* (Cambridge, 1984). On Austrian policy in the seventeenth century, see especially Max Braubach, *Prinz Eugen von Savoyen,* 5 vols. (Vienna, 1963–1965); on Prussian, Otto Hintze, *Die Hohenzollern und ihr Werk,* 4th ed. (Berlin, 1915), and, brief but useful, Sidney B. Fay, *The Rise of Brandenburg-Prussia* (New York, 1937). A classic essay on great-power politics in the early modern period is Leopold von Ranke, *Die grossen Mächte,* which can be found in English translation in the appendix of Theodore von Laue, *Leopold Ranke: The Formative Years* (Princeton, 1950). The standard work on *raison d'état* is Friedrich Meinecke, *Die Idee der Staatsräson,* 3d ed. (Munich, 1963), trans. by Douglas Scott as *Machiavellianism* (New Haven, 1957).

On the origins and development of diplomacy, see D. P. Heatley, *Diplomacy and the Study of International Relations* (Oxford, 1919); Leon van der Essen, *La Diplomatie: Ses origines et son organisation* (Brussels, 1953); Ragnar Numelin, *Les Origines de la diplomatie,* trans. from the Swedish by Jean-Louis Perret (Paris, 1943); and especially Garrett Mattingly, *Renaissance Diplomacy* (New York, 1951), and Heinrich Wildner, *Die Technik der Diplomatie: L'Art de négocier* (Vienna, 1959). Highly readable is Harold Nicolson, *Diplomacy,* 2d ed. (London, 1950). An interesting comparative study is Adda B. Bozeman, *Politics and Culture in International History* (Princeton, 1960).

There is no modern edition of *L'Ambassadeur et ses fonctions par Monsieur de Wicquefort* (Cologne, 1690); but Callières's classic of 1776 can be found: François de Callières, *On the Manner of Negotiating with Princes,* trans. A. F. Whyte (London, 1919, and later editions).

Suggestive on the limitations of policy is Geoffrey Parker, *The Military Revolution: Military Innovation and the Rise of the West* (Cambridge, 1988).

2

Eighteenth-Century Diplomacy

During the first half of the nineteenth century, a period in which the forces of nationalism were still relatively undeveloped, a book that enjoyed a considerable vogue among students of international politics was the Göttingen historian A. H. L. Heeren's *History of the Political System of Europe*. The author contended that for more than a century, the component states of Europe had been moving insensibly but inevitably toward federation, a process that was encouraged both by their similarities—the fact that they "resembled each other in manners, religion, and custom and were connected by reciprocal interests"— and by their diversity, which, he said, "preserved practically in circulation a greater compass of political ideas" and, more important, created a general repugnance to the idea of dominance by a single power.

Heeren did not hesitate to suggest that the creation of a European system had been all but consummated in the eighteenth century. He admitted that "a rightful condition among the several states, such as might be projected in theory, was at all times far from being established." Nevertheless, he added,

> As a gradual result of the progress of culture, a system of international law was developed, which, reposing not merely on express treaties, but also on silent agreements, enjoined the observance of certain maxims in peace, but more especially in times of war, and which, though often violated, were still eminently beneficial. Even the strict, and sometimes excessive, etiquette, mutually observed by states toward one another, was by no means a matter of indifference on the part of states, often the most unlike in power and constitution.

The most important results of this, Heeren argued, were, first, the acknowledgement of the sacredness of rightful possession, which he said was "the support of the whole system," and, second, the recognition of the principle of the balance of power, "that is, the mutual preservation of freedom and independence, by guarding against the preponderance and usurpation of an individual.'' To Heeren, maintenance of the balance was "the constant problem of higher policy" and the principal preoccupation of the diplomats who made and executed it; and the consequences of this were beneficial, resulting in

> a constantly wakeful attention of the states to one another, and various consequent relations by means of alliances and counteralliances, especially of the more distant states; the greater importance of the states of the second and third order in the political system; and, in general, the preservation of a feeling of the value of independence, and the elevation of politics above gross selfishness.

Heeren's view that after centuries of conflict, the European states had succeeded in the eighteenth century in moderating their anarchic tendencies and forming a system based upon mutual respect and recognition of the balance of power was bound to arouse a certain incredulity in the mind of anyone who had studied the politics of that century. How could one speak of a European system when the principal powers were engaged in almost continuous warfare against each other? The eighteenth century is often called the Age of Enlightenment or the Age of Reason, and we know that its greatest thinkers, impressed by Isaac Newton's discoveries concerning the laws that ran the universe, were curious to discover rules of rational behavior for human society. Yet between these earnest efforts and the actualities of international politics there seemed to be no vital connection. La Bruyère wrote mockingly that the diplomats of the age "spoke only of peace, alliance, and public tranquillity . . . and thought only of their special interest," and the same thought was voiced by a contemporary statesman who described the conditions of his time as "a continuous quarrel between people without morals, intent on taking and perpetually hungry."

The gulf that existed between the Enlightenment and politics, and the duplicity and greed that characterized great-power diplomacy in the eighteenth century, may be illustrated by some reference to the early policy of Frederick II (the Great) of Prussia. In many ways, Frederick was the quintessential product of the Enlightenment. To the distress of his father, the soldier-king Frederick William I, he appeared to spend his time as crown prince on matters that were remote from statecraft and the art of war. He corresponded with French *philosophes* like Voltaire, who was later his guest at San Souci; he studied poetry and music, becoming an excellent flutist; and he wrote a long treatise on politics in which he attacked the principles of Machiavelli on ethical and rational grounds, like any other advocate of the *Aufklärung*.

Yet the young Frederick's thoughts were not as remote from politics as his fretful father supposed. In 1731, in a letter to one of his aides, he wrote that Prussia occupied an exposed and defenseless position in the center of Europe and that it would be the plaything of the other major powers if it did not increase and consolidate its territory. *Corriger la figure de la Prusse* (to correct the shape of Prussia) was the important thing, a process that, given the nature of Prussia's scattered holdings, was required by the honor of the Hohenzollern house, so that its leaders "could cut a good figure among the great of this world and play a significant role." This letter was a curious blend of cold realism and youthful idealism, as when the prince talked of "Prussia's raising itself from the dust into which it has fallen" and bringing the Protestant faith to bloom in Europe and the Reich so that it could represent "the future for the oppressed, a refuge for widows and orphans, a support for the poor, and a terror for the unjust." On the whole, the realism was the stronger note, as the sequel showed.

In 1740, Frederick succeeded his father on the throne of Prussia. The same year saw the death of the Austrian emperor, Charles VI, an ineffectual ruler whose extravagance had weakened Austrian finances and whose wars in eastern Europe had decimated the army. With Charles the main male line died out, and the throne passed to his daughter Maria Theresia. The emperor had feared that her claim might be contested and had therefore asked the European powers to subscribe to a document called the Pragmatic Sanction, in accordance with which they engaged to observe and defend the integrity of the Austrian possessions under Maria Theresia's rule. Frederick of Prussia had signed this document along with most of the other rulers.

Nevertheless, neither his signature nor the arguments against immorality that he had used in his *Anti-Machiavel* treatise deterred him now from taking advantage of what seemed to be an ideal opportunity for aggrandizement—an opportunity which he seemed, indeed, to think it would be criminal to let slip. Without hesitation, he ordered his armies to invade and seize the rich Austrian province of Silesia, a territory to which Prussia had some vague historical claims that could give a screen of legal plausibility to what was quite patently an act of aggression and is, indeed, remembered as "the rape of Silesia."

Before embarking on this adventure, Frederick, in order to still the doubts of his ministers, wrote a remarkable memorandum that should be quoted *in extenso* for the light it throws on him and upon eighteenth-century diplomatic practice.

> Silesia is the portion of the Imperial heritage to which we have the strongest claim and which is most suitable to the House of Brandenburg. The superiority of our troops, the promptitude with which we can set them in motion, in a word, the clear advantage we have over our neighbors, gives us in this unexpected emergency an infinite superiority over all other powers of Europe. If we wait till Saxony and Bavaria start hostilities, we could not prevent the aggrandizement of the former which is wholly contrary to our interest. . . . [As for the other powers], England and France are foes. If France should meddle in the affairs of the empire, England could not allow it, so I can always make a good alliance with one or the other. England could not be jealous of my getting Silesia, which would do her no harm, and she needs allies. Holland

will not care, all the more since the loans of the Amsterdam business world secured on Silesia will be guaranteed. If we cannot arrange with England and Holland, we can certainly make a deal with France, who cannot frustrate our designs and will welcome the abasement of the imperial house.

Russia alone might give us trouble. If the empress lives . . . we can bribe the leading counsellors. If she dies, the Russians will be so occupied that they will have no time for foreign affairs. . . . All this leads to the conclusion that we must occupy Silesia before the winter and then negotiate. When we are in possession we can negotiate with success. We should never get anything by negotiations alone except very onerous conditions in return for a few trifles.

This memorandum really requires no comment. Here is a mind completely dominated by *Staatsräson,* a mind that admits no legal or ethical bounds to state ambition. That Frederick's relations with Maria Theresia had been wholly amicable up to this time and that he was bound by treaty to respect the integrity of her possessions were, in 1740, wholly irrelevant to him. The opportunity for gain was imperative, and Frederick began his invasion. In the event, his gamble paid off: Prussia won and retained Silesia, a fact that had profound influence upon the structure and future of Germany. For when Austria lost Silesia, with its large population and important resources, the western half of the Austrian Empire ceased to be a predominantly German state, and the whole balance of forces in Germany tilted in Prussia's favor. But this result was gained only as a result of two wasting wars in which the Silesian issue at times seemed to drop out of view. In the first of these, the so-called War of the Austrian Succession, which extended from 1740 to 1748, Prussia was joined by France, Spain, Bavaria, and Saxony (although Saxony changed sides in 1743), all of which saw an opportunity of gaining some territory in the Netherlands or Italy or Bohemia at Austria's expense, whereas Austria was supported by Great Britain, which sent some troops to the Low Countries but devoted more of its energies to attacking French and Spanish possessions in the New World. The second was the Seven Years War, which extended from 1756 to 1763, in which Prussia, as a result of the brilliant diplomatic revolution effected by the Austrian chancellor Kaunitz, found itself opposed by Austria, France, Russia, Saxony, Sweden, and (after 1762) Spain and supported only by Great Britain and Hanover. In this war too, both Frederick's opponents and his supporters were motivated by a lust for gain, and it is significant that some of the most important battles took place not in Bohemia and Moravia, the main arena for the confrontations of the Austrian and Prussian armies, but in North America and India. It is difficult to read of the casualties demanded by these titanic struggles, in which Frederick confirmed Prussia's title to great-power status by bleeding his country white, and in which the other powers changed sides without the guidance of any but the meanest of principles, without thinking of the eighteenth century as an age of anarchy and rapine.

And yet it is important to note that much of what Heeren said about the elements of an emerging European system was also true. Despite the wars that pitted the European states against each other, there was a general assumption that they were members of a comity of states that were bound together by common ties of family relationship, religion, and historical tradition. These connections, it was often argued, were more significant than their sporadic enmities, which were evanescent. Clausewitz, the military theorist, was speaking in the spirit of the eighteenth century when he later wrote:

> If we consider the community of states in Europe today, we ... find major and minor interests of states and peoples interwoven in the most varied and changeable manner. Each point of intersection binds and serves to balance one set of interests against another. The broad effect of all these fixed points is obviously to give a certain amount of cohesion to the whole. ... The fact that Europe, as we know it, has existed for over a thousand years can only be explained by the operation of these general interests.

Some eighteenth-century publicists did not hesitate to talk of the great powers of Europe as forming a society or a federation (a term that frequently occurs) or a concert. And although it was difficult to prove that such a concert actually existed, they were fond of pointing out that on certain principles or rules of the diplomatic game there was enough broad agreement to indicate that some kind of concerted thinking could be mobilized.

For instance, there was a general agreement that it was normal and right that there should be five great powers. The thought that one of them might disappear—that Prussia might actually be destroyed in the Seven Years War, for example—was resisted by all major powers. There seemed to be an unconscious feeling (it was Ranke who first used this comparison) that the disappearance of one of the great powers would have the same kind of disastrous effect as that caused by the death of the first violinist in a quintet that had played together for a long time.

In the second place, there was general agreement that although the powers might fight against each other, the way in which they fought should be subject to some regulation. The codification of the so-called laws of war, begun in the sixteenth and seventeenth centuries, was carried further in the eighteenth. The laws were extended from such things as rules governing military booty and the treatment of wounded and prisoners to relations between the military and civilian society. Efforts were made to determine under what conditions of war it was permissible for a commander to order the destruction of crops or livestock, or to destroy civilian dwellings, or to take hostages. There was no authority to see that these rules were respected, and they were often violated, but by and large they were fairly effective, and they represented a general feeling that if it was at all possible, this was the way soldiers were to behave and that unless circumstances seemed to demand it, civilian society should be spared the horrors that accompanied any war. In the eighteenth century, this control or limitation of the effects of military action on society reached its peak when even Frederick the Great, who was a daring and single-minded practitioner of war, declared that he wanted to fight his wars without the peasant behind his plow and the towns-man in his shop ever being aware of them.

Finally, there was a general recognition of the principle of the balance of power, which took two forms. The first was a general wariness about anything that looked like an attempt at universal domination by a single power. Consider once more the case of Frederick II in 1740. That the attack on Silesia was an act of aggression was palpable; but it should be noted that it was designed as a limited aggression. Frederick could even argue—indeed, he did argue—that he was not violating the principle of the balance of power by invading Silesia but vindicating it, by correcting it and making it sounder. He knew that that argu-ment was plausible enough to appeal to third powers, many of which felt that Austria was too big anyway.

But Frederick also knew that if he carried his aggression to the point of seeking to destroy Austria or, even further, to the point of seeking an ascendancy over all Europe, he would be stopped by a coalition of all other powers. This was, of course, never his intention. Like other European rulers of his time, balance of power meant to him a denial of universal ambitions. It also meant something else in the eighteenth century, this century of reason and mechanical rules. It was generally agreed that for the balance of power to work properly, a territorial gain effected in war by one power should be balanced by compen-satory gains for other major powers.

The application of this rule involved such elaborate territorial arithmetic that it is almost impossible to describe some of the arrangements. Consider the case of the War of the Polish Succession, which was fought in the years 1733–1735. Just as Turkey was the Sick Man of Europe in the nineteenth century, so did Poland, which in the seventeenth century had been potentially a great power, become the Sick Man of Europe in the eighteenth, with all powers anxious about its condition and eager to have a share in the spoils if it fell to pieces. In 1733, the Polish Diet, tired of being ruled by Saxons, elected a Pole, Stanislaus Lesz-czynski, as king. This annoyed both the Russians, who sent an army of thirty thousand men to Poland to protest, and the Austrians, who had got along well with the Saxon rulers and who also mobilized. The Russians succeeded in de-posing Leszczynski and forcing a rump diet to elect August III of Saxony as king, but the French, whose young King Louis XV had married Leszczynski's daughter, would not accept this result and declared war on Austria with the support of Sardinia (the House of Savoy) and Spain. The war was fought mostly in Baden and Italy and went badly for the Austrians. When it threatened to grow and involve England, the French called a halt, and a peace settlement was made.

In the interests of the balance of power, everybody, except the Poles over whom the war had started, received some compensation. Leszczynski gave up the throne of Poland but kept the courtesy title king and was given the Duchy of Bar. Later, in 1740, when Duke Francis of Lorraine, the husband of Maria Theresia, became emperor of Austria and gave up Lorraine in order to acquire Tuscany, Leszczynski got Lorraine too. It was agreed, however, that when he died both Bar and Lorraine would pass to his daughter, the wife of the French king, and would thus become part of France. The Habsburgs, through Duke Francis, acquired not only Tuscany in Italy but also Parma and Piacenza. The Spanish got Naples, and the king of Sardinia was fobbed off with some minor frontier rectifications. It was a big pie, and everybody got a piece.

In 1735, the Russians did not bother to claim a share in the spoils, for they were not interested in Italy or the Franco-German borders. But they had demonstrated their ability to depose one Polish king and put a creature of their own in his place. They had advertised the weakness of Poland, and they were willing to wait until the situation was ripe for a real land grab there. But they were prepared also to recognize the principle of sharing the booty when that time came. The most spectacular of the eighteenth-century applications of balance to territorial aggrandizement was to come with the division of Poland among Russia, Austria, and Prussia in the three partitions of 1772, 1793, and 1795.

It can be maintained, therefore, that the eighteenth century was not completely anarchic and that the great powers acknowledged certain rules of international intercourse, such as the necessity of the existence of the normal quota of five great powers, the view that the rigors of war should be ameliorated by restrictions upon the freedom of commanders in the field, and the belief that it was important to observe the balance of power as a limitation upon ambition and as a guide in territorial partition. But this hardly justifies Heeren's contention that a European system existed in the eighteenth century. The most that can be said is that the *idea* of a system of a European federation, of a concert of powers, was in men's minds. Writers on politics often talked of it as a desirable thing, in the sense that if it really existed, it might be able to develop the already recognized rules of international behavior into a more effective code of law that would restrain international violence and reduce the constant drain that war imposed upon state resources.

For the most part, this was publicists' talk, the discourse of philosophers and theorists. It was not reflected in the deliberations and activities of governments, which went their violent ways without bothering themselves with thoughts of federations and concerts. To make them concern themselves over such matters, something was needed that was capable of shocking and frightening them into real collaborative action, something that would force them to convert the dream of a European concert into a working reality.

That was supplied by the French Revolution and the foreign policy of the Republic and the Napoleonic Empire. Yet so entrenched were the European powers in their customary ways that the significance of the revolution was lost on them when it took place. Their first reaction was one of satisfaction—a feeling that the events in Paris would not last but that, while they did, France would be paralyzed and incapable of conducting foreign policy, a situation from which they would derive advantages. The idea that the revolution might threaten them never occurred to the powers. The same Kaunitz who had effected the diplomatic revolution of 1756 wrote a pamphlet called ''Reflections on the Pretended Dangers of Contagion with Which the New Constitution of France Menaces Other Sovereign States,'' in which he scornfully dismissed the very idea of the revolution having external consequences.

This relaxed attitude almost proved fatal for them in the end, for it enabled the revolutionary forces in France to survive the awkward period when they might have been put down easily by foreign intervention. It gave the revolution a chance to consolidate itself and then to go on the offensive, as it did in 1792 with the decrees that declared its intention of liberating Europe from absolute rulers.

Even these decrees and the subsequent movement of French armies toward the Rhine did not unduly alarm the other powers. The Austrians and Prussians sent armies to block the French, but their efforts in the campaigns of 1793–1795 were uncoordinated and lamed by their nervous concern lest the Russians, while their backs were turned, decide to seize Poland. The war in the west was really a kind of Austro-Prussian competition for spoils in the east. In 1793, Prussia managed to participate in the second partition of Poland, while Austria was left in the lurch; and, in 1795, knowing that another partition was pending, the Prussian government did not hesitate to make a private deal with the French in order to extricate itself from the war before all Poland was gone. By the secret peace of Basel in 1795, the Prussians sold out their Austrian ally and promised the French that they could have the left bank of the Rhine (which Louis XIV had never been able to conquer) if they gave Prussia compensation in western Germany. Then they terminated hostilities and scrambled back eastward just in time to share in the third and final partition of Poland.

It is unnecessary to continue the story in any detail. This kind of selfish and short-sighted behavior enabled the French republican armies to conquer the Rhineland and to penetrate into southern Germany, Switzerland, and Italy. When the Republic gave way to the Consulate of Napoleon Bonaparte and then to the Empire, this French imperialism gained in momentum and intention. As Ranke wrote later, ''Everything that had happened in Louis XIV's time had now been far exceeded. The old liberties of Europe were submerged. Europe seemed about to be swallowed up by France. The universal monarchy, that had hitherto seemed only a remote danger, was almost realized.''

Yet the other great powers still seemed incapable of understanding the dimension of the danger. Although England strove to form anti-French coalitions and received the support of Austria, the Russians were unreliable allies, and the Prussians remained neutral until 1806 and then, choosing the wrong moment to fight Napoleon, were smashed and rendered powerless for another seven years. Napoleon was well on his way to complete domination of Europe, having turned both Austria and Prussia into near satellites, when he overreached himself in Russia in 1812. And it was only in the wake of that setback that the other powers finally formed the Grand Alliance that would encompass his defeat.

When they had done so and when they had won their first great collaborative battle at Leipzig in 1813, quarrels and dissension threatened to divide their union. But their awareness of the danger that they had not yet fully escaped not only kept them together but, at long last, induced them to take the first real step toward converting the eighteenth-century aspiration for a concert into an effective working arrangement. In the French town of Chaumont on 1 March 1814, the governments of Austria, Prussia, Russia, and Great Britain, largely under the influence of the British foreign secretary, Castlereagh, signed a treaty in which they agreed not only to continue the war against Napoleon until a definitive victory had been gained, but also to continue their alliance after their victory. The language of the treaty is significant as showing their motivation: "The present Treaty of Alliance having for its object the maintenance of the balance of Europe, to secure the repose and independence of the Powers, and to prevent the invasions which for so many years have devastated the world, the High Contracting Parties have agreed among themselves to extend its duration for twenty years from the date of signature."

This treaty held the allies together until the Corsican was banned from Europe and until the great settlement of 1814–1815 was completed. And at the Congress of Vienna and in the Second Peace of Paris, the stipulations of the Treaty of Chaumont served as the basis for the first notable experiment in institutionalizing the principles of concert and balance in behalf of European peace.

Bibliographical Essay

Heeren's treatise is available in English: A. H. L. Heeren, *History of the Political System of Europe and Its Colonies,* 2 vols., trans. from the German by George Bancroft (Northampton, Mass., 1829). A fundamentally different view will be found in the classic account of eighteenth-century diplomacy, Albert Sorel, *L'Europe et la révolution française,* 8 vols., 4th ed. (Paris, 1897).

An excellent survey of developments in the eighteenth century is M. S. Anderson, *Europe in the Eighteenth Century* (London, 1961). The years of relative peace are treated in Penfield Roberts, *The Quest for Security, 1715–1740* (New York, 1947); those of conflict in Walter L. Dorn's masterful *Competition for Empire, 1740–1763* (New York, 1940), which is particularly good on Kaunitz and his contemporaries. On Frederick II, see the account in Friedrich Meinecke, *Die Idee der Staatsräson,* 3d ed. (Munich, 1963);

Gerhard Ritter, *Frederick the Great,* trans. from the German by Peter Paret (Berkeley, 1968); G. P. Gooch, *Frederick the Great: The Ruler, the Writer, the Man* (New York, 1947); and Theodor Schieder, *Friedrich der Große* (Frankfurt am Main, 1983), which has a fascinating discussion of the mixture of idealism and realism in Frederick's policy. Useful also is Christopher Duffy, *The Military Life of Frederick the Great* (New York, 1986).

For the period of the American and French revolutions, see R. R. Palmer's classic *The Age of the Democratic Revolution,* 2 vols. (Princeton, 1959, 1964); Leo Gershoy, *From Despotism to Revolution, 1763–1789* (New York, 1944); and Crane Brinton, *A Decade of Revolution, 1789–1799* (New York, 1934). On the diplomacy of the Napoleonic age, see especially Enno E. Kraehe, *Metternich's German Policy,* vol. 1, *The Contest with Napoleon, 1799–1814* (Princeton, 1963), and C. K. Webster, *The Foreign Policy of Castlereagh, 1812–1815* (London, 1931). Geoffrey Bruun, *Europe and the French Imperium, 1799–1814* (New York, 1938), is still useful.

The best edition of Clausewitz's classic treatise is Carl von Clausewitz, *On War,* ed. and trans. Michael Howard and Peter Paret (Princeton, 1976).

3

Balance of Power, 1815–1914:
Three Experiments

During the nineteenth century, the greatest challenge to statecraft was the task of devising a political system that would contain international violence and prevent war from threatening once more, as it had during the Napoleonic period, to assume its absolute form. Three generations of statesmen struggled with the problem of establishing a viable equilibrium of forces in Europe, and their efforts found expression in three quite different systems of balance of power, each of which reflected the characteristic tendencies of its time. The first of these experiments was made by the negotiators who gathered in Vienna in 1814 and 1815; the second by the German chancellor Otto von Bismarck at the end of the 1870s; the third by the harried diplomats in the years after 1890. In terms of effectiveness, the first came closest to fulfilling the purposes for which it was formed. The second embodied all of the ingenuity of its creator but was too complicated to have much inherent stability; and the third was little more than an exercise in desperation.

I

One of the most famous paintings ever made of a diplomatic conference is the one that the French portraitist Jean-Baptiste Isabey made of the Congress of Vienna. In the center of this large canvas, standing with a proprietary air and a look of satisfaction on his handsome face, is the host of the meeting, the Austrian chancellor Prince Metternich, while around him are grouped the chief representatives of the other powers: Castlereagh, the British foreign secretary, with his legs crossed negligently; the king of Prussia, Frederick William III, looking gloomily at the phlegmatic Englishman; the czar of Russia, Alexander I, wearing a uniform with epaulettes so big that one wonders how he will be able to lift himself out of the chair in which he is sitting; and the representative of France, Talleyrand-Périgord, with his clubfoot, his badly powdered wig, his pendulous lips, and his sardonic eyes. In the background, in bestarred and bemedalled clusters, stand the lesser figures of the congress—resident ambassadors, diplomatic secretaries, military aides, and the like—all bearing on their faces that arch and condescending smirk that is worn by persons who wish to give the impression that they are privy to mysteries that they are pledged not to reveal.

It is well to consider the faces of these bedecked and bedizened statesmen, for they were pathbreakers. There had been other conferences and congresses before Vienna, like Münster and Osnabrück in 1648, and Utrecht in 1713. But those meetings had been for the purpose of ending hostilities and dividing spoils. The statesmen at Vienna had set themselves another task. Metternich made this clear when he said:

> No great political insight is needed to see that this Congress could not be modelled on any which had taken place. Former assemblies which were called congresses met for the express purpose of settling a quarrel between two or more belligerent powers—the issue being a peace treaty. On this occasion, peace had already been made [he was referring to the First Peace of Paris, which had ended hostilities] and the parties meet as friends who, though differing in their interests, wish to work together towards the conclusion and affirmation of the existing treaty.

What did he mean by "conclusion and affirmation"? Clearly, that the main task of this congress was to move from a mere ending of past hostilities to a settlement that would prevent future conflict. This was the assigned task, and it was accomplished.

This did not mean that the peacemakers of Vienna utterly neglected the kinds of things that had preoccupied their predecessors at Osnabrück and Utrecht. They made sure that the members of the Grand Alliance were rewarded in accordance with the degree of their sacrifice and their contribution to the victory, and they devoted considerable time also to the complicated business of restoring titles and territory to rulers who had been deprived of them by Napoleon. But they did not allow this attention to the principles of compensation and legitimacy to obtrude upon what Metternich had defined as their more important obligation—that of constructing a new international system that would be able to resist any renewal of the kind of subversion and aggression that Napoleon had practiced against them; and in seeking to fulfill that obligation, they refused to allow themselves to be distracted by the greed of petty princelings or the desire for revenge against France. They did not, for example, attempt to restore, in facsimile form, the Europe that Napoleon had destroyed. They did not clutter up the international landscape with scores of rehabilitated petty principalities. And they did not succumb to the temptation to be vindictive toward the French people. Wilhelm von Humboldt, the Prussian ambassador to Vienna, who was to play a leading role in devising the agenda for the congress, had been in Paris when the Silesian army of Blücher and Gneisenau had entered the conquered city, and he had been distressed when the Prussian soldiers had wanted to blow up all the bridges over the Seine because they were named after Napoleonic victories. This kind of pettiness Humboldt and his colleagues in Vienna succeeded in excluding from the deliberations. They had no desire to cripple France in any serious way, least of all to make it so weak that it could not play its appropriate role as a great power in the postwar period.

The two principal architects of the new order were Viscount Castlereagh, the British foreign secretary, and Prince Clemens von Metternich, the chief minister of the emperor of Austria. Both were convinced that the key to the new international settlement must be the principle of the balance of power. The core of this doctrine was to them, as it had been to their predecessors who had fought against Louis XIV in the seventeenth century, a readiness on the part of the powers to resist unilateral attempts at universal domination. But they also believed that there should be such an equilibrium of forces among the major powers as to discourage such attempts, and they did not think that the eighteenth-century procedure of allowing territorial aggression on the part of the individual states, provided everybody else received compensation, had been a good way of attaining that. In general, the eighteenth-century territorial equilibrium had, in their view, been too loosely defined and too full of dangerous imbalances (like the one that goaded Frederick into such bloody action in 1740).

Under their leadership, therefore, the negotiators at Vienna went through enormous efforts to adjust territory, resources, and population as equitably as possible among the major powers—balancing off Russian gains in Poland with Austrian gains in Italy and Prussian acquisitions in the Rhineland, constructing buffers between the great powers in the Low Countries (by joining Belgium and Holland into one state) and in the German states that lay between Prussia and Austria. Germany, one delegate said later, had to serve as a kind of shock absorber and hence had to remain disunited in the interests of peace, preserving the "balance through an inherent force of gravity." The labors expended upon this elaborate redrawing of the map of Europe were onerous and protracted, and the results were written into the final act of the Congress of Vienna.

The men who guided this work were not, however, so naive as to believe that they had insured themselves against future trouble by this elaborate exercise in cartography. They were well aware that a new Frederick or a new Napoleon might arise, and they believed that some executive body must be established that would be capable of dealing with threats to the balance as soon as they occurred. In the eighteenth century, no such body had existed; and although publicists like Voltaire were fond of writing articles in which they argued that the rulers of Europe were tied together by bonds of religion, common history, and intermarriage and thus constituted a European federation or concert of Europe, this was always an ideal rather than a reality. Metternich and Castlereagh and their colleagues now actualized it by building upon the Treaty of Chaumont of March 1814. The Quadruple Alliance of November 1815 (later broadened to include France) not only reiterated the key features of Chaumont but stipulated that the great powers would hold periodic conferences of their foreign ministers "for the purpose of consulting upon their interests, or for the consideration of measures which . . . shall be considered the most salutary for the purpose and prosperity of Nations and the maintenance of the Peace of Europe." Thus, the new order was in a sense given both a constitution and a constitutional watchdog—a balance of power (as defined by the final act) and a concert of powers to watch over it.

In the form in which it was conceived, the system did not last long. When Metternich and Czar Alexander of Russia became concerned over the threat that liberalism posed to existing thrones of Europe, they tried to turn the Quadruple Alliance into an agency that would automatically intervene in the affairs of any country in which there was a revolution or an agitation against the status quo and suppress by force the revolutionary or democratic or liberal movements. These attempts the British government viewed as a subversion of the true purpose of the Quadruple Alliance; and in a powerful note of 19 October 1818, Castlereagh protested that "nothing would be more immoral or more prejudicial to the character of governments generally than the idea that their force was collectively to be prostituted to the support of established power without any consideration of the extent to which it was abused." The eastern powers were not, however, to be stayed, and the British felt compelled to refuse to attend further meetings of the foreign ministers.

This withdrawal from the concert was more apparent than real. In a note of 5 May 1820, protesting against the Metternich policy, Castlereagh made it clear that, while Great Britain could not countenance a policy of joint meddling in the internal affairs of small states, its cooperation could always be counted upon when there was a genuine threat to the peace of Europe and the balance of power; and his successors periodically repeated this pledge as late as the mid-century. In 1852, Lord John Russell said in the House of Commons:

> We are connected, and have been for more than a century, with the general system of Europe, and any territorial increase of one Power, any aggrandisement which disturbs the general balance of power in Europe, although it might not immediately lead to war, could not be a matter of indifference to this country and would, no doubt, be the subject of conference, and might ultimately, if that balance was seriously threatened, lead to war.

Nor were these only words. In every crisis that threatened the peace between 1815 and 1854, the British were represented and played a leading role in finding a solution short of war. This was true in the Belgian crisis of 1830, the Near Eastern crisis of 1838, and the first Schleswig-Holstein crisis of 1850, to mention only the uglier disputes of this period. In all those cases, and in others, the European concert was able, with British participation, to demonstrate its effectiveness in preserving the Vienna balance and the public order.

There can be little doubt that the balance-of-power system worked more effectively in the years from 1815 to 1854 than at any later period in the nineteenth century, and we must ask ourselves why this was so.

In the first place, statecraft in this period was not subject to certain pressures that subsequently caused governments, often reluctantly, to do things that were bound to arouse the suspicion and fear of other powers and to invite violent retaliation. For the most part, the governments of these years did not have to worry about public opinion as they set their course in foreign affairs. There were exceptions to this, of course. Turkish atrocities against Christians in the Balkans could and did cause popular agitation for reprisals in Russia; and French boulevard opinion got very worked up in 1840 about a minor setback in the Near East and almost stampeded the government into war. But in general, Metternich's view that "foreign affairs is not for the plebs" seemed to be reasonably sound, and foreign ministers did not concern themselves overmuch about what might be in tomorrow's headlines.

Governments were free also from pressure from organized economic interests. Industrialization and capitalism had not evolved to the point where business firms were forming lobbies and seeking to influence political decisions; in this period most businessmen were convinced that the best thing that the government could do for them was to leave them alone. The problem of reconciling desirable foreign policy initiatives with the desiderata of powerful private interests, which in our own time often makes the use of economic pressures ineffective (as was true in the case of the U.S. grain embargo against the Soviet Union in 1980–1981), did not plague foreign offices in the first half of the nineteenth century.

Again, there was no agitation on the part of military establishments for an increased rate or level of armament. Indeed, the country with the biggest army after 1815, Russia, actually proposed a general scaling down of armaments one year after the Congress of Vienna had completed its work. This proposal did not find favor with the other powers—the British said they believed that each power should be its own judge when it came to setting limits to its armed forces, although they added that they would be ready at all times to inform others of their force levels; the Austrians were not even prepared to go that far, because of what Metternich called "the perpetual difficulty of obtaining any true data from Russia"—but on the other hand, if they wouldn't disarm, there was no disposition on the part of any of the powers to launch a program of military expansion; and the war offices of the various powers seemed completely content with this situation. There were no military pressure groups, any more than there were economic pressure groups, to complicate the policy-making process and disturb international relations.

In the second place, there were no ideological differences of any importance between the powers. There were moments, to be sure, when it seemed that divisions of this kind were on the point of becoming real. After the revolutions of 1830, which brought a liberal regime to power in France, Europe seemed to be divided into two camps: a liberal one of England and France, and a conservative one comprising Russia, Prussia, and Austria. The British foreign secretary, Lord Palmerston, admitted that this was the apparent drift of international politics when he said, "The three and the two think differently and therefore they act differently."

If one examines the record of the years 1830–1854, however, it is clear that the powers ignored their ideological differences more than they observed them. If cooperation with France was, as Lord Palmerston once said, the axle upon which British policy turned, he had no compunction about concluding agreements with the Eastern powers in moments when he felt the French were threatening British interests; while on the French side, Louis Philippe showed a growing desire—once his regime was firmly established—to seek an accommodation with the Eastern powers even at the expense of his entente with England. When Metternich became worried about the czar's policy in the Near East, he consulted the British about ways of restraining him; when the czar became annoyed with his Prussian ally's Baltic ambitions, he collaborated with the British to frustrate them. If Europe was divided after 1830 along ideological lines, they were not so rigidly drawn as to prevent a high degree of interpenetration of combinations and a considerable amount of collaboration between the Eastern and Western powers.

Finally, all differences between the powers were subordinated to the high degree of consensus among them. With the possible exception of France, which did not dare admit its uniqueness, all powers accepted the balance of power—that is, the territorial arrangements made at Vienna and the broader principle that no single state should be allowed to increase its possessions except with the consent of others. The acceptance of this implied certain other things: a high degree of restraint on the part of single powers (Czar Nicholas could probably have exacted a higher price for his aid to the Turks in 1833 but refused to do so because he feared such unilateral action might lead to emulation); a willingness to accept the validity of existing treaties (in no age in modern times was there greater respect paid to the principle *Pacta sunt servanda*); and a willingness when single powers seemed on the point of seeking unilateral aggrandizement (as was true of France in 1840) to participate in concerted action to restrain them.

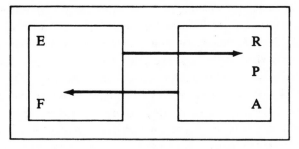

Figure 1

This consensus was the essential strength of the international system of the years 1815–1854. Figure 1 is a reasonably accurate visual expression of the way in which the balance of power was maintained in the early nineteenth century. The inner squares represent the Anglo-French entente on the one hand and the combination of the northern courts on the other; the arrows signify the interpenetration and intercamp collaboration that went on throughout the period; and the outer rectangle represents the consensus that held all of the major powers together in an effective concert that preserved the Vienna settlement in its major outlines and maintained the equilibrium of forces in Europe.

II

The strength of this Vienna system was seriously eroded by the revolutions that took place during 1848, a year of profound political convulsions that undermined confidence in all legal structures, including the international ones. After 1848, a new spirit prevailed in the chancelleries of Europe, one that found its strongest expression in the policies of a new generation of young men in a hurry who were ambitious for their own countries and no longer willing to abide by the collaborative principles and practices invented and followed by the statesmen of Vienna. These newcomers included Felix zu Schwarzenberg in Austria, Camillo di Cavour in Piedmont, Otto von Bismarck in Prussia, and Louis Napoleon in France. The event that opened the way to the fulfillment of the ambitions of these *Realpolitiker* (to use the term invented in the 1850s by Ludwig von Rochow) was the outbreak of war between Russia and Britain (supported by France and Piedmont) in 1854. The two powers whose collaboration had prevented the revolutions of 1848 from degenerating into a major international conflict now slipped into one themselves—a senseless struggle that resulted not from any deliberate threat to the interest of either power, but from a series of escalating moves to ward off imaginary dangers. The Crimean War by itself caused more deaths than any other conflict between 1815 and 1914; more important, it left

Europe in an anarchical situation in which more powers were interested in revising what was left of the balance than were interested in preserving it. After 1856, Russia, France, Prussia, and the rising power of Piedmont could all be considered as revisionist powers, and only Austria and Great Britain as supporters of the existing order, and the second of these, wearied by its exertions in the Crimea, was in a pronouncedly isolationist mood. In this situation, the European concert could not exert effective restraint against aggressors, and its failure was illustrated in the fact that within fifteen years, four major wars were fought in Europe: the Italian war of 1859, between Austria on the one hand and Piedmont and France on the other; the war between Denmark and the German states in 1864; the Austro-Prussian War of 1866; and the Franco-Prussian War of 1870. As a result, the old European balance was destroyed.

Moreover, the task of making a new balance and building an effective new international system to maintain it was much more difficult than that which had confronted the men of Vienna. There was no relaxation of tension after 1870, as there had been after 1815. The resentments and frustrations left by the wars of unification were great—the French unable to forget the annexation of Alsace and Lorraine by Germany, the Austrians seeking to make good their losses in Germany by a forward policy in the Balkans that aroused Russia's anger and distrust, the Italians dissatisfied with the extent of their new united kingdom and burning to despoil the Austrians of areas inhabited by Italian minorities.

The opportunities for friction between the powers were many after 1870, not only because all of the free territory in Europe, all of the buffers and shock absorbers, had disappeared with the completion of Italian and German unification (so that the great powers now had common borders and rubbed up against each other uncomfortably), but also because the age of free trade was coming to an end and the age of neomercantilism and imperialism dawning, so that tariff wars and colonial competition between powers would soon be the order of the day. The psychological mood of the years after 1871 was not one of appeasement, but rather one of hypersensitive nationalism and combativeness, which was fed by the widespread currency of Darwinism and by the sensationalism of a newspaper press that pandered to a gullible and excitable new reading public that had been created by the spread of free compulsory elementary education. Governments that were interested in following sensible collaborative foreign policies were no longer as free of external pressures as Metternich had been. Public opinion still exercised only a sporadic influence upon policy determination, but economic interests were now organized and were developing techniques for persuading governments to alter policies in their interest. Bismarck, for example, found that he could not simply ignore industrial and agricultural pressure for tariffs in the seventies and colonies in the eighties. Also, in an age in which warfare had become mechanized and increasingly technical, governments were discovering that they had to consult their military staffs more frequently and that it was increasingly difficult to disregard the advice they received, even when it had questionable political implications. In all countries, war offices now tended to become pressure groups for the increased armaments that were a feature of the age.

In view of all this—and of the increased incidence of ideological differences between powers that came with the growth of French *revanchisme,* Pan Slavism, Pan Germanism, irredentism, and integral nationalism—it is clear that there could be no real consensus between the powers as there had been in the period before the Crimean War; and, this being so, it was unlikely that the concert of Europe, even if it could be reassembled, would be effective in maintaining the uneasy balance of power that the wars of the sixties had created.

This was a source of concern to the leading statesman of the country that had been the principal beneficiary of those wars. Otto von Bismarck, who had contributed so powerfully to the destruction of the old European balance, was a changed character after 1870, a man who was determined to keep the gains his country had made but who wanted nothing more for it but peace, since he regarded Germany now as a sated power. It became rapidly apparent to Bismarck, however, as he became aware of the unreliability of old friends during the crisis of 1875 and of the possibility of an Austro-Russian conflict in the Balkans that would almost certainly involve Germany, that wishing for peace was not enough. When he acted as an honest broker in 1878, inviting the contentious powers to a congress in Berlin and successfully averting a war in the Near East, the Russian government took the line that the settlement was a blow to its vital interests and a betrayal of past friendship and began to talk of an alliance with France. It was clear to Bismarck that the traditional friendship among Prussia, Austria, and Russia, forged in the war against Napoleon, could no longer be relied upon. If the existing balance of power, and Germany's place in it, was to be preserved, it would have to be by some new means.

Bismarck reluctantly concluded that the only effective way of escaping from his dilemma would be the elaboration of a system of secret alliances that would, at a minimum, relieve Germany of potential isolation and might, if things went well, give him some measure of control over the policies of enough of the other powers to prevent their embarking upon actions that would threaten the general peace. Later on, he was to define his policy by saying that one must not lose sight of "the importance of being one of three on the European chess-board. That is the invariable objective of all cabinets and of mine above all others. Nobody wishes to be in a minority. All politics reduce themselves to this formula: to try to be one of three as long as the world is governed by an unstable equilibrium of five great powers."

This was probably a rationalization after the fact. After the Congress of Berlin, when Germany was in a state of near isolation, Bismarck had more limited objectives. He decided that Germany needed one reliable ally, and he

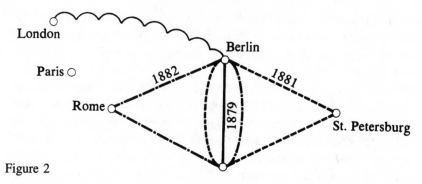

Figure 2

reached out to Austria-Hungary, concluding a secret treaty that stipulated mutual defense in the event of an attack by Russia and benevolent neutrality if either ally were attacked by a power other than Russia. But this treaty of 1879 rather unexpectedly brought him the kind of control that was to secure the European balance for the next twelve years. For although the Austrian treaty was a secret, its conclusion was not, and it startled the Russians into changing their tune and asking for a renewal of the Three Emperors' League, which Bismarck granted. And that success brought the Italians, hat in hand, to Berlin, asking for protection against French attacks on their interests in North Africa—to which Bismarck agreed on condition that the Italians also make a treaty of accommodation with Austria. Assured by his Austrian treaty of assistance in case of a Russian attack upon Germany, Bismarck had, by means of his other new engagements, blocked the possibility of a Franco-Russian alliance and greatly reduced the chance of a war between Austria and Russia in the Balkans or a conflict between Austria and Italy in the Trentino. Simultaneously, his support of British interests in Egypt completed the isolation of France.

A graphic illustration of Bismarck's balance of power would be markedly different from that of the Vienna system. It would look something like Figure 2. Here there is no outer all-embracing consensual frame-work. The suspicion between the powers was so great that consensus was impossible. At the same time, there are no opposing but interconnected subsystems. In this model, all powers, with the exception of France, are bound one way or another to Berlin, and bound on Bismarck's terms. The Austrians, for instance, were assured of German support in the event that their Balkan interests were subjected to Russian attack, but they were at the same time held on a very short leash by Bismarck's warning that he would not support them if they took the initiative in causing an Austro-Russian war.

The Bismarck way of maintaining the post-1871 equilibrium of forces was a complicated one, and that was its chief weakness. It operated by means of secrecy, constant maneuver, and a high degree of disingenuousness. During the tense Bulgarian crisis of 1886–1887, when a renewal of Austro-Russian antagonism in the Balkans dissolved the Three Emperors' League and a simultaneous wave of *revanchisme* in France made a Franco-Russian alliance seem possible, Bismarck was able to contain these dangers and repair his system only by the most questionable means: a deliberately manufactured war-scare designed to intimidate the French and professed support of Russian objectives in the Balkans that was belied by covert connivance with third powers and stock market manipulations that rendered his promises meaningless. Bismarck's performance in this affair has often been described as a tour de force, but the course that he followed was so subterranean and devious that, while it is unnecessary to accept the judgment of a distinguished British scholar who held ''that the old gentleman had slightly lost his head,'' it is difficult to avoid the suspicion that he was beginning to prefer tactical virtuosity to plain dealing. Certainly his methods in the Bulgarian affair saved his system only in a formal sense, while increasing the feeling of the Russians in particular that they had been lied to. As a result, the days of the Bismarckian model of balance of power were numbered. Even if the chancellor had remained in office after 1890, it is impossible to believe that it could have stood the strain of his manipulations much longer.

III

The third systematic form assumed by balance of power came in the years from 1907 to 1914, when all of the major European powers, including Great Britain, which had abandoned the ''splendid isolation'' upon which it had prided itself during most of the nineteenth century, were ranged in two hostile and highly armed coalitions. It was this manifestation of the politics of equilibrium that fastened itself upon the imagination of later generations and, because of its catastrophic end, made balance of power an opprobrious term in the postwar period, particularly in the United States.

It is possible—and not entirely unjustified—to place the blame for the emergence of the 1907–1914 system, with all of its deplorable consequences, upon the nature of German policy after Bismarck's dismissal in 1890. That event had been followed almost immediately by the German government's decision to simplify its foreign commitments by dropping the connection with Russia, which appeared to be incompatible with obligations assumed toward Austria in the Dual Alliance of 1879. This was a reasonable enough step to take and one that certainly did not justify the loud predictions of doom voiced by the Bismarck *fronde.* Had the German government maintained its aplomb when the Russians did the natural thing and began to move toward an accommodation with France, much later harm might have been avoided. Instead, the nervousness and tactical maladroitness of German policy destroyed what was left of Bismarck's system and left Europe in a much more unstable and fragile condition. This result the

German government of William II, particularly in the period when Bülow was chancellor and Tirpitz chief of the imperial Naval Office, effected in two ways.

In the first place, it conducted an aggressive and offensive policy in the overseas areas of the world, interfering in the spheres of influence of other powers in Africa, the Pacific, and the Middle East in such a way as to annoy everybody and to convince old associates that the Germans were unreliable. The Russians, who tended still to be closer ideologically to the Germans than to the western powers and who regarded the British as their chief antagonist in the Middle East, were unpleasantly surprised, at the end of the nineties and the beginning of the next decade, to find the Germans moving into their sphere of interest in the Persian Gulf, and they began to revise their views. The British and the French, who were at loggerheads in Africa after 1882 and came uncomfortably close to war in the Sudan in 1898, discovered that Germany was becoming a nuisance and a potential threat to both of them and began to mend their fences. Meanwhile, Britain loosed its ties with Germany's junior partners out of irritation over German tactics.

In the second place, the stability of the German government at home and its security against socialism depended upon an alliance of conservative political parties and groups that derived financial support from heavy industry and big agriculture. Those economic interests had desiderata and knew how to combine their forces so as to get what they wanted. Specifically, their pressure was instrumental in persuading the German government to launch a heightened naval armaments program in 1900 which could not help concerning and worrying the English and in the end alienating them. They were also able to mobilize enough votes in the Reichstag in 1902 to force the passage of a new tariff bill that virtually excluded Russian grain from German markets. This tariff struck a blow against the economic interests of that class in Russia that had always been the most friendly to Germany, and when that happened any chance of reconciliation between Germany and Russia came to an end. Since the early 1890s, there had been a military tie between France and Russia. This now became stronger, and both powers turned to Britain, which was waiting to receive them.

It would be a mistake, however, to think of this fateful course as having been caused solely by German clumsiness and impercipience. Even had William II, Bülow, and Tirpitz been wiser and more responsible leaders, it is difficult to believe that the British apprehensiveness about Germany would have been any different. In his masterly study of the rise of Anglo-German antagonism, Paul Kennedy has pointed out that basically, it was the transformation of Germany from a cluster of second-rate states under insignificant princelings to a united empire with a population greater than Britain's, impressive industrial resources, and advanced technology that was the root cause of the deterioration of its relations with Great Britain. By the end of the nineteenth century, Germany was

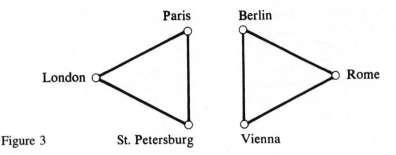

Figure 3

"not only growing out of its European 'skin' but also acquiring the early attributes of a world power. . . . All this necessarily implied a relative diminution in Britain's own commercial/colonial/maritime position unless it in turn was able to export more, colonize more, and build more ships so as to preserve the original relationship."

To the British this change brought new anxieties and new resentments. The nervousness characteristic of German policy after 1890 was no less pronounced in Great Britain. It was all too easy to believe that Germany was infringing upon British interests, even when this was more a question of perception than of actuality. British decision makers concerned about "saving the empire" slipped easily into the habit of regarding Germany not as a rival but as a future foe. Lord Esher was not alone in thinking "there is no doubt that within measurable distance there looms a titanic struggle between Germany and Europe for mastery. The years 1793–1815 will be repeated, only Germany, not France, will be trying for European domination. She has 70,000,000 of people and is determined to have commercial pre-eminence. To do this *England* has got to be crippled and the Low Countries added to the German Empire." It was this kind of deepseated *Angst* that led the British governing class to conclude in the first years of the new century that Britain could no longer maintain its security by its own resources but must seek to contain the German threat by entering into partnership with Germany's antagonists.

The result was the Entente Cordiale with France in 1904 and the Anglo-Russian Agreement of 1907, which effected a radical transformation of the European balance and a confrontation between Triple Alliance and Triple Entente (Figure 3). The salient characteristics of this new system were, as was true of the Bismarckian experiment in equilibrium, a lack of any consensus between the powers and a reliance upon formal secret alliances rather than informal combinations. But this new variant was a bipolar system, in contrast to the Bismarck system, in which everything had centered upon Berlin; and this bipolarity made it as much more unstable than the Bismarck system as that system had been more unstable than the Vienna one. For there was no interpenetration

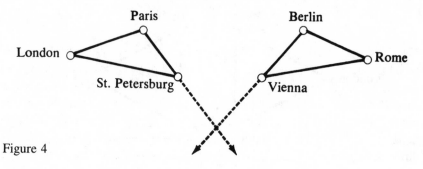

Figure 4

here, as there had been in the Vienna system, and there was no control by a strong alliance leader, as there had been in the Bismarck system. In the years 1907–1914, the predominant characteristics of both parts of the new bipolar system were a constantly accelerating armament program and a growing fear in both coalitions of losing allies to the opposite camp and thus being placed at a dangerous disadvantage, or being encircled and destroyed.

The German government, aware that the Italians were unreliable (there was lots of evidence of this after 1900) came to fear isolation and to place an excess valuation upon the Austrian alliance (hence William II's talk about the necessity of Nibelungen loyalty). Because the Germans did so, they abandoned Bismarck's wise limitation upon his commitment to Austria, namely, that Germany would support it against Russia only if it were attacked by the latter power and not if it took the initiative itself. In 1909, during the last stages of the Bosnian crisis, the German chief of general staff, Moltke the younger, specifically told his opposite number in Vienna that he could rely upon German support, regardless of the origins of the conflict, an assurance that was patently dangerous but seemed necessary in the circumstances. The British and the French began to have similar apprehensions about losing the Russians to the Germans (this was the constant fear of the permanent undersecretary of the British Foreign Office, Sir Arthur Nicolson), and they tended, in consequence, to give them a dangerous degree of freedom of action, instead of warning them that, if they were foolhardy, they would have to stand alone. The details of the various crises from the Bosnian affair of 1908–1909 to the Sarajevo crisis of 1914 need not be spelled out. It is enough to say that, in the simplest terms, the First World War resulted from the inflexibility of the alliances and the lack of control by the senior members over the most irresponsible of their partners. Once more the result can be shown schematically (Figure 4), the triangles indicating the opposed alliances and the arrows indicating the irresponsible drives of the two junior partners, which drew the whole family of nations into war after the murder of the heir to the Austrian throne in Sarajevo on 28 June 1914.

IV

The three experiments contrived by European statesmen in the nineteenth century to construct and operate a viable balance-of-power system differed, as noted, in significant respects. The earlier variant of that system, described in chapter 2, was even more competitive and less regulated by common conventions, practices, and institutions and, perhaps partly for that reason, more vulnerable to Napoleon's drive to replace it by a hegemonic system. These differences notwithstanding, all variants shared certain essential features to a greater or lesser extent, and these general characteristics of the multipolar European balance-of-power system deserve brief mention.

The major "rule" of the European balance-of-power system was that each of the five great powers should cooperate as necessary to preserve the balance, for this was the principal means for discouraging any one state from seeking hegemony. It was understood that considerable flexibility in making alliances and shifting alliance partners was necessary to this end. Permanent, rigid alliances were to be avoided, a rule violated with disastrous consequences in the variant of the system that came into being during the years 1907 to 1914. Similarly, to ensure that the five major actors remained of roughly equal power and to dampen the competition among them, several other rules and practices were institutionalized as necessary means for the operation and maintenance of the system. One of these, the principle of compensation, as already noted, worked as follows: when one of the great powers acquired—or wished to acquire—additional territory or resources, it was understood that the other powers also had to receive appropriate payoffs of territory, population, or resources, usually at the expense of weaker states inside or outside of Europe.

Another rule of the system that operated to maintain balance and stability was the understanding that war involving the great powers should be fought for strictly limited objectives. A related rule was that punitive peace terms were to be avoided in terminating such wars and that the great power that was defeated in such a contest had to be readmitted to the system as a regular member to participate once more in the balancing process. In these and other ways, the competition and conflicts among the great powers were regulated in the interest of preserving the balance-of-power system and, in turn, the essential security and survival of each of them.

The European balance-of-power system of the eighteenth and nineteenth centuries displayed a number of distinctive characteristics that are not found in hegemonic international systems, such as that centered on Manchu China during roughly the same period, or in systems of world government that have been advocated from time to time. Thus, the European system was a *decentralized, self-regulating system*—one in which power and responsibility remained in the hands of the constituent state actors. There was, in other words, no supranational political or governmental authority at the apex of the system to keep the major powers in line, to regulate their quarrels, to ensure that international politics did not become anarchic, to act in order to enforce the rules of the system. All these were, indeed, important requirements for the maintenance of the European system, but they had to be achieved by the great powers themselves by coordinating and regulating their own behavior.

Furthermore, the management of the European system in the interest of maintaining the balance was understood to be a responsibility that all of the great powers should assume. Awareness of the responsibility emerged with greater clarity and conviction particularly after the nearly disastrous experience with Napoleon. Before that, there was a tendency to assume that the balancing and equilibrium the system required would follow more or less automatically from unrestrained competition among them—a reflection, one is tempted to say, of the Smithian and physiocratic belief in the virtues of perfect, unregulated competition. Afterward, European statesmen felt the need to create an institutional framework and practices—embodied in the concert of Europe—to promote the kind of cooperation and coordination of foreign policies needed to ensure the efficiency of a balance-of-power system. When the concert proved to be ineffective in the decade after 1871, Bismarck attempted to fill the vacuum by developing a different variant of the system in which he arrogated to himself unilateral responsibility for "managing" it.

A third characteristic of the European system was that the competition among the major actors was not conceived of, or pursued, in terms of a "zero-sum" game. That is, the great powers did not perceive each other as implacable enemies engaged in an elimination contest, one in which any gain for one side could only be at the expense of the other. Rather, the actors viewed each other as "limited adversaries": not only was a gain for one not necessarily a loss for the other, but the principle of compensation was invoked as a means of moderating the competitiveness of the game.

Efforts to preserve the character of a non-zero-sum game were facilitated by another feature of the European system, which can be highlighted by invoking the colorful distinction in economic analysis between the "constant pie" and an "expanding pie." For much of the eighteenth and nineteenth centuries, the amount of territory and resources available to be contested and divided up among the great powers was not fixed and finite. The struggle over "who gets what" was alleviated because the European powers were competing for an expanding pie. Thus, the competition did not (and was not permitted to) jeopardize the vital interests of any of the great powers. Rather, it was conducted in good part at the expense of third parties—that is, weaker European states, declining major powers (such as Spain and the Ottoman Empire), and non-European territories in Africa, Asia, and America. Toward the end of the nineteenth century and in the decade before the outbreak of World War I, however, opportunities for further expansion at the expense of third parties narrowed, and some statesmen began to view the competition with their great-power rivals in terms approaching a constant-pie analogy, a development which contributed to the rigidification and polarization of the two alliance systems.

Finally, it should be noted that the European balance-of-power system did _not aim at eliminating war as an instrument of foreign policy._ Instead, a distinction was made between permissible and impermissible wars. War and the threat of military action were often regarded as permissible if the objectives were limited and did not threaten the stability of the balance-of-power system. Thus, one could make war, or threaten it, in order to achieve useful marginal gains (or to avoid irksome losses) that did not threaten the vital interests of other major powers or undermine their status as such; but wars were impermissible if they aimed at, or created the possibility of, drastically weakening any of the great powers or their essential allies. On the other hand, resort to threats of war and actual war were legitimate, indeed in a sense became necessary, if one state attempted to achieve predominant power and domination of the system, for this would destroy the balance-of-power system itself and replace it with a hegemonic international system. With the passage of time, and particularly in the rigid bipolar version of the system at the turn of the century, the distinction between permissible and impermissible war faded. This was nowhere more evident than in July 1914, when the great powers for a variety of reasons could not agree whether the Austrian declaration of war upon Serbia was permissible or not.

Bibliographical Essay

The literature on the reconstruction of Europe after the Napoleonic wars is very rich. Most useful on the Vienna negotiations are C. K. Webster, *The Congress of Vienna* (London, 1919), and Harold Nicolson, *The Congress of Vienna* (London, 1945). Illuminating on the men who made the settlement are C. K. Webster, *The Foreign Policy of Castlereagh, 1815–1822,* 2d ed. (Oxford, 1937); A. Duff Cooper, *Talleyrand* (London, 1932); Henry A. Kissinger, *A World Restored: Metternich, Castlereagh and the Problems of Peace, 1812–1822,* new ed. (New York, 1964), an excellent account; and the biographies of Metternich by H. Ritter von Srbik, 4 vols. (Munich, 1925ff.), H. du Coudray (London, 1935), G. Berthier du Sauvignon (London, 1962), and Algernon Cecil (New York, 1933). On the Austrian statesman, see also E. L. Woodward's provocative essay in *Three Studies of European Conservatism* (London, 1930). On the congress system, the old but still useful authority is G. Allison Phillips, *The Confederation of Europe,* 2d ed. (London, 1920), but see also H. G. Schenk, *The Aftermath of the Napoleonic Wars: The Concert of Europe—an Experiment* (New York, 1947). For the course of international politics before 1848, H. W. V. Temperley, *The Foreign Policy of Canning, 1822–1827* (London, 1925), and Paul W. Schroeder, *Metternich's Diplomacy at Its Zenith, 1820–1823* (New York, 1962), give interesting contrasting views; and C. K. Webster,

The Foreign Policy of Palmerston, 1830–1841, 2 vols. (London, 1951), is essential. For general coverage of the middle years, see Gordon A. Craig, "The Great Powers and the Balance of Power, 1830–1870," in *New Cambridge Modern History,* vol. 10 (Cambridge, 1960), and Paul W. Schroeder, *Austria, Britain, and the Crimean War: The Destruction of the European Concert* (Ithaca, N.Y., 1972); on disarmament, see Gordon A. Craig and Peter Paret, "The Control of International Violence: Some Historical Notes," *Stanford Journal of International Studies* 7 (1972): 1–21; E. L. Woodward, *War and Peace in Europe* (London, 1929); and J. Headlam-Morley, *Studies in Diplomatic History* (London, 1930).

For the second half of the century, see especially A. J. P. Taylor, *The Struggle for Mastery in Europe, 1848–1918* (Oxford, 1954), sometimes a bit sweeping in its judgments; R. C. Binkley, *Realism and Nationalism, 1852–1870* (New York, 1935), a brilliantly executed study; and W. L. Langer, *European Alliances and Alignments,* new ed. (New York, 1950), and *The Diplomacy of Imperialism,* 2d ed. (New York, 1951). Bismarck's diplomacy is treated in the biographies by A. J. P. Taylor (New York, 1955), Erich Eyck, 3 vols. (Zurich, 1941–1944), Lothar Gall (Frankfurt am Main, 1980), Otto Pflanze, 3 vols. (Princeton, 1990), and Ernst Engelberg, 2 vols. (Berlin, 1986, 1990); but see also W. N. Medlicott, *Bismarck, Gladstone and the Concert of Europe* (London, 1956), and George F. Kennan, *The Decline of Bismarck's European Order: Franco-Russian Relations, 1875–1890* (Princeton, 1979). On the Congress of Berlin, see B. Humphrey Sumner, *Russia and the Balkans, 1870–1880* (London, 1937), a splendid book. On the deterioration of the balance of power after 1890, see the first chapters of the much discussed Fritz Fischer, *Griff nach der Weltmacht* (Dusseldorf, 1961), translated in abbreviated form from the German as *Germany's Aims in the First World War* (New York, 1967); James Joll, *The Origins of the First World War,* 2d ed. (London, 1992), a remarkably comprehensive book for its modest size; Zara S. Steiner, *The Foreign Office and Foreign Policy, 1898–1914* (Cambridge, 1969), and *Britain and the Origins of the First World War* (London, 1977); and Paul Kennedy, *The Rise of the Anglo-German Antagonism, 1860–1914* (London, 1980), a masterly study.

Useful general works are F. H. Hinsley, *Power and the Pursuit of Peace: Theory and Practice in the History of Relations Between States* (Cambridge, 1963), which concentrates upon the nineteenth-century system; E. V. Gulick, *Europe's Classical Balance of Power* (Ithaca, N.Y., 1955); F. R. Bridge and R. Bullen, *The Great Powers and the European States System, 1815–1914* (London, 1980); and Paul Kennedy, *The Rise and Fall of the Great Powers: Economic Change and Military Conflict from 1500 to 2000* (New York, 1987).

4

System-Building, 1919–1939

In 1814–1815, after almost twenty-five years of intermittent warfare, representatives of the European powers had been able to sit down together—in Metternich's phrase, ''as friends''—and to lay the foundations for a diplomatic system that worked effectively for thirty-five years and, after a period of reorganization by war between 1854 and 1871, reasonably effectively for another forty. The war that brought that system to its calamitous end lasted only four years, but when it was over at last and the statesmen of the belligerent nations came together in another great diplomatic congress, this time in Paris, their achievement fell far short of that of their predecessors at Vienna. No viable system emerged from their labors and, although they tried at times to pretend that it had, the fact that a greater war than that of 1914–1918 broke out within twenty years was proof of their failure.

The peacemakers of 1919 were, to be sure, confronted with a situation of unprecedented difficulty. For one thing, the conflict that had just come to an end had not been contained and completed by the powers that began it, nor did some of them survive the fighting of it. That the war had expanded from its European center to every part of the world was not, of course, surprising. We have seen that that happened even in the wars of the eighteenth century, and that then, and during the great age of imperialism in the nineteenth century, the great powers often sought to regulate their intra-European relations by means of action in colonial areas. But in this war, the former colonial areas came into their own as independent actors in world politics, and they emerged from the war with policies and objectives of their own. Canada, Australia, New Zealand, and South Africa, as well as Japan and the United States, had played a secondary and sporadic or discontinuous role in international affairs before the war; their part was to be greater from now on. But how much greater it was still difficult to say; and the question of how to fit them into his political calculations confronted the system maker with grave structural problems.

Moreover, after the war there was not much left of the known entities of international relations. Of the five great powers that had dominated the old system, three—the German Empire, the Russian Empire, and the Austro-Hungarian Empire—had succumbed to revolution, and the third of these had dissolved into its component parts. How was one to work into any new system such untried elements as the Bolshevik state of Russia and the new German and Austrian republics, to say nothing of such nations as Hungary and Czechoslovakia, Yugoslavia and the revived Poland?

Any attempt to do so was bound to be complicated by political passions that had been unknown in 1814. There was no question now of former friends and foes sitting down together to lay the foundations of peace, as they had at Vienna. The war of 1914–1918 had far exceeded the conflicts of the nineteenth century in duration and ferocity, and in other senses it was revolutionary: it was not a limited but a total war that involved the whole of the resources at the command of the participants, and it broke down the old division between the military and civilian parts of society. Indeed, there were really no noncombatants in this war, and the suffering of civilian populations was greater than it had been since the horrors of the Thirty Years War. That war, as we have seen, started as a religious conflict and ended as a political one. One could say of the First World War that it marked a reversal of that process, beginning as a political conflict and ending as a religious one, in which each side began to view the other not as an opponent who must be defeated, but as a kind of anti-Christ who must be extirpated. This transition, which was much more marked in the case of civilian populations than in that of the fighting men themselves, was the result of suffering and sacrifice on the one hand and wartime propaganda on the other, and it had serious results, turning the war for many people into what has been called above a zero-sum game. When it was over, there was little sentiment among the victors for reconciliation with the beaten foe. The impulse was rather to punish him, to place burdens upon him that would prevent his recovery or delay it for an indefinite period.

This is why events at Paris in 1919 took a different course than they had a hundred years earlier in Vienna. In 1814–1815, the settlement had been a two-stage process. The war was ended by the First Peace of Paris, and certain arrangements were made to establish a government in the defeated country with which the others could have relations. Only after that was done was a congress held for the purpose of making a comprehensive and viable peace settlement, and during the negotiations for this the former enemy was allowed to participate on equal terms with the victors. The original intention in 1919 was to have a similar procedural model: a preliminary conference to make peace and some tentative decisions about new territorial arrangements, as well as about penalties and compensations, followed by a second conference, with the participation of the defeated powers, to consider these and other matters and to draw up the definitive settlement. But the peacemakers never got to the second stage, and many decisions that were tentative and made in the expectation that they would be revised in a followup conference became definitive by default, with grave consequences later on.

This was due partly to the failure of the victorious powers to realize how complicated a task it would be to make peace after so protracted a war, or how long it would take, a discovery that led them in the end to abandon their original intention. But the deeper reason lay in the passions engendered by the war. Too many of the participants were unreconciled and bent solely upon the most Draconian forms of punishment against the Germans or the Austrians or the Turks. The enemy powers were not given the chance to express their views during the deliberations, and in the end they were simply handed peace terms that were in large part vindictive, and told to accept them. When the victors' will to revenge seemed to falter or when they sought to moderate their treatment of the enemy, their representatives were attacked by their own newspapers and threatened with reprisals at the next elections. During the whole of the peace conference, the *Daily Mail* in Great Britain carried a box on its first page that read "The Huns will cheat you yet!" This was meant as a warning to British negotiators, and it persuaded them to be unforgiving in their attitude and savage in their demand for reprisals. The head of the British government in 1919 was David Lloyd George, and his election slogan of 1918 is indicative of the temper of the times. It was "We will squeeze the orange till the pips squeak!"

During the peace conference and afterward, the former enemy powers were relegated to a kind of limbo. It should be remembered, for instance, that Germany—although it was no longer the same Germany that had caused the war, but a new republic—was not allowed to become a member of the League of Nations until 1926. If one recalls that Russia, in its new form as a union of Socialist Soviet states, was also excluded, since it was considered to be a subversive threat to the Western nations, which had only intermittent relations with it and generally regarded it as lying outside the comity of nations, one can understand that it was extremely difficult to construct an international system that promised to be as effective as the one that had been destroyed in 1914; and it became more difficult when the United States, despite its leading role in the years 1917–1919, voluntarily withdrew into isolation.

This became clear even before the future course of the United States was determined. One of the problems confronting the peacemakers was to find a theoretical basis for a new international order. The negotiators in Vienna a hundred years earlier had invoked the principle of the balance of power, and there were statesmen in Paris, particularly the French, who continued to think in those terms, as also in terms of treaties of guarantee and of alliance, the traditional support of the balance. But this idea found an eloquent and powerful antagonist in the president of the United States, Woodrow Wilson, who like many Americans before him believed that balance-of-power politics was a contrivance of states that had always been prone to absolutism, militarism, and antidemocratic behavior and that the coming of the war in 1914 was rooted in its acrobatics and intrigues. He had made his determination to eliminate the old system abundantly clear in his speech to the United States Senate on the essentials of peace on 22 January 1917, in which he had called for "a peace without victory" and declared:

> There must be not a balance of power but a community of power. . . . I am therefore proposing that all nations henceforth avoid entangling alliances that draw them into competitions of power, catch them in a net of intrigue and selfish rivalry, and disturb their own affairs with influences intruded from without. There is no entangling alliance in a concert of power. When all unite to act in the same sense and with the same purpose, all act in the common interest and are free to live their own lives under a common protection.

One month after the Armistice, he made the same point clear to his associates in the peacemaking process. In his speech at the Guild Hall in London on 28 December 1918, he said that the soldiers of the Allied armies had

> fought to do away with an older order and to establish a new one, and the center and characteristic of the old order was that venerable thing which we used to call the "balance of power"—a thing in which the balance was determined by the sword which was thrown in the one side or the other; a balance which was determined by the unstable equilibrium of competitive interests; a balance which was maintained by jealous watchfulness and an antagonism of interests which, though it was generally latent, was always deep-seated. The men who have fought in this war have been the men from free nations who were determined that that sort of thing should end now and forever.

This was, of course, a biased view, and Wilson's picture of the balance-of-power system was a restricted one, based entirely upon the unstable post-Bismarckian model. But in these speeches, the president was less a historian than a visionary, inspired by a conviction held by many Americans since the beginning of their nation that relations of the peoples of the world should be regulated not by the outworn standards of Europe, but by democratic principles. "The old nonsense about balance of power," an American journal had announced in 1852, "is wholly out of date, and the doctrine of the solidarity of mankind is beginning to spread; popular sovereignty is on the point of overcoming legitimacy quickly; every day the system, which is now restricted to Europe and America, is expanding; and soon it will embrace Asia, Africa and Oceania." This vision had persisted in American thinking about foreign affairs, although challenged by realists like Alfred Thayer Mahan and Theodore Roosevelt; and after the debacle of 1914–1918 it inspired Wilson and the members of the U.S. delegation to the peace conference. They came to Paris in a militant mood, as suspicious of European motives as the founding fathers had been (John Adams once said, "It is obvious that all the powers of Europe will be continually maneuvering with us, to work us into their real or imaginary balances of power") and intent, as Walter Lippman wrote at the time, upon "teach[ing] the European mind . . . that back of all our physical display lies a purpose which strikes at the roots of the old European system."

In its place, Wilson desired to establish a community of free nations that would adjust their relations with each other without resort to the modalities of the old European order, and the basis of this was to be a League of Nations, with permanent institutions for the discussion of matters of interest to the international community, for the revision of the peace treaties when inequities became apparent, and for the regulation of disputes. The establishment of this body was the president's principal objective during the Paris negotiations, but the potential advantages that he claimed for it proved to be less than attractive to the representatives of the Allied powers. Premier Clemenceau of France remained an intransigent supporter of the balance-of-power system, convinced that history had shown it to be the most effective regulator of relationships between nations; and he was not prepared to abandon it because of sermons by a man whom he regarded as an idealistic schoolmaster from a country with no experience in world affairs. The British and the Italians and the Poles were inclined to agree. They wanted to punish the enemy, to be compensated for their sacrifices, and to construct a new system on the basis of treaties and guarantees.

The Paris Peace Conference became, therefore, the scene of a protracted conflict between President Wilson and his former associates. In the end, he gained his major objective, the establishment of the League of Nations, but only at the expense of so many compromises that vitiated his own declared principles—particularly the Fourteen Points of the peace program that he had announced in his address to Congress on 8 January 1918—that it was difficult to talk any longer of a peace without victory and with justice for all parties. The discrepancies between what the Fourteen Points had promised and what the Treaty of Versailles stipulated were so palpable that Wilson's critics in the United States had no difficulty in mounting a powerful offensive against the settlement. In the debate over the treaties in Congress, the League was attacked not only as a tool in the hands of selfish and greedy powers, rather than a symbol of a new international order, but as a conspiracy to involve Americans in the corrupt old system of secret treaties and irresponsible commitments. Membership in such a body would, in the view of one elder statesman, "entangle the American nation in a European–Asiatic balance of power"; and in the end the Senate rejected the treaties and forbade American membership in the League.

This was a fatal blow to Wilson's dream of a new international system. The

League survived until the coming of another world war, but it was weakened irreparably by American abstention at the outset, as well as by the fact that two other major powers stood outside its membership, namely, Germany (until 1926) and the Soviet Union (until 1934). Nor did it show any capacity for growth, since the British and French governments could not agree upon its right to apply sanctions in moments of aggression by single powers. The French tried periodically to put teeth into the League covenant by having its members sign guarantees to act automatically when peace was threatened; this was the purpose of the Draft Treaty of Mutual Assistance of 1923 and the Geneva Protocol of 1924, the latter of which was intended to bind League members to take action against states that refused to arbitrate disputes or were designated as aggressors by the League Council. The British consistently defeated these attempts, taking the line that the League would not survive if too great a strain were placed upon it and that it would be advisable to regard it, not as a body that took punitive action against wrongdoers, but as a clearinghouse for differences.

The British attitude was perhaps influenced by a veiled resentment over the equality rule in the League Assembly. From Salisbury's time to the Sudeten crisis of 1938, the British showed periodic disrespect for the pretensions, and even the rights, of small powers; and it was said of Austen Chamberlain that when he spoke in the Assembly, he sometimes seemed to be saying, "We are perfect. We are British. And yet you, you dagoes, dare to come here and criticize US!" To vest too much authority in a body that listened as intently to the speeches of Benes of Czechoslovakia and Titulescu of Rumania as it did to those of their own representatives must, to the British, have seemed injudicious. Finally, even if they had been more receptive to arguments for something like the Geneva Protocol, the British government would have been restrained by the attitude of the Dominions, which now claimed the right to be consulted on policy matters and were firmly opposed to any new European commitments by the home country. In consequence, the British steadfastly opposed reform of the League, which tended as time passed to become a mere debating club.

In exasperation, the French began to build up their own security system by concluding alliances with Belgium and, since Russia lay outside the new international system, with Poland and the so-called Little Entente (Yugoslavia, Rumania, and Czechoslovakia). But France's resources were not sufficient to support these eastern allies unless the British were prepared to give some assistance; and the British were not ready to do any such thing. In 1925, when the British government, in order to encourage an alleviation of tension, signed the Rhineland Pact at Locarno guaranteeing the common boundary between Germany on the one hand and France and Belgium on the other, it made it clear that it was unprepared to enter into any similar engagements with respect to eastern Europe. In private, the British were brutally frank about this. Sir Austen Chamberlain told the Committee of Imperial Defence that the Rhineland Pact would actually reduce British liabilities on the continent, for "by making it perfectly clear that we were prepared to make our maximum effort . . . in the case of one frontier . . . it was implied that in the case of the other frontier we were not." This, Chamberlain suggested, would eventually make France see that it would be advisable to reduce its commitment to Poland, since it could not now count upon British support in a Franco-German conflict that had resulted from a French attempt to prevent Germany from overrunning its eastern ally. Weakened by this British attitude and by the high cost of military assistance to its eastern members, the French system lost even more credibility after the conclusion of the Nazi-Polish Pact in 1934; and the French government cast doubt upon its own confidence in the system by its subsequent efforts to complete the Maginot Line, a gigantic defensive rampart along its eastern frontier from the Swiss border to Belgium, and, as we shall see, by the nature of its commercial policy in the 1930s.

A word more should be said about the British attitude toward eastern Europe. In 1925, when it became clear that the British government was going to oppose the Geneva Protocol because that arrangement would oblige it to intervene anywhere in Europe where aggression occurred, the historical adviser to the Foreign Office, Sir James Headlam-Morley, struck a dissenting note. It would be a mistake, he wrote, for Britain to dissociate itself from European problems, nor was the argument that the Dominions did not desire new involvements in Europe compelling. In the future, the danger point in Europe was likely to be not the Rhine but the Vistula, and consequently no security pact would be effective if it were not European rather than regional in scope. These were prophetic words and intended as a warning that the principle of the European balance of power had always been central to Great Britain's foreign policy. They were, however, disregarded, and the British government not only restricted itself in European affairs to a regional arrangement (the Rhineland Pact) but for the rest sought to create a system of its own that was essentially non-European in nature, based upon the closest possible political and, after 1932, economic relations with its empire and upon cooperation with the United States in the Far East to protect their joint interests against Japanese ambitions.

These French and British experiments in system-making did not restrain the aggressive tendencies of Fascist Italy and National Socialist Germany after 1935 or of Japan after 1937. In the face of these new totalitarian threats, both the French security system and the League system crumbled, while the British gave themselves over to an increasingly dangerous policy of seeking peace by appeasing the dictators. These tendencies found their ultimate form in the belated attempt by Neville Chamberlain to ignore both the League and the Soviet Union (which after 1934 was a League member and a supporter of collective security) and to settle European affairs at least (Far Eastern affairs were by then in a hopelessly dangerous condition) by means of a Four Power Directorate of Britain, France, Germany, and Italy. Created at the Munich Conference in September 1938, this experiment was, to all intents and purposes, dead by March 1939, when Hitler's troops marched into Prague, at which time the world was only six months away from another great war.

In large part, the failure to build an effective international system after 1919 was due to the absence of any real measure of collaboration between the powers that had won the war. The British and the French pursued separate, and at times antagonistic, lines of policy, while the United States withdrew itself as far as possible from the world arena. Yet a major complicating factor in this, as in all aspects of diplomacy in these years, was what has been called in the introduction to this volume the diplomatic revolution, the complex of technological, socio-economic, and political changes that impinged upon the behavior of members of the international community, the most dramatic of which—beginning during the war and continuing until the present—were the steady growth in the number of active members in the international community and the simultaneous break-down of its internal homogeneity.

Before 1914, there were only about a dozen nations in the whole world that took a continuous interest and share in world affairs, and most of these were European. The Paris Conference was the first clear demonstration of how radically that condition was changing, and from that time onward the number of states that were determined to play independent roles upon the world stage increased steadily until the Second World War, which brought an explosive acceleration in its train, so that today there are almost 190 nations listed as members of the United Nations. Long before that result was achieved, it had become apparent that it was more difficult to convert the larger community into a working system than it had been when the participating states were fewer in number.

Along with the numerical expansion went another fateful change. An important reason for the relative effectiveness of the nineteenth-century system was that its members were bound together by a common historical tradition, by cultural and religious ties, and by familial relationships. Its statesmen spoke the same language and, in general, played the game of diplomacy according to the same rules, and all of this greatly facilitated communication and cooperation. This kind of homogeneity did not survive the war, largely because of the intrusion into international politics of new ideologies unknown in the nineteenth century. The victory of bolshevism in Russia in 1917, of fascism in Italy in 1922, and of national socialism in Germany in 1933 put an end to the commonly accepted norms of behavior. The Chicherins and Mussolinis, as we shall see, did not accept the rules of the club; they were constantly experimenting with the possible advantages of rule-breaking. This had subversive effects. It is difficult to play chess with someone who insists upon moving his bishops like rooks; and it was equally hard to reach agreement in negotiation with a vis-à-vis who employed all of his diplomatic guile to make agreement impossible. The British permanent undersecretary for foreign affairs in the 1930s, Lord Vansittart, once summed up his experience of dealing with diplomats from totalitarian regimes by saying in exasperation, "I have 'done' many conferences in my life but never went into one without some hope of a fairly quick result. No one could say the same today. Results are often not expected and often not even desirable." In an ideological age—and such an age opened in 1919—the possibility of creating an effective international system was remote.

Bibliographical Essay

On the organization and procedures of the peace conference, see especially F. S. Marston, *The Peace Conference of 1919* (Oxford, 1944); on the problems caused by them, Harold Nicolson, *Peacemaking 1919,* new ed. (New York, 1939), and Paul Birdsall, *Versailles Twenty Years After* (New York, 1941); and on the broader problems of the conference and the interests of the participants, Arno J. Mayer, *Politics and Diplomacy of Peacemaking: Containment and Counterrevolution at Versailles, 1918–1919* (New York, 1967), an informative though tendentious study. The literature on Wilson is almost unmanageable in bulk, but an excellent guide is provided by the editor of the Wilson papers, Arthur S. Link, in *Wilson the Diplomatist,* rev. ed. (Chicago, 1965). See also Arno J. Mayer, *Political Origins of the New Diplomacy* (New Haven, 1959), and Gordon A. Craig, "The United States and the European Balance," *Foreign Affairs* 55 (1976): 189–198. Important also is Alexander L. George and Juliette L. George, *Woodrow Wilson and Colonel House: A Personality Study* (New York, 1956).

On Anglo-French differences after the war, there are three important books: Arnold Wolfers, *Britain and France Between the Wars: Conflicting Strategies of Peace* (New York, 1940); Piotr Wandycz, *France and Her Eastern Allies, 1919–1925* (Minneapolis, 1962); and W. M. Jordan, *Great Britain, France and the German Problem, 1918–1939* (London, 1943). On the League of Nations, the standard history is F. P. Walters, *A History of the League of Nations,* 2 vols. (London, 1952); but see also Jon Jacobson, *Locarno Diplomacy* (Princeton, 1972), and Jonathan Haslam, *The Soviet Union and the Struggle for Collective Security in Europe, 1933–39* (New York, 1984). On the diplomatic revolution, See Gordon A. Craig, "The Revolution in War and Diplomacy," in *War, Politics and Diplomacy: Selected Essays* (New York, 1966), and, in general, Gordon A. Craig and Felix Gilbert, eds., *The Diplomats, 1919–1939* (Princeton, 1953).

For valuable overviews of the interwar period, see G. Ross, *The Great Powers and the Decline of the European States System, 1914–1945* (London, 1983); R. J. Sontag, *A Broken World, 1919–1939* (New York, 1971); and Paul Kennedy, *The Rise and Fall of the Great Powers: Economic Change and Military Conflict from 1500 to 2000* (New York, 1987), pt. 6.

5

Public Opinion and Foreign Policy

One of the salient features of the interwar period was the heightened influence that public opinion exercised upon the formulation and execution of foreign policy. Particularly in democratic countries, this manifested itself in an excessive preoccupation with the mood of the electorate and a consequent tendency of governments to follow rather than lead opinion. It also had the effect of changing the conduct and forms of diplomacy in ways that were not always conducive to efficiency.

This deference to public opinion would have seemed strange to nineteenth-century statesmen. Otto von Bismarck did not allow the vagaries of the mass mind to influence his policy, although he was adroit in manipulating it through his controlled press and was not above explaining that actions that he had taken for other reasons (the refusal to allow France to annex the Grand Duchy of Luxemburg in 1867, for instance, the seizure of Alsace and Lorraine in 1871, and the beginning of German colonialism in 1884) were demanded by public opinion. The British government paid lip service to the principle of popular sovereignty in the realm of foreign affairs, and Benjamin Disraeli told the House of Commons in August 1880 that "any human conclusion that is arrived at with adequate knowledge and with sufficient thought is entitled to respect, and the public opinion of a great nation under such conditions is irresistible, and ought to be so."

He was quick, however, to add a caveat, with the words, "But what we call public opinion is generally public sentiment," and it was clear that in his view, public expressions of opinion about foreign affairs were generally emotional and ill-informed and hence unworthy of attention. Salisbury, Lansdowne, and Grey tended to agree. Indeed, one of the most striking characteristics of the men who molded British policy in the fateful days before the outbreak of war in 1914 was their lack of interest in what the public might be thinking about the drift of affairs and their irritated contempt for press views. Sir Arthur Nicolson, the permanent undersecretary for foreign affairs, complained that "the public are as a rule supremely indifferent to and very ignorant of foreign affairs," although— as Zara Steiner has written—neither Nicolson nor anyone else in the Foreign Office ever took any special pains to enlighten it. As for the press, the Foreign Office view was that its members were not gentlemen, their views were unsound, and their meddling in foreign affairs was deplorable. The "enlightened public," which was the only public that counted, didn't need the press in any case and could be counted on to agree with the professional elite in the Foreign Office.

Attitudes like these could not be maintained after the world war. The sacrifices caused by that conflict made the man in the street more insistent upon his right to express an opinion about what the foreign policy of his country should be, and politicians or officials who appeared to disregard this ran the danger of being swept away by public indignation, even when they could claim that they had acted in the national interest. During the interwar period, there were any number of distinguished victims of this kind, and their example served *pour encourager* (or rather *décourager) les autres.* Woodrow Wilson was one such, a man hailed as a world savior in 1918 and then forced to see his design for a democratic world system rejected by an American electorate whose ardor for a role in the world community cooled when its prospective costs were realized and which then retreated precipitately toward the supposed blessings of what Warren G. Harding called "normalcy." Aristide Briand, an earnest worker for conciliation with Germany, fell before a similar wave of irrational feeling when rumors spread after the Cannes Conference of 1922 on reparations that he had become a pawn in the hands of Lloyd George, an accusation that seemed to be corroborated by newspaper photographs showing him apparently receiving golfing lessons from the British prime minister. Lloyd George himself, who had been the author of victory during the Great War, was the victim of a public outcry against his handling of a crisis in the Middle East (the so-called Chanak crisis of September 1922). The objections were based not on a reasoned understanding of his policy, which was undoubtedly questionable, but rather on a supposition that he was really trying to drag Britain into another war.

Moral indignation sometimes played an important part in public sentiment, and the case of Sir Samuel Hoare, British foreign secretary in 1935, is instructive in this regard. Hoare was driven from office by a surge of public indignation whose violence astonished seasoned political observers after he had, with Pierre Laval of France, worked out a plan for ending the war in Ethiopia. This involved the loss to the ruler of that country of about two-thirds of his empire, part of which would go to Italy outright, the rest being reserved as a sphere of Italian economic interest. The thought of Haile Selassie being thus despoiled and left with a mere fragment of territory connected to the sea by a narrow passage that the *Times* called "a corridor for camels" revolted the public conscience. In an able speech, Hoare sought to defend himself by pointing out that Great Britain was the only country that had placed military and naval units on alert for possible support of League action in defense of Ethiopia; no one else was stirring; and, since Britain could not carry the burden of war alone, the Hoare–Laval plan was not unreasonable. No one listened to this argument, and Hoare fell; but no one called, or at least not for very long, for real sanctions against Italy, certainly not after Hitler had taken advantage of the continuation of the war to move his troops into the Rhineland. Ethiopia was forgotten after that, and the emperor lost not just two-thirds of his realm, but all of it.

The retribution that public feeling could wreak upon statesmen and diplomats seeking to deal with complicated international problems in accordance with the rules of *raison d'état* or national interest was, therefore, real, and this was intimidating. It tended to make the people who were charged with the conduct of foreign policy more cautious than their nineteenth-century predecessors had been. It induced them to alter the way they did their business. And in several ways, it made them less effective than their predecessors.

Examples of governmental timidity in the face of a possibly vindictive public opinion are not hard to find. In Great Britain, the fall of Lloyd George in 1922 had a depressing effect upon his successors, and the Bonar Law, MacDonald, and Baldwin governments all showed a nervous tendency to seek to appease the public at any cost, even if this meant reversing positions regardless of the effect upon ongoing negotiations and the ultimate cost to the national interest. During the ticklish Lausanne negotiations of January and February 1923, which finally liquidated the Chanak crisis and arranged a settlement with Turkey, the chief British negotiator, Foreign Secretary Lord Curzon, was handicapped at every turn by a fearful and bitterly critical public opinion and a cabinet that seemed more than once on the verge of disavowing him. By brilliant diplomacy, Curzon gained all of his objectives, but he wrote: "I found Bonar [the prime minister] longing to clear out of Mosul, the Straits, and Constantinople, willing to give up anything and everything rather than have a row, astonished at the responsibility I have assumed at Lausanne, and prepared for me to back down everywhere."

The passage of time did not make British governments more willing to place national interest above public mood, as the story of the peace ballot of 1935 makes clear. Sponsored by the League of Nations Union, this was intended to determine the public attitude toward the League and collective security in general. Five questions were asked: (1) Should Britain remain a member of the League? (2) Were respondents in favor of all-round reduction of armaments by international agreement? (3) Did they favor general abolition of national military and naval aircraft by international agreement? (4) Should the manufacture and sale of armaments for private profit be prohibited by international agreement? and (5) Did respondents believe that if a nation attacked another, the other nations should compel it to stop by economic and nonmilitary measures or, if necessary, by military means?

Eleven and a half million people voted, and of these the great majority voted affirmatively on the first four questions and the first part of the fifth. On the question of military sanctions, however, only 6.75 million votes were affirmative.

It was clear that a lot of thought had gone into the voting—the ballot came close to satisfying Disraeli's criteria of reflective public opinion—but the discrepancy between the 11,090,387 votes for League membership and the 6,784,368 for military measures to preserve its principles was striking; and to the government in power, and its prime minister Stanley Baldwin, it seemed clear that this reflected a strong aversion to war and to building up the armaments to support it. Baldwin was aware that Great Britain's armed strength was dangerously low, too low for it to go beyond its present modest effort to persuade Mussolini to withdraw from Africa. What line should he, as a responsible leader, take in the forthcoming parliamentary elections? With an eye to public feeling, he took all lines. He declared that the League of Nations would continue to be the cornerstone of British foreign policy and that, in the dispute over Ethiopia, there would be "no wavering in the policy we have hitherto pursued." (The Hoare–Laval plan was still months away.) Gaps in the national defense would be filled, but the prime minister pledged that "there will be no great armaments" and that the government would continue to work for general disarmament.

With this trimming of sail to catch every breath of popular feeling, Baldwin sailed to an easy victory in the parliamentary elections. A year later, when many things had gone wrong—when disarmament was dead, Ethiopia conquered by Italy, Hitler in the Rhineland, and the arms gap wider than ever—Winston Churchill accused Baldwin of irresponsibility in failing to call in 1935 for a heightened armaments effort. The prime minister answered in a speech in the House of Commons: "Supposing I had gone to the country and said that Germany was rearming and we must rearm, does anyone think that this pacific democracy would have rallied to that cry at that moment? I cannot think of anything that would have made the loss of the election from my point of view more certain."

In Britain's sister democracy across the Atlantic, the government was no more eager to risk offending public sentiment by adopting firm positions in foreign affairs. In 1932, when the disarmament conference opened in Geneva, hope of a successful conclusion was weak from the outset because the French government refused to consider any real reduction of armaments or any kind of concession to Germany on the question of equality unless it were given additional guarantees of security by the other powers. There were two ways in which the United States government might have tried to persuade the French to modify this negative stance, and both, at various times, were suggested. The first would have been to agree to a consultative pact—that is, a commitment to consult with other signatories of the Pact of Paris if there were a crisis caused by some state that threatened to resort to war. The second would have been to offer to reduce or abandon war debts owed to the United States if the beneficiaries of that action would scale down their armaments. President Hoover rejected both ideas because he believed that they would be politically unacceptable in the United States. Like Baldwin, he was afraid of losing the election.

Hoover's successor proved during his first term to be equally reluctant to defy the isolationist temper of American voters. During his second, however, Roosevelt became increasingly concerned about the deterioration of the world situation and convinced that the United States should be doing something to check it. He said this plainly for the first time in a speech in Chicago on 5 October 1937: "The epidemic of world lawlessness is spreading. When an epidemic of physical disease starts to spread, the community approves and joins in a quarantine of the patients in order to protect the health of the community against the spread of the disease." He suggested that the peace-loving nations must act in the same way against the current epidemic and said, "There must be positive endeavors to preserve peace." The response to this appeal was immediate, massive, and negative. The White House was flooded with mail from groups of veterans, pacifists, and mothers and from church congregations and organized isolationists, deploring this apparent attempt to involve the United States in the morass of world intrigue and war; and the administration felt it expedient to disavow the true intent of the speech and to retreat into an inactivity that lasted until the very eve of the European war.

In addition to its tendency to lame the resolution of governments, particularly in critical situations where risks of war were involved, the power of public opinion had a significant effect upon the conduct of diplomacy itself. For one thing, it ended the virtual monopoly of the professionals. One of the striking features of postwar opinion about foreign affairs in the democratic countries was the unanimity of the view that professional diplomats and their way of doing business had been largely responsible for causing the recent conflict and that the sooner their control was broken the better. Diplomats, the French ambassador Jules Cambon wrote sadly, were not regarded with any affection. Indeed, in the United States they were, both in Congress and in the press, ridiculed as social butterflies and attacked as persons of ambiguous loyalty, while in England the Labour party regarded the whole diplomatic establishment as a consciously aristocratic instrument, dedicated to the defeat of truly democratic policy.

In the face of this feeling, political leaders thought it wise to reduce the public role of the professionals, which generally meant that they took over their functions themselves. The fashion was set by Lloyd George, who shared the popular prejudice against the professionals and who also believed, as he once said, that "diplomats were invented simply to waste time. . . . It is simply a waste of time to let [important matters] be discussed by men who are not authorized to speak for their countries.'' During the peace conference and the three years that followed, Lloyd George bypassed the Foreign Office and to a large extent ignored the missions abroad and traveled about Europe with his own staff, conducting negotiations with other heads of state on complicated matters that he did not always perfectly understand. The meager and sometimes disconcerting results of these methods did not discourage others from imitating them. Instead of letting chiefs of mission abroad do what they were trained to do, foreign ministers and secretaries of state took to doing their business for them, either by using the telephone (the enemy of reflection, which became generally accepted as a means of diplomatic communication in the 1930s) or by traveling themselves to their posts to take over the conduct of negotiations. The latter practice was to become increasingly frequent after World War II, particularly in the United States, where people joked about Secretary of State John Foster Dulles's infinite capacity for taking planes and—with a play upon the words of an old music hall song—asked, ''I wonder where's Kissinger now?''

The results of this diplomatic activity by political leaders, ministers, and special missions of prominent politicians or private citizens (another device much resorted to in the United States) were disappointing. After World War II, a commission established by the French Constituent Assembly to investigate the political, economic, diplomatic, and military events that contributed to the defeat of 1940 did not hesitate to underline the deficiencies of the so-called new diplomacy. Its report noted that

> after the conclusion of the treaties of 1919, ministers had the habit of multiplying their contacts with their colleagues in other countries. The abuse of direct conversations opens the door to numerous dangers. Engagements are taken too easily. They are often improvised. It is better to define the course of a negotiation by a note which has matured in the silence of the ministry than by chance exchanges that are likely to be imprecise.

There were many ministerial meetings during the interwar period that testified to the truth of that statement and were the cause of subsequent confusion and misunderstanding—Stresemann's meeting with Briand at Thoiry in 1926, for example, and that of Pierre Laval with Mussolini in January 1935. Nor was imprecision the only danger inherent in this kind of diplomacy. When politicians engaged in the process of negotiation, they were apt to feel that their reputations were at stake and that a successful result was imperative. Some of Lloyd George's negotiations ended with ringing declarations that were plainly designed to convince a credulous public that great objectives had been achieved—which later, however, proved to be insubstantial. A striking example of this kind of disingenuousness can be seen in the case of the negotiations for an Anglo-Soviet agreement in 1924. The salient issue was the question of compensation for

British properties confiscated and debts repudiated by the Bolsheviks, and when the Soviet representatives showed no inclination to give any assurances on this point, the British Foreign Office decided that the talks should be broken off. At this point, a deputation from the Labour party, which had itself been in contact with the Russians, intervened, arguing that failure to reach a result would have unacceptable political results and producing a compromise that conveniently papered over all the irreconcilable differences between the parties. This the MacDonald government accepted, and a treaty was signed.

Along with the changes in the personnel charged with the conduct of important foreign business went a change in format. During the war, Woodrow Wilson had called for "open covenants openly arrived at," and it soon became an article of public faith that "open diplomacy" was the only acceptable procedure for any state that claimed to be a democracy. This was, of course, based upon a misconception, since government action in the Western democracies had long been controlled by the people, working through their elected representatives and by means of their power to change governments by periodic elections and to dismiss those whose performance in office had been unsatisfactory. In such a system, foreign relations, like all other aspects of policy, were subject to periodic review. To the advocates of open diplomacy, this was not enough. In effect, they were demanding the right to watch over policy as it emerged, to have a window into the rooms where the negotiators were at work, to know what was going to be said tomorrow and what their government intended to do if the other side did not like its proposals. This was a demand that Metternich or Bismarck would have regarded as preposterous and which Disraeli would have described as palpably dangerous.

It was, however, widely granted, and the result was a rapid growth of diplomacy by conference. This took two basic forms: large meetings, in which many states participated in discussions of matters of general interest, like the Genoa Conference of 1922, the disarmament conference of 1932, and the world economic conference of 1933; and what came in time to be called summit conferences, meetings of the foreign ministers or heads of state of great powers to deal with particular crises or opportunities, like the Locarno Conference of 1925, the Bessinge meeting of 1932, the Stresa meeting of 1935, and the Munich Conference of 1938.

Such meetings gratified the public desire for openness, but that was their greatest weakness. The large conferences often met, as in the case of the disarmament conference, under the pressure of public impatience and without adequate preliminary talks to lay a basis for fruitful negotiation. They often, indeed, seemed to be planned more for their public effect than for the substantive issues at stake. There were too many newspapermen and photographers on hand, and too many press conferences, inspired leaks, and other inventions of modern public relations. Because of the presence of the journalists, all conferences began with public statements by the heads of the various delegations, in which they made their objectives clear. This often had the effect of so fixing their positions that they had no subsequent room for maneuver or concession, since an alteration of position might seem, to a vigilant public, to be a humiliating retreat. In these circumstances, not much could be expected, except a final communiqué that sought to record a success where none existed.

As for summit conferences, surely the most unfortunate invention of the new diplomacy, even when they were successful, they were apt to have unhappy results. What Richard Nixon wrote about the Peking and Moscow summit meetings of 1972 could be applied with equal force to the Locarno Conference of 1925: "Creation of a willowy euphoria is one of the dangers of summitry. Many people embraced the naive notion that . . . we would all live happily ever after. . . . The euphoria also made it more difficult to gain support for the decisive actions and strong military forces that were needed to make détente succeed." So in 1925, the apparent success of the Locarno Conference diverted public attention from the problems that had not been solved there and that soon undermined the accord.

More often than not the summit meetings failed for reasons once outlined by a shrewd critic of diplomatic practice, Sir Harold Nicolson. The participants in summits were always, he pointed out, particularly busy men. "The time at the disposal of these visitors is not always sufficient to allow for patience and calm deliberation. The honors which are paid to a minister in a foreign capital may tire his physique, excite his vanity, or bewilder his judgment." In 1932, during the first phase of the disarmament conference, there was what was in effect a loosely structured summit meeting in the villa of U.S. Secretary of State Henry Stimson at Bessinge, in which Prime Minister Ramsay MacDonald of Great Britain, Premier André Tardieu of France, Chancellor Heinrich Brüning of Germany, and Foreign Minister Dino Grandi of Italy met with Stimson. Nothing but confusion resulted from their conversations. Secretary Stimson concluded from them that Brüning was so conciliatory in temperament and so modest in his demands for concessions that a Franco-German agreement was imminent. Tardieu went back to Paris with the feeling that Brüning "wouldn't commit himself to anything." Brüning claimed later that MacDonald had agreed to support the German claim for equality of treatment in armament. The British prime minister did not believe that he had said anything of the sort. There was no way of resolving the discrepancies, since no record was made of the conversations, and the Bessinge summit had a negative effect upon the hope of reaching a disarmament agreement.

Lack of precision also marked the Stresa summit of 1935. This meeting had been called in order to decide what response the Locarno powers would make to Hitler's repudiation in March of the arms clauses of the Versailles Treaty. Failing to discover an effective means of retaliation, the participants drew up a statement expressing their determination to oppose any further acts of aggression. Into this statement, Mussolini proposed the insertion of the words "in Europe," a suggestion that Prime Minister MacDonald accepted without any attempt to clarify Italian motives. The duce interpreted this silence to mean that he need fear no British opposition to his already well-matured plans to acquire an empire in Africa, and the Stresa Conference, which had been designed to build a front against Hitler, turned out to be a kind of prologue to the Italian aggression in Ethiopia.

As for the Munich summit, which resembled more a dictated peace than a negotiating situation, it produced a classic illustration of the folly of taking hastily drafted and ill-considered agreements seriously. This was the so-called Anglo-German Declaration which, on the morning after the conference proper, was hastily drafted by Lord Strang, the permanent undersecretary for foreign affairs, and rewritten by the prime minister before being submitted to Hitler who, after a moment's hesitation, signed it. It was this loosely stated pledge of future cooperation that Chamberlain waved to the welcoming crowd at Croydon Airport as proof that he had secured "peace for our time" and which sustained his faith in the appeasement policy until Hitler showed the unreliability of pledges that are not guaranteed by invading rump Czechoslovakia in March 1939.

A final result of the heightened importance of public sentiment in the interwar period was a new emphasis upon what might be called diplomacy by public declaration. This was the technique of using a public address to send a message, not to another government, but to public opinion in another country, in the hope of influencing it to bring pressure upon its own government in the interest of the message's initiator. Generally speaking, democratic states were less effective at this sort of thing than totalitarian ones, because they had to worry about both the foreign audience and the one at home. Woodrow Wilson, whose appeals to other peoples during the war had an exciting effect, and who in some ways could claim to have dissolved the Austro-Hungarian Empire by his eloquence, was singularly unsuccessful in his attempt to appeal to peoples over the heads of their governments during the peace conference, partly because of mounting evidence that he had lost the support of his own. When Heinrich Brüning was chancellor of the Weimar Republic, he sought desperately to gain a foreign policy success—a further scaling down of reparations or the grant of parity, at least in principle, in armaments—that might shore up his position at home, and for this end he used public diplomacy to convince the Western governments and their public that he was a man of good will who believed in peace and international collaboration, and one to whom they could safely make concessions. But for every speech that Brüning made in this vein for foreign consumption, he had to make another in order to appease domestic opinion by sounding the nationalist strain, talking about Germany's grievances, and promising to be un-yielding in his demands for rectification.

Herbert Hoover, who believed that the world of the 1930s was suffering from mass insanity, tried to cure this by appealing to "world opinion" in various ways; but if such a thing existed, it didn't seem to be listening.

The past master of this kind of diplomacy was Adolf Hitler. Whenever he did something particularly outrageous, such as casting off the arms restrictions of the Versailles Treaty or declaring that he no longer recognized the provisions of Locarno, he could be counted on to make a major address in which he appealed to the uneasy conscience of the West by recalling the harsh provisions of the peace settlement. He would explain that far from being a provocative or aggressive action, what he had just done was a means of opening up opportunities for a sounder peace, in preparation for which he was ready to enter into any kind of treaty the Western powers might desire, providing that it was a bilateral one. (He never bothered to explain that bilateral treaties are the easiest ones to break.)

These speeches were remarkably effective, principally because people in the West did not want war; and they helped to dissuade Western governments from proposing active resistance to his aggressions. After all, what could they do about the Rhineland invasion, when Hitler's speeches and sympathetic reaction in their own newspapers, some of which were secretly financed by German agencies, had persuaded a good part of their electorate that Hitler was "only going into his own backyard"? What could they do about the *Anschluss,* when many of their voters had been persuaded that Austria was German anyway?

There is no doubt that the emergence of public sentiment as an important factor in foreign policy made Western governments in the 1930s vulnerable to German and other propaganda that worked on the feelings of their peoples in such a way as to jeopardize national interest. The fact that most people felt more than they thought and had strong hostilities and fears that could be easily mobilized increased this vulnerability. This was most apparent in France in 1938 and 1939, when an appreciable number of people became convinced that to resist Hitler was to invite Stalin to Paris and, for that matter, that a Hitler victory was preferable to a government by Léon Blum, which would involve France in an unwinnable war.

Bibliographical Essay

Details about the impact of public opinion upon postwar American foreign policy can be found in the rich literature on the fight over the League of Nations. See, among many works on the subject, Thomas A. Bailey, *Woodrow Wilson and the Lost Peace,* new ed. (Chicago, 1963), and *Woodrow Wilson and the Great Betrayal,* new ed. (Chicago 1963).

On the British susceptibility to public moods, compare Zara S. Steiner, *The Foreign Office and Foreign Policy, 1898–1914* (Cambridge, 1969), with Gordon A. Craig, "The British Foreign Office from Grey to Austen Chamberlain," in *The Diplomats, 1919– 1939*, ed. Gordon A. Craig and Felix Gilbert (Princeton, 1953), and "The Professional Diplomat and His Problems, 1919–1939," in *War, Politics and Diplomacy: Selected Essays* (New York, 1966). On the League of Nations Union peace ballot, see Winston S. Churchill, *The Gathering Storm* (Boston, 1948); Harold Macmillan, *The Winds of Change, 1914–1939* (New York, 1966); and Keith Middlemas and John Barnes, *Baldwin, a Biography* (London, 1969). On the Hoare-Laval Pact and its effects, see Anthony Eden, *Facing the Dictators* (Boston, 1962), and Middlemas and Barnes, *Baldwin.*

On conference diplomacy and summitry, see the comments of Charles W. Thayer, *Diplomat* (New York, 1959), and Richard Nixon, *The Real War* (New York, 1980). On the Genoa Conference, see J. Saxon Mills, *The Genoa Conference* (New York, 1922); Harry Kessler, *Walter Rathenau, His Life and Work* (New York, 1930); and Jane Degras, ed., *Soviet Documents on Foreign Policy*, vol. 1, *1917–1924* (Oxford, 1952); on Locarno, Gustav Stresemann, *Vermächtnis*, 3 vols. (Berlin, 1932–1933), and Peter Krüger, *Außenpolitik der Republik von Weimar* (Darmstadt, 1985); on the disarmament conference and the Bessinge meeting, the articles of Michael Geyer and Gordon A. Craig, in *Internationale Beziehungen in der Weltwirtschaftskrise 1929–1933*, ed. Josef Becker and Klaus Hildebrand (Munich, 1980); and on the Munich Conference, John W. Wheeler-Bennett, *Munich: Prologue to Tragedy* (New York, 1948), Telford Taylor, *Munich: The Price of Peace* (New York, 1979), and Lord Strang, *At Home and Abroad* (London, 1956).

6

Economics and Foreign Policy

In the failure of the collective security system in the years from 1919 to 1939, economic problems and the way in which the various powers reacted to them played a major part. Without attempting to deal with this subject as comprehensively as it deserves, we can at least note that the structural and psychological stability of the postwar international system was from the beginning affected by the horrendous human costs of the conflict—8 million men killed in combat, 7 million permanently disabled, 15 million "more or less seriously wounded," and probably, in Europe exclusive of Russia, as many as 15 million civilian casualties—and the unprecedented destruction of dwellings and farms, livestock and forests, communication networks and equipment, industrial plants and shipping, all of which had to be rebuilt or replaced. Equally daunting were the financial problems that resulted from the fact that most of the belligerents had relied upon borrowing rather than taxation to meet the costs of war and were now confronted with staggering debts and the threat of mounting inflation caused by depreciating currencies.

It cannot be said that the victorious powers had any appreciation of the dimensions or the potential international consequences of these problems; on the contrary, the short-sightedness and narrow nationalism of their approach to them contributed powerfully to their failure to establish effective defenses against political threats to the public order. Two aspects of this deserve special emphasis. First, the economic tactics that the victors used against the most important of their recent antagonists were so unrealistic and uncoordinated that they fatally weakened the possibility of genuine appeasement in the early postwar years. Second, after the international system was already in grave jeopardy, they underestimated the purpose and effectiveness of German economic diplomacy and thus lost the ability to maintain by economic means a viable balance of forces between the status quo and the revisionist powers.

This sorry story had its origins in the decision of the Allied powers at Paris in 1919 to impose upon the beaten foe a burden of reparations. It is understandable enough that they should have done so. The war had cost them heavy losses of life and property and had consumed their financial resources and foreign investments. In the postwar temper, democratic leaders felt it impossible to ask their own people to assume these liabilities, and it seemed logical to conclude that their former antagonists should be made responsible.

Even so, the decision was taken without a rigorous examination of its potential results. It overlooked previous experience with the use of reparations, which was not exactly heartening, Napoleon's financial exactions in Prussia after 1806 having been a major factor in inflaming the powers of resistance in that defeated country, and the reparations paid by France after its defeat in 1870 having contributed to the speculative boom in Germany that culminated in the financial crash of 1873. It ignored the psychological effects that were bound to flow from the unhappy notion of attributing to Germany and its allies the sole responsibility for having caused the war, an arguable and needlessly provocative hypothesis which John Foster Dulles, a member of the United States delegation at Paris, later believed was one of the principal causes of Germany's turning to Hitler. And it failed to appreciate the lack of logic in a procedure that set out to punish not the imperial government that had been in power in 1914 (which it might have done by being more insistent upon the surrender of its leaders), but rather the new republican regime that had been founded in 1919 and was guiltless as far as the war was concerned.

Moreover, the way in which the decision was implemented flew in the face of Woodrow Wilson's Fourteen Points, which had promised "the removal as far as possible of all economic barriers" between nations, and ignored the advice of the British economist John Maynard Keynes that the first order of business at Paris should be to restore the freely functioning world economy that had brought general prosperity before 1914. The reparations burden bore no relation to Germany's ability to pay. Because the British government insisted that the liability should include, not only shipping losses and damages to property, which the Germans themselves were resigned to paying, but the cost of pensions and disability payments made to British citizens during and as a result of the war, the resultant total was twice as large as the original estimate. In other parts of the treaty, the Allies also deprived Germany of all of its colonial empire, some of its richest mining districts, and its merchant marine, deprivations that would make it difficult if not impossible for the new German government to raise and transfer the sums demanded. In the face of these conditions, there was no question that Germany was separated by very formidable barriers from normal economic activity.

This in turn posed the question of the purpose of the reparations. Were they intended merely to pay the costs of the war and to enable the Allies to liquidate the debts that they had contracted to the United States during the course of the conflict, or did they mask a political purpose, a desire not merely to punish Germany but to keep it in a position of economic and hence political weakness for a long period? During the negotiations at Paris, there was no discernible clarity of motive. The American expert Norman Davis wrote: "Some of the delegates wanted to destroy Germany, some wanted to collect reparations, and some wanted to do both. Some wanted to collect more than Germany had agreed to pay or could pay; and others wanted to take all her capital, destroy her, and then collect a large reparation bill." In the years that followed, this muddle disappeared and, among the principal powers, a basic difference emerged between the French, who quite clearly regarded reparations as a political weapon, and the British, who deplored this and felt that even the financial motive had become dubious. The United States, which had not signed the treaty, occupied a detached position.

It was over the question of treatment of Germany that the disarticulation of Anglo-French policy, which soon had unfortunate effects in other areas, particularly the Near East, first became pronounced. At Paris, the French had been denied the territorial compensation along the Rhine that they felt they had deserved and had been forced to be content with an Anglo-American pledge of support in the event of a future German attack. But in consequence of the American decision not to accept the treaty, that guarantee had never been ratified, and the French felt cheated of their legitimate security requirements. They found it necessary, therefore, to insist upon the strict observance of the Versailles Treaty, and particularly of those articles that called for the disarmament of Germany and its liability to pay reparations. The strongest advocate of this position was Raymond Poincaré, the dominant figure in French foreign policy from 1921 to 1924. A representative of the Conservative-Nationalist tradition in French politics and the wartime president of the Republic, Poincaré had been convinced of Germany's aggressive tendencies well before 1914. After the war, his suspicion was not modified, and he believed that the Germans must be kept down by a program of treaty enforcement, military alliances, and a strong army. As R. D. Challener has written, Poincaré was known for his impassioned orations during dedications of war memorials, which always culminated with the insistence that the Germans could and must pay every sou of their reparations obligation.

The British had increasing reason to doubt the possibility and even the advisability of full repayment. The first effect of reparations upon the British economy had not been fortunate. The acquisition of the German merchant marine had contributed to the postwar slump of the domestic shipping industry, and German reparations in coal were destroying Britain's European markets for that commodity. In addition, the British had a keener appreciation than the French of the transfer difficulties confronting the Germans and of the dangers implicit in the course that they were compelled to take in order to keep up with their financial liabilities—namely, resort to the printing presses with resultant depreciation and inflation.

From 1920 until his fall from office in 1922, therefore, Lloyd George sought to convince the French of the advisability of revising the treaty terms in Germany's favor. He called a series of conferences for that purpose, at Spa in 1920, at Cannes in 1922, and—a larger meeting, designed to discuss the European economy in general, including relations with the Soviet Union—at Genoa in the same year. He had no success in persuading the French to moderate their attitude, partly because of the maladroitness of the Germans themselves. At Spa, their delegation included not only General von Seeckt, in uniform, but the industrialist and banker Hugo Stinnes, the first of a long series of businessmen who played an important role in interwar diplomacy. On this occasion, he destroyed any possibility of the Germans receiving a sympathetic hearing by berating the Allies and accusing them of suffering from "the disease of victory." At Genoa, perhaps in a desperate attempt to break out of their isolation, the Germans absented themselves from conference business long enough to make a pact of friendship with the Soviet Union. Such an action could only confirm the French in their suspicion of German intransigence, the more so because it was soon rumored that there were secret military arrangements between the two new partners.

Lloyd George's efforts thus came to nothing, and the hard line followed by the French was allowed to take its ultimate and self-defeating form. This came in January 1923, when French and Belgian troops entered the Ruhr, Germany's last productive mining area. The reason for this invasion, which had been authorized over British objections by the Reparations Commission, was a German reparations default in coal and timber deliveries, but Poincaré had for some time suspected that the German government, by doing nothing to control the mounting inflation in its country, was steering toward a fraudulent bankruptcy as a means of escaping from the reparations obligation. He believed that an occupation of the Ruhr and the seizure of its mines and forests as "productive guarantees" was the only way that France could be assured of German compliance with the treaty. His action was strongly supported by the French steel industry, which wanted to secure a reliable supply of coke, and by soldiers like Marshal Foch and War Minister Maginot, who saw an opportunity of gaining permanent possession of the area.

Stephen Schuker has called the Ruhr invasion and the passive resistance with which it was met a renewal of war between France and Germany by economic means. This is the way Marshal Foch saw it and, in September 1923, when the German government was forced to call off the policy of passive resistance, he said, "Armistice! Von Hoesch [the German *chargé d'affaires* in Paris] at the Quai d'Orsay is like Erzberger coming to my railway car in the

Rethondes station.'' There was really no reason for jubilation. The costs of supporting passive resistance had compelled the German government to resort to the printing presses in earnest, and the resultant runaway inflation, by victimizing the bulk of the German *Mittelstand,* had struck a fatal blow to the stability of the Republic and enormously strengthened the nationalist, anti-Weimar, anti-Versailles elements in the country. This could be a source of satisfaction for no one who believed in peace and collective security.

Moreover, even if regarded in narrower and more selfish terms, it was difficult to think of the French operation in the Ruhr as a victory. Certainly its objectives had not been attained. There was no assurance that German reparations payments would be resumed soon or would ever reach the proportions that a too-optimistic French legislature had hoped would relieve them of the responsibility for recasting an inefficient financial structure and devising a system of taxation capable of reducing France's dangerously swollen burden of debt. Four months after the German capitulation, in January 1924, belated realization of the true weakness of the French fiscal situation came to the financial community, and the franc collapsed with a bang that shook Poincaré's government to its foundations. In the weeks that followed, panic was widespread and bankruptcy was near, and in the end the currency was saved only by the government's ability to float loans with the banking houses of J. P. Morgan in New York and Lazard Brothers in London.

This desperate expedient was of more than economic significance. The British government, unwilling to leave the Ruhr in French possession, had revived a suggestion originally made in 1922 by U.S. Secretary of State Charles Evans Hughes that an independent committee of business and financial experts inquire into all of the ramifications of reparations. Under British and American pressure, Poincaré had consented in December 1923. Whatever such a commission might recommend, he was resolved to fight for the retention of productive pledges in the Ruhr and even of some form of military control. After the onset of the financial crisis in Paris, however, this became impossible. France's dependence upon foreign loans that had to be approved by the United States and British governments sharply reduced the bargaining power of both Poincaré and Herriot, who succeeded him in May, when dealing with the findings of the experts, which were ultimately incorporated in the Dawes Plan of 1924.

The consequences became clear at the London Reparations Conference, which met in July 1924 to amend and put into effect the provisions of the Dawes Plan. In the history of postwar diplomacy, this conference was notable for being the first European diplomatic gathering since 1919 in which the United States government participated formally and the first at which the Germans appeared as equals. But more interesting—and illustrative of the enhanced diplomatic presence of financiers in a period when governmental decisions were so heavily influenced by economic considerations—was the role played at the meeting by bankers, particularly Sir Montagu Norman of the Bank of England and Thomas W. Lamont of J. P. Morgan and Company. Since the resumption of reparations payments in accordance with the new and less onerous schedules devised by the experts could only be effected by means of a loan to Germany that was floated in the United States through the house of Morgan, the New York bankers insisted that all possibility of another Ruhr invasion be eliminated, for reasons summed up in the *Wall Street Journal:* "The average investor is disinclined to 'buy into a quarrel,' and, if there is no assurance that France will not reenter the Ruhr at some future date with the avowed purpose of compelling Germany to live up to the letter of the law in connection with its reparation payments . . . a German loan offering in this country will fall flat."

At the conference, Lamont pushed this point vigorously from behind the scenes, with the at first hesitant support of the American delegation and the more enthusiastic backing of the MacDonald government, prompted by the virulently anti-French Norman and by the Foreign Office, which had long felt that French fears for security were exaggerated. Uncertain of their own financial future, the French did not dare antagonize what again might be their only sources of support. In the end, although minor concessions were made to save Herriot's face, the powers of the Reparations Commission were amended so as to make reprisals impossible except in the case of a clearly flagrant reparations default (although dispassionate observers of the German scene believed that the nationalist passions inflamed by the French action in January 1923 would not be appeased by the Dawes Plan and that new defaults were bound to come sooner or later). Since at the same time the French were forced to give up their productive pledges and to agree to withdraw their troops from the Ruhr within a year of the implementation of the plan, their ability to compel the Germans to observe the terms of the Versailles Treaty had been seriously diminished, although not perhaps so fatally as to warrant Stephen Schuker's statement that at the London Conference, "the era in which France could lay claim to great power status also effectively came to an end."

The conference widened the already significant differences that marked Anglo-French attitudes toward the Germans. In the period that followed, despite the apparent rapprochement reached at the Locarno Conference in 1925 and the close relationship that came to exist between Aristide Briand and Gustav Stresemann, French suspicion of Germany and disinclination to make further concessions in the question of reparations or that of the military occupation of the Rhineland remained strong. The British, on the other hand, inclined increasingly to the view that everything possible should be done to strengthen the faltering German Republic by restoring its full sovereignty in foreign affairs. In the last years of the Weimar Republic, this divergence of view became particularly acute over the question of armaments, the British taking the position that the arms clauses of the Versailles Treaty should be modified to give Germany equality of status and, in time, equality in substance, the French adamantly refusing any change unless it were accompanied by formal guarantees of French security by the other great powers. This failure to agree prevented any scheme of arms control based upon general reductions from emerging from the disarmament conference in 1932, and that failure in turn led, after Hitler's accession to power, to Germany's departure from the conference and from the League of Nations in October 1933 and its subsequent repudiation of the arms clauses of the Versailles Treaty in March 1935.

The disarmament conference of 1932 brought the United States back temporarily to European councils and raised the possibility that it might use its financial resources to effect a favorable diplomatic result. President Herbert Hoover had long been a personal advocate of disarmament and was aware of the strong popular support that it enjoyed in the United States. He was convinced, moreover, that reduction of armaments was the best way of promoting recovery from the world depression and, in a speech before the International Chamber of Commerce in May 1931, had recited figures to show how heavily armaments bore on the economies of the principal powers. He concluded with the words, "Of all the proposals for the economic rehabilitation of the world, I know of none that compares in necessity or importance with a successful result of the [forthcoming disarmament] conference."

When it became clear in preconference talks that the French were disinclined to agree, some of the president's advisers urged him to use economic weapons to gain his point. His ambassador in Paris, Walter E. Edge, wrote: "It is my conviction that France will continue to throw monkey wrenches in the gear box until she is forced by such colossal and general pressure that even she will find difficulty in resisting." The time was probably coming, he suggested, when the deepening depression would cause a repudiation of both reparations and the war debts owed to the United States. Why not anticipate that and, while the debts still offered some leverage, provide remission or reduction as a reward to those powers willing to cut back their armaments, a form of pressure that the French would surely be unable to resist?

The president had no great sympathy for the French, and the idea of using debts as a weapon was not new to him. In 1924, when he was secretary of commerce in the Coolidge administration, he had been disappointed when the State Department had failed to withdraw its approval for further private lending to countries like France, Belgium, and Italy that had not made debt-funding arrangements with the United States. He said then that the "financing operations of those governments were merely covert schemes of finding money for unproductive purposes, largely for military purposes." In 1931, however, Hoover was unwilling to follow the logic of his earlier position, because he knew that any suggestion of debt reduction, even as a means of pressure to promote disarmament, would arouse a storm in the Senate and in the general public, where there was no inclination to dissolve the European obligation and widespread agreement with the sentiment attributed to President Coolidge, "They hired the money, didn't they?" Nor, when Edge repeated his suggestion, did it appeal to Hoover's secretary of state, Henry L. Stimson, who seemed shocked at the thought of using such an unconventional and even ungentlemanly method of diplomacy. "Other countries," Stimson wrote, "would flare up at being asked to sell their independent right to fix their own armaments by a bargain with another nation." As a result of the president's reluctance to jeopardize his electoral chances and the secretary of state's distaste for economic arm-twisting, American statecraft proved incapable of breaking the impasse in the Geneva Disarmament Conference and preventing the fateful consequences that flowed from it.

The American example of 1931–1932 suggests that economic diplomacy was not congenial to the diplomatic establishments of the Western democracies and not a weapon that they used effectively. This is borne out by a comparison between Adolf Hitler's use of economic diplomacy in eastern Europe and that of Great Britain and France.

Even before the coming of the National Socialist regime, the Germans had evinced a lively awareness of the political goals that could be achieved by economic means. The ill-fated Customs Union plan of 1931 with Austria, which failed because of clumsy diplomatic preparation and spirited French and Polish opposition, may have been regarded by Chancellor Heinrich Brüning, who authorized it without ever being deeply committed to it, as a means of recouping his political fortunes after the electoral setback of September 1930 and as a useful way of combating the depression. But in the Foreign Office, State Secretary Bülow, who was to survive Brüning and continue in office in Hitler's first years, had no doubt about its wider political significance. In a memorandum of January 1931, he wrote:

> Once the German-Austrian customs union has become a reality I calculate that the pressure of economic necessity will within a few years compel Czechoslovakia to adhere to it in one way or another. I would see in this the beginning of a development which would be likely to lead to a solution, scarcely conceivable by other means, of vital political interests of the Reich. In this I am thinking of the German-Polish frontier problem. If we should succeed in incorporating Czechoslovakia in our economic bloc, and if meanwhile we should also have established closer economic relations with the Baltic States, then Poland with her unstable economic structure would be surrounded and exposed to all kinds of dangers; we should have her in a vise which could perhaps in the short or long run make her willing to consider further the idea of exchanging political concessions for tangible economic advantages.

Once Hitler had taken power, the integration of economic diplomacy with political objectives became both closer and more successful. From 1934 onward,

Germany's economic life was based upon *Wehrwirtschaft* (war economy), and in August 1936, in the long memorandum that formed the basis of the Four Year Plan, Hitler made this more explicit. Those charged with making economic decisions should remember, he said, that their sole duty was to enable the German people to assert itself in the world of politics. The time was past for fruitless debates over economic theory and for irresponsible suggestions for solving shortages of foodstuffs and raw materials at the cost of the national armament program. The task confronting the nation was to find provisional solutions for the problems of food and raw materials and to create the basis for "the struggle for self-realization." Hitler called for an economic mobilization comparable to the military one, which would maintain living standards without jeopardizing the military effort and would attain self-sufficiency in strategic materials. "The German army must be operational in four years. The German economy must be capable of supporting war in four years."

German success in achieving these goals was due in part to the skillfulness of economic strategy in eastern Europe. Because of the weakness of the Reichsmark on international exchanges, the Germans were forced to institute exchange controls and to reserve hard currency for purchases of strategic materials in short supply. But this weakness did not handicap them in eastern Europe, where the currencies were also weak and controlled, where there was a willingness to accept the Reichsmark for sales made to Germany, and where—most important—there was an ardent desire for weapons. German penetration of eastern Europe proceeded on the basis of these facts and took the form of exchanges of foodstuffs and raw materials for arms made in Germany, a trade that not only kept the German people well fed until the war began but protected the German arms industry from the alternative dangers of overproduction and stagnation. This German strategy was so successful that by 1938, the Western powers were ready to acquiesce in German economic hegemony in the area.

This was, however, a victory by default. In his informative study of economic diplomacy before World War II, David E. Kaiser argues that the British and French never shared the German belief in the primacy of foreign policy and that under the pressures of the world depression, they allowed economic considerations to take precedence over basic principles of foreign policy that were vital to their future security. Between 1931 and 1934, the British government made a conscious decision to stimulate domestic and empire production at the expense of trade with foreign countries, a decision that was implemented by the abandonment of the traditional policy of free trade and by the Ottawa Agreement of 1932. The consequences of this were foreseen in a Foreign Office memorandum of December 1931, which stated that "a high protective tariff, combined with Empire preference, implies a measure of dissociation from Europe, a corresponding diminution of our influence over European affairs, and possibly a growth of economic nationalism." Despite these risks, the new policy was not only adhered to but elaborated upon with other features that were bound to make trade with Europe, and especially eastern Europe, difficult: an agricultural marketing bill that empowered the Board of Trade to restrict European imports of selected commodities in the interest of British agriculture, and a stubborn resistance by the Treasury and the Bank of England to clearing agreements that might have facilitated trade with countries with managed currencies.

France showed the same short-sighted parochialism as Great Britain, although one might have thought that the fact that it had allies in eastern Europe might have counselled a more reflective coordination of foreign and economic policy. Yet tariff and quota policies continued to favor the French empire over foreign markets throughout the 1930s, and although France imported between 1.0 and 1.5 million tons of cereals annually and hundreds of millions of francs worth of timber, relatively small amounts of these came from eastern Europe. An attempt to change the pattern and to follow the German example of trading weapons for grains was prevented by the slow pace of French rearmament, which started only in 1936 and took another two years to get into high gear.

Particularly after the extent of German penetration of eastern Europe became clear, there were people in the foreign offices of both countries who tried to galvanize their governments into meeting the German challenge. In Great Britain, Laurence Collier of the Northern Department and his colleague in the Southern Department, E. M. B. Ingram, argued the need for a more aggressive commercial and foreign policy. In a strong memorandum in 1938, Ingram wrote:

> It has always been the traditional policy of His Majesty's Government to prevent one Power from attaining a predominant position on the Continent. It is true that conditions change and that England no longer stands in exactly the same relation to Europe as she did either in the 18th or 19th centuries. Nevertheless it will no doubt be generally conceded that it remains very much to her interest—indeed, it will be argued in some quarters that it is vital to her interests—that Germany should not attain a virtual hegemony in Europe.

With a reference to the recent extension of credit to Turkey, Ingram continued:

> That the situation is not hopeless is shown by the fact that we have already managed, so we hope, to prevent one power at least in this part of Europe from falling under German influence . . . and the success we have had in this direction leads us to hope that it may not be impossible to take similar action in respect to other minor European states. Even where it is not possible to prevent German influence playing a very large part, it might be all-important to convince the countries concerned that they are not completely abandoned by the Western Powers and that the latter still offer them a loophole of resistance to the German stranglehold which they dread.

In France, the political director of the Quai d'Orsay, René Massigli, had long shared the same views. In July 1936, he wrote a strong appeal to the government, in which he warned that, already partially dependent on the Reich economically, Central and Eastern Europe is now menaced by its military influence. Having begun its intensive rearmament, Germany can offer arms in payment of its commercial debts. By doing so she can also keep her arms factories running and improve her own materiel. She is also interested in assuring her supplies of raw materials from the neighboring countries, which are not separated from her by the sea—which she does not command—and which are in fact her commercial creditors.

It was high time, he argued, that France had an economic plan to meet the German hegemonial drive. Despite its current economic troubles, "the moment has come to furnish our allies with tangible proof that we intend to put our economic relations in harmony with our political ones, and practise our alliances."

That these arguments fell on deaf ears was due in part to the administrative disarticulation of policy and the high degree of bureaucratic jealousy in the Western democracies. In economic matters in particular, policy had been allowed to fall into the hands of agencies other than the Foreign Office—the Board of Trade and the Treasury and the Bank of England in Great Britain, the ministries of Finance, Commerce, Agriculture, and Public Works in France—and these bodies were frequently blind to the broader aspects of the policies they managed and resentful of any interference with their sphere of activity. The lack of any proper machinery for coordinating views aggravated the situation and made it possible for individual ministries to veto trade policies of political significance, as the French Ministry of Agriculture was able to do in 1938–1939 in the case of trade concessions to the Danubian states.

Had the Foreign Office and the Quai d'Orsay possessed the prestige that was theirs before 1914, this bureaucratic competition might have been reduced. But in both Britain and France, the traditional ministries for the conduct of foreign relations fell upon evil days in the 1930s. Even during the Baldwin years, Foreign Office advice was both neglected and resented, since it appeared to invite conflict with the dictators when nothing of the sort was desired; and once the appeasement policy had triumphed with the accession of Neville Chamberlain as prime minister, the Foreign Office was considered to be too pro-French and anti-German to be trusted on any matter of importance. After 1936, the same attitude prevailed on the French ministerial level, and it was no accident that uncomfortable views about competing with the Germans were not welcomed and that René Massigli lost his post in 1938.

The failure of the French and British governments to devise an effective economic diplomacy for eastern Europe underlined the lack of any French determination to make a vigorous attempt to support its own eastern alliance system. It also provided striking evidence of how completely Great Britain abandoned in the years from 1919 to 1939 the principle of the European balance of power that had guided nineteenth-century British foreign policy. The beneficiary of this failure was Adolf Hitler.

Bibliographical Essay

For a general discussion of the economic characteristics and problems of the postwar period, see Paul Kennedy, *The Rise and Fall of the Great Powers: Economic Change and Military Conflict from 1500 to 2000* (New York, 1987), pt. 6.

The reparations debate began with John Maynard Keynes, *The Economic Consequences of the Peace* (London, 1920), and has continued ever since. See, for example, Etienne Mantoux, *The Carthaginian Peace* (New York, 1952); Gustav Stolper, *The German Economy, 1870–1930* (New York, 1940); Sally Marks, "Reparations Reconsidered," *Central European History* 5 (1972): 358–361; Charles S. Maier, *Recasting Bourgeois Europe: Stabilization in France, Germany and Italy in the Decade After World War I* (Princeton, 1975); and Herman J. Rupieper, *The Cuno Government and Reparations, 1922–1923* (London, 1979). On Anglo-French differences and their diplomatic consequences, see W. M. Jordan, *Great Britain, France and the German Problem, 1918–1939* (London, 1943); Harold Nicolson, *Curzon: The Last Phase, 1919–1925,* new ed. (New York, 1939); the brilliant study by Stephen Schuker, *The End of French Predominance in Europe: The Financial Crisis of 1924 and the Adoption of the Dawes Plan* (Chapel Hill, N.C., 1976), upon which the account of the London Conference above is based; and, for the period after Locarno, Jon Jacobson, *Locarno Diplomacy* (Princeton, 1972), J. W. Wheeler-Bennett, *Information on the Reparation Settlement, Being the Background History of the Young Plan and the Hague Agreements, 1929–1930* (London, 1930), Philip Snowden, *An Autobiography,* 2 vols. (London, 1934), Gustav Stresemann, *Vermächtnis,* 3 vols. (Berlin, 1932–1933), and Peter Krüger, *Außenpolitik der Republik von Weimar* (Darmstadt, 1985).

On economic aspects of the disarmament conference, see Gordon A. Craig, "Die Regierung Hoover und die Abrüstungskonferenz," in *Internationale Beziehungen in der Weltwirtschaftskrise 1929–1933,* ed. Josef Becker and Klaus Hildebrand (Munich, 1980), and Heinrich Brüning, *Memoiren, 1918–1934* (Stuttgart, 1970).

On German economic diplomacy, see Edward W. Bennett, *Germany and the Diplomacy of the Financial Crisis, 1931* (Cambridge, Mass., 1962), which has the most satisfactory explanation of the Austro-German Customs Union plan; Hjalmar Greeley Schacht, *Confessions of "the Old Wizard"* (Boston, 1956); Dieter Petzina, *Autarkiepolitik im Dritten Reich: Der nationalsozialistische Vierjahrsplan* (Stuttgart, 1968); and, especially, David E. Kaiser, *Economic Diplomacy and the Origins of the Second World War: Germany, Britain, France and Eastern Europe, 1930–1939* (Princeton, 1980), from which the quotations from Ingram and Massigli are taken.

7

Totalitarian and Democratic Diplomacy, 1919–1939

In September 1938, when Neville Chamberlain went to Godesberg, carrying his allies' approval of the terms for a settlement of the Sudeten question that Hitler and he had agreed on at Berchtesgaden two weeks earlier, he was disagreeably surprised to find that his host had changed his mind and had drafted much more Draconian conditions for the Czechs. When Chamberlain was handed a paper embodying these, he is reported to have said angrily, "This is an ultimatum, not a negotiation!" Pointing to the title page, Hitler replied mildly, "It says memorandum."

This incident illustrates how faulty real communication was apt to be between the democracies and the totalitarian states in the interwar period. Indeed, these diplomatic conversations and negotiations often resembled what the French call a *dialogue des sourds,* a conversation between deaf people, or more properly a conversation in which one side misheard what was being said while the other side wasn't really listening.

The basic reason for this condition was a profound difference in values and aspirations. Great Britain, France, and the United States had developed in the liberal-democratic tradition, and their approach to international relations after 1919 was strongly influenced by the faith in the primacy of reason that is part of that tradition and the repugnance to war that is common to liberal-democratic societies. Western diplomats regarded great-power politics as a rational pursuit and assumed that it would, as in the past, operate according to reasonable and generally accepted rules of procedure and accommodation. They believed that in an age that followed the most terrible war in history, any person competent enough to rise to the leadership of a great nation would be intelligent enough to see that war was not to anyone's advantage. And they assumed that the task of diplomacy would continue to be one of seeking the peaceful settlement of disputes without the sacrifice of one's own interest and security. In contrast, from the beginning of their existence, the totalitarian states rejected these values and assumptions and operated according to rules of their own.

In the case of the Soviet Union, this rejection was recognized and resented in the West, and Soviet–Western relations were consequently so heavily burdened by distrust and hostility that even when both sides were confronted with a common danger in the 1930s, no *modus vivendi* between them was possible. In contrast, Western statesmen long failed to recognize the true nature of Fascism and National Socialism and to appreciate how different the basic values of those movements were from their own. This misunderstanding and the persistence with which the West sought an accommodation with the dictators was the source of much frustration and tragedy.

I

If the West had fewer illusions about relations with the Soviet Union than about those with Fascist Italy and Nazi Germany, this was largely because the new regime in Russia had quickly made its own position abundantly clear. It did this not only by repudiating the debts owed by the czarist government to its Western allies and by confiscating all foreign properties in Russia without compensation to the owners, but also by officially rejecting all the forms and usages of traditional diplomacy. When Leon Trotsky assumed the office of commissar for foreign affairs, he announced that it was his intention "to issue a few revolutionary declarations to the peoples and then shut up the joint [the Foreign Office]"; and, when he led a delegation to the Brest-Litovsk Conference of 1918 to make peace with the Germans, he flatly refused to observe any of the amenities of the old diplomacy. He insisted that the Bolshevik delegation dine alone, that it accept no invitations of any kind from its hosts, that the forms of courtesy customary in diplomatic intercourse be dispensed with, and even that the word "friendship" be deleted from the preamble to the draft treaty. "Such declarations," he stated, "copied from one diplomatic document into another, have never yet characterized the real relations between states."

When this defiance didn't work and the revolutionary regime began to realize the true extent of its weakness and vulnerability to external pressures, it reconsidered its attitude toward diplomatic formalities and began to cultivate the traditional usages in order to be able to maintain contact with the bourgeois states. This seemed to be the best way of detecting and even influencing their behavior and of securing the loans and credits that Russia sorely needed. But the damage had already been done and was compounded by the activities of the Comintern—that "general staff of the world revolution of the proletariat" that Lenin had founded in 1919 with the mission of coordinating the activities of Communist parties abroad and encouraging subversion against non-Communist governments—and Soviet approaches to the West were regarded with lively suspicion. In August 1920, U.S. Secretary of State Bainbridge Colby wrote in a note to the Italian government:

> It is not possible for the Government of the United States to recognize the present rulers of Russia as a government with which the relations common to friendly governments can be maintained. This conviction . . . rests upon . . . facts . . . which none dispute [and which] have convinced the Government of the United States, against its will, that the existing regime in Russia is based upon the negation of every principle of honor and good faith, and every usage and convention underlying the whole structure of international law, the negation, in short, of every principle upon which it is possible to base harmonious and trustful relations, whether of nations or of individuals. . . . There cannot be any common ground upon which [the United States] can stand with a Power whose conceptions of international relations are so entirely alien to its own, so utterly repugnant to its moral sense. There can be no mutual confidence or trust, no respect even. . . . We cannot recognize, hold official relations with, or give friendly reception to, the agents of a government which is determined and bound to conspire against our institutions.

Other governments were not so adamant, and in the case of Great Britain both Lloyd George and Ramsay MacDonald sought agreement with the Soviet Union on the basis of economic collaboration, the former because he was convinced that the Bolsheviks could be "tamed" in this way, the latter because of the strong sentiment in his party for rapprochement with the great revolutionary country of the East. The history of these attempts was not happy, for they did not satisfy Western desires concerning debts and confiscations, and they brought no cessation of Comintern activities, which the Soviet government always disavowed as emanating from an independent organization for which it bore no responsibility.

It was clear, from the very beginning of contacts with the Soviet Union, that Soviet negotiators had a fundamentally different approach toward diplomacy from that of their Western colleagues. To them it was more than an instrument for protecting and advancing national interest; it was a weapon in the unremitting war against capitalism. Diplomatic negotiations could not, therefore, aim at real understanding and agreement. On the eve of the signature of the Anglo-Soviet Trade Agreement of 1921, L. B. Kamenev said, "We are convinced that the foreign capitalists, who will be obliged to work on terms we offer them, will dig their own graves."

In Soviet practice, negotiations were often intended not to reach settlements but to block or delay them until the situation elsewhere had changed in such a way as to improve the Russian position. Sometimes they were entered into in a spirit of speculation or in an effort to test the objectives and will of the other side; sometimes they were designed for propaganda purposes, in order to ingratiate the Soviet Union with third parties. In large conferences in particular—this was true of the Genoa Conference of 1922 and the Geneva Disarmament Conference of 1932—the Soviet delegation was apt to follow a line that, in the Western view, was neither practical nor conducive to progress in the discussions. The Soviets' favorite ploy was to universalize their position in the hope that the peoples of colonial areas and significant parts of the populations of Western nations would identify themselves with it. This was in accordance with the advice given by Marx and Engels in *The German Ideology,* where they held that since "increasingly abstract ideas hold sway" in the modern world, the revolutionary class was compelled "to represent its interest as the common interest of all the members of society, put in an ideal form; it will give its ideas the form of universality and represent them as the only rational, universally valid ones," and it will seek to speak "not as a class but as a representative of the whole society."

In pursuing this tactic, Soviet negotiators kept the conversations on the level of general principles as long as possible, knowing that this made for endless debate and gave frequent opportunities for rhetorical fireworks. At the same time, they tried to place the Western states on the defensive by questioning their good faith and inserting into the record statements by public figures in Western countries which, they claimed, showed a fixed determination to resist peaceful agreement. Refutations of these allegations they blandly disregarded and, in general, they admitted no obligation to answer rational arguments.

Even when they desired a settlement, Soviet negotiators made accommodation difficult. They did not subscribe to the view, common to Western diplomacy since the Renaissance, that negotiation was a bargaining process in which agreement was reached through mutual concession, what Callières had called a *commerce d'avis réciproque.* After World War II, Nikita Khrushchev once called this "a huckster's approach" and said that Soviet negotiators did not have "to make any concessions because our proposals have not been made for bartering. We act on the principle that sensible solutions must be found that would not damage any country. . . . Those who really strive for peace must not use methods of petty bargaining in the talks." In the interwar period, Soviet diplomats like Chicherin, Litvinow, and Molotov were guided by similar principles, and Soviet negotiators, bound by rigid directives that allowed little flexibility, regarded with suspicion the freedom of maneuver permitted to their Western counterparts. Proposals from the other side of the table met with automatic opposition, followed by persistent and uncompromising advocacy of the Soviet point of view.

The tactic of initial rejection was carried at times to ridiculous extremes, as it was in September 1929, when British Foreign Secretary Arthur Henderson presented the Soviet envoy Dovgalevsky with a list of questions that he felt should be discussed and settled before the resumption of formal relations between their two countries was considered. Dovgalevsky came to the second meeting with his own list, on which the same questions appeared in different order, and proceeded to fight tenaciously for his proposed agenda. So also, in December 1929, the British minister in Moscow complained that "anyone accustomed to dealing with M. Litvinow will remember how he frequently appears to be on the point of agreeing to suggestions made to him, but in practice, when pressed for any definite statement, he invariably reverts to his original point of view."

These methods reinforced the conviction that it was difficult under any conditions to carry on political discussions with the Soviet Union and impossible to rely on any agreements made. The belief proved to be a heavy handicap to any revision of view in the years when the Soviet Union, alarmed by the threat of National Socialism, placed the Comintern under restraint and began to seek agreements with the West that might strengthen the system of collective security. This shift in policy was marked by a new spirit of accommodation in Soviet diplomacy, and it had some success: diplomatic recognition by the United States in 1933, Soviet admission to the League of Nations in 1934, and the negotiation of the Franco-Soviet Pact in 1935. Even so, Western suspicion of Soviet motives remained unabated.

Recognition by the United States did not, for instance, lead to any effective collaboration against the totalitarian states until after the war had broken out; nor did Soviet membership in the League diminish the British government's growing disenchantment with that body. The strongest man in the National government, Neville Chamberlain, was not impressed by Litvinow's eloquent speeches at Geneva in behalf of collective security or by Soviet proposals for the containment of Hitler before it was too late. He dissuaded the French from seeking to elaborate their flimsy pact with the Soviets by means of military engagements, and he brushed aside Soviet proposals for four-power talks after Hitler had seized Austria in March 1938, stating that "the Russians [were] stealthily and cunningly pulling all the strings behind the scenes to get us involved in war with Germany." During the Sudeten crisis, Chamberlain discouraged those who believed that the Soviet Union might play a positive role; and the exclusion of the Soviet Union from the Munich Conference was in full accordance with his view that the security of Europe could be maintained by a directory of great powers, but not one that included the Soviets.

Even when that experiment collapsed and English voices were raised in behalf of attempts to secure an Anglo-French-Soviet alliance, Chamberlain remained unmoved. "I must confess," he wrote on 26 March 1939, "to the most profound distrust of Russia. I have no belief whatever in her ability to maintain an effective offensive, even if she wanted to. And I distrust her motives, which seem to me to have little connection with our ideas of liberty, and to be concerned only with getting every one else by the ears."

It would be a mistake to blame the British prime minister for driving the

Soviet Union into Hitler's arms and making the Second World War inevitable. There is no assurance that, had he been eager to forget the past and enthusiastic about an alliance with the Soviets, their course would have been any different than it was. The Soviets' policy was animated by their ideological hatred of all bourgeois regimes; their diplomatic strategy, however, was determined by considerations of relative danger, which made it necessary for Russia to throw its support to one or the other of its ideological opponents.

Chamberlain's attempt to exclude the Soviet Union from his own plans for the consolidation of European peace, however, probably persuaded the Soviet government that the Western powers were not serious about opposing Hitler but hoped to turn his aggressive tendencies toward the east. This made Russia anxious to make its own deal with Hitler. Vice Commissar Potemkin's words to the French ambassador Coulondre after Munich were revealing in this respect. "My dear friend," he said, "don't you see what you have done? You have made a fourth partition of Poland inevitable."

Absent from that worried remark was any intimation of recognition that Soviet behavior from 1919 onward may have contributed to this unhappy state of affairs. Criticism of Western policy toward the Soviet Union before 1939 must be tempered by an awareness of how sharp the memory was in Western capitals of Soviet deviousness and double-dealing. This distrust, even more than the practical difficulties that the negotiations of 1939 revealed, was the main obstacle to a last-minute marriage of convenience in the face of the threat of Adolf Hitler.

II

In contrast to the West's attitude toward the Soviet Union, its views of the other principal totalitarian states were remarkably tolerant, and London and Paris seemed for a long time eager to excuse Hitler's and Mussolini's breaches of treaty law without recognizing the threat posed to their own national safety. The explanation is to be found, in the first place, in the stubbornness with which the British government adhered to the policy of appeasement and compelled its French ally to go along. But the fallacies of British policy would have become apparent long before 1939, even to its authors, if it had not been for the diplomatic skills of Adolf Hitler, who proved to be adroit in playing to the prejudices and partialities of the British and French governments and in postponing the time when the scales finally fell from their eyes.

The appeasement policy was the invention of Neville Chamberlain, who as chancellor of the exchequer during the last years of Stanley Baldwin's prime ministership had become steadily more dismayed by what he considered to be the mistaken premises of British foreign policy. A politician who had made his way to cabinet rank by distinguished service in a number of domestic ministries, Chamberlain had no experience with foreign affairs before becoming prime minister in 1937 and, indeed, had once been interrupted while airing his views on foreign subjects by his brother Austen, one of the authors of the Locarno treaties, who said, "Neville, you must remember you don't know anything about foreign affairs."

This was proved in the end to be tragically true. But Neville Chamberlain was a strong-willed and self-confident man in a government of ministers weaker than himself. As early as May 1934, he was writing in his diary, "Unhappily it is part of my nature that I cannot contemplate any problem without trying to find a solution for it. And so I have practically taken charge of the defence requirements of this country." A year later, he was confiding to his sister that he had become "a sort of acting P.M.," telling the indecisive Baldwin what he should do; and in June 1936, he showed that he did not exclude foreign affairs from the sphere of his intervention by calling in the House of Commons for an end to the policy of sanctions against Italy for its aggression in Ethiopia, in a speech which he had not bothered to clear with Foreign Secretary Anthony Eden because he was sure that Eden would beg him not to make it. Shortly before he became prime minister, he told Lady Astor that "he meant to be his own Foreign Minister."

The statement implied a fundamental change in the direction and methods of British foreign policy. In a Europe in which the power balance had been sensibly altered by Hitler's repudiation of the arms clauses of the Versailles Treaty, by the Ethiopian and Spanish conflicts, and by the remilitarization of the Rhineland, Chamberlain felt it idle to go on talking as if the Versailles system could be maintained and the League of Nations revivified. In a moment of brutal candor, he said, "We must not try to delude small weak nations into thinking that they will be protected by the League when we know that this will not be the case." The time had come to find a new basis for European order, and the way must be paved by a vigorous attempt to appease the revisionist powers in the interest of détente. Instead of invoking outworn ideals, one should bring into play the practical virtues of realism and accommodation. Like a good businessman seeking to make a deal, one should try to find out what the true objectives of the dictators were and then use this knowledge as the basis for a bargain that would bring them back into the international comity by satisfying their wants. That this might involve the recognition of Mussolini's African conquests and an end to demands that he withdraw his "volunteers" from Spain, that it could probably be effected only by giving Germany back its colonies and making adjustments in the boundaries of eastern Europe, Chamberlain acknowledged and accepted, on the ground that the détente that would follow would be to everyone's advantage.

There was no dearth of critics of these ideas. Foreign Secretary Anthony

Eden, the permanent undersecretary for foreign affairs Lord Vansittart, Winston Churchill, the former ambassador in Berlin Sir Horace Rumbold, and other persons of wide European experience pointed out at various times that the basic flaw of appeasement was its assumption that the dictators could be appeased. They argued that on the contrary Hitler was still animated by the desire for *Lebensraum* that he had articulated in *Mein Kampf* and that Mussolini would, as far as possible, model his behavior on the Führer's; that an attempt to buy them off could only be made at the expense of small states; and that it was a mistake to think that they placed as high an evaluation on peace as Chamberlain did himself. These were shrewd arguments (and the last was corroborated by no less a person than Hermann Goering, who once said to Lord Halifax, "I should like to discuss these things with Mr. Chamberlain some time, but I suppose all he would want to talk about is peace"). But Chamberlain was too headstrong to take these criticisms seriously, and he resented the fact that they were made. His feelings were reflected in his kicking Vansittart upstairs and forcing Eden's resignation and his subsequent preference for bypassing the Foreign Office as much as possible. Like other outsiders, Chamberlain resented professionals, and he convinced himself that the Foreign Office was too pro-French and anti-German, too bound to the old Versailles system, and too unrealistic. He preferred to choose for advisers and associates people whose views agreed with his own, like Sir Horace Wilson, who came from the Treasury Department and had little prior knowledge of foreign affairs, and his ambassador in Berlin, Sir Nevile Henderson, who had none of the objectivity and skepticism of his predecessors Rumbold and Sir Eric Phipps.

In the end, Chamberlain's critics were proven to be right, and the appeasement policy helped to bring on the war that the prime minister was seeking to avoid. This was not, however, due solely to his gullibility. Hitler's gifts of persuasion were considerable, and Chamberlain was not the only European statesman who was deluded by his ability to mask his true intentions until he felt strong enough to be able to disregard potential opposition.

In the uses of diplomacy, Hitler was easily the most skillful of the totalitarian leaders. The Soviets often showed technical competence but were always handicapped by ideological rigidity and a tendency to alienate their negotiating partners by their inveterate suspicion, the tediousness of their tactics, and their deviousness. Mussolini and his diplomats brought nothing new to the art of negotiation, and Fascist diplomacy, after the duce's son-in-law Galeazzo Ciano had taken over the Palazzo Chigi, was characterized by an emphasis upon the sensational rather than the substantive, an inordinate degree of posturing and bombast (that was what the *tono fascista* on which Ciano insisted really amounted to), and a not inconsiderable amount of slipshodness in detail, as in the drafting of the Pact of Steel with Germany in May 1939, which imposed rigid conditions upon Italy without defining the *casus foederis,* providing escape clauses, or stipulating the necessity of consultation. In contrast, Hitler showed both skill and inventiveness in using the resources and techniques of diplomacy to advance his purposes.

For the sake of brevity, one can speak of Hitler's diplomacy as going through four distinct phases. The first of these, which followed immediately upon his accession to power, may be called the diplomacy of concealment or obfuscation, for it was designed to convince the other powers that the *Machtübernahme* would bring with it no fundamental change in German foreign policy. The personnel in the Foreign Office and the embassies remained unchanged; intensive propaganda was beamed abroad to convince other governments and peoples that the unpleasant things going on inside Germany (the *Gleichschaltung* process that was destroying all of the elements of potential resistance to the new regime) had no foreign political connotations; *Mein Kampf* and its arguments were played down; and every possible attempt was made to stress common bonds with the West by means of cultural exchanges and inducements to Western tourism. All of this was intended to prevent external interference while Germany was vulnerable and until *Gleichschaltung* was completed and secret rearmament was begun.

In the second phase, which began at the end of 1933 and extended through the next year, Hitler's diplomacy was intended to disengage Germany from obligations assumed by previous governments and to protect the country from the possible consequences of doing so. This began with Germany's departure from the disarmament conference and the League of Nations in October 1933, an action which Hitler carefully prepared by playing upon the bad conscience of the West with regard to Germany's remaining disabilities under the Versailles Treaty and the resentment that existed in some countries over France's reluctance to make concessions. He also used with effect tactics that were to be employed again during the Sudeten crisis of 1938, constantly raising the level of his demands at the disarmament conference so that a settlement became impossible and then withdrawing from the conference and the League on the grounds that the German people would no longer tolerate an imposed inequality. As in 1938, he subsequently held a plebiscite in Germany to demonstrate that he had full public support.

During the year that followed, Hitler's main diplomatic efforts were devoted to avoiding any attempt to punish him for his actions. This took the form of a flurry of public and private assurances that Germany was willing to make new engagements and enter into new pacts with any power. His promises had such a ring of sincerity that they reassured Western statesmen; even as late as the spring of 1939, Neville Chamberlain was telling journalists that he expected Hitler to return to the League and disarmament talks before the end of the year. To escape from diplomatic isolation, Hitler himself (for it was his own idea rather than that of the Foreign Office) negotiated a pact of friendship with Poland in January 1934, an arrangement that proved its worth later in the year, when his new partner helped scuttle French Foreign Minister Louis Barthou's plan to contain Germany by means of an eastern Locarno.

The third phase, which extended from the beginning of 1935 until the end of 1937, was characterized by a diplomacy of testing, designed to discover how much resistance could be expected once Hitler had unmasked his plans for expansion in the east. It began with the Saturday Surprises of March 1935, when, on successive Saturdays, Hitler announced that Germany had a new air force and that it would no longer be bound by the arms clauses of the Versailles Treaty. It continued, when no retaliatory spirit evinced itself (the Stresa front of April 1935 collapsed, and the British government proved perfectly willing, despite Hitler's violation of the treaty, to sign a naval accord with him in June), with the remilitarization of the Rhineland and the intervention in the Spanish Civil War.

It was during this period of testing that Hitler showed how skillful he could be in disarming potential antagonists. When Foreign Secretary Sir John Simon and Anthony Eden went to Berlin in late March 1935 to remonstrate with him concerning his recent actions, he managed to persuade Simon that his behavior had been actuated by a sense of honor and a desire to regain the kind of equality that would enable Germany to return to the League with pride; and on 21 May 1935, in a brilliant example of public diplomacy, he offered to conclude bilateral agreements with his neighbors, to recognize the independence of Austria and refrain from interfering in its internal affairs, and (less than a year before he unashamedly reversed himself) to observe the Locarno treaties, including the demilitarization of the Rhineland. Even the usually skeptical Phipps, then ambassador in Berlin, was won over, as his advice to his government showed. He wrote:

> His Majesty's Government may decide that it is now undesirable to conclude any convention with this country. . . . I earnestly hope that they will not allow themselves to be deterred by the mere contemplation of Herr Hitler's past misdeeds or breaches of faith. After all, he now leads nearly 70 millions of industrious, efficient and courageous, not to say pugnacious people. He is, like most men, an amalgam, and he may, like many men, have evolved since the old, somewhat gangster-like days at Munich. His signature, once given, will bind his people as no other could. It need not bind Great Britain to any state of undue weakness; it need not blind her to the undoubted dangers lying ahead. And if the worst befall, and Hitler decide to break his freely-given solemn pledge, surely our battleground would be all the firmer for having put him to the test?

The fourth phase was the period of aggression, heralded by Hitler's secret meeting with his military and diplomatic advisers on 5 November 1937 and by the reorganization of the army command and the appointment of Joachim von

Ribbentrop as foreign minister in February. These actions were implemented by the *Anschluss* in March, the acquisition of the Sudetenland in September 1938, the absorption of rump Czechoslovakia in March 1939, and the preparations for war with Poland. Although the emphasis was now shifting to military action, diplomacy was still important to Hitler. By its means, he reassured Mussolini that the loss of Austria was tolerable in view of the other advantages that the duce would gain from their collaboration; and it was indispensable in carrying the British and French with him, despite momentary flashes of resistance in London and Paris, until the invasion of Prague proved the bankruptcy of appeasement. Not the least of Hitler's achievements was his ability to exploit Chamberlain's naive belief in his own realism. No word bulked larger in the German diplomatic vocabulary during the months when Hitler was explaining the reasonableness of his claims in central Europe, the irresponsibility of people like Schuschnigg and Benes who opposed them, and the wisdom of accepting the inevitable. Scarcely veiled threats and references to the invulnerability of German arms now began to mingle with the reassurances, but these did not become obtrusive until March 1939, when Hitler tired of the game and sent his tanks into Prague.

Even after that, however, and the beginning of the agitation against Poland, Hitler did not rely entirely upon the military weapon. Indeed, his most stunning diplomatic stroke came in August 1939 when, after a long period of careful sounding, he suddenly made up his mind to make an alliance with the Soviet Union and carried this plan through with blinding speed literally under the noses of French and British negotiators who were, clumsily and belatedly, seeking the same end. With that treaty in his pocket, Hitler had no further use of the diplomatic art. In contrast to his opposite numbers in London and Paris, he had never regarded it as a means of preserving peace but merely as an instrument for preparing the way for the war that he had always wanted. "After all," he said once the war had begun, "I did not raise the army in order *not* to use it." The statement underlines the fact that all of his diplomatic intercourse with the Western governments, upon which they had placed such high hopes, had been nothing but a deliberately contrived *dialogue des sourds,* in which the words he used had secret meanings that the other side could not hear.

Bibliographical Essay

This chapter is based in part upon Gordon A. Craig, *On the Diplomatic Revolution of Our Times* (The Haynes Foundation Lectures, University of California, Riverside, April 1961), and on his essay "Totalitarian Approaches to Diplomatic Negotiation," in *War, Politics and Diplomacy: Selected Essays* (New York, 1966).

On Soviet diplomacy, see Theodore von Laue, "Soviet Diplomacy: G. V. Chicherin, People's Commission for Foreign Affairs, 1918–1930," in *The Diplomats; Russian For-*

eign Policy: Essays in Historical Perspective, ed. Ivo J. Lederer (New Haven, 1962); George F. Kennan, *Russian and the West Under Lenin and Stalin* (Boston, 1961); Adam B. Ulam, *Expansion and Coexistence: The History of Soviet Foreign Policy, 1917–1964* (New York, 1968); and Jonathan Haslam, *The Soviet Union and the Struggle for Collective Security, 1933–39* (New York, 1984). See also Alan Bullock, *Hitler and Stalin: Parallel Lives* (New York, 1991).

On the appeasement policy, there is much background material in Keith Middlemas and John Barnes, *Baldwin, a Biography* (London, 1969), and Anthony Eden, *Facing the Dictators* (Boston, 1962); and Keith Feiling, *Life of Neville Chamberlain* (London, 1946), is still essential. J. R. M. Butler, *Lord Lothian* (London, 1960), and A. L. Rowse, *All Souls and Appeasement* (London, 1961), tell us much about the assumptions of Chamberlain and his associates; and *The History of "The Times,"* vol. 4, pt. 2 (London, 1952), is even more revealing. Special studies of value are Martin Gilbert, *The Roots of Appeasement* (London, 1966), and Martin Gilbert and Richard Gott, *The Appeasers* (London, 1963). Telford Taylor charts the course of Chamberlain's policy in detail in *Munich: The Price of Tragedy* (New York, 1979). For a defense of Chamberlain's policy against those who fail to take into account the circumstances of the time and the gap between Great Britain's responsibilities and its strength, see David Dilks, " 'We must hope for the best and fear the worst': The Prime Minister, the Cabinet, and Hitler's Germany, 1937–1939," *Proceedings of the British Academy* 53, no. 9 (1987). The best and most even-handed explanation of the failure of the Chamberlain policy is Donald Cameron Watt, *How War Came: The Immediate Origins of the Second World War, 1938–1939* (London, 1989). Instructive is Brian Bond, *British Military Policy Between Two World Wars* (Oxford, 1980).

The rich literature on Hitler's foreign policy is summarized and reference is made to the principal works in chapter 19 of Gordon A. Craig, *Germany, 1866–1945* (Oxford, 1978). Special reference should be made to A. J. P. Taylor, *The Origins of the Second World War* (New York, 1962), an ingratiating but tendentious book; Eberhard Jaeckel, *Hitler's Weltanschauung,* trans. from the German (Middletown, Conn., 1972); and Gerhard L. Weinberg, *The Foreign Policy of Hitler's Germany,* vol. 1, *Diplomatic Revolution in Europe, 1933–1936* (Chicago, 1970), and vol. 2, *Starting World War II, 1937–1939* (Chicago, 1980). Also of interest are Andreas Hillgruber, *Germany and the Two World Wars* (Cambridge, Mass., 1981), and Klaus Hildebrand, *Das vergangene Reich: Deutsche Außenpolitik von Bismarck bis Hitler* (Stuttgart, 1995).

8

A Postwar System of Security:
Great-Power Directorate
or United Nations?

The war that began when Hitler's columns sliced into Poland in September 1939 lasted for almost six years and, long before it was over, had proved to be more truly global than its predecessor, more total in its demands upon resources and in its impact upon all classes of society, more sophisticated in its weaponry, and more destructive in its results. At least 17 million soldiers, sailors, marines, and airmen died in action during the conflict, and 18 million noncombatants met their deaths; and, as if that were not enough, the war ended with the revelation of the existence of a new category of terrible weapons that promised to multiply these dreadful statistics beyond the limits of human comprehension if interstate conflict on a major scale ever recurred.

Even before this discovery was made, it had become clear to Allied statesmen that in this war victory was not enough. They realized that they must succeed where their predecessors after the First World War had failed: they had to establish effective barriers against a repetition of the cataclysm. Long before the hostilities had come to an end, two methods of achieving this end, related but different in emphasis, had assumed a semblance of form and attracted supporters. One was Franklin Delano Roosevelt's "Great Design" for a great-power directorate to maintain peace. The other was a plan to establish a second but more effective League of Nations, the United Nations organization that had been forecast in the declaration that followed the conference of Allied foreign ministers in Moscow in October 1943.

I

Roosevelt's "Great Design," as he himself called it, for the postwar world was based to a remarkable extent on lessons of the past that he and his closest advisers—indeed, many others as well—had drawn from various failures of policy after the First World War which had led to the Great Depression, to the emergence of aggressive totalitarian governments in Germany, Italy, and Japan, and finally to another great war.

As Roosevelt and others saw it, one of the mistakes made by the Allies in 1918 was to enter into an armistice with the existing German government without completely defeating its armed forces and occupying the entire country. As a result, German nationalists could afterward claim that Germany had not really been defeated but that the army had been "stabbed in the back" by the new liberal democratic government in Berlin that came into power at that time. The first lesson for Roosevelt, therefore, was that it was essential this time to defeat completely, disarm, and occupy those countries that had started World War II. This was one of the first things Roosevelt, Churchill, and Stalin discussed and quickly agreed upon as their joint war aim, and they succeeded in carrying it out. But, as we will note, it had important consequences for the structure of the postwar world and for the task of creating a viable new security system.

Other important lessons from the failure of peacemaking after World War I also had to be kept in mind. The total defeat and occupation of Germany, Italy, and Japan would amount to little in the long run if economic conditions of the kind that had helped bring totalitarian governments to power in the 1930s were allowed to occur again. Hence a second requirement for a more lasting peace was to develop economic policies and cooperation that would avoid future depressions. Reconstruction of the world's economy on a durable basis was a prime objective of American wartime planning for the postwar era. Plans were made to remove or sharply reduce barriers to trade among nations. American planners also took up the important matter of reforming the international monetary system. They developed detailed plans for creating mechanisms and institutions that would stabilize international currencies and facilitate the flow of capital across national boundaries in order to expedite postwar reconstruction and economic development.

There was, as one would expect, a strong element of national self-interest behind these economic measures. Roosevelt and his advisers knew perfectly well that his New Deal policies before the war had not solved the problem of unemployment in the United States. It took the war to do that. And there was real concern that, once the war was over and the stimulus of war production to the economy removed, large-scale unemployment would reemerge. Roosevelt wanted to stimulate free trade and healthy economies elsewhere in the world, not only because he believed this essential for developing a viable international system but also because he hoped that foreign markets would absorb the vast amount of goods that American industry would have to continue to produce to maintain employment at a high level at home. We need not go into the details of these economic plans, except to say that with some modifications they were put into effect after the war and were for a number of years generally successful.

Perhaps the most important lesson Roosevelt and his advisers drew from the bungling of the peace after the First World War had to do with the fact that the United States not only had failed to join the League of Nations but also had pursued a generally isolationist foreign policy. American unwillingness to co-operate with other peace-seeking countries had indirectly contributed to the worldwide Great Depression of the 1930s and to the rise of the totalitarians. This time, Roosevelt believed, it was essential that the United States should not return to an isolationist foreign policy once World War II ended. But by no means could he take it for granted that American public opinion and Congress would not press for a return to the traditional American policy of avoiding "entangling alliances."

Thus, even while the war was going on, Roosevelt had to lay the groundwork to ensure a postwar internationalist policy. He had to define such a policy, at least in broad outlines, and to gain legitimacy and public acceptance for it. He did so by conducting the war and justifying it in ways that would lead naturally to an internationalist foreign policy thereafter. In this he was successful in general terms and could, indeed, take satisfaction in the fact that, by the war's end, the old isolationist opposition to an active foreign policy was, if not dead, then seriously weakened. At the same time, the most articulate and influential voices calling for American participation in the creation of a new international system were neo-Wilsonians who favored a new and stronger League of Nations, and this was a view that Roosevelt rejected as idealistic and impractical. His approach to constructing an international security system was based on the realities of power. In Roosevelt's view, it was important that the states that possessed preponderant military power agree to cooperate to preserve the peace.

Roosevelt's thinking was strongly influenced by his concern about the situation that would confront the peacemakers when the war was over. Once Nazi Germany was defeated, there would be an important power vacuum in Central Europe. The question of *who* and *what* would fill this vacuum would pose the most serious implications for the vital interests of both the Soviet Union and the Western powers. If the two sides could not quickly find a mutually acceptable approach to the power vacuum, then they would almost certainly enter into the sharpest kind of competition and conflict over the control of Central Europe.

Such an ominous prospect was all the more likely because the weak and divided international system of the interwar years had collapsed with the outbreak of World War II. The military alliance between the Western powers and the Soviet Union had been forced upon them by circumstances—the danger of defeat at the hands of Nazi Germany and its allies. After the enemy was beaten, all the mutual suspicion and the long-standing differences in ideology between the West and the Soviet Union would have an opportunity to emerge once again. Roosevelt was aware that the postwar world would contain only victors and vanquished; there would be no international system to provide a framework within which the Western powers and the Russians could work out a solution to the power vacuum created by their victory. So Roosevelt had to tackle two important and difficult tasks at the same time: to create a new international system and to find a way of preventing dangerous competition for control of Central Europe.

What were the various ways to accomplish these critical tasks? One approach was to try to create a new balance-of-power system in which there would be a great deal of competition among the major powers. Such a system had existed during the eighteenth century and had failed to deter Napoleon from trying to achieve hegemony; it had also failed for many years to form the kind of coalition needed to bring him down. Roosevelt believed that that kind of system for the postwar period would be neither desirable nor feasible. England would be too weak by itself to provide a military counterweight to Russia on the European continent. In Roosevelt's view, the United States, even with all its military power, would not want, or be able, to bolster England for the purpose of balancing Soviet pressure in Europe. One must keep in mind that Roosevelt operated on the premise—which seemed completely justified at the time—that American public opinion would not tolerate leaving large American military forces in Europe very long once the war ended. So the grim prospect he had to contend with, and to avoid if possible, was that the Soviet Union could end up dominating Europe unless the Russians were brought into a different kind of balance-of-power system.

Another possibility was to try to reduce the potential for conflict in a new balance-of-power system by giving each of the major powers generous spheres of influence in areas of special interest to them. This approach was favored by Winston Churchill, the British prime minister during the war. At his private meeting with Stalin in Moscow in October 1944, Churchill attempted to work out a mutually acceptable understanding that would take into account both the interests of the two sides in the Balkans and the power realities. Churchill provides a vivid description in his memoirs of one of his meetings with Stalin, which began at ten o'clock on the evening of 9 October: "The moment was apt for business." Churchill took out a sheet of paper and wrote next to the name of each of the Balkan countries the percentage of influence each side should have there: Romania, 90 percent Russian; Greece, 90 percent British; Bulgaria, 75 percent Russian; Hungary and Yugoslavia, 50 percent British and Russian. Churchill pushed the paper across the table to Stalin, who looked it over and then proceeded to make a check mark to signify his approval. Churchill then said, "Let us burn the paper." Stalin replied, "No, you keep it." Although Churchill did obtain Stalin's approval for a spheres-of-influence agreement between their two countries covering the Balkans, Roosevelt—though initially sympathetic—felt he could not approve of such an arrangement.

For several reasons, Roosevelt rejected both the model of a highly competitive balance-of-power system and the idea of minimizing its potential for conflict by creating spheres of influence. First of all, he doubted—and in this he was unquestionably right—that domestic public opinion, given its historic antipathy to the European balance of power, would agree to American participation. Besides, for Roosevelt to endorse or to participate in a spheres-of-influence agreement would have directly contradicted the principle of self-determination and other historic American ideals that he had written into the Atlantic Charter. This document had been issued by Churchill and him early in the war, and the Soviet Union had later given it a qualified endorsement. The Atlantic Charter was the major statement of Allied war aims and a major means by which Roosevelt secured public support for an internationalist U.S. foreign policy. Having done so, he could not turn around and support postwar plans that violated those principles.

Secondly, Roosevelt did not believe that a traditional balance-of-power system or spheres-of-influence arrangement would really eliminate competition among the major powers for very long. He thought any such arrangement would be unstable and that the world would soon become divided into two armed camps—a Western democratic one and a Soviet-led one. An arms race would ensue that would at best result in a dangerous armed truce and would at worst lead to another world war. Roosevelt, one might say, foresaw the possibility of the Cold War unless some alternative could be devised.

The only alternative, as Roosevelt saw it, was a version of the balance-of-power system modeled on some aspects of the concert system established by the European powers in 1815 after defeating Napoleon. He hoped to maintain the unity and cooperation of the Allies after the defeat of the totalitarian states. This was the option the president favored from an early stage during the war—he called it his "Great Design"—and he persuaded Churchill and Stalin to cooperate in trying to bring it about.

Roosevelt's Great Design deserves closer attention. The president wanted to establish a postwar security system in which the United States, Great Britain, and the Soviet Union—and, it was hoped, eventually also China—would form a consortium of overwhelming power. These major powers, forming an executive committee, would cooperate in meeting threats to the peace, from either the defeated powers or any other states. The "Four Policemen"—the term was Roosevelt's own—would have a monopoly of military power; all other states would be prevented from having military forces that could pose a serious threat to others. The fact that this would encroach on the principle of the sovereign equality of states did not seem to concern the President greatly.

The Great Design also called for the United States, Britain, and the Soviet

Union to work out mutually acceptable settlements of the important territorial issues and political problems in Europe. These would be reached through joint consultation and agreement, that is, through a system of collective rather than unilateral decision making. Once again, this was reminiscent of the *modus operandi* of the old European concert system. (Roosevelt also hoped that the Russians would participate in arrangements to deal with trade, currency stabilization, and other economic problems.)

Whatever the merits of the president's design, the problem remained of winning public support for this kind of realism. It is worth noting that Roosevelt himself was most cautious about attempting to publicize his Four Policemen concept, largely because he felt it necessary, if he was to maintain a domestic consensus for an internationalist foreign policy, to blur the differences between his own plan and the desire of the idealists for a system of collective security based upon another, stronger League of Nations. The president spoke about his own plan with a number of influential opinion leaders; but when he launched a trial balloon in order to publicize the idea, in an interview with Forrest Davis that appeared in the *Saturday Evening Post* in April 1943, there was a sharply negative reaction. As a result, Roosevelt backed away from further efforts to educate public opinion in order to gain legitimacy for his Four Policemen concept.

Indeed, in the end, his sensitivity to public opinion weakened his originally strong opposition to a revival of the League of Nations. Despite his private view that the task of enforcing the peace would have to be left to the strongest powers, in order to avoid political trouble at home, Roosevelt yielded to the pressure of the vocal groups who were calling for the establishment before the war was over of the United Nations organization promised in the Moscow Declaration of October 1943. He went along when his secretary of state, Cordell Hull, gradually transformed the Four Policemen idea into what became the Security Council of the United Nations. The president consoled himself with the thought that what was critical was not the early establishment of that organization, or the precise format of the Security Council, but rather that the United States and the Soviet Union should preserve a friendly and co-operative relationship, and that they should settle all important issues between them outside the Security Council and work together to maintain the peace.

Roosevelt, as mentioned earlier, could not approve a spheres-of-influence arrangement in Europe. He feared that Americans would perceive it as another example of how the cynical, immoral European powers periodically made secret arrangements to divide up the spoils at the expense of weaker states, and hence as a violation of the principle of national self-determination and independence. Such a development in American opinion, Roosevelt foresaw, could jeopardize his postwar plans right from the beginning. At the same time, however, he recognized that the Soviet Union's legitimate security needs in Eastern Europe would have to be satisfied. Since the Red army was occupying Eastern Europe and would likely move into Central Europe as well, the Soviet Union could do as it wished there in any case. The United States was not going to employ force or threats of force to prevent or dissuade the Soviets from creating friendly regimes and making territorial changes in Eastern Europe. This was understood and accepted even by those of Roosevelt's advisers who were most negative in their attitude toward Soviet communism.

From the standpoint of maintaining domestic support for his postwar policy, it was terribly important for Roosevelt that the Soviet Union define its security needs in Eastern Europe in *minimal* terms, and that it go about securing friendly regimes in Eastern Europe in ways that the United States and Britain could agree to and that would not flagrantly conflict with the principles of the Atlantic Charter. At stake for Roosevelt was the legitimacy of his entire plan for a postwar security system based on cooperation with the Soviet Union. If the American public saw Russian behavior in Eastern Europe as contradicting the principle of national self-determination and independence, it would come to regard the Soviet Union as expansionist and untrustworthy.

Roosevelt hoped, perhaps somewhat naively, that the potential conflict between Soviet security requirements and the principles of the Atlantic Charter could be avoided or minimized. He attempted to persuade Stalin that the complete defeat and disarming of Germany and the arrangements the Allies were making to weaken and control postwar Germany would do more to guarantee Soviet security than would the imposition of tight-fisted Soviet control over Eastern Europe. He also tried to make Stalin understand the difficult problem that would face his administration if the Soviet Union imposed arrangements in Eastern Europe that flagrantly conflicted with the charter commitments. In effect, Roosevelt was pleading for Stalin to show self-restraint; he hoped that Stalin would cooperate at least to the extent of providing a "cosmetic" façade to the creation of pro-Soviet regimes in Poland and other Eastern European countries by going through the process of "free elections" and the like. And in fact Stalin was disposed to cooperate. Cosmetic solutions were devised several times. Thus, Roosevelt and most of his advisers thought they had achieved their goal at the Yalta Conference in February 1945. But their optimism was quickly shaken by new difficulties with the Russians over interpretation of the Yalta agreements regarding Poland. Within a few months of becoming president, Truman patched up this disagreement, but once the war with Japan was over, distrust of Soviet intentions mounted in Congress and among the public. Russian behavior in Eastern Europe was increasingly perceived as a harbinger of more ambitious expansionist aims, and it became difficult to arrest the drift toward the Cold War.

After this became a reality, many people felt that Roosevelt had been naive or foolish in believing that the Soviets would cooperate in the kind of international system he had desired. It is true that the exigencies and pressures of the wartime situation—the need to get along with the Russians in order to ensure the defeat of the enemy powers—had encouraged the president and others to develop a benign, optimistic image of the Soviet Union. But the naiveté that Roosevelt has been charged with was much more apparent after the failure of his hopes for postwar cooperation with the Russians than before. During the war itself, and even for some time after Roosevelt's death, many specialists on the Soviet Union (Charles Bohlen, for one) and other foreign policy experts were by no means sure that his policy would fail. Many of the beliefs, hopes, and expectations regarding the Soviets that appeared to support the president's Great Design enjoyed a considerable measure of plausibility and support; and even skeptics thought that Soviet leaders might cooperate out of self-interest. The generally successful wartime collaboration encouraged such hopes, and they were further reinforced by Roosevelt's assessment of Stalin's postwar intentions and the general endorsement he obtained from Stalin of the concept of a co-operative postwar security system.

It should be noted, further, that despite his generally optimistic personality and outlook, Roosevelt realized that his image of the Soviets might prove to be defective and that his hopes for postwar cooperation might eventually prove to be unfounded. He knew that he was taking a calculated risk, and he remained sensitive to any Soviet actions that threatened the success of his postwar plans. Roosevelt was also quick to undertake remedial measures to bring Stalin back into line whenever necessary, although these were not always successful.

II

If the public reaction to the Four Policemen project was decidedly cool, things were quite different when the United States government turned its energies toward the creation of the United Nations. Roosevelt addressed a joint session of Congress after his return from the Yalta summit, declaring:

> The Crimea Conference . . . ought to spell the end of the system of unilateral action, the exclusive alliances, the spheres of influence, the balances of power, and all the other expedients that have been tried for centuries—and have always failed. We propose to substitute for all these a universal organization in which all peace-loving nations will finally have a chance to join.

Roosevelt's address was greeted with something approaching nationwide enthusiasm, and this was sustained not only during the months that followed, as the outlines of the organization were delineated and it was launched in San Francisco in April 1945, but even after it had become evident that the new organization could neither prevent nor solve all international problems. National polls in February and September 1948, for example, showed majorities of 50 percent to 60 percent believing in the United Nations as the best hope for peace in a world that seemed to be becoming dangerous again.

But this was a transient phenomenon. Some of the popular enthusiasm for the new organization was doubtless selfish and based on the hope that it would reduce American responsibilities in foreign affairs. Much more of it was the result of unreasonable expectations. Brian Urquhart, a long-time civil servant posted to the United Nations and after 1974 the organization's undersecretary, wrote at the end of his career that, in the optimism that attended its birth, there was an impression that the new organization would be able to act on the international level in much the same way as a government acts on the national level. This was a profound misunderstanding, for "the UN is nothing like a government. It has no sovereignty or power of sovereign decision-making. It is an association of independent, sovereign states which depends for its effectiveness on the capacity of its members to agree and to cooperate," and this capacity is likely to be quite limited.

This was certainly true in the case of the most powerful of its members. The great-power unanimity that formed the basis of Franklin Roosevelt's Four Policemen idea, which, it had been hoped, would be the driving force of the new organization, never materialized. As a result, as Urquhart has written, the political life of the UN became, to a large extent, "the story of a continuous effort to improvise around, and to sidestep, the obstacle of fundamental great-power differences" and to find substitutes for the harmony that could not be reached in the organization's Security Council, of which they were the permanent members. This was not fully understood in the West, and particularly in the United States, where the original enthusiasm for the UN eroded rapidly and was replaced by a continuing crisis of legitimacy that was manifested in many forms, among which may be mentioned public outrage when the General Assembly did not agree with American positions, congressional complaints about the UN's failure to prevent crises that Congress itself had not foreseen, investigations of the political views of UN staff members during the McCarthy period, and a tendency on the part of successive administrations to belittle the UN's successes while blaming their own foreign policy failures upon it.

In the critical years that saw the beginning of the Cold War, the self-styled realists in Washington were inclined to leave the United Nations almost completely out of their calculations. President Truman's secretary of state, Dean Acheson, was always contemptuous of what he called "universal Plumb plans," among which he included the UN, and in the crisis caused by Great Britain's admission that it could no longer support the governments of Greece and Turkey against external threats, he bypassed the UN and eliminated all but the barest reference to it in the Truman Doctrine. Joseph Marion Jones, one of Acheson's aides, later justified this, in terms that are less persuasive now than they may have been when they were written, by arguing,

> In 1947 the prestige of the United Nations was important, but there was one thing even more important, and that was a fearless confrontation of the American people with the responsibilities involved in the use of the tremendous and unique power of the United States to promote peace and well-being and preserve freedom.

A similar disregard, bordering upon contempt, came a year later, when the UN was desperately seeking a plan for partitioning Palestine that might avert a war between the Arabs and the Jewish settlers, whose numbers were being rapidly augmented by refugees from Europe. This time the United States negated the negotiations and precipitated hostilities in the area by abruptly recognizing an independent state of Israel without even informing its own UN delegation of its intentions.

The UN suffered greatly in public esteem during the Korean War, which was begun as a UN operation intended to repulse and punish the invaders from the north and then to restore the *status quo ante bellum*. The problem here was that the UN forces were under American command and the supreme American commander, General Douglas MacArthur, did not feel bound by the original objectives. MacArthur's willfulness, his newspaper appeals to the American public against the policy of his superiors, and his eventual dismissal aroused much emotion in the United States and, in conservative circles, led to charges that "the Korean War was the only war ever lost by the United States" and that this was due to the restrictions placed by Truman and the UN upon their military hero. Dean Acheson, who was also a target of conservatives' criticism, was at one with them in their scorn for the UN, largely because of what he felt was its inadequate support of the American position after the Chinese had entered the war. This led him to write later,

> The proceedings in both Washington and New York were not helpful in rallying the country to meet major military reverses and to bear the vagaries of a recalcitrant general. I wished then, as often before and since, that the headquarters of the United Nations were anywhere except in our own country.

In retrospect, much of the criticism suffered by the UN in its first two decades seems mean-spirited and ill-informed. Leaving aside the solid record of accomplishment made by its sixteen subsidiary organizations, which specialized in relief operations, cultural activities, and various kinds of "people-to-people diplomacy," the UN was the one place in the world where all blocs and ideologies were represented, the one permanent diplomatic community, and the one piece of diplomatic machinery that could be put to work at a moment's notice. It had great importance as a place in which informal contacts could be made and hints and signals passed outside of official diplomatic channels, and it was such signals and private talks between Philip Jessup and Jacob Malik in 1949 that prepared the way for the termination of the Soviet blockade of Berlin. The UN was also the one body in which both traditional and democratic, bilateral and parliamentary forms of diplomacy could be brought to bear upon critical problems, so that, in moments of great danger, parliamentary diplomacy in the General Assembly could freeze a situation until a solution could be found for it. This is essentially what happened in the Suez crisis of 1956, when the cease-fire called for by the General Assembly and subsequent negotiations by UN Secretary General Dag Hammarskjöld were the means of allowing the aggressors to extricate themselves from the fiasco with some dignity. The Suez affair was not the last occasion on which the UN saved major powers from the possible consequences of their own mistakes. Two years later, after an anti-government coup in Iraq, the landing of U.S. Marines on the shores of Lebanon (which was made to avert a threat that never materialized and, in retrospect, never seems to have been very likely) might have invited a Soviet response had Hammarskjöld not devised a face-saving formula by which the United States withdrew its troops in Lebanon (and Great Britain its forces in Jordan) in return for an assurance that the UN would take steps to ensure the peace and security of those countries.

The UN's greatest success came after the precipitate withdrawal of Belgium from the Congo, leaving that strategically important and mineral-rich area vulnerable to either Soviet takeover or a superpower conflict. Hammarskjöld's determined effort to build an independent nation eventually triumphed, although at the time of his death in an airplane crash in September 1961 this success was by no means clear, and his policy appeared to have as many enemies in the U.S. Congress as it had in the Kremlin. Walter Lippman wrote later:

> The cause of the opposition from East and West is a determination not to have the UN succeed in what it is attempting to do. For if the UN succeeds, there will not be a communist government in the Congo. That is what Khrushchev hated about Hammarskjöld and the Secretary General's office. And if the UN succeeds, there will not be a restoration of white supremacy in the Congo, and that is why money, propaganda, and clandestine intervention are being employed to frustrate the UN.

Soviet premier Nikita Khrushchev's rage took the form of an attempt during the fifteenth session of the General Assembly in 1960 to unseat the secretary general and replace his office with a three-man directorate, or *troika*, representing the main power blocs. This was frustrated in part by a noble rejoinder by Hammarskjöld, in which he vindicated his duty to resist great-power pressure when it was necessary in behalf of the UN Charter. More significant, perhaps, was the solid support that the secretary general received from the delegates of the Third World member states, a sign that these countries were no longer happy about having the agenda of the UN determined by the great powers. Indeed, the increased number of such countries represented in the world organization—which increased the membership to 110 by October 1962—marked a significant shift in the nature of its work, since the newly independent nations were interested primarily in developmental, environmental and other global problems, rather than in the political and military questions that absorbed the attention of the superpowers and their allies. In his superb autobiographical history of the UN, Urquhart notes that this change contributed to the crisis of legitimacy that the UN suffered from in the Western countries, which, as they lost their majority in the General Assembly, were even less inclined than they had been in the past to view the UN as a major instrument of foreign policy.

Thus, in the years that followed, the UN received much more criticism than praise, a fact that is not easy to justify by any objective review of the record. Indeed, when one considers the organization's achievements in peacekeeping and peacemaking in Cyprus, where a UN contingent arrived in 1964 and was still holding the contentious parties apart more than two decades later, and on the border between India and Pakistan in 1966, or its relief operation in Bangladesh in the early 1970s, or the services of the UN Disengagement and Observer Force on the Golan Heights in the wake of the October War of 1973, or those of the UN Interim Force in Lebanon in all but impossible circumstances after 1978, one feels constrained to ask where we would all be without the UN. Yet throughout these same years ran a current of carping from the Western powers, which in moments of frustration blamed the UN for situations in which they had themselves been impercipient before the event and unwilling to act after it. Thus, Hammarskjöld was criticized for not having averted the Soviet invasion of Hungary in 1956 and U Thant for not having prevented the Arab-Israeli war of 1967 by refusing to withdraw the UN force in the Sinai when Egypt's Nasser demanded it and for being timorous at the time of the Soviet invasion of Czechoslovakia in 1968.

It cannot be denied that the UN was partly responsible for its own decline in popularity in the West, and particularly in the United States, although this was the fault not of the secretary general's office, but of the General Assembly, whose Third World majority was inclined to assume attitudes that were objectionable to the West. The most notorious example of this came in 1975, when, in a gesture of sympathy with the Palestine Liberation Organization (PLO), the General Assembly passed a resolution declaring that Zionism was a form of racism and racial discrimination. This led to an explosion of outrage in the American press and in the U.S. Congress and had widespread and lasting repercussions in public opinion, strengthening the hand of those who firmly believed that the UN was an alien and dangerous presence that should no longer receive government support. This was not without influence upon the Reagan administration's later decision to withhold a large part of its assessed contribution to the world organization.

This small-minded and short-sighted decision remained in force during the years that followed, despite the fact that UN performance more than proved its indispensability in a time of mounting international complexity. The year 1988, for example, saw a string of UN successes that were so impressive that the *New York Times* declared it "the year of the UN." In April, after seven years of peace talks led by a UN mediator, the Soviet Union agreed to withdraw its forces from Afghanistan by mid-February 1989. In August, on the basis of a UN Security Council plan, Iran and Iraq agreed to a ceasefire in a bloody and wasting conflict that had lasted for ten years. In the same month, UN Secretary General Javier Pérez de Cuéllar secured the agreement of Greece and Turkey to hold new talks on the problem of uniting Cyprus, which had poisoned relations between the two NATO allies for more than twenty years. The secretary general also began talks in August that promised to end the war between Morocco and the Algerian-backed Polisario guerrillas for control of the western Sahara. In December, UN forces began to monitor the withdrawal of Cuban forces from Angola in accordance with the terms of an agreement between the Angolan, South African, and Cuban governments mediated by the United States. On 7 December 1988, the General Assembly in New York was the scene of Mikhail Gorbachev's most breathtaking announcement, that of the Soviet Union's intention, without the necessity of any treaty, to demobilize 500,000 troops, 10,000 tanks, 8,500 artillery pieces, and 800 aircraft within two years. Also in December, Yasir Arafat's declaration before a meeting of the General Assembly in Geneva that his Palestine Liberation Organization (PLO) recognized the binding nature of pertinent UN resolutions and the right of the state of Israel to exist created the necessary conditions for Secretary of State George Shultz's decision to establish formal contact with the PLO in the hope of alleviating the Palestine problem. To complete the list, in September 1988 the UN peacekeeping force was awarded the Nobel Peace Prize.

Two years later, when Saddam Hussein of Iraq invaded Kuwait, it was the UN Security Council, in what has been called one of the most important meetings in the organization's history, that authorized the use of force, if necessary, to expel Iraqi troops from the territories they had occupied and "to restore international peace and security to the area." Subsequently, when diplomatic and economic pressure failed to persuade Saddam to yield, the UN carried out a massive military operation that accomplished its objective.

In the United States, this was popularly hailed as an American victory because the bulk of the air and ground operations were launched by American troops. But it is clear enough that the United States could not have borne the military and financial requirements of the operation alone, and it was realized afterward that unilateral action would be equally unavailing in other situations that arose in the wake of the collapse of the Soviet Union and its traumatic effects on international order in the first half of the 1990s. In the face of dangerous new crises in Europe (the dissolution of Yugoslavia and the civil war that followed), Africa (the famine and tribal warfare in Somaliland, and the genocidal massacres in Ruanda and Burundi), and the Far East (North Korea's attempts to escape from international restrictions upon proliferation of nuclear weapons), it became clear that the best hope of resolving these and similar problems lay in the UN's ability to coordinate action between the major powers. It was perhaps natural for individual governments to blame their own reluctance to become, or remain, involved in critical situations upon supposed inadequacies on the part of the world organization, as the United States did in the cases of Somaliland and Bosnia, but it was obvious enough by the middle of the 1990s that any hope of advancing toward a viable international order must depend upon the support that the major powers gave to a UN that had over the years represented the best interests of all parts of the international community. Indeed, in a special issue entitled "Beyond the Year 2000: What to Expect in the New Millennium," *Time* predicted in 1992 that "cooperation with the UN will be the norm" and that "the world will have to utilize the powers of the UN" to solve its problems.

Bibliographical Essay

Section I of this chapter draws upon a previous publication: Alexander L. George, "Domestic Constraints on Regime Change in U.S. Foreign Policy: The Need for Policy Legitimacy," in *Change in the International System,* ed. O. R. Holsti, R. M. Siverson, and A. L. George (Boulder, Colo., 1980).

The account of Roosevelt's plans for a postwar security system draws on a large number of secondary analyses, among them John Lewis Gaddis, *The United States and the Origins of the Cold War, 1941–1947* (New York, 1972); Willard Range, *Franklin D. Roosevelt's World Order* (Athens, Ga., 1959); Roland N. Stromberg, *Collective Security and American Foreign Policy* (New York, 1963); and Robert A. Divine, *Roosevelt and World War II* (Baltimore, 1969). On spheres of influence, see Daniel Yergin, *Shattered Peace* (Boston, 1977), p. 59.

Roosevelt discussed his "Great Design" in considerable detail in background interviews with a journalist, Forrest Davis; see "Roosevelt's World Blueprint," 10 April 1943; "What Really Happened at Teheran-I," 13 May 1944; and "What Really Happened at Teheran-II," 20 May 1944, in the *Saturday Evening Post.*

On the United Nations, see Gaddis, *The United States and the Origins of the Cold War;* Louis J. Halle, *The Cold War as History* (London, 1967); and Bradley F. Smith, *The War's Long Shadow: China, Russia, Britain, America: The Second World War and Its Aftermath* (New York, 1986). Also helpful and informative are such standard works as David McCullough, *Truman* (New York, 1993); Dean Acheson, *Present at the Creation: My Years in the State Department* (New York, 1969); Joseph Marion Jones, *Fifteen Weeks: An Inside Story of the Genesis of the Marshall Plan* (New York, 1955); Alan

Bullock, *Ernest Bevin, Foreign Secretary* (Oxford, 1983); Robert A. Divine, *Eisenhower and the Cold War* (New York, 1981); Arthur M. Schlesinger, Jr., *The Thousand Days: John F. Kennedy in the White House* (Boston, 1965); and Theodore C. Sorenson, *Kennedy* (New York, 1965). W. W. Rostow, *The Division of Europe After World War II* (Austin, 1981), invaluable for its analysis of the relationship between ideas and action in the evolution of United States policy in Europe, has some interesting revelations about early opposition to the UN by American policy makers like George Kennan. Of special interest in pleading the indispensability of the organization is Thomas Hovet, Jr., "United Nations Diplomacy," *Journal of International Affairs* [special issue, "Diplomacy in Transition"] 17 (1963): 29 ff. What is said in this chapter about UN activities and great-power attitudes toward the organization is largely based on Brian Urquhart, *A Life in Peace and War* (New York, 1987), a splendid book as is his *Ralph Bunche, an American Life* (Boston, 1993). See also Paul Gordon Lauren, "Diplomacy and Diplomats of the United Nations," in *The Diplomats, 1939–1979*, ed. Gordon A. Craig and Francis L. Loewenheim (Princeton, 1994).

9

The Cold War as International System

I

Even during the Second World War, as noted in the last chapter, the United States and Great Britain took exception to Stalin's attempts to create pro-Soviet regimes in Eastern Europe, particularly in Poland. These disagreements persisted after the war and contributed to the steady erosion of the wartime alliance between the Soviet Union and the Western powers. Much more serious was the split that developed with the Soviet Union over occupation policies in Germany. In the face of deepening economic chaos in that country and the failure of repeated efforts to win Soviet adherence to joint measures to check it, President Truman felt compelled, in collaboration with the British and French governments, to restore the German economy in the Western occupation zones and eventually to take steps toward setting up a separate West German government. The Soviets reacted strongly to these developments, which they felt marked the beginning of a revival of German militarism. They imposed tighter controls over Eastern European countries occupied by their troops, ruthlessly eliminating potential political opponents and placing reliable Moscow-oriented Communists in power, and in February 1948 they dismantled the democratic government of Czechoslovakia and installed a puppet government of their own. Four months later, in a forcing play designed to disrupt the process of consolidation in West Germany, they imposed a blockade upon West Berlin, cutting off Western ground access to the city. In response, the Truman administration accelerated the efforts to strengthen Western Europe that had begun with the launching of the Marshall Plan for economic assistance in 1947, opened the negotiations that led to the establishment of the NATO alliance in 1949, and began serious discussion of the advisability of rearming the West Germans, whose manpower would be needed if NATO were to achieve a viable military capability.

The events of the period could be traced in much more detail, but enough has been said to illustrate the way in which a vicious cycle of action and reaction occurred in the relations between the West and the Soviet Union. Its effect was to initiate and escalate what came to be called the Cold War. Each side believed that it was behaving in a justifiably defensive manner in response to obstructionist and threatening behavior on the part of the other. The images Soviet and Western leaders held of each other hardened; each side perceived the other increasingly as harboring hostile intentions. This is not to say that the Cold War was caused merely by mutual distrust and misperception—its origins lie deeper than that, as has already been suggested, in the real and important conflicts of interest that existed between the two sides—but there is no doubt that they were seriously exacerbated by the psychological dynamics of conflict escalation.

False perception and psychological phenomena of this kind are, unfortunately, familiar in international relations, as they are in everyday life. Oliver Wendell Holmes once remarked that in any argument between two persons, six persons are involved: the two as they actually are, each of the two as he sees himself, and each of the two as he sees the other. No wonder, Holmes exclaimed, that the two talk past each other and become angry! In international affairs, the same sort of psychological multiplication process is apt to take place, with much the same effects.

At the end of the war, the dominant view of the Soviets held by American leaders was that they were pursuing limited objectives and were not embarked on an expansionist global policy. Soviet actions in Eastern Europe in 1945 and early 1946 were disturbing but not seriously damaging to U.S.–Soviet relations; and President Truman and many others in the United States were inclined to believe that even Russian behavior in Poland was explicable in terms of the Soviet Union's justifiable security needs. This view of Soviet intentions started to change for the worse, however, when the USSR began to bring strong pressure to bear upon the governments of Turkey and Iran and Greece, when Stalin revived the historic Russian demand for guaranteed passage through the Straits of Bosphorus, when he delayed removing his troops from northern Iran, and when Greek Communists, with outside help, engaged the government in civil war. These developments alarmed American officials. Perhaps erroneously, they believed that Stalin was supporting the Greek Communists, and they regarded this and the Soviet pressures on Ankara and Teheran as efforts to extend control over areas that lay outside the range of legitimate Soviet security needs. Evidence of expansionist aims seemed further confirmed by Soviet obduracy over the German question, which has already been mentioned, and by the Czech coup of 1948 and the Berlin blockade.

The American image of the Soviet Union steadily darkened during the first postwar years, and the American attitude toward Soviet—American relations became increasingly alarmist. As early as February 1946, in a now-famous telegram from the U.S. embassy in Moscow, George F. Kennan attributed to Soviet leaders a compulsion to probe any "soft spot" in neighboring countries in an effort to discover whether they could advance Soviet power and influence at an acceptable risk. He suggested that if their probes met with firm opposition, they would withdraw, that they could in fact be contained by firmness and by a Western effort to reduce potential "soft spots" in strategically important parts of the non-Communist world. This theory and the arguments with which Kennan supported it assumed increasing credibility in the minds of policy makers in Washington, although it was not until 1949 that the concept of containment was fully translated into new foreign policy commitments and specific policies.

Containment was implemented relatively slowly in part because Truman could not easily obtain congressional and public support for replacing Roosevelt's policy with a tougher approach to the Soviets. There was still much friendly feeling toward the Soviet Union, a carryover from the wartime admiration of the Red Army's resistance to the Nazis. Many people had an uneasy feeling that Truman was betraying Roosevelt's ideals and blundering into a dangerous conflict with the Russians that was really avoidable. Henry Wallace, a former vice president under Roosevelt and secretary of commerce under Truman, was so outspoken in his criticism of the drift toward the Cold War that the president finally dismissed him. The Truman administration was, indeed, so hard-pressed to find congressional and public support for its major containment policies that it found it necessary deliberately to exaggerate the Soviet threat. This later led revisionist historians to criticize the president for having initiated the process that led to the anticommunist hysteria and the phenomenon of McCarthyism in the late 1940s and early 1950s.

In his memoirs, Dean Acheson, Truman's secretary of state, admits that he consciously denigrated Soviet intentions and portrayed Russia as aiming at world domination in order to gain approval for the president's policies. With a touch of sarcasm toward those who criticized him for oversimplification, Acheson argued that this is sometimes necessary in order to conduct foreign policy effectively in a democracy. "The task of a public officer seeking to explain and gain support for a major policy is not that of a writer of a doctoral thesis. . . . If we made our points clearer than truth, we did not differ from most other educators and could hardly do otherwise."

II

Cold War is a descriptive term that was generally adopted in the late forties to characterize the hostile relationship that developed between the West and the Soviet Union. While loosely employed, the term had an exceedingly important connotation: it called attention to the fact that, however acute their rivalry and conflict, the two sides were pursuing it by means short of another war and that, it was hoped, they would continue to do so. As some commentators noted, however bad the Cold War was, it was better than a hot one, and few would deny that the Cold War was an acceptable substitute for a thermonuclear war with the Russians, if that indeed were the only alternative.

For our purposes we need to go beyond the meaning and significance of the term to consider whether and in what sense this prolonged period of acute and dangerous hostility between the West and the Soviet Union can be regarded as an "international system." We will argue here that the state of Western–Soviet relations during the period of the Cold War, while certainly not an ideal international system, did indeed constitute a primitive one in which certain restraints and norms were present and adhered to. This can be seen if we recall the three prerequisites of an effective international system discussed in the Introduction to this book—agreed aims, appropriate structure, and commonly accepted procedures—and if we employ them to analyze the state of Western–Soviet relations during the Cold War.

The Western powers and the Soviet Union had only one major objective in common: the prevention of World War III. Although the Cold War was an extremely conflict-laden type of international system, this single common objective provided an effective counterweight to the differences and rivalry between the two sides. The desire to avoid a thermonuclear war exerted so powerful an effect on Soviet–American relations because it was coupled with mutual fears than *any* shooting war between American and Soviet forces, no matter at how modest a level initially, could escalate. As a result, both sides gave highest priority to managing effectively the confrontations and crises that developed during the period.

For the reasons indicated, cooperation in "crisis management" quickly became one of the most important means by which the international system achieved its aim and thereby maintained itself. The other important means, employed by each side against its opponent, was deterrence. Some efforts were made to develop other methods of regulating rivalry and promoting some cooperation, but they were far less effective so long as the Cold War persisted in its acute form up to, and including, the Cuban missile crisis. These included efforts to develop arms control; crisis prevention (as against crisis management); accommodation (that is, use of negotiation to arrive at agreements to settle or moderate certain conflicts of interest); and economic cooperation.

As relations between the Western powers and the Soviet Union deteriorated in the late forties, a bipolar structuring of the international arena emerged. Each of the two superpowers moved quickly to organize and dominate a worldwide alliance system. There were not enough major powers of relatively equal strength to make possible the reemergence of a multipolar balance-of-power system. (Besides, as noted in the preceding chapter, Roosevelt and others thought that such a system would be neither feasible nor desirable.) Each superpower dominated its weaker allies and attempted to keep its alliances under tight control. There was very little flexibility in making alliances or, for the weaker states, in switching them. The United States and the Soviet Union viewed any possible loss of an ally, even a small one, with great apprehension for fear of its effects on the rest of their alliances. Not all states, it is true, were absorbed into one of the two systems; there were some neutrals, buffer states, and neutralized countries. But it is no exaggeration to say that two powerful hegemonic alliance systems emerged, giving a bipolar structure to the international system that went well beyond that which had characterized the two-alliance variant of the European balance-of-power system at the turn of the century.

III

American foreign policy under successive administrations, beginning with Truman's, pursued two basic objectives: first, to prevent the further spread of international communism (and, if possible, to roll it back); second, to avoid World War III. High priority was attached to both of these objectives, but there was a built-in conflict between them that emerged sharply in certain situations. On these occasions, U.S. policy makers experienced a serious dilemma and the necessity to choose a preferred objective.

Thus, for the United States to adopt assertive policies to stop the spread of communism or roll it back in certain situations was perceived as increasing the risk of a thermonuclear war. On the other hand, there were situations in which, if the United States gave priority to avoiding the risk of war, it might well have to accept the possibility of further spread of communism or its consolidation. During the Cold War, American policy makers, in Democratic and Republican administrations alike, attempted to cope with this dilemma by considering whether in a given situation the *balance of power* between the Soviet bloc and the free world alliance was at stake. If a Communist success in a certain area was regarded as something that would critically weaken the ability of the non-Communist world to contain the further spread of communism, then the balance of power was threatened. American policy makers then felt inclined to do what they could—always, though, without triggering World War III—to prevent that particular Communist success, even though to do so meant accepting some danger of war. This was the case, for example, in the Berlin crises of 1948, 1958–1959, and 1961.

If, however, a Russian success in a given area would not seriously undermine the ability of the Western alliance to contain the future spread of communism, then American policy makers were generally inclined not to react in ways that would risk World War III. This alternative way of dealing with the policy dilemma is illustrated by Eisenhower's unwillingness to intervene when East Germans rebelled against the Communist regime in 1953. Eisenhower stood aloof once again, despite all the talk from his administration of "liberation" of Eastern Europe, during the Hungarian revolution in 1956 when the new Nagy government took itself out of the Warsaw Pact and called for help from the West. Far from attempting to deter Soviet military intervention in Hungary, Eisenhower was concerned lest Khrushchev, if kept uncertain about U.S. intentions, might become rattled and somehow trigger a general war. Accordingly, Eisenhower told Dulles to find a way of assuring Khrushchev that while the United States did not approve of the Soviet intervention, it would not interfere.

It may be noted that this use of the balance-of-power criterion in making critical foreign policy decisions during the Cold War was similar to its employment by the major powers during the old European balance-of-power system. One difference, however, was that the fear of a thermonuclear holocaust, which had no counterpart in the old system, discouraged both the United States and the Soviet Union from resorting to war as a way of preventing an undesired change in the existing balance of power if to do so would result in a direct clash between American and Russian forces.

IV

In later years, critics of the containment strategy pursued by the West during the Cold War argued that, despite its optimism and steadfastness, it was curiously utopian and in its prescriptions abstract. Thus, as Henry A. Kissinger was to point out, containment assigned to the United States, at the height of its military superiority, a purely reactive role and seemed to foresee no place for diplomatic initiative. This strategy may have led to lost opportunities. In the early 1950s, for example, Winston Churchill believed that, as Josef Stalin began in his last years to realize the economic potential and staying power of the West, it may have been possible to explore the outlines of a general settlement and that the Soviet Peace Note of March 1952, raising the possibility of uniting Germany on the basis of neutrality, may have been a first step in that direction. But the West, feeling that progress toward political and military integration would be jeopardized by the onset of negotiations, rejected the note without thorough investigation, as it did other Soviet feelers after Stalin's death. In April 1953, Secretary of State John Foster Dulles wrote to a member of the White House staff,

There's some real danger in our just seeming to fall in with these Soviet overtures. It's obvious that what they are doing is because of outside pressures, and I don't know anything better we can do than keep up these pressures right now.

Whether or not opportunities for the negotiation of a general settlement were missed by this attitude is impossible to say with any assurance at this late date. The fact remains, however, that the Western governments failed to make proper use of their diplomatic resources and fell into the habit of leaving the initiative to the Soviet Union, a practice that became dangerous after the West lost its military advantage. This was particularly true in the years from 1955 to 1963, when Nikita Khrushchev was secretary of the Communist party in the Soviet Union.

A new and aggressive spirit became apparent in Soviet policy as soon as Khrushchev's authority was consolidated. This was not the result of temperament, but basically a reaction to the uncertainty and lack of direction that affected all aspects of policy in the two years following the death of Josef Stalin in March 1953. The change in attitude was almost made necessary by new factors at work in the world of communism that appeared to threaten Soviet ascendancy. One of these was growing restiveness on the part of the satellite states of Eastern Europe. Dissatisfaction became so serious in East Germany in June 1953 that Soviet tanks had to be sent in to restore order, and it was reflected in growing discontent in Poland and Hungary. A second was the challenge of the People's Republic of China, whose leaders remained true to Stalinist principles at a time when Soviet leaders seemed to be turning away from them, and who criticized the Soviet Politburo for not being aggressive enough in its relations with the West. Moscow was worried by this disaffection, and when Khrushchev emerged as the strongest force in Soviet politics in 1955, he seems to have concluded that a hard line might calm the criticism in Peking and contain the trouble in the satellite capitals.

Khrushchev inaugurated his policy with energy and a variety of techniques that testified to Soviet versatility and aroused some trepidation in the West. He rapidly built up the strength of the Warsaw Pact, the Soviet counterpart to NATO, while simultaneously making much of the recent acquisition of the hydrogen bomb and publicizing new Soviet jet planes as the best in the world. Throughout 1955 and 1956, the air was blue with Soviet boasting about their superiority in conventional forces, nuclear weapons, and delivery systems. At the same time, Khrushchev began a massive program of economic aid and technical assistance to countries like Egypt, Iran, Afghanistan, Cambodia, Laos, North Vietnam, and Burma—a "ruble diplomacy," as a Princeton economist dubbed it, that made many people in the West believe that by winning the Third World, communism might well succeed in burying the West, as Khrushchev in his cheerful manner said it was going to do.

In launching his policy, the Soviet leader was greatly aided by the misguided Anglo-French-Israeli attack upon the Suez Canal in 1956. The provocation suffered by the British and French at the hands of the Egyptian leader Nasser had doubtless been great, but this could not disguise the fact that the operation both violated the principles of the United Nations and was characterized by deliberate deceit toward their American ally. It was also marked by a degree of military bungling on the French and English side that made a quick success impossible. The result was a fiasco, which Khrushchev exploited with great skill. The Suez crisis diverted the attention of the West from Poland, where there were clashes between the workers and the police, and from the open revolt against the satellite government in Hungary that erupted in October. Khrushchev was able to contain the Polish troubles by means of economic and political concessions and to suppress the fighting in Budapest brutally without having to worry about Western intervention. More important, the crisis shook NATO to its foundations and gave enemies of the West the pleasure of seeing the United States collaborating with the Soviet Union in haling its own allies before the bench of justice in the UN.

Khrushchev seems to have believed that the Western alliance was dissolving and that a few doses of what came to be called atomic blackmail would complete the process. He was doubtless encouraged by the panicky Western reaction to the launching of the first Soviet intercontinental missiles and particularly of the space satellites, an event that led many Western opinion-makers to talk as if the Soviets were on the point of winning scientific and hence military mastery of the world. In any event, he now began to make covert threats to NATO members like the one delivered to the British government in December 1957, complaining about the stationing of American bombers with nuclear weapons in Britain and expressing surprise that a country so vulnerable by its geographical position and so defenseless "against modern weapons" should permit this. Six months later, in July 1958, when NATO troops landed in Lebanon to shore up a disintegrating situation there, he sent an official warning to the American and British governments, reminding them of the atomic strength of the Soviet Union; and he was reported to have said privately that, if American forces made a move toward Iraq, where a pro-Western government had just been overthrown, he would see that the United States Sixth Fleet was reduced to a mass of molten steel.

All of this was designed to weaken the will and unity of the West. The real offensive was opened on 27 November 1958, when the Soviet Union sent a note to the Western powers reopening the German question. At inordinate length but with considerable vehemence, it pointed out that although thirteen years had passed since the end of the war, the German situation was still unregulated. It was now time for the West to recognize that two German states had come into existence and also to end the anomalous position of West Berlin, an enclave in the territory of East Germany still occupied by Western troops. The Soviet Union was willing to allow West Berlin to exist as a free demilitarized city, but not in its present condition. It proposed, for the next six months, to make no changes in Western access to the city; but if no agreement was reached in that period, it would sign a separate treaty with the German Democratic Republic (GDR) and relinquish its occupation rights and powers. The Western powers would then have to negotiate with the GDR over their rights of access, and the GDR, as a sovereign state, would have the right to make whatever conditions it desired.

This note came to be called the Berlin ultimatum, although it was very long for an ultimatum and although time was to show that it wasn't as ultimative as it sounded. It appears to have been motivated in part by the desire to eliminate the escape hatch that West Berlin provided for people in the GDR, who were fleeing to the West in ever-larger numbers, and in part by the fear that the United States might decide to supply the new German army with nuclear weapons (the note suggested that a nuclear-free and neutralized Germany might be considered as a possible solution to the German question). It is possible that Soviet–Chinese relations provided another motive. The Chinese were becoming increasingly independent of Soviet control and were now well on their way to acquiring nuclear weapons. Khrushchev may have hoped that a spectacular victory in the German question would enable him to persuade Peking to recognize his leadership and to give up nuclear weapons as too expensive.

Success, however, depended on a Western cave-in, and this did not materialize. President Eisenhower, to be sure, did seek to appease the Soviet leader by telling him that the United States did not intend to stay in Berlin forever and that, indeed, he regarded the situation in Berlin as "abnormal." But Khrushchev was not to be fobbed off with generalities: he wanted his demands to be met, preferably at a summit conference. But the Western allies would not give in, at least not until there had been preliminary talks between the foreign ministers, and their successful stone-walling took the energy out of the Soviet offensive. Foreign ministers' meetings and Chinese distractions took up a good part of 1959, and the Soviet leader became increasingly frustrated and at the same time increasingly anxious for a summit meeting that would give him some kind of a success. But when he finally secured President Eisenhower's assent to such a meeting and a date in May 1960 was set, an American U-2 observation plane was shot down deep inside Soviet territory, and the president immediately assumed responsibility for it. Khrushchev aborted the summit.

He did not, however, as some feared at the time, carry out the threats made in the note of November 1958. It was not until May 1961, when a new president was in office and American policy was in disarray as a result of the fiasco at the Bay of Pigs, that Khrushchev felt the time propitious for a new drive toward his German objective. In a meeting with President Kennedy in Vienna, he delivered a new ultimatum. Unless a viable treaty could be negotiated by December, the Soviet Union would sign a separate treaty with the GDR. West

Berlin could continue as a free city, but if Western troops were stationed there the Soviets would have to have the same privilege, and access rights would have to be negotiated with the GDR. This time Khrushchev was not seeking to appease the Chinese, who had by now gone their own way, or to persuade the West to agree to a neutral Germany. His eyes were concentrated on Berlin alone, where the number of refugees had reached flood proportions (thirty thousand fugitives from East Germany were to pass through West Berlin in July) and was bringing East Germany to the verge of collapse. Hence Khrushchev's new urgency and the menacing tone of his conversation with the president.

Kennedy was shaken but not cowed. He left Khrushchev with the words "It will be a cold winter" and, instead of bolting into negotiations, he returned home to push the armaments program that had started in February. Some classes of reservists were called up, an earnest of American intentions that elicited floods of new threats from Moscow and a military response of the same nature.

The crunch came in August 1961, and it took an unexpected turn, for on the thirteenth of that month the East German government began the construction of a wall along the boundary between the two halves of Berlin, cutting off mutual access. While this action did not come as a complete surprise to Western authorities, it was not President Kennedy's policy to oppose such a development, and nothing was done to prevent the construction of the wall. This in itself was a success for Khrushchev. He had stopped the drain on the energies of East Germany, he had forced the West to condone a violation of the Potsdam Agreement, and he had greatly increased the number of people in the West who felt that West Berlin could not be protected.

It may be that Khrushchev believed this too, for he kept up the pressure after 13 August. Two weeks after the wall went up, he invited C. L. Sulzberger of the *New York Times* to come to Moscow for an interview, and there asked him to take a private message to President Kennedy stating that he "would not be loath to establishing some sort of contact with him to find a means, without damaging the prestige of the United States, to reach a settlement. But on the basis of a peace treaty . . . and a free city of Berlin." He added that if it came to a showdown, Britain, France, and Italy, which he described as "figuratively speaking, hostages of us," could not be expected to support the United States. When Sulzberger repeated the substance of this conversation to U.S. Ambassador Llewellyn Thompson, Thompson said, "This means war! All of us are going to be dead!" The president's reaction, when Sulzberger saw him at the beginning of October, was almost equally gloomy.

Why Khrushchev did not make good on his threat is by no means clear. It may be that an incident in Berlin at the end of October had a sobering effect upon him. On 25 October, when two American officers in civilian clothes were denied access to East Berlin because they refused to show their papers to East German guards, General Lucius D. Clay, whom Kennedy had sent to Berlin to hearten the shaken population, decided on a show of force to dramatize Allied rights in all parts of the city and sent an armored contingent to Checkpoint Charlie on the wall. The Soviet commander in East Berlin responded in kind (thus proving that the Soviets were *not* ready to relinquish their rights in the city to the East Germans). It was a frightening confrontation, for behind the tanks stood all the nuclear force in the world.

If this incident induced second thinking on Khrushchev's part, it also deeply alarmed the Kennedy administration, which now felt it so urgent to settle the Berlin question that they became incautious. In the spring of 1962, after lengthy negotiations with Soviet Foreign Minister Andrei Gromyko and Soviet Ambassador Anatol Dobrynin, Secretary of State Dean Rusk concocted a plan for regulating access to Berlin that aroused the liveliest apprehension in Germany, not least of all among American diplomatic representatives there who regarded it as a sell-out, and which was blocked only when Chancellor Konrad Adenauer took public issue with his Washington ally.

If Berlin had been lost during those dangerous years, the course of the Cold War would probably have turned definitively against the West. That it was not lost was due to a number of complicated factors, not least of all the behavior of Charles de Gaulle, whose unwavering refusal to negotiate under the pressure of ultimata prevented the Western powers from agreeing on a program of concessions to the Soviet Union, and of Konrad Adenauer, whose stubborn opposition to and detailed criticism of all Allied plans for meeting the Soviets half way slowed the process and whose hints that he might meet with Khrushchev himself alarmed his allies and prevented them from overruling him. More important were Khrushchev's disinclination to back his threats with force; his mistake, after the U-2 incident, in breaking up the Paris summit in 1960, where he might have gotten much of what he wanted; his decision in August 1961 of settling for half of what he wanted by authorizing the building of the Berlin Wall; and his subsequent folly in abandoning a concentrated strategy for a diffuse one and becoming involved in the Cuban affair, hoping apparently to win Berlin as a by-product of an American humiliation in the Caribbean. That was a grave miscalculation, and it not only put an end to Khrushchev's German hopes but, very soon after the liquidation of the Cuban missile crisis, to his political career as well.

V

Khrushchev's secret deployment of some forty-two medium-range and between twenty-four and thirty-two intermediate-range ballistic missiles in Cuba during the late summer and early fall of 1962 brought the superpowers to the brink of thermonuclear war. Unforeseen and unwanted by either side, the tense confrontation was resolved through careful crisis management by both Washington and Moscow. Forgoing an immediate air strike against the missile sites but threatening to make one if necessary, Kennedy undertook a naval blockade of Cuba instead. In the end, the president's use of the strategy of coercive diplomacy to persuade Khrushchev to remove the missiles proved effective. The crisis ended with a hastily arranged quid pro quo in which Khrushchev agreed to take out his missiles in return for a conditional pledge by Kennedy not to invade Cuba in the future as well as a secret agreement to remove U.S. Jupiter missiles from Turkey.

The crisis was the culmination of the long-standing practice of employing strategic nuclear threats as an instrument of Cold War policy. It does not require much imagination to understand the frustration Kremlin leaders must have felt during the years of American strategic superiority when Washington relied implicitly or explicitly on the threat of "massive retaliation" or to appreciate Moscow's determination to neutralize this American advantage and, if possible, to turn the practice of strategic threats against its makers. We have already noted Khrushchev's efforts to do so in the 1950s as the Soviet Union acquired medium-range nuclear missiles that targeted Western Europe.

Americans were uncertain of the pace at which the Soviets were acquiring long-range strategic nuclear missiles that could reach the United States. Their anxiety provided Khrushchev with an all-too-tempting opportunity to neutralize and reverse the Cold War advantage such capabilities had given the United States. The Soviet leader increasingly played on American and Western fears that the Soviets were outdistancing the United States in nuclear rocket capabilities and creating a "missile gap" in their favor. From 1957 to 1962, the Soviet government engaged in a deliberate, systematic, and sustained campaign of deception, issuing grossly exaggerated claims regarding the production and deployment of ICBMs. Khrushchev put these claims to use to invigorate his assertive foreign policy; this was, as we have seen, nowhere more evident and threatening than in the Berlin crises.

Finally, when Khrushchev continued pressure against Berlin after erecting the Berlin Wall, Kennedy publicly disclosed in the early autumn of 1962 that new intelligence conclusively laid to rest the missile gap fear and thoroughly discredited the Soviet leader's bombastic strategic claims. The facts of the matter were that the Soviets had deployed very few ICBMs and that the United States would retain a clear strategic advantage for at least several more years. Kennedy's disclosure did, indeed, quickly defuse the Berlin crisis and put an end to Khrushchev's claims and threats. But it also left the Soviet leader in a difficult position. Not only did he suffer the embarrassment of having his deception unmasked, but he was forced to abandon temporarily the vigorous thrust of his foreign policy until he developed a real strategic capability. There is also reason to believe that his relations with the Chinese Communist leaders were further strained by the affair.

Under considerable psychological and political pressure to recoup this situation and to reinvigorate his foreign policy, Khrushchev succumbed to the temptation to secure a "quick fix" of the strategic imbalance by deploying medium- and intermediate-range missiles, of which he had plenty, in Cuba. The story of the belated discovery of the missile sites in Cuba and the deliberations of Kennedy's Executive Committee, which led to a decision to seek the removal of the missiles by means of a naval blockade coupled with coercive diplomacy, is well-known and need not be repeated here. (But see the case study of the Cuban missile crisis in chapter 15 on coercive diplomacy.) Instead, let us turn to a discussion of the impact of this brush with thermonuclear war on the Cold War policies of the two superpowers.

VI

The Cuban missile crisis may well be regarded as one of the turning points of recent history, for it facilitated a transition from the era of the acute Cold War to a search for a less dangerous and more viable international system. Thus, one may speak of the missile crisis as having had a "catalytic" effect. That international crisis can have positive results in improving relations between previously antagonistic states is often overlooked in our natural preoccupation with and concern over the danger of war created by tense diplomatic confrontations. But crises often offer statesmen opportunities for constructive change. It is interesting to recall in this connection that the Chinese character for "crisis" has two meanings: the first is the same as the standard meaning of the word in English—that is, threat or danger to important values. The second connotation, however, is something quite different—not "threat" but "opportunity." There is something quite profound in the double meaning which, in the context of international relations, suggests that a crisis can loosen things up; it can lead policy makers to question and to revise if not totally discard some of the old beliefs and policies that led to the impasse; it can make them willing to strike out in new directions.

The Cuban missile crisis had precisely this kind of effect on Khrushchev and Kennedy. Samuel Johnson once remarked to Boswell that nothing concentrates the mind so well as the prospect of being hanged in a fortnight. It is not an exaggeration to say that the horror of the missile crisis was a kind of shock therapy for both leaders. It brought to a head long-standing dissatisfactions with the Cold War on both sides and strengthened their determination to move away from its worst aspects toward a better alternative.

This new spirit and determination led within nine months to the signing of the limited test ban treaty—the first major arms control agreement between the two nuclear superpowers. Even more significant perhaps was the fact that the American image of the Soviet opponent began to undergo significant modification. Kennedy and other American leaders began to view the Soviet Union as a *limited adversary* rather than as a total enemy, as they had during the height of the Cold War. This change was conveyed dramatically by Kennedy in a moving speech at the American University in Washington, D.C., on 10 June 1963, in which he called upon the American people to reexamine their views on the Cold War. He warned his listeners not to take "a distorted and desperate view of the other side, not to see conflicts as inevitable," and not to regard "accommodation as impossible and communication as nothing more than an exchange of threats." He went on to say about the Soviet Union that "no government or social system is so evil that its people must be considered as lacking in virtue."

Heartening as this sounded, the alleviation of tensions between the superpowers was of short duration. The assassination of John Kennedy in Dallas in November 1963 robbed the movement for new measures of nuclear arms control of its momentum, and during the administration of Lyndon B. Johnson no further progress was made. Meanwhile, both governmental and popular thinking continued to be dominated by the philosophy of containment and particularly by its tendency to overlook distinctions and see problems in universal terms. It was the pervasive assumption that all Communist regimes were identical, linked, and under Moscow's hegemony and that all must be opposed that drew the United States into the long agony of the Vietnam War. For this involvement, which was made without any careful assessment of costs and possible outcomes, Kennedy was as responsible as his successor was for its continuation and expansion. As a result, the Cold War was prolonged for almost thirty years. Twenty years after John Kennedy's speech at American University, cautioning Americans against thinking the worst of their antagonists, another president was assuring them that the Soviet Union was still "the evil empire."

Bibliographical Essay

The development of the Cold War generated a great deal of political controversy that quickly spilled over into scholarly studies and has not yet run its course. Herbert Feis provided an early "orthodox" interpretation of the origins and development of the Cold War. Among the many important criticisms of the orthodox viewpoint are the "revisionist" interpretations provided by William A. Williams, Walter LaFeber, Gabriel and Joyce Kolko, Barton J. Bernstein, Lloyd C. Gardner, and Thomas G. Paterson. The present chapter views the origins and development of the Cold War in analytical terms rather than with any intention to attribute responsibility to either of the superpowers.

There are many useful histories of the Cold War, written mostly from the standpoint of American policy. See, for example, Walter LaFeber, *America, Russia, and the Cold War, 1945–1967,* 4th ed. (New York, 1980); Seyom Brown, *The Faces of Power: Constancy and Change in United States Foreign Policy from Truman to Johnson* (New York, 1968); John Spanier, *American Foreign Policy Since World War II,* 7th ed. (New York, 1977); Daniel Yergin, *Shattered Peace* (Boston, 1977); Stephen E. Ambrose, *Rise to Globalism* (New York, 1976); and Thomas G. Paterson, *On Every Front: The Making of the Cold War* (New York, 1979). See also David McCullough, *Truman* (New York, 1993).

A critical account of the operational aspects of containment can be found in Henry A. Kissinger, *Diplomacy* (New York, 1994). See also Gordon A. Craig, "Konrad Adenauer and His Diplomats," in *The Diplomats, 1939–1979,* ed. Gordon A. Craig and Francis L. Loewenheim (Princeton, 1994); Detlev Felken, *Dulles und Deutschland: Die amerikanische Deutschlandpolitik, 1953–1959* (Bonn, 1993); and Frank A. Mayer, "Adenauer and Kennedy: An Era of Distrust in German-American Relations," *German Studies* 17, no. 1 (February 1994).

To his earlier study, *The United States and the Origins of the Cold War, 1941–1947* (New York, 1972), John Lewis Gaddis has added a detailed analysis of the different versions of U.S. containment policy in the years since 1946: *Strategies of Containment* (New York, 1982). See also his volume of essays, *The Long Peace: Inquiries into the History of the Cold War* (New York, 1987), which seeks, among other things, to delineate elements of stability that emerged in the postwar international system and persisted despite the continuation of the Cold War. The gradual transition to a Cold War image of the Soviet Union on the part of President Truman and his close advisers is traced in detail and explained partly with reference to cognitive psychological theory in a fine study by Deborah W. Larson, *Origins of Containment: A Psychological Explanation* (Princeton, 1985).

The emphasis placed on deterrence strategy in American Cold War policy is examined in detail in Alexander L. George and Richard Smoke, *Deterrence in American Foreign Policy: Theory and Practice* (New York: 1974), which also includes twelve detailed case studies of Cold War crises.

10

From Détente to the End
of the Cold War

I

The year 1969 saw two important political changes within the Western alliances and two corresponding initiatives that were intended to make significant changes in the international system. In Washington the Republican administration of Richard M. Nixon succeeded the Democratic administration of Lyndon B. Johnson and embarked upon a radically new policy of *détente*, a term which in classical diplomacy referred to a process of relaxation, but as used by Nixon and his National Security Adviser Henry A. Kissinger had a wider meaning, involving not only relaxation but accommodation with former antagonists in the hope of eventually creating a new international system. In Germany, at the same time, a major political change brought the Socialists to power for the first time since the founding of the Federal Republic, with the creation of a Socialist-Liberal government (SPD/FDP) with Willy Brandt as chancellor. After consulting his Western allies, Brandt inaugurated the so-called New Eastern Policy (*Neue Ostpolitik*), which was designed to bring a formalization and consequential relaxation (*Entspannung*) of relations with the governments of the Soviet bloc in Eastern Europe.

In the case of Nixon and Kissinger, they were both convinced that the world would be a better place if all of the powers conducted their business on the basis of national interest and that a global balance of power—in the president's words, "a stronger, healthy United States, Europe, Soviet Union, China, Japan, each balancing the other, not playing one against the other, an even balance"—would be the best assurance of peace. To be able to play their part in such a balance, Kissinger and Nixon felt that they had to refocus the strategy of containment on its original target and purge it of the ideological distractions that had led to the Vietnam involvement, which by now had lost both public and congressional support.

As John Lewis Gaddis has written, the essence of the problem facing Nixon and his adviser was

> to find a way to withdraw from Vietnam without appearing to have been forced to do so; to regain the initiative in world affairs without giving evidence of ever having lost it; and to accommodate all this within the awkward institutional framework that the American constitution demanded.

As far as Vietnam was concerned, Nixon and Kissinger sought to prevent a precipitate American disengagement while building up the strength of the South Vietnamese government and simultaneously, through diplomacy, bombing, and mining harbors, applying pressure to the North Vietnamese to make peace. It was the hope of receiving help in persuading the recalcitrant enemy to negotiate seriously that led to the greatest diplomatic coup of the Nixon administration, the breakthrough in China in July 1971. This opening did not have the results in Vietnam that had been hoped for, but it was a prelude to Kissinger's grandiose experiment in reforming the containment policy by triangular diplomacy, the elaboration of a policy of linkage, and détente with the Soviet Union.

In going to China, Kissinger's calculation was that the Soviet Union would be induced by the move to improve its relations with the United States as a measure of self-protection. Having established a measure of friendly relations with both of the great Communist rivals, the United States would obtain some leverage with each that could be advantageous to American foreign policy. The threat posed to the world position of the United States by the policies of either of these two Communist powers would be moderated by engaging each of them in a process of détente and accommodation. In addition, the United States could hope to reduce further the potential threat to its interests emanating from either and to induce their cooperation with American policy by using its unique middle position in the triangular relationship to tilt or threaten to tilt in favor of one or the other.

This is not to say that Nixon and Kissinger viewed the Soviet Union in the same terms as they did the People's Republic of China (PRC). The major potential threat to American security and worldwide interests was perceived to emerge from the growing power of the Soviet Union. China was not, and would not for many years become, a superpower on a par with the United States and Russia. And so the major reason behind Nixon's opening to China was to obtain leverage for developing a more satisfactory relationship with the Soviet Union. The threat of positive U.S. relations with China was to be part of the "stick" which, coupled with various inducements held out to the Soviet Union, would draw it into a more constructive relationship in which the Soviets would restrain themselves from employing their growing power to make advances at the expense of U.S. interests and those of its allies.

II

What, then, was the strategy that Nixon and Kissinger employed to achieve this new kind of constructive relationship with the Soviet Union? It had four major components, including an element of "appeasement," a term that they carefully avoided.

The first of these called for acknowledging that the Soviet Union was entitled to the same status as a superpower that the United States enjoyed. The Soviets had long wanted to achieve equality of status with the United States; and President Nixon now recognized this, rhetorically and in various symbolic ways, for example, in summit meetings with them. But while such recognition granted the Russians the position and the prestige that they desired, it left undefined what the new status was to mean in practice. The Soviet leaders proceeded to interpret political equality with the United States as meaning that they were justified in pursuing a more assertive foreign policy; American leaders and public opinion in the United States came to view this as a violation of the basis of the détente.

A second element in the Nixon strategy was a conditional willingness to legitimize the present division of Europe in a formal diplomatic manner. A cardinal objective of Soviet policy since 1945, such legitimation was bound to be difficult for American public opinion to accept, and for a long time it had been rejected by American policy makers. The sticking point for the United States was West Germany, where the United States had found it expedient during the Eisenhower administration to insist that reunification was inevitable and desirable and to support the so-called Hallstein Doctrine maintained by the Adenauer government. This doctrine, in the name of reunification, denied any legitimacy to the German Democratic Republic, and under it the West Germans refused to have dealings with any state that extended recognition to the East German regime. There was always an element of disingenuousness about American support of reunification and about the lip service paid by the Soviet Union to the same principle. In reality, neither the United States nor the Soviet Union would have tolerated a fusion of the two Germanies unless it was sure that the new united nation would end up on its side in the Cold War struggle. But neither said this openly for fear of arousing German nationalist feeling, and the United States avoided any statements that might be taken to suggest that the present division of Europe was acceptable.

By the end of the 1960s, however, the situation was different than it had been in the days of Eisenhower and Adenauer, and in Germany the Hallstein

Doctrine had lost most of its credibility. In a famous speech in Tutzing, during a meeting on German unification, Egon Bahr of the Social Democratic party had called in 1963 for a new approach to the East, a policy of "small steps" that would lead to "change through rapprochement." It was in this spirit that, when the Social Democratic party came to power in 1969, Willy Brandt initiated a policy aimed at closer relations with all the states of Eastern Europe (which led in 1970–1971 to new treaties between the Federal Republic and the Soviet Union and Poland) and an accommodation with the East German regime or, as Brandt put it, an agreement about "practical questions . . . that could alleviate the life of people in divided Germany." The United States government was not at first enthusiastic about Brandt's *Ostpolitik,* but it placed no obstacles in his way, while at the same time insisting that any new treaty between the two Germanies should be preceded by a new Four Power Agreement which guaranteed the rights of the Western powers in West Berlin. Such a treaty was negotiated and signed in August 1971 and was followed, in December 1972, by a new Basic Treaty between the two German states.

From the beginning there was an inherent contradiction in *Ostpolitik.* Its long-term goal was the reunification of the two parts of Germany. But it was also designed to advance the coming of a European peace order by way of the full recognition of the sovereignty and frontiers of existing East European states, including, paradoxically, the German Democratic Republic, and to bring to these countries economic and political reform. As the years passed, the practitioners of *Ostpolitik* tended to become so deeply involved in promoting the latter objective—a task that required much complicated negotiation and the synchronization of the Federal Republic's diplomacy with Moscow, the Eastern states, the GDR, and Washington—that they tended to neglect and even to forget the former. This explains why governmental circles and the general public in West Germany were so completely unprepared when unification suddenly became a live issue in 1989.

But, meanwhile, there is no doubt that *Ostpolitik* created an atmosphere that encouraged détente and removed a barrier that had inhibited Soviet–American discussions of the division of Europe. President Nixon could now, in pursuance of his own détente goals, agree in principle to discuss the long-standing Soviet desire for a formal document, signed by all European countries as well as the United States, that would recognize existing borders and thereby confirm the Soviets' dominant influence in Eastern Europe and the German Democratic Republic. The discussion was eventually to lead to the Helsinki Agreement, signed at the 1975 Conference on Security and Cooperation in Europe, which, as we shall see in a later chapter, obliged the signatories to refrain from using force in order to change frontiers, to facilitate greater movement of peoples and ideas between the two parts of Europe, and to observe and promote the human rights of populations (although the clauses dealing with this last subject were sufficiently abstract as to cause much later controversy).

The third element in Nixon's détente strategy called for the United States to enter into a variety of formal agreements with the Soviet Union that would further mutual cooperation and make available economic and technical assistance. The rationale was that the Soviets would acquire from the agreements a strong stake in maintaining a constructive relationship with the West. These agreements and the prospect of additional ones were supposed to create a "web of incentives" that would motivate Soviet leaders to behave with restraint and to moderate their tendency to "probe the soft spots" and seek gains in third areas at the expense of the United States. It was hoped that concessions to the Soviets in the economic and commercial sphere would "spill over" to improve Soviet-American political relations. With this in mind, the two countries concluded a major grain deal in July 1972 and a trade agreement in October.

This was merely the beginning of an impressive record of successful negotiation between America and Russia. It is interesting to note that of the 105 treaties and other agreements that the United States had made with the Soviet Union since 1933, when President Roosevelt extended diplomatic recognition to the USSR, 58, or over half the number, were concluded between 1969 and 1974; and 41 of those were signed between May 1972 and May 1974.

The fourth element of the strategy was especially important to Nixon and Kissinger, for in a sense it was the long-range payoff that they hoped would follow from the other three. This was the development of a set of new norms and rules for the competition between the two superpowers. The détente policy placed great emphasis upon working out strategic arms control limitations and other types of agreements to reduce the danger of a new world war. Two agreements in particular illustrate the nature of the Nixon–Kissinger effort to develop norms for sustaining a new constructive relationship with the Soviets. At the summit meeting in Moscow in May 1972, Nixon and Brezhnev signed an agreement called "Basic Principles of Relations," which Kissinger, in a press conference immediately after the summit, described as defining new rules of conduct for both sides. In this document, the two powers agreed to prevent the development of situations that might dangerously exacerbate their relations; they were to do their utmost to avoid military confrontations and the outbreak of nuclear war; and they further agreed that henceforth they would "exercise mutual restraint in their relations and [would] be prepared to negotiate and settle differences by peaceful means." Negotiations on outstanding issues were to be conducted in a spirit of reciprocity, mutual accommodation, and mutual benefit—that is, neither side would seek one-sided advantages but would work to achieve compromises.

A second agreement emerged one year later, in June 1973, at the summit meeting in Washington between Nixon and Brezhnev. On that occasion, they signed an "Agreement on the Prevention of Nuclear War," the content of which repeated some of the provisions of the earlier agreement, emphasizing the need to consult on an urgent basis in situations raising the threat of nuclear war.

The détente policy progressed reasonably well until late 1973, but the expectation that the Soviets would act with greater restraint in their foreign policy was not fully realized. In particular, it was the failure of the Soviet Union to prevent its client states, Egypt and Syria, from initiating war against Israel in October 1973, and the ample military supplies it provided them to conduct that war, that seemed inconsistent with these agreements. In part, the trouble was that the agreements of 1972 and 1973 defining rules of conduct were highly general and inevitably vague. But perhaps the problem was a more fundamental one. The Russians defined détente (or "peaceful coexistence," as they often preferred to call it) differently than did the Americans. To them, détente did not require that they cease support for "progressive" and "liberation" movements in the Third World.

For these and other reasons, the momentum of the détente process slowed down. American support for it declined after the Arab-Israeli War of October 1973, and even more after Soviet assistance to Cuban military intervention in Angola in 1975. As for the Russians, they resented the efforts of Senator Henry Jackson and others to make the Senate's approval of increased U.S. trade with the Soviet Union contingent on its willingness to allow an increase in the emigration of Jews.

After Gerald Ford became president, he was not able to do much to rejuvenate détente, although he did try to move toward a SALT-II agreement by entering into the interim Vladivostok agreement with Secretary Brezhnev. The president also tried for a time to defend détente against the increasingly vocal domestic criticism. During the contest for the Republican presidential nomination in 1976, however, Governor Ronald Reagan made détente the focus of his effective attack upon the Ford administration. Ford eventually thought it prudent to announce that he was dropping the term from his political vocabulary and that henceforth his policy would be called "peace through strength."

The questions raised about détente in the United States were varied and insistent. Had there been a basic modification of Soviet ambitions and intentions? Was the Soviet Union using détente merely to gain an advantage over the United States? Were the Soviets winning more concrete benefits from the policy than the United States? Were the agreements that had been concluded, or were pending, lopsided? Should the United States put pressure upon the Soviet Union in order to force a liberalization of its policies at home and in Eastern Europe in return for any benefits it derived from détente? Was the Soviet Union taking advantage of détente and the SALT negotiations to surpass the

United States in strategic capabilities and to increase its influence in the Third World at its expense and that of its allies?

The necessity of securing legitimacy for long-range foreign policy had, as we have seen, preoccupied Franklin Delano Roosevelt as he made plans for his postwar security system. The problem was well-known to Kissinger and had been touched on in his incisive analysis of the eventual failure of the policies of Castlereagh and Metternich in the post-Napoleonic years. "The acid test of a policy," he had written there, "is its ability to obtain domestic support. This has two aspects: the problem of legitimizing a policy within the government apparatus . . . ; and that of harmonizing it with the national experience." Ironically, Kissinger's détente policy was to encounter, and fail to pass, the same acid test.

Why was the Nixon–Kissinger policy so difficult to legitimize, and why did such legitimacy as it acquired erode so badly? The fact is that the Nixon administration succeeded in creating neither normative nor cognitive legitimacy for its policy. The former it sought to achieve by arguing that détente was necessary in order to prevent a third world war; but although everyone agreed with this objective, few persons thought that the danger was so imminent as to require the United States to bestow important concessions and benefits on the Soviet Union. The cognitive legitimacy of the détente policy was somewhat stronger but, as we shall note, it rested on premises that were increasingly questioned by important elements of the public.

It was more difficult to win public legitimacy for détente than it was for the Cold War, a fact that becomes understandable if one compares the objectives and strategy of the latter with those of the former. During the Cold War, the American objective was simply to contain the Soviet Union until the force of Soviet ideology had spent itself; and to achieve that goal, the United States had relied almost exclusively on deterrent strategy. The détente policy, on the other hand, was more ambitious and more complicated. It aimed at persuading the Russians to mend their ways and to enter into a new constructive relationship with the United States. To this end, Nixon and Kissinger made use of conciliation and accommodation as well as deterrence—employing, in other words, the carrot-and-stick approach.

The Cold War was also easier to legitimize than détente because it rested upon a simple negative stereotype, the devil image of the Soviet leaders. The détente policy imposed on the government the more difficult task of getting people to view the Soviets as a limited adversary, neither friend nor foe but something in between. The nature of that something was not easy for many people to understand.

The idea of bestowing benefits on the Soviet Union in order to create a web of incentives may have been a good strategy in principle. But in practice, as implemented by Nixon and Kissinger, it aroused increasing concern in the United States. Critics of détente argued that Nixon and Kissinger were giving Moscow many tangible benefits in return for vague promises of good behavior and pious hopes that the Soviets would be induced to limit their ambitions and meddling in third areas. To be fair, this criticism overlooked the fact that the policy did not rely solely on rewards and bribes. Nixon and Kissinger stood ready whenever necessary to reinforce the incentives with measures of the kind associated with traditional containment policy and deterrence strategy. There were a number of occasions when the Nixon–Ford administration reacted firmly, as in response to the Syrian tank invasion of Jordan in September 1970, in the Indian-Pakistani conflict in December 1971, in the case of the possible Soviet submarine base being built in Cuba in late 1970, in the Arab-Israeli War of 1973, and in Angola in 1975.

This did not, however, allay the growing dissatisfaction, and the incidents themselves seemed to underline the absence of discernible change in Soviet behavior. Some critics of détente contend that Kissinger overestimated the leverage available to him for accomplishing his objective. Perhaps it was overly optimistic to believe—and dangerous to encourage the American public to believe—that the web of incentives and penalties available to the Nixon administration would suffice to create a stake in détente so valuable to Soviet leaders that they would give up opportunities to extend their influence in the world. Interestingly, this was among the aspects of détente policy that was most sharply challenged by opponents who charged that Kissinger had ''oversold'' détente.

The legitimacy of détente strategy also suffered because its implementation confused the public. It was perhaps predictable that many members of Congress and the public would fail to grasp the subtleties of a strategy that combined threats and penalties with efforts at conciliation and bestowal of benefits. If the Soviets behaved so badly on some occasions as to warrant threats or penalties, why then reward them in other respects? Should there not be more explicit quid pro quos whereby the Soviets would give up something concrete for each benefit they received? Criticism of this kind not only eroded the legitimacy of détente policy; it brought increasing pressure to bear on the administration to abandon, or at least make significant changes in, the strategy employed. The domestic politics of détente within the United States, magnified by Reagan's unexpectedly strong challenge in the Republican presidential primaries of 1976, forced the Ford administration to drive harder bargains with Moscow and to apply more exactly standards for acceptable agreements. And this constraint applied equally to President Carter's approach to the Soviets.

But perhaps the worst consequence of the way in which Kissinger applied the complex strategy of conciliation and deterrence was that it tended over time to polarize American public opinion. Both the anti-Soviet hawks and the antiwar doves became dissatisfied with the détente policy for different reasons, and with the passage of time they attracted growing public and congressional support. Thus, whenever Kissinger bestowed benefits on the Soviets, the hawks protestd. And whenever Kissinger confronted the Soviets—as in the Arab-Israeli War of 1973 and over Angola—the doves sounded the alarm that the administration was about to start down the slippery slope into another Vietnam.

As a result, Kissinger found himself caught in an increasingly severe whiplash between hawk and dove critics of his policy. Those members of Congress and the public who did understand and sympathize with the intricate logic and rationale of the dual strategy, and who made up the centrist constituency whose support Kissinger so badly needed to maintain the momentum of the détente process, were gradually neutralized by the growing strength and louder voices of the others.

Kissinger's difficulties with his hawkish critics were compounded by other adverse developments which he was unable to control and to which he sometimes inadvertently contributed. These developments included the Soviet leaders' repeated insistence—in part no doubt to quiet the opposition to détente from their own hawks—that détente did not mean that they were betraying their Communist ideology and would forgo support for "national liberation" movements. American hawks interpreted such Soviet statements as exposing the fallacy of the premises underlying Kissinger's hopes for a new constructive relationship with the Soviets. Soviet insistence on defining détente in terms of their own concept of "peaceful coexistence" also revived concern over their intentions. And this concern over the premises of détente policy was much strengthened by the continuing buildup of Soviet strategic and other military capabilities coupled with the failure of the SALT negotiations to limit the arms race. Thus, the question of Soviet intentions, which has periodically agitated American foreign policy experts and public opinion since the end of World War II, emerged once again as a highly salient and controversial issue.

For all of these reasons, the legitimacy of the détente policy eroded badly, a development which enormously strengthened the various domestic constraints associated with democratic control of foreign policy. As a result, Kissinger's ability to conduct a coherent, effective policy on behalf of the laudable objectives of détente was shattered well before the end of the Ford administration. With the deterioration of the stable domestic consensus on détente, Kissinger could no longer count on minimal public acceptance of the variety of actions that implementation of his strategy required. Not only was he no longer given the benefit of the doubt, but some of his activities engendered suspicion that they were designed to serve his personal interests or the political fortunes of his administration. His secretive approach to decision making and his diplomatic style did much, of course, to enhance the distrust.

No doubt Kissinger believed that his détente policy fell victim to the public's impatience for quick results and its unreasonable demands for frequent concrete indications that the policy was succeeding. It is certainly true that given the ambitious character of the détente objective, which required resocialization of Soviet leaders and their acceptance of the norms of a new regime in U.S.–Soviet relations, it was only reasonable to assume that considerable time and repeated efforts would be needed to accomplish that goal, and that, before Kissinger's behavior modification therapy took full effect, the Soviets would occasionally misbehave. But if so, how could one evaluate whether the strategy was succeeding? Kissinger's critics pointed to instances of Soviet meddling in third areas as evidence of the failure and unsound character of the strategy. Kissinger himself could only retort that Soviet behavior would have been perhaps even more aggressive and the confrontations more dangerous had it not been for détente. Neither side could prove its case, but the critics may have pronounced the strategy of inducing self-restraint in Soviet foreign policy a failure prematurely.

In his own defense, Kissinger quite properly complained that Congress had weakened both the carrot and the stick available to him for influencing the Soviets. First, it had undermined the possibility of increased trade and credits that the Nixon administration had held out to the Russians, and second, in response to Vietnam, it had gradually hamstrung the president's ability to generate credible threats of force to cope with Soviet-backed encroachment in third areas. Furthermore, Watergate and the ensuing downfall of Nixon crippled the energies of the United States in many ways, ruining the domestic credibility of the government, destroying its authority with other governments, and paralyzing key instrumentalities of foreign affairs. The generalized antigovernment feeling aroused in the United States militated against an effective foreign policy. The American people seemed tired of diplomacy in the grand manner, weary of the acrobatics of balance-of-power maneuvers, and eager for a simpler style that would accord with recognizably American values. This kind of policy—Wilsonian rather than Hamiltonian, let alone Bismarckian or Metternichian—Jimmy Carter promised to give them.

It is worth noting that, in contrast to the American experience, détente as practiced by the German Federal Republic was subject to little public criticism, and that, when the Socialist-Liberal coalition collapsed in 1979 and was succeeded by the CDU/CSU/FDP coalition, the new Chancellor Helmut Kohl made no effort to terminate the policy, although he balanced it with a more energetic *Westpolitik* that was designed to improve relations with Washington. One might have supposed that some of the questions asked of Kissinger might have been directed to his West German counterparts. What exactly did Bonn get back in return for the trade agreements, commercial contracts, and the floods of hard currency that it lavished upon the Eastern governments through *Ostpolitik?* It is easy to point to one undeniable success—that travel restrictions between the two Germanies were greatly eased and that travel visas for Germans from countries in Eastern Europe increased from a mere trickle in the 1970s to 200,000 in 1988. But when one looks at the larger objective—to use trade agreements and government-guaranteed credits to promote economic and eventually political reforms in the Eastern countries—it is clear that it did not work. Timothy Garton Ash has written:

> Western trade, credits and technology transfers were overwhelmingly transferred through organs under the central control of the party-state. They were used less to facilitate economic reform than as a substitute for such reform. As a result of this systematic misapplication, the Western ''carrots,'' far from setting these states on the path of sustained growth, with political modernization following economic modernization, instead helped them down the path to economic crisis.

In general, *Ostpolitik* legitimized and brought tangible benefits to the Eastern regimes without significantly improving the lot of the common people. Paradoxically, the West German government was not interested in human rights issues and distanced itself from popular protest movements, like the Polish revolution of 1980–1981, which it feared might bring a Soviet intervention that would end détente. Similarly, the West German government desired no repetition in the GDR of the workers uprising of 17 June 1953. It took comfort in the fact that its relations with the Eastern regimes had improved and that the atmosphere was crisis-free; it was also confident that *Ostpolitik* was moving Eastern Europe toward an era of peace and cooperation. Because this seemed to be so, *Ostpolitik* remained popular in West Germany, even as the issue of German unification became remote if not irrelevant. It is not surprising, therefore, that the failure of détente in the United States alarmed many West Germans, as did the sharp deterioration of Soviet–American relations that followed.

III

The major challenges facing the Carter administration were to reinvigorate public support for a liberal internationalist foreign policy, to overcome national self-doubts as to whether the United States still had a constructive role to play in world affairs, and to counter the drift toward neoisolationism. Carter tried to do all this by downgrading the priority Nixon and Ford had given to nourishing the connection with the Soviet Union and by giving greater priority to developing relations with other countries and to ''world order'' objectives. To be sure, Carter did not eschew reconstructing détente on a more realistic and sober basis, but he and his advisers gave little evidence of having any well-developed, coherent design or consistent strategy for doing so. The linchpin of Carter's policy toward the Soviet Union—indeed, its only clear and consistent objective—was the conclusion of SALT-II. But whereas the Ford administration had brought negotiations for a new SALT agreement close to completion, Carter and his secretary of state, Cyrus Vance, immediately set back the SALT process by launching a new proposal for reduction of strategic weapons in such a manner as to shock and dismay Soviet leaders. To the distrust and hostility already aroused in the Kremlin by Carter's earlier proclamation of a "human rights" campaign, which Russian leaders understandably perceived as the initiation of political warfare against their system, was now added the grim possibility that the new administration would complicate, if not prevent, the achievement of a second SALT agreement, to which the Soviets attached great importance.

The search for a way of reviving and reorienting the détente relationship never recovered from these initial blows. Negotiation of the SALT-II treaty was finally completed and the document signed by the president and Secretary Brezhnev at a summit meeting in mid-1979. But by then public and congressional support had seriously weakened, and Senate ratification was probably dealt a fatal blow by the unexpected discovery of a Soviet combat brigade in Cuba. President Carter's attempt to take a strong line and demand the removal of the brigade or a change in its status was ineffectual, and the Soviet rejection of his demands caused a further waning of public confidence in the administration's competence and a hardening of opposition to the ratification of SALT-II. A few months later, when the Soviets sent troops into Afghanistan, the fate of the treaty was sealed.

From our present vantage point, we can see that the Soviet invasion of Afghanistan was an act of overextension similar to the American involvement in Vietnam but more serious in its consequences, indeed, an act that betokened the end of the Soviet empire; but this was not apparent at the time, and the invasion rocked Washington. The beleaguered American president, with his hopes of arms control in ruins and soon to be faced with the humiliation of seeing the U.S. embassy in Teheran invaded by Iranian militants and its personnel taken into captivity, reacted with anger and frustration. In a televised interview with Frank Reynolds of ABC News, President Carter said:

> My opinion of the Russians has changed most drastically in the last week.
> . . . It's only dawning upon the world, the magnitude of the action the Soviets
> undertook in invading Afghanistan. It's even more profoundly important than
> their going into Hungary [in 1956] and Czechoslovakia [in 1968], because
> they went in, overthrew an existing government, installed a puppet, put mas-
> sive forces in, and created a direct confrontation between an atheistic govern-
> ment on the one hand and a deeply religious people on the other who have
> historically fought for their own independence and freedom.

This Soviet invasion, he said, was "the greatest threat to world peace since the second world war."

However that may be—and when under strong emotion politicians are given to hyperbole—it was clear that the president was deeply disappointed. He had expected better of the Russians, and now he had to admit that, despite all of his hopes, détente was finally dead.

IV

Ronald Reagan, who assumed the presidency in January 1981, possessed none of the intellectual sophistication of presidents like John Kennedy and Richard Nixon, and his proneness to oversimplification, particularly in fiscal policy, imposed a burden of debt on the nation that was so large that it hampered the activities of his successors. Yet no individual deserves more credit than he for bringing the Cold War to an end. This he accomplished by investing the containment policy with an aggressive spirit that it had lacked since its earliest days and recovering the initiative in the long contest with the Soviet Union.

In an admiring assessment of Reagan's policy, Henry Kissinger has written that the new president was bored with the details of foreign policy. On the other hand, he had a literal belief in American exceptionalism, in the unique position of his country as the greatest force for good in history, and in the duty that this imposed upon it to oppose evil wherever it was to be found. In the contemporary world, the agent of evil was the Soviet Union, which, as Reagan told his first press conference was prepared to ''commit any crime, to lie, to cheat'' to achieve its goals. To attempt to deal with this ''evil empire,'' as he called it in 1983, until it had changed its ways and expressed an honest desire to be a peaceable member of the world community, was not only illogical but morally wrong. Understanding this must be the principal determinant of United States foreign policy.

It was in this spirit that the Reagan administration launched a counteroffensive against Soviet expansionism, sending aid to the Muslim rebels in Soviet-occupied Afghanistan, aiding anti-Communist forces in Ethiopia and Angola, supporting the Contras against the Communist-backed Sandinistas in Nicaragua, and checking and increasing the costs of the Soviet attempt to spread its influence in the Third World. Some of Reagan's agents were not overly scrupulous in their efforts to promote this fight, and the campaign against the Sandinistas in particular was financed in part by highly questionable arms contracts with the same Iranian revolutionaries whose capture of American diplomatic personnel had destroyed President Carter's popular support. But critics of individual aspects of Reagan's foreign policy were vastly outnumbered by Americans who were inspired and heartened by the fact that movement had been restored to American policy after a decade of setbacks and disappointments.

Reagan's most formidable challenge to the Soviet Union came in the area of armaments. From the beginning of his first term, arms expenditures increased sharply. The administration began the deployment of the land-based intercontinental MX missile and restored weapons systems that had been eliminated from the American armory during the Carter administration, like the B-1 bomber. More important still was a major shift in the line of battle in Europe. Reagan always maintained that the Soviets had cheated during the détente period, using the relaxation of East–West tension to build up a large number of land-based missiles (SS-20s) that were capable of reaching all parts of Europe. He now insisted upon the implementation of the so-called NATO double-track decision of 1979, which, largely under the inspiration of the German Chancellor Helmut Schmidt, called for the deployment of intermediate missiles (Pershing IIs and cruise missiles) if the Soviets did not agree to remove the SS-20s. Negotiations to achieve the latter purpose had been unavailing, and under American pressure NATO now made the decision to deploy.

The Reagan arms build-up and the rhetoric with which it was accompanied alarmed many Europeans, who regretted the passing of détente and feared the coming of a new ice age. This is particularly true of Germany, where the Social Democratic party repudiated its own chancellor, Helmut Schmidt, because he remained true to the double-track decision. A large and well-coordinated peace movement fought against deployment and urged withdrawal from NATO if it were insisted on. The Soviets took advantage of this situation to rain threats down upon the new German government of Helmut Kohl, warning of a sharp deterioration of relations between Moscow and Bonn and the end of the arms control talks in Geneva. Kohl elected to stand firmly on the side of his American ally, and the deployment went forward. It was a stunning victory for the Reagan policy, and combined with the simultaneous announcement of his support for a new defense against long-range missiles, the Strategic Defense Initiative (SDI), one that threatened to nullify the Soviet offensive potential. After the dissolution of the Soviet Union, Timothy Garton Ash interviewed Helmut Kohl, Helmut Schmidt, and former West German Foreign Minister Hans Dietrich Genscher, and all three told him that the crucial factor in forcing a revision of Soviet policy was the deployment of the Pershings and the cruise missiles, and Kohl added that Mikhail Gorbachev had told him that he agreed.

Despite the ideological cast of his rhetoric, Reagan does not seem to have believed that the gulf between the United States and the Soviet Union was unbridgeable. Indeed, he hoped that the Soviet leaders would one day see the light and give up their expansionist and subversive intentions, and he dreamed periodically of a summit meeting in which the two powers could reconcile their differences. On two occasions—in personal letters to Leonid Brezhnev and to his successor Yuri Andropov—he actually hinted at such a resolution of the Cold War. But it was not until Mikhail Gorbachev became secretary general of the Communist party that this became a real possibility.

More energetic, more critical, less reverential of the ideological stereotypes of the past than his predecessors, Gorbachev became secretary in 1985, just as it began to be apparent that a major economic and political crisis was engulfing his country. At long last, the debilitating effects of military and territorial over-expansion on the one hand and bureaucratic stultification and mismanagement of the economy on the other became obvious. In the age of the computer revolution, Soviet communications were hopelessly backward; the much vaunted planned economy suffered from both lack of planning and coordination and, more basically, from an almost total absence of accountability, and the nature of the political system discouraged independent thinking and initiative. Soviet production bore no rational relationship to the rich natural resources of its vast empire, which could neither feed itself nor produce goods that were competitive in world trade. Meanwhile, in addition to the strains imposed by the armaments competition with the United States, other commitments drained away the vital energies of the nation: the war in Afghanistan, which came more and more to resemble in its effects the American debacle in Vietnam; the effort to support its programs in the Third World, now under increasing attack from the United States; the necessity of maintaining a large armed force on the Sino-Soviet frontier; and the not inconsiderable political and military strain of buttressing order in the increasingly restless satellites in Eastern Europe.

There is no reason to believe that Gorbachev appreciated the dimensions of the problem when he first took office, and he seems to have been confident that a thorough purge of the party and the introduction of some elements of market-economy into central planning would revitalize the system. But it was not easy to discover who the progressive elements in the party were, and the bureaucrats in the administration were skilled at resisting reform. It was soon clear that it would be a long time before Gorbachev's prescriptions could be expected to work, and that he did not have much time at his disposal, for the internal crisis became steadily more serious.

Almost unavoidably, then, Gorbachev was forced to seek an alleviation of Soviet ills by a reform of foreign policy in the hope that, if this were spectacular enough, it would induce foreign countries to help solve Soviet domestic difficulties. He did so by announcing his intention of pursuing a policy of *peaceful coexistence*—not as a temporary expedient, a breathing space in which the Soviet Union could regroup its forces, which had been the case when previous Soviet leaders from Malenkov to Brezhnev had used the term, but as an end in itself, stripped of any ideological connotations. Reacting with a healthy skepticism, Western leaders were nevertheless impressed by the earnestness with which Gorbachev urged an end to confrontational strategies that threatened the superpowers with mutual destruction and the acceptance of a new philosophy of global interdependence. Ronald Reagan was sufficiently moved by what seemed to be a vision that coincided with his own that he met with the Soviet leader in a remarkable summit meeting in Reykjavik, Iceland, in 1986, in which the two statesmen found themselves in such close accord that they agreed in principle to reduce all strategic forces by 50 percent within five years and to destroy all ballistic missiles within ten. Indeed, Reagan might have agreed to the abolition of all nuclear weapons, a possibility that terrified his European allies, had not Gorbachev caused the essential failure of the conference by insisting on American abandonment of SDI, which Reagan refused.

Reykjavik marked the end of any hope of Gorbachev's ending the arms race quickly and reaping the economic and political advantages. From now on, his policy was one of what the Germans call *Flucht nach vorne*—a flight forward—a process of improvisation in the hope that something would work to relieve his domestic situation. Unfortunately, this did not happen; his attempt to establish normal relations with China by offering to withdraw most of the forces in Mongolia met a cool response and a demand that the Soviets withdraw from Afghanistan, which he did not dare do, and his announcement at the UN's General Assembly in December 1988 of unilateral cuts in the Soviet armed forces also failed to elicit any reciprocal response. Meanwhile, he had become tremendously popular in the West, where his appearances were accompanied by enthusiastic crowds crying "Gorby! Gorby!" and where his book *Perestroika* became a bestseller and was awarded the book prize of the Friedrich Ebert Stiftung in 1988. Inevitably, his anti-ideological stance raised the hopes of opposition leaders in the satellite states of Eastern Europe and increased the difficulties of the Communist regimes there. Since 1968, when Soviet tanks rolled into Prague, those regimes had had the assurance that if they were too hard pressed, the Brezhnev Doctrine, which stipulated a Soviet right to intervene in Eastern Europe, would be invoked in their favor. But Gorbachev could not give them that assurance without damaging his image and adding to his economic difficulties. He could only urge the beleaguered party leaders to reform their regimes, which they sought ineffectually to do. In Poland, General Jaruzelski, who had suppressed the workers movement Solidarity in 1981, now permitted it to share in elections on 4 June 1989, in which it won a landslide victory over the Communist party. This was a significant turning point in the history of Eastern Europe, encouraging liberal forces in other satellite countries to follow Poland's example. They did so. In Budapest, on 16 June 1989, as massive crowds celebrated the thirty-first anniversary of the burial of Imre Nagy, who had been murdered by the Kadar regime for his leadership of the revolution of 1956, the failure of the police to intervene showed that the authority of the Communist party was broken in Hungary. In Prague, students were already planning agitations that were to precipitate the "velvet revolution" in November. Meanwhile, any possibility that Soviet forces would intervene to save the satellite empire seemed remote after Gorbachev, in a speech to the Council of Europe in July, had rung the death knell of the Brezhnev Doctrine by declaring that in the new Europe "any interference in domestic affairs and any attempts to restrict the sovereignty of states—friends, allies, or any others—are inadmissible."

V

The strongest and most loyal of the Soviet satellites was the German Democratic Republic, and it was generally expected that it would be the most resistant to change. Indeed, at the beginning of October 1989, the Socialist Unity (SED) regime celebrated its fortieth year in power with pomp and fanfare and praise of its leader Erich Honecker. Yet behind all the rhetorical flourishes lay an uncomfortable realization that the country was ripe for an explosion. According to opinion polls, popular discontent had increased from 17 percent to 68 percent in the last two years, and in the course of 1989 thousands of people, drawn generally from the most energetic and best educated sections of society, had fled to the West, a number that increased to over 300,000 when the Hungarians opened their frontier to Austria and facilitated the exodus.

The effects of this loss upon industrial production and the efficiency of social services was comparable to that of the great pre-1961 emigration that had led to the building of the Wall. This exodus was demoralizing for the leadership of the SED and encouraged an interparty plot to unseat Honecker which was finally carried out on 17 October. The mass migration also encouraged the growth of a citizens movement (*Bürgerbewegung*) that began to demonstrate in the streets of Berlin, Dresden, Leipzig, and other large cities. Inspired by a desire to reform socialism and make emigration unnecessary, this movement encountered the brutal use of police force in its first street appearances, but as they grew in size (there were 70,000 people in the streets of Leipzig at the beginning of November and five times that number at its end), it soon became clear that neither the SED nor the secret police (STASI) had the stomach to resort to anything on the scale of the operation in Tiananmen Square in Beijing in May. Instead, Honecker's bumbling successors became panic stricken and, in their attempts to appease the crowds, muddleheaded. This explains why the new travel regulations that they issued in the hope of stemming the steady depletion of the population were so ambiguous and contradictory that they led, surely against their intentions, to the opening of the Wall on 8 November.

It was this dramatic event that made German unification a political issue again, after years of being stifled in the East and all but forgotten in the West, largely as a result of *Ostpolitik* and the acceptance of the legitimacy of the two Germanies. Helmut Kohl, with the sureness of political instinct that was characteristic of him, resolved to make the issue of unification his own, a decision that divided and eventually defeated the citizens' movement in the East.

Kohl would not have been successful had it not been for the firm and consistent support of the United States. The opening *démarche* in his policy—his Ten Point Program of 28 November 1989 for accelerating European integration by encouraging the formation of "confederal structures" between the two Germanies—was greeted with consternation and ill-disguised anger by the other powers. Great Britain's prime minister, Margaret Thatcher, intimated that it might be proper to talk of German unification in five or ten years, but not before, a view shared by the Belgians and the Dutch. France's president Mitterrand seemed to think even that estimate of the time that would be needed was over-generous and set off to Kiev to consult Mikhail Gorbachev, who gave him an ambiguous answer. The only exception to this chorus of disapproval was the United States. President George Bush had already made it clear in April 1989, and again in press interviews in September and October, that he endorsed uni-fication and saw no reason for the fears of revived German nationalism ex-pressed by his allies. This made Europeans unhappy, and there was press talk about a new Fourth Reich with a statue of Hitler in every town, but this did not change the president's mind. Elizabeth Pond has written:

> The United States was . . . totally supportive of reunification and played a crucial activist role in achieving it, both in reversing British and French op-position and in persuading the Russians that they could survive German unity with their dignity preserved.

The documents are not yet available to explain the American motivation for taking so strong a stand, but it is not unlikely that the Bush administration was moved both by its belief in Helmut Kohl's dedication to the cause of European unity and his firm Western orientation and by the opportunity to remove the Soviet presence from central Europe.

As Kohl went his way with American support, the movement in East Ger-many for a reformation of socialism that would assure the GDR an independent existence and might permit it to find a third way between communism and capitalism wavered and declined. The almost daily revelations of the true state of the economy and of the extent of ecological disaster in the factories and the farms deeply shocked the population and eroded the kind of identification with the GDR that would have been needed to spark revitalization. At the same time, the prestige of the *Bürgerbewegung* began to decline rapidly among the working class, who saw no results coming from the endless discussions and relapsed into their innate suspicion of intellectuals. "Instead of a more humane world," Kon-rad Jarausch has written, "most people wanted prosperity through unification. . . . Demonstrators began to defect from the civic movement. They intoned a new chant: "Neither brown nor red—Helmut Kohl [is] our bet!""

The rush to unification was accelerated and made unstoppable by two events. The first was the tremendous victory of the Christian Democrats in the March 1990 elections for the GDR parliament. This was helped by the failure of the cit-izens' groups either to protest effectively against the intrusion of the Western party organizations in the election campaign or to organize themselves as electoral parties, and it was greatly aided by the disarray of the SPD and its ambivalence on the unification issue. But essentially it was Helmut Kohl's triumph, won by his impressive performances in Erfurt, Chemnitz, Magdeburg, Rostock, Cottbus, and Leipzig during the last week of the campaign, when he reached almost one million people, almost 10 percent of the electorate. Later, he may have regretted that he had been so exuberant in describing the benefits that would flow from unification, but politicians rarely have scruples about painting bright futures.

The second event was Kohl's meeting with Gorbachev in Moscow, and then in Stavropol in the Caucasus in July 1990, which cleared away the last diplomatic barriers to Germany's unification. The agreement between the two leaders stipulated the right of the expanded German republic to make its own security arrangements, that is to continue the old GFR's membership in NATO, which was a Western condition of unification. It was agreed also that the joint German army after unification should be reduced to a strength of 370,000 men and that German NATO units should not be stationed in the former GDR until Soviet occupying forces had been withdrawn. Kohl's foreign policy adviser Horst Teltschik has called this "the miracle of Moscow" and described it as a victory for Kohl's personal diplomacy. But it was very much a team effort, with Foreign Minister Hans Dietrich Genscher and his staff preparing the way by a skillful use of promises of financial aid and with George Bush in the background, applying pressure on Moscow when it was needed.

There was nothing left to do now but tie up the loose ends, which was quickly done. In August 1990, the two German governments set rules for the first all-German elections and concluded their unification agreement; in September, the foreign ministers completed the so-called two-plus-four negotiations, between the two Germanies plus the four occupying powers, the United States, the Soviet Union, Great Britain, and France, which terminated their "rights and responsibilities for Berlin and Germany as a whole." On 3 October, the formal unification ceremony was held in front of the old Reichstag in Berlin, and on 2 December the first truly national elections since Hitler's time resulted in a triumph for the center-right coalition in Bonn.

VI

Whatever his private feelings about this great turning point in Europe's history, Mikhail Gorbachev was in no position to object. In July, as the Soviet satellite empire was well on its way to dissolution, he was appealing to the G-7 summit of the leaders of the industrial democracies for economic assistance.

> Our perestroika is inseparable from a policy aiming at our full participation
> in the world economy. The world can only gain from the opening up of a
> market as big as the Soviet Union.

This appeal was virtually an admission, as Henry Kissinger has written, that his hope that liberalization would modernize the Soviet Union and enable it to hold its own internationally as a great power had failed, and that he was now dependent on international good will. The Moscow agreement with Helmut Kohl a year later proved that, if further proof was needed.

Gorbachev was never bereft of expedients. He now thought that revitalization at home might be better served by shifting the center of power in the Soviet Union from the Communist party, which had steadfastly opposed reform, to the government, where he would function as president of the Soviet Union. New energies might be released also, he thought, if the central planning agencies were bypassed, and regional and local autonomy and initiative were encouraged. This was ingenious but impractical, flying in the face of forty years of centralized party control. The attempt to bypass the party led only to confusion, resistance, and sabotage, and was in all probability the basic cause of the bizarre and ineffectual *coup* against Gorbachev in August 1991. The encouragement of regionalism led to a flaring up of ethnic and national ambitions long suppressed by centralized control. The movement for independence from communism that had by now completed its conquest of the satellite empire, with revolutions in Bulgaria and Romania, now spread to the Soviet Union itself. The Baltic states broke away in the course of 1990, and independence movements began to grow in other Soviet republics.

It was this that finally brought Mikhail Gorbachev down. As the Soviet Union began to dissolve into its component parts, Boris Yeltsin, the president of Russia, declared the independence of the Russian republic and, by extension, of all the others as well. In one stroke, both the Soviet Union and Gorbachev's position as its president were abolished. His attempt to save his country's status as a great power by ending the Cold War had failed.

Bibliographical Essay

This chapter draws on previous publications: Alexander L. George, "Domestic Constraints on Regime Change in U.S. Foreign Policy: The Need for Policy Legitimacy," in *Change in the International System*, ed. O. R. Holsti, R. M. Siverson, and A. L. George (Boulder, Colo., 1980), and Alexander L. George, ed., *Managing U.S.–Soviet Rivalry: Problems of Crisis Prevention* (Boulder, Colo., 1983).

In addition to numerous contemporary statements by President Richard Nixon and Henry Kissinger articulating and defending their détente policy, valuable retrospective materials are provided in their memoirs. Kissinger's *White House Years* (Boston, 1979) and *Years of Upheaval* (Boston, 1982) are particularly valuable; see also R. M. Nixon, *RN: The Memoirs of Richard Nixon* (New York, 1978). For critical views, see Walter Isaacson, *Kissinger: A Biography* (New York, 1992), and John Lewis Gaddis, "Rescuing Change from Circumstance: The Statecraft of Henry Kissinger," in *The Diplomats, 1939–1979*, ed. Gordon A. Craig and Francis L. Loewenheim (Princeton, 1994).

A useful collection of documents, addresses, and other official statements on the détente policy is provided by Robert J. Pranger, ed., *Détente and Defense* (Washington, D.C., 1976). Among the many published commentaries and critical appraisals of the détente policy, the most useful for present purposes is Stanley Hoffmann, *Primacy or World Order* (New York, 1978), pp. 33–100, which contains observations regarding the difficulty of gaining legitimacy for the détente policy similar to those offered in the present chapter. Important data and analyses are presented in Dan Caldwell, *American–Soviet Relations from 1947 to the Nixon–Kissinger Grand Design* (Westport, Conn., 1981). An insightful analytic treatment of the détente experience is provided in Kjell Goldmann, *Change and Stability in Foreign Policy: The Problems and Possibilities of Détente* (Princeton, 1988). See also Stephen A. Garrett, "Nixonian Foreign Policy: A New Balance of Power—or a Revived Concert?" *Polity* 8 (1976): 389–421, and Robert Osgood, ed., *America and the World*, vol. 2, *Retreat from Empire? The First Nixon Administration* (Baltimore, 1973).

On *Ostpolitik,* see A. James McAdams, "The New Diplomacy of West German *Ostoplitik,*" in *Diplomats,* ed. Craig and Loewenheim; and Timothy Garton Ash, *In Europe's Name: Germany and the Divided Continent* (New York, 1993).

On President Carter's policy toward the Soviet Union, see Francis L. Loewenheim, "From Helsinki to Afghanistan: American Diplomats and Diplomacy," in *Diplomats,* ed. Craig and Loewenheim. On U.S. policy in the 1980s, see William G. Hyland, *Mortal Enemies: Superpower Relations from Nixon to Reagan* (New York, 1987), and *The Reagan Foreign Policy* (New York, 1988); Michael Howard's more critical view in the "America and the World, 1987–1988" issue of *Foreign Affairs;* and, for arms control, John Newhouse's two-part article "The Abolitionist," *New Yorker,* 2 and 9 January 1989.

On Gorbachev, see Mikhail Gorbachev, *Perestroika* (New York, 1988), and "Gorbatschow, Mann des Jahres, Mann der Stunde," *Der Spiegel,* no. 50 (1988), as well as Alexander Dallin, "Gorbachev's Foreign Policy and the New Political Thinking in the Soviet Union," in *Gorbachev's Reforms,* ed. Peter Juwiler and Hishi Kamura (Hawthorne, N.Y., 1988). See also, on Reagan and Gorbachev, Henry Kissinger, *Diplomacy* (New York, 1994); Margaret Thatcher, *The Downing Street Years* (New York, 1993); Denis Healey, *The Time of My Life* (London, 1989); George P. Shultz, *Turmoil and Triumph: My Years as Secretary of State* (New York, 1993); and Alexander L. George, "The Transition in U.S.–Soviet Relations, 1985–1990: An Interpretation from the Perspective of International Relations Theory and Political Psychology," *Political Psychology* 12, no. 3 (1991).

On the revolution in Eastern Europe, the best book is Timothy Garton Ash, *The Magic Lantern: The Revolution of 1989 Witnessed in Warsaw, Budapest, Berlin and Prague* (New York, 1990).

On German unification, see the overview by Konrad H. Jarausch, *The Rush to German Unity* (New York, 1994) and, for the foreign policy aspects, the perceptive book by the *Christian Science Monitor* reporter Elizabeth Pond, *Beyond the War: The Road to German Unification* (New York, 1993). Helmut Kohl's foreign policy adviser, Horst Teltschik, has written an account of the unification process that throws much light on the diplomatic story: *362 Tage: Innenansichten der Einigung* (Berlin, 1991). For the two-plus-four negotiations, see Richard Kiessler and Frank Elbe, *Ein runder Tisch mit scharfen Ecken: Der diplomatische Weg zur deutschen Einheit* (Baden-Baden, 1993).

For a detailed account by two U.S. officials who participated in the Bush administration's success in helping to bring about the unification of Germany, see Philip Zelikow and Condoleeza Rice, *A Study in Statecraft: Germany Unified and Europe Transformed* (Cambridge, Mass., 1995).

11

The Evolving International System

In mid-July 1990, as the revolutions in Hungary, Poland, Germany, and Cze-choslovakia consolidated themselves and the Soviet Union began to betray signs of dissolution, observers in the Middle East noted an ominous massing of Iraqi forces along the border of the independent state of Kuwait and concluded that military action might well be imminent. For some time now, it had become obvious that the Iraqi dictator Saddam Hussein's ambitions had not been diminished by the long and wasting conflict that he had waged against Iran, which had ended with a cease fire arranged by the UN in August 1988. Almost immediately he had begun to interfere with Syrian interests in Lebanon, by shipping arms to Christian forces there, and to pressure Kuwait for concessions on the islands of Bubiyan and Warbah, and it was known that he was building up a stockpile of biological and chemical weapons and had already used the latter against his rebellious Kurdish subjects.

This was enough to cause some concern in the United States, which had tended to support Iraq during the Iranian war and had supplied it with weapons, but this was not strong enough to effect a change in current policy. In the foreign policy community there was a tendency to play down Saddam's excesses, the predominant view being that he was a pragmatist who, if handled in the right way, would see that there was a natural congruence between his own and American interests. The Reagan administration therefore turned a deaf ear to the argument that international law required a strong response be made to Saddam's gassing of the Kurds and continued to grant licenses for dual-use technology exports to Iraq as well as for the export of military equipment that Saddam had requested for his personal protection.

When the Bush administration came to power at the beginning of 1989, no significant change of policy took place. The new president authorized a review of policy toward Iraq, but when it was over he and his Secretary of State James

Baker opted for a diplomacy of delicate pressures combined with assurances of friendship. This was a failure for a number of reasons that are analyzed at some length in chapter 12, not the least important of which was a profound misunderstanding of their opponent. Saddam seems to have concluded from the American behavior that he could pursue his ambitions without any fear of serious opposition, let alone military reprisals, and his military buildup along the Kuwaiti border in July 1990 followed logically from that assumption.

The U.S. government then sought to implement a strategy that would deter Saddam but made little progress, largely because the leaders of the friendly Arab states took the line that the Iraqi leader had no intention of attacking Kuwait but was merely applying pressure in order to win concessions in on-going disputes with that country. They urged the United States not to become involved in these controversies but to allow the "Arab brothers," to work out a peaceful resolution of their differences. How misguided this advice was was shown within weeks when Saddam's troops crossed the Kuwaiti border.

From that moment on, there was no further hesitation on the president's part. He threw himself energetically into the task of mobilizing world opinion against Saddam, a task made easier for him by the unequivocal nature of Iraq's breach of international law, for the sovereignty of Kuwait had long been formally recognized by all of the Arab states, including Iraq. In early August, then, the UN Security Council denounced Iraq's aggression and, in a series of resolutions, voted to impose progressively stiffer sanctions. (Subsequently, in late November, it was to authorize the use of force if necessary to expel Iraqi forces from Kuwait and to restore peace to the area.) With this backing, President Bush skillfully built up a military coalition ("Desert Shield") to prevent further Iraqi aggression and, after some delicate negotiations with a fearful and hesitant Saudi government, dispatched a large ground force, backed by naval units, to Saudi Arabia. As he proceeded, Bush had his detractors at home and abroad. In Germany, for example, there were large demonstrations, with people holding up placards that read "No war for oil!"; in the United States congressional critics and liberal journalists, aroused by the president's doubling of the ground forces in the Middle East in November, argued that he wanted war in order to shore up his political fortunes, which had been set back by the disappointing showing of the Republicans in the mid-term elections. But stability of oil prices and supply was a matter of vital interest to many members of the international community, and George Bush was not the first American president to acknowledge that preventing the area from falling under the control of a single power was a vital Western interest. As for the troop buildup, which transformed "Desert Shield" to "Desert Storm," it was surely Saddam's stubborn intractability that was responsible for it. The president and his advisers had little faith in the power of economic sanctions to make the Iraqi dictator disgorge his spoils, and they probably feared that the longer the crisis lasted the greater the tendency would be for the painfully achieved coalition to develop differences and grow weaker in will.

This was what Saddam was counting on, and it explains why he was misguided enough to remain unmoved by a personal visit to Baghdad by UN Secretary General Pérez de Cuéllar and to disregard even the 15 January deadline for withdrawal set by the president and supported by a resolution of the U.S. Senate. On 16 January American and allied war planes began to bomb command and control centers in Baghdad and Iraqi military positions in Kuwait. It was soon clear that Saddam could not oppose these raids effectively, and his attempt, by firing SCUD missiles into neutral Israel, to goad the Israelis into retaliating and then appealing to the other Arab states for support in a jihad against Israel, failed miserably when the Tel Aviv government, with great steadfastness, elected to follow American advice and remain on the sidelines. The bombing continued until 23 February when—after an attempt by Gorbachev to broker a settlement on conditions that proved unacceptable to the U.S. government—the president gave Saddam until noon on 24 January to pull out of Kuwait and, when this too was refused, launched the ground offensive, which lasted less than one hundred hours and cost astonishingly few allied casualties: fewer than 100 Americans were killed. Ten thousand Iraqi prisoners were taken in the first day's fighting, and Saddam's Republican Guard, whose formidable fighting spirit had occasioned so much purple prose in the American media, simply put its tanks in trucks and fled to Baghdad. There was, for reasons that will be discussed later, no pursuit and hence no destruction of Saddam and his armed forces, a disappointing political conclusion to a highly satisfactory military campaign, but Kuwait was liberated, and peace returned to the area.

These tremendous events and the progressive decline and finally, in December 1991, the formal dissolution of the Soviet Union induced a sense of euphoria in the West, particularly in the United States. One academician, in an essay that was widely quoted, wrote that recent events amounted to "the end of history," at least in its past forms, and the final victory of American capitalism. A Pentagon draft study released in March 1992 ("Defense Planning Guidance for the Fiscal Years 1884–1999") echoed the same kind of triumphalism by describing as a desirable objective of American policy a unipolar world in which the remaining superpower, the United States, would guarantee global order, while deterring any other nation or group of nations from challenging its primacy.

President Bush was more modest in describing American goals. In his speech to the United Nations on 23 September 1991, he told his audience that

> the United States has no intention of striving for a Pax Americana. However, we will remain engaged. We will not pull back and retreat into isolationism. We will offer friendship and leadership and, in short, we seek a Pax Universalis, built upon shared responsibilities and aspirations.

These words sounded noble while remaining noncommittal. Clarification was provided soon enough, when the international community was called upon to face up to the problems of Somalia, Bosnia, and Ruwanda.

At the end of 1992, it became apparent that in the African nation Somalia foodstuffs were in such short supply that the people were faced with widespread starvation unless they received large-scale emergency aid. On 3 December, President Bush decided to send troops to Somalia to distribute food to overcome the crisis. The president was reported by the *New York Times* to have said that

> because the United States is now the world's only remaining superpower, it cannot ignore responsibility for grave humanitarian crises in which American actions, and only American actions, could well mean the difference between life and death for hundreds of thousands of people. Even though the United States has no military, economic or political interests at stake in such crises, it must respond anyway....

Almost immediately problems arose concerning the scope of the American mission. The *New York Times* reported on 13 December that UN Secretary General Boutros Boutros-Ghali was unhappy because no mention was made in the American announcements of a private understanding reached with the Bush administration, after the Security Council had authorized the American intervention on 3 December, that the American troops would disarm the rival gangs in Somalia that were interfering with the distribution of food. This question was unresolved as the American mission went forward. In due course—some months after Bill Clinton assumed the presidency—American troops did become involved in an effort to disarm the gangs and also to capture the leader of the largest and most obstructionist of them. Operational mistakes were made, and American casualties were suffered; and immediately there were strong demands in the American press and in Congress that the troops be withdrawn and the mission aborted. This in effect happened amid mutual recriminations between the UN and the U.S. government and congressional demands that American troops participate in no further UN operations unless upon their own terms and under their own command.

This was all the more disturbing because it revealed a deep ambiguity in American attitudes toward the use of force. At the end of the Gulf War, George Bush declared that ''we'' (the United States) had ''kicked the Vietnam syndrome once and for all.'' Even at the time, this was a dubious statement, for certainly one of the reasons for the hasty termination of hostilities against Saddam Hussein was the desire to avoid a prolonged ground war that might involve heavy American casualties. After Somalia, whenever there was discussion of the possibility of using American troops for peacemaking abroad, congressional speeches, newspaper articles, and the commentaries of television pundits began to bristle with the fatal words "slippery slope," "quagmire," and "body bags," stereotypical references to the Vietnam experience and warnings against pro- longed involvement in situations in which military victory could not be assured almost immediately. As we shall see in chapter 19, the question of when force should be used, and under what conditions, had been a subject of debate within the American military ever since the Korean War, and during the Reagan ad- ministration it had caused a sharp exchange of views between the secretary of defense and the secretary of state. After Somalia, it entered the realm of public debate.

This was true, of course, not only in the United States. Other countries also worried about the usability of force in foreign affairs, for different reasons. The British and the French were perhaps less prone to the sensitivity to casualties shown by the American Congress and media, realizing that readiness to resort to force was often politically unavoidable and even desirable. Thus, in 1982, the British fought a war against Argentina in the Falkland Islands that might have been avoided by diplomacy, and again in 1991 participated in the Gulf War, with clear awareness of the fact that to act otherwise might cast doubt upon their status as a great power; and the French government considered it a matter of honor and prestige, and a sign that its claim to European leadership was valid, to show its flag in the Gulf and later in Bosnia and Ruwanda. The government of the newly united Germany, on the other hand, was virtually immobilized at the time of the Gulf War by a militant peace movement that denounced George Bush as a war criminal. For the foreign policy of the new Germany, it was not a very promising beginning and was made worse by the Socialist leader Oscar Lafontaine's remark that to ask Germany to send troops to the Gulf would be like offering brandied chocolates to a reformed alcoholic. Many Germans agreed. Guilt about their own historical past combined with self- distrust was not the least of the factors that prevented Germany from acting together with other nations in the Gulf.

The same reluctance to resort to force was to be observed during the pro- tracted and wasting war in Bosnia. Although the roots of this war were to be found in age-old ethnic rivalries, the European powers themselves bore some responsibility for the immediate origins of the conflict. In December 1991, as quarrelling mounted between the nationalities that Marshal Tito had united in one nation, Croatia and Slovenia moved toward declaring their separation from Yugoslavia. The West European governments and the United States hesitated to recognize their independence, for, although Slovenia's borders included no significant Serb minority, this situation was not the case in Croatia, and the Western governments feared that their acquiescence would lead to a war be- tween the Serb minority, backed by Belgrade, and the Croatian majority. There was, however, no unity of view between the Western governments. In June

1991, U.S. Secretary of State James Baker visited Belgrade and indicated his support for the continued unification of Yugoslavia, an action that encouraged the Serbs to believe they had American support for their attempts to suppress efforts by the other nationalities to win independence. On the other hand, German Chancellor Helmut Kohl and his foreign minister, Hans-Dietrich Genscher, influenced by strong pro-Croat public sentiment at home, became convinced that unity was no longer viable and that the European governments must support the principle of self-determination, as laid down in the Paris Charter of the KSZE of December 1990. At the Maastricht meeting of the European Union, Germany persuaded its reluctant allies to support the independence of Croatia and Slovenia, without insisting, however, that the Croats assure the rights of their Serb minority.

The result was that the declaration of Croatian independence was followed by a bloody passage of arms in which the Serbs succeeded in taking control of that part of the country that they inhabited and put into effect the ghastly process that was soon known everywhere as "ethnic cleansing." Eventually, after a degree of bloodshed that shocked the world, a cease-fire was negotiated between the opposing forces in January 1992, and the UN sent a peacekeeping force into the country.

The initial failure to ensure the rights of the Serb minority in Croatia was repeated shortly thereafter in Bosnia-Herzegovina, where Serbian and Croatian Christians and Serbs and Croats who had been converted to Islam centuries earlier had lived together in uneasy balance. In order to prevent a civil war here, a special commission of the European Union negotiated a partition plan in 1992, which received the support of Bosnia-Herzegovina's Serbs, Croats, and Muslims. The Bush administration, however, balked at this solution and urged that Bosnia-Herzegovina should remain a single multiethnic state, which, it intimated, it was prepared to recognize. According to Warren Zimmerman, who was at the time the U.S. ambassador to Yugoslavia, Washington argued that partition would set a bad example, especially for the successor republics of the former Soviet Union, where ethnic violence was already spreading. The American view prevailed; in April 1992 the European governments joined Washington in granting diplomatic recognition to Bosnia-Herzegovina, and the partition talks collapsed. As Zimmerman later explained, "Our hope was that the Serbs would hold off if it was clear Bosnia had the recognition of Western countries. It turned out we were wrong."

The Bosnian Serbs, fearful of being marginalized, attacked, supported by the Serbian government and the bulk of the Yugoslav army. The conflict might have been frozen in place if a plan for a mixed Bosnia devised by Cyrus Vance, formerly President Carter's secretary of state, and David Owen, former leader of the British Social Democratic Party, had received the swift and unanimous approval of the major powers, but it did not. Alternatively, the Serbs might have been forced to halt their advance if the Western powers had resorted to bombing strikes against their supply routes, but this approach was not tried either. Eventually the Serbs controlled so much of Bosnia that they could be expelled only by the commitment of ground troops, and whenever that was mentioned the discussion was soon dominated by slippery slopes, quagmires and body bags. Nevertheless, the UN, the EU, the Russian Federation, and the U.S. persisted in seeking a solution and in December 1994, partly as the result of a special mission of former President Carter, a ninety-day cease-fire was agreed upon between the belligerents. The prospects for securing an agreement on the territorial division of Bosnia remained, as of May 1995, obscure.

It might be mentioned here that members of the European Union seemed to feel no moral imperative to intervene by force (or, if they did, did not yield to it), although the Bosnian war was being waged in the middle of Europe and was accompanied by atrocities the like of which had not been seen since World War II. This attitude was also true of the Western reaction to the frightful tribal warfare that broke out in the African state of Ruwanda in 1994, which observers on the scene reported had cost the lives of hundreds of thousands of people. The tendency of Western nations was instinctively to announce that their vital interests were not involved in this remote and primitive struggle, and it was reported that the United States government had let it be known that it would oppose any official description of events in Ruwanda as genocide, lest this increase the pressure upon it to intervene.

The general reluctance on the part of the major powers to resort to force out of fear of public and congressional disapproval, reasons of military doctrine, historical guilt, too narrow a definition of national interest, or a blunted sense of moral purpose indicated that it was not going to be easy to attain George Bush's "Pax Universalis, built upon shared responsibilities and aspirations." Yet that goal was so desirable that, while politicians temporized, statesmen, civil servants, international agencies, and scholars continued to think about the means by which progress toward the ideal could be made. One example of this goal is President Bill Clinton's Partnership for Peace, a plan for broadening the membership of NATO and extending its influence by inviting the new nations of Eastern Europe and the Russian Federation to become apprentice, and in time full, members. Another is the plan, of which Helmut Kohl is the most enthusiastic supporter, to extend the European Union to include the Scandinavian states and those Eastern states that are the most economically and politically developed. Of particular interest are two more comprehensive plans, the global plan for security adumbrated by former Secretary of State Henry A. Kissinger, and UN Secretary General Boutros Boutros-Ghali's *Agenda for Peace.*

At the outset of his book *Diplomacy,* published in 1994, Kissinger stated that the challenge confronting world leaders in the wake of the Cold War was to bring order to the multistate world that was emerging, a task with which none of them has had much experience.

> Never before has a new world order had to be assembled from so many different perceptions, or on so global a scale. Nor has any previous order had to combine the attributes of the historic balance-of-power systems with global democratic opinion and the exploding technology of the contemporary period.

Where are they to turn for guidance as they approach this task? Kissinger is convinced that the only resource they have is the history of the ways in which states have regulated their relations with each other in the past, and that they must study this with an eye to the light it casts on their present perplexities. This will require a willingness to lay aside old prejudices and *idées fixes*—the American conviction, for example, that arrangements that are too logical are by their nature suspicious and that balance of power and *raison d'état* are alien to American values.

Writing primarily for Americans, whose country, he believes, will have the greatest stake in, but also the greatest responsibility for, the building of a new international system, Kissinger is sure that in the new post–Cold War world traditional American idealism will need the leaven of geopolitical analysis, and that

> America, like other nations, must learn to navigate between necessity and choice, between the immutable constants of international relations and the elements subject to the discretion of statesmen,

and will have to recognize that foreign policy must begin with clear definitions—of interests, objectives, and the limits of national policy. And, above all, America must be preoccupied with balance of power whether it likes it or not.

> Geopolitically, America is an island off the shores of the large landmass of Eurasia, whose resources and population far exceed those of the United States. The domination by a single power of either of Eurasia's two principal spheres—Europe or Asia—remains a good definition of strategic danger for America, Cold War or no Cold War. For such a grouping would have the capacity to outstrip America economically and, in the end, militarily.

Protection from that danger lies in an active balance-of-power policy.

In an intriguing passage early in his book, Kissinger suggests that, in the post-Communist world, the American temperament will probably find the Bismarck approach to balance of power more congenial than the British. If we were to try to imitate the British "disciplined aloofness from disputes and ruthless commitment to the equilibrium in the face of threats," we would, he thinks, find it difficult to summon up either the aloofness or the ruthlessness. On the other hand, the Bismarck policy of restraining the exercise of power in advance by some consensus on shared objectives with various groups of countries would be more our style.

Thus, for example, the Atlantic Alliance and the European Union might extend a security umbrella over the new democracies in Eastern Europe. More generally, the likely and most constructive model would be

> partially overlapping alliance systems, some focusing on security, some on economic relations. The challenge for America will be to generate objectives growing out of American values that can hold together these various groupings.

In general, this can be described as a conservative, even traditional plan, making few concessions to new problems in the modern world (the ecological dilemmas facing industrial nations, the role of powerful independent actors in the economic sphere, and others), and assuming that great-power rivalries will continue to be the main threats to peace and will be contained by measures validated by history. It is Bismarckian in its inspiration, although it may owe something also to the policy of Dwight David Eisenhower and John Foster Dulles, with their passion for regional alliances, and it assumes a determination and a skill in orchestration in the United States that hardly accords with recent examples of American unwillingness to make large commitments that may involve the use of force. Moreover—and this is a graver flaw—it does not address the problem posed by the fact that in the present world peace is less often threatened by conflicts between states than by friction, power contests, and the breakdown of order within states. In an interesting article, J. Stremlau has pointed out that, of the 184 states comprising the UN, "very few—including tiny mini-states—today fear external threats to their physical safety." But he adds, "Ironically, this success has had the unintended consequence of inspiring more and more dissident forces within states to seek sovereignty, by force if necessary."

This problem receives more adequate attention in Boutros Boutros-Ghali's *An Agenda for Peace*. First published in June 1992 as a Report of the Secretary General of the UN, this document was widely discussed and debated in the parliaments of the member states and in the Security Council, and on the basis of the comments and criticisms that he received, the secretary general prepared another report which was issued in the summer of 1993 under the title *An Agenda for Peace: One Year Later*.

The document is exactly what its title suggests: a list of suggestions about "how the international community can best equip itself to respond to a world in a rapid state of transition." Unlike Kissinger, Boutros-Ghali is not prepared to put his faith in the leadership or direction of any single power, however great. On the contrary, he believes that

> history is accelerating. The pace is alarming. The direction is not entirely known. At this time of stress, the hard fact is that no power or combination of powers is prepared to take on its shoulders the responsibility for collective security worldwide.

This leaves only the United Nations to pursue a more secure world by its work in four principal areas: preventive diplomacy, peacemaking, peacekeeping, and peacebuilding, and the *Agenda* briefly reports on progress in each of these.

The UN's peacemaking and peacekeeping functions are known well enough to make any discussion of them here unnecessary. It might be noted that, with 100,000 peacekeepers deployed at the end of 1993 in thirteen different parts of the world, increasingly heavy burdens have been placed upon member states in recent years, and it has become even more difficult to find states willing to supply military and police units. But such costs must be balanced against the costs to the general peace of situations entirely bereft of control, and it ill becomes nations that are seriously in arrears with their assessed UN contributions, like the United States, to accuse the UN of assuming too many obligations. Bad as the situation in Bosnia had become by 1994, it would certainly have been infinitely worse without the UN peacemaking and peacekeeping teams that had been sent there.

Important as these activities have been, however, they are no more so, Boutros-Ghali argues, than the functions of preventive diplomacy and peacebuilding. The former seeks to resolve disputes between and within countries before violence breaks out. Thus, in 1992, UN observers working in close cooperation with the National Peace Secretariat in South Africa helped reduce tensions, control demonstrations, and stop clashes from getting out of control. Boutros-Ghali admits that preventive diplomacy is still an elusive concept which, for its full development, will need refinement and the elaboration of techniques of early warning, fact finding, confidence building and the establishment of good offices. To be effective it must take account of the multidimensional roots of conflict in today's world, which is not an easy task. Even so, in the Secretary General's opinion,

> it is impossible to overestimate the value of preventive diplomacy. While it is true that the United Nations cannot get involved in every problem around the world, the field of preventive diplomacy is infinitely expandable. It is a key that can lock the door against chaos and open the way to peace.

As for peacebuilding, it aims at strengthening those institutions within nations that do most to consolidate a sense of confidence and well-being, with the most important elements in this process being democracy and development. By giving new nations advice and assistance in devising their constitutional arrangements, by organizing and supervising elections, and by providing various sorts of technical assistance, international agencies can promote democratization, and since democracies almost never fight each other, this is a service to peace. Peace in turn encourages development, which, under the right conditions, helps democracy consolidate itself. How to discover those conditions and make the most of them may, in Boutros-Ghali's opinion, be the most compelling challenge of our time, and the peace and security of the world will depend, in ways that we have not yet fully realized, on our ability to face it.

Of the various proposals for attaining a Pax Universalis, Boutros-Ghali's *Agenda* is the most modest. It promises little more than slow painful steps toward the ultimate goal and the hope of small successes that are always at the mercy of local conditions, like the UN's successful peacemaking operation in Cambodia in 1992. And it depends upon the cooperation and sacrifice of the wealthier members of the international community, which cannot, unfortunately, always be counted on. Even so, its logic is unmistakable and compelling, and it offers hope in a dangerous world.

Bibliographical Essay

On the Gulf War, see the interesting book by Rick Atkinson, *Crusade: The Untold Story of the Persian Gulf War* (Boston, 1993). Norman H. Schwarzkopf, *It Doesn't Take a Hero* (New York, 1993), discusses the military aspects of the conflict and gives a not entirely convincing rationale for the termination of the conflict. See also Stanley A. Renshon, ed., *The Political Psychology of the Gulf War: Leaders, Publics, and the Process of Conflict* (Pittsburgh, 1993), particularly the article by Alexander L. George, "The Gulf War's Possible Impact on the International System."

For American attitudes toward Iraq before the war, see Bruce W. Jentleson, *With Friends Like These: Reagan, Bush and Saddam, 1982–1990* (New York, 1994). For national attitudes toward the use of force, see Denis Healey, *The Time of My Life* (London, 1989), and Margaret Thatcher, *The Downing Street Years* (London, 1993) (the Falklands War); Christian Hacke, *Weltmacht wider Willen, Die Außenpolitik der Bundesrepublik Deutschland*, rev. ed. (Frankfurt-am-Main, 1993), and Arnulf Baring, *Deutschland, was nun? Ein Gespräch mit Dirk Rumberg und Wolf Jobst Siedler* (Berlin, 1991) (the Gulf War); and Thomas L. Friedman, "In Somalia, New Criteria for U.S. Role," *New York Times*, 5 December 1992, Paul Lewis, "UN Chief Says Letter to Bush Outlines U.S. Commitment," *New York Times*, 13 December 1992, and Steven Greenhouse, "U.S. View of Sanctions," *New York Times*, 3 July 1994 (on Somalia and its consequences). On Bosnia, see A. M. Rosenthal, "Preventing More Bosnias," *New York Times*, 25 May 1993, and on the background to the recognition of Croatian independence, Hacke, *Weltmacht wider Willen*, pt. 9, chap. 4.

On preventive diplomacy, see the book by Australian Foreign Minister Gareth Evans, *Cooperating for Peace: The Global Agenda for the 1990's and Beyond* (St. Leonards,

Australia, 1993), and the soon-to-be published article by J. Stremlau, "Antidote for Anarchy." On prescriptions for the future, see Henry Kissinger, *Diplomacy* (New York, 1994), and Boutros Boutros-Ghali, "An Agenda for Peace: One Year Later," *Orbis,* 37, no. 3 (Summer 1993). On the expansion of the UN's peace-making function, see Paul Lewis, "Peacekeeper Is Now Peacemaker: UN Wrestles With Its New Roles," *New York Times,* 25 January 1993.

II

Maintaining the System:
Problems of Force and Diplomacy

12

Knowledge for Statecraft: Lessons of History

The distinguished historian of the Renaissance, Jacob Burckhardt, once remarked that the true use of history is not to make leaders more clever for the next time but to make them wiser forever. Admittedly, it is not easy to learn from history, though almost every statesman and general has professed to have done so. In the first place, people often disagree about the correct lesson to be drawn from a particular historical experience. For example, American leaders and scholars drew quite different lessons regarding a strategy for dealing with limited conflicts such as the frustrating experience of the Korean War. Second, even if people agree on the correct lesson to be drawn from a particular case, they often misapply it to a new situation that differs from the past one in important respects.

If it is hazardous for policy makers to rely, as they sometimes do, upon a single historical analogy in deciding what to do in a new situation, how then can historical experience be utilized to deal effectively with a new situation that appears to bear a certain resemblance to past cases but also possesses unique (or at least some different) features? To make proper use of historical experience is admittedly a challenging task. The answer lies in synthesizing "lessons" from a broader range of experience, which can be done by drawing upon a variety of historical instances of a particular phenomenon, be it deterrence, coercive diplomacy, crisis management, détente, cooperation, or some other aspect of relations between states. The task is to convert the "lessons of history" from a larger number of cases into a comprehensive theory and general knowledge that encompasses the complexity of each of these activities. By comparing successes and failures of a particular strategy under different circumstances, one can identify conditions under which that strategy is likely to work or fail. Such a differentiated theory regarding the efficacy of strategies and instruments of policy is all the more necessary since, as any historian or literate person knows, the "lessons" of history are often inconsistent, if not contradictory, and generalizations are hazardous if not carefully qualified.

Despite considerable efforts in the past few decades to revive and systematize the study of foreign policy strategies, progress in conceptualizing many of these strategies, accumulating general knowledge of their uses and limitations, and identifying conditions on which success in their employment depends remains uneven and often poorly developed. There are, of course, many excellent individual historical studies that illuminate the employment and outcome of a given strategy, such as appeasement, in particular situations. But seldom does one see studies of several historical cases of a given type of strategy which are conducted within a well-defined conceptual framework that permits systematic comparison and cumulation of the results of individual cases.

Part II of the book indicates how individual historical instances of a particular strategy can be studied in order to contribute to a broader appreciation of its uses and limitations and to identify problems that may arise in attempting to implement the strategy and conditions that appear to favor its success or contribute to its failure. Before proceeding to chapters on individual strategies and undertakings that constitute some of the tools of statecraft, let us illustrate the inadequate knowledge base employed in the conduct of American foreign policy by examining the policy the Bush administration pursued unsuccessfully toward Iraq after the end of the Iran–Iraq war in 1988. Four of the six strategies that were employed failed in part because administration leaders operated with a poor understanding and conceptualization of their logic and requirements. They also lacked adequate general knowledge of the operational requirements, and their efforts were further handicapped by an incorrect image of Saddam Hussein.

These deficiencies cannot be attributed to the failure of policy officials to use available knowledge of the strategies in question that the scholarly community had already accumulated. In fact, such knowledge did not exist because the research needed to produce it had not yet been done. The strategies in question addressed the following four tasks: resocializing an outlaw state and reforming a rogue leader; deciding whether and how to employ appeasement; the proper use of reassurance of a possible dangerous opponent in conjunction with or in lieu of relying upon deterrence to dissuade him from encroaching on your interests and, finally, how best to conduct and terminate a military conflict in order to achieve the political as well as the military objectives of a war. The following pages provide a brief indication of how an inadequate understanding of these strategies contributed to the Bush administration's inability to make effective use of them in dealing with Saddam Hussein. In each case, the administration's flawed image of the Iraqi leader also played an important role.

Resocialization of Outlaw States

Great powers have often been confronted by ambitious states which were not socialized into the norms of the international system and posed a threat to its orderly working and stability. Addressing the problem at the outset of his book, *A World Restored,* Henry Kissinger held it to be of critical importance for the stability of the international system that all major states and their leaders should share a common concept of "legitimacy." This he defined as "international agreement about the nature of workable arrangements and about the permissible aims and methods of foreign policy." States that rejected the norms and practices of the existing international system Kissinger referred to as "revolutionary" states. More recently, such states are often referred to as "outlaw" states and their leaders as "rogue" leaders. What strategies are available for dealing with outlaw states and rogue leaders? Which strategies have been tried in the past and with what results? There is, in fact, no systematic, comparative study of this historical experience that would provide today's policy makers with conceptual and generic knowledge of this phenomenon. One can identify several possible strategies:

1. Military action, coercive pressures, and/or covert action to replace the outlaw regime with a more acceptable government or at least eliminate its rogue leader.
2. Long-range containment, which if pursued effectively, as it was toward the Soviet Union, might help eventually to bring about changes in the ideology and internal composition of the outlaw state that leads it to accept the norms and approaches of the international system.
3. A strategy of rewards and punishments designed to bring about fundamental changes in behavior and attitudes of the outlaw regime.

The third of these strategies can be viewed as an adaptation of the psychological technique of behavior modification for use in diplomacy. A confused and ineffective version of it was employed by the Bush administration toward Saddam Hussein following the end of the Iran–Iraq war until the attack on Kuwait.

One way of conceptualizing the strategy is conveyed by the notion of "conditional reciprocity," a practice that demands meaningful changes in policy and behavior in return for each and every concession or benefit bestowed upon the outlaw state. Clearly, the strategy of resocialization and the levers it employs must be conceptualized in a sophisticated way and carefully implemented. There exist hardly any systematic analyses of efforts of this kind to serve as a basis for formulating policy-relevant generalizations to guide decision makers.

What one "gives" the outlaw state and what one demands in return requires strategic planning that maps out and/or provides materials for improvising a series of incremental steps. Conditional reciprocity must be implemented flexibly; it must make use of monitoring and feedback. Those who employ the strategy must be aware of its risks and find ways of minimizing and controlling those risks. Finally, they must remain sensitive to indications that the strategy is not working or needs prompt reassessment. The Bush administration's effort to make use of the strategy of resocialization, which it referred to as a policy of "friendship," was lacking in all these respects.

Perhaps enough has been said to call attention to the need for detailed comparative studies of past efforts of this kind, some successful others not. The absorption of Kemal Atatürk's Turkey into the international system is perhaps an example of successful integration of what was regarded initially, particularly by the British, as a possible outlaw state or, at least, as one situated outside the international community. The Nixon–Kissinger policy of détente toward the Soviet Union can be studied as an example of a strategy of resocialization that was flawed both conceptually and in implementation insofar as its objectives included the long-range goal of encouraging the Soviets to mend their ways and enter into a new "constructive relationship" with the United States. Examples of failed attempts to reform a rogue leader probably include Neville Chamberlain's effort not merely to appease Hitler, but also to bring Germany back as a responsible actor into a reconstituted European system. Other outlaw states and rogue rulers that have been and appear to continue to be seriously at odds with the existing international system include Khomeni and his successors in Iran, Khaddafi's Libya, Assad's Syria, and Kim II Sung's North Korea.

More systematic knowledge regarding the uses, limitations, and risks of the several alternative strategies for dealing with outlaw states and their rogue leaders, therefore, is not merely for historical interest. The problem continues to have considerable relevance for contemporary U.S. foreign policy and poses a challenge to scholars and policy specialists to develop knowledge for statecraft.

Appeasement

Elements of appeasement can be seen in the policy of "friendship" the Bush administration pursued toward Saddam Hussein until the Persian Gulf crisis erupted in late July 1990. A review of that policy warrants the observation that it was neither well conceptualized nor implemented.

A moment's reflection on this case points to an anomaly. The historical case *against* appeasement is well understood and deeply etched in the consciousness of generations of policy makers and foreign policy specialists. In contrast, the case *for* appeasement is not well understood and lacks an analytical basis derived from historical instances when it was successfully employed in the interest of avoiding conflict and developing positive relations. Policy makers who believe it may be expedient to "conciliate" a possible dangerous adversary or to engage in "constructive engagement" with him do not have available a historically grounded theory regarding the conditions under which what is essentially a *policy of appeasement,* though the term itself cannot be used, is likely to be a viable strategy.

Put another way, the unfinished task is to replace with a more differentiated analysis the simple generalization so strongly rooted in the post-Munich era: "if appeasement then World War III" (or as it is sometimes rephrased: "if appeasement now, then it is likely to be necessary to fight a more difficult war in the future"). Instead, *two* "conditional generalizations" are needed: under what conditions is appeasement a dangerous policy that will increase the likelihood of war or a worse war in the future? But, also, under what conditions is appeasement a viable strategy that will reduce conflict with another state and markedly lower or eliminate the possibility of war? As a historically well-informed observer reminded us many years ago, "To show stubborn unyieldingness to an opponent who possesses a real sense of grievance over specific issues may be as dangerous as to make concessions to an opponent whose ambitions are endless." Only now, however, is a scholarly effort finally underway to make a systematic analysis of historical cases of appeasement in order to identify those conditions under which it is likely to be a viable conflict avoidance strategy and other conditions in which appeasement is likely to be misguided and contribute to the eventual onset of war.

In the classical European balance-of-power system, appeasement had a much more ambitious goal than some other ways of moderating a conflictual relationship. As will be noted in chapter 18 on Détente, there existed a gradation of steps for improving relations between two states that was incorporated into well-defined and well-understood concepts and practices of diplomacy. The process of improving relations might begin with "détente," which referred merely to a relaxation of tensions, and possibly develop into "rapprochement," whereby one or both sides expressed a desire to address some or all of their disagreements with a view to possible agreement. This, in turn, could lead to an "entente"—a limited, but significant improvement in relations in which the two sides at least recognized a similarity of some views and interests but with understandings between them limited to certain issues and an improvement in relations that stopped short of an alliance. Entente could then lead to "appeasement"—the methodical removal of the principal causes of the conflict—and possibly to alliance.

Following the breakup of the European system, the precise definition and sharp distinction among these concepts and practices were badly eroded. For example, the term *détente,* which came back into fashion after the effort Kennedy and Khrushchev made following the Cuban missile crisis to improve U.S.–Soviet relations, acquired an elasticity and ambiguity that often confuses its old meaning of a mere relaxation of tensions with what used to be called rapprochement, entente, and indeed also appeasement. Elements of all three objectives and practices were implicit in Nixon's so-called détente policy, but, in the atmosphere of the Cold War, it would have been most imprudent to refer to the more far-reaching objectives of U.S. policy toward the Soviet Union in these terms.

Comparative studies of successful and unsuccessful appeasement can help identify the conditions under which it may be a viable strategy, the risks of the strategy, and the ways of coping with it. Such insights can be gained, as will be noted in the chapter on détente, by comparing British appeasement policy toward Hitler with the gradual improvement in Anglo-French relations after the Fashoda crisis of 1898, and Chancellor Willy Brandt's successful *Ostpolitik* policy toward the Soviet Union and Eastern Europe.

An examination of the history of international relations should easily identify many other instances in which appeasement and conciliation either worked or did not, thereby enabling scholars to produce the conditional generalizations that will refine an understanding of when this strategy is and is not likely to be a viable one and how best to implement it.

Reassurance

In the several weeks before Iraq invaded Kuwait on 2 August 1990, the Bush administration attempted to deal with the emerging threat by a combination of deterrence and reassurance. It did not expect Saddam Hussein to attack. Yet in the face of the worrisome deployment of large Iraqi forces to the Kuwait border and Saddam's bellicose rhetoric, the administration felt it necessary to undertake an effort at deterrence. For some reason, it was thought necessary to accompany deterrence with reassurance. Reassurance took the form of diplomatic signals to Saddam indicating a desire for continued friendship. The deterrence component of the administration's response to indicators of possible aggression was not only extremely weak, it was further diluted by the effort to assure Saddam of Washington's desire for a continuation of friendly relations.

Resort to reassurance as a strategy on this occasion was questionable and probably counterproductive. When an adversary who is contemplating aggression regards the deterring state as basically hostile and as opposed to his "legitimate" foreign policy aspirations, he may interpret reassurance as an insincere effort to mask hostility. Such a response to reassurance is all the more likely if the adversary's mind-set is tainted with a touch of paranoia. As is well known, paranoid personalities tend to be very suspicious of friendly gestures. Another possible misinterpretation by the adversary of efforts to reassure him is that one may regard them, as Saddam possibly did in this instance, as a sign of irresolution. This, in turn, may encourage the rogue leader to question the credibility and significance of deterrence directed toward him.

Besides, the reassurance that Washington conveyed was very weak since it did not address the economic difficulties and needs, driven surely in part by Saddam's expensive military programs, that he had been voicing with increasing urgency beginning in the spring of 1990. Nor does it appear that the Bush administration urged the Kuwaiti government to be more forthcoming in dealing with Saddam's demands. As already suggested, it is not clear why the administration chose to convey reassurances in this situation and what it expected to accomplish thereby. Perhaps by iterating its policy of ''friendship'' toward Iraq the administration intended to convey an indirect warning that continuation of its policies of economic and military assistance would depend on Iraq's good behavior. But if so, the warning was so attenuated as to raise questions whether it was perceived as such and whether it could serve as a lever in the situation.

Reassurance can take different forms and is used for a variety of purposes in different situations in international relations. It indeed constitutes an important lever for use in diplomacy in certain circumstances. The possibility of coupling reassurance of some kind with deterrence, or substituting some form of reassurance for deterrence, has recently been highlighted in the writings of political scientists. But the systematic study of the strategy has only begun and the scholarly contribution of historians will be essential. Reassurances were frequently employed in the European system, often successfully, but at times ineffectively. This rich varied experience appears to be available only in descriptions of specific historical episodes. Needed is a systematic comparative study of its many different uses and its limitations, and the development of conditional generalizations that identify the circumstances and modalities that favor its success and seek to explain its failures.

War Termination: Integrating Military and Political Objectives

War should indeed be understood, as Clausewitz emphasized, as a continuation of politics by other means. But the task of selecting military objectives and strategy that will facilitate the achievement of broader political war aims has repeatedly encountered difficulties that led to disappointment with war outcomes, frustration, and acute domestic controversy. Paradoxically, it appears easier to use overwhelming military force to achieve very ambitious goals of total war than it is to achieve the more modest political objectives of a limited war. In some limited conflicts, as in the recent Persian Gulf War, even a resounding battlefield success cannot be easily converted into a wholly satisfactory political outcome. To be sure, the Allied coalition in the Gulf War was successful in achieving its military objectives. Kuwait was liberated, the Iraqi army was routed, Iraq's military capability and its infrastructure were greatly weakened. Achievement of these military objectives also accomplished the most important of the Allied coalition's political objectives. Thus, the regional threat posed by Iraq's powerful military forces was sharply reduced. And the general objective of establishing "peace and security" in the Middle East called for by the Security Council Resolution of 29 November 1990 that authorized use of force to liberate Kuwait was furthered by stiff cease-fire terms that imposed on Iraq the obligation to destroy all nuclear, chemical, and biological weapons and production facilities, and missiles capable of reaching other countries in the region.

However, an important political objective—the removal of Saddam Hussein from power—was not accomplished. To be sure, the objective was not explicitly authorized by the Security Council nor was it an official objective of the Bush administration. That is, it was not among the military objectives formally assigned to General Schwarzkopf's forces; accordingly, military strategy did not include pursuit, capture, or elimination of the Iraqi leader. Nonetheless, there can be no question that Saddam's ouster was an aim and an outcome of the war keenly desired by the Bush administration and, indeed, by some of Washington's coalition partners.

Here is not the place to attempt a detailed explanation for the limitation of military operations that enabled Saddam to survive. There were good reasons why the coalition armies were not authorized to pursue their advance into Iraq all the way to Baghdad to ensure the removal of Saddam from power. The UN coalition did not seek—in fact, it wished to avoid—a break-up of the Iraqi state into several smaller entities or a "Lebanonization" of the internal situation within the country. Early in its war planning, Washington had come to a firm, well-considered decision not to wage a total war against the Iraqi state that would lead, as in World War II, to its total defeat and a prolonged occupation which would require responsibility for its administration after the war ended. Rather, the objective was to leave in place a defeated, much weakened Iraqi state that could continue to balance Iran. This policy was defended by administration officials after the cease-fire, in response to criticism for not intervening on behalf of the Kurd and Shiite rebellions. As White House spokesman Marlin Fitzwater put it: "We don't intend to involve ourselves in the internal conflict in Iraq." One of Bush's close advisers reminded the critics that "our mission was to liberate Kuwait, not to reform Iraq. We had no intention of getting bogged down in that mess."

The determination not to go all the way to Baghdad or to intervene on behalf of the Kurd and Shiite rebellions was strongly influenced by post-Vietnam U.S. military doctrine that warned against military interventions on behalf of ambitious–amorphous political objectives. According to the doctrine, force should be used only for achieving strictly military objectives and employed in accord with professional military judgment. The United States should avoid becoming involved militarily in situations in which it could not be successful in a relatively short period of time with minimal casualties. Most civilian leaders of the Bush administration shared the military leaders' inhibitions and, also for broader political and diplomatic reasons, were strongly determined to minimize U.S. involvement in postwar Iraq. The Bush administration believed that political support for the war was geared to limited military objectives and might erode rapidly if Washington embarked on more ambitious goals. Nor could UN and coalition support for a more far-reaching military campaign be counted upon. Besides, when the cease-fire was declared on 28 February, it did not seem necessary to do anything more by way of military action to bring about Saddam's downfall. It was widely believed within the administration and elsewhere that Saddam could not survive in power after suffering so savage and humiliating a defeat.

Finally, a few general observations will perhaps provide a framework for considering the difficult problem of integrating military and political objectives in a limited conflict. It is misleading and conceptually incorrect to pose the problem, as is often done, as that of "matching" military and political objectives. Such a formulation assumes—and begs the question—that acceptable military means can always be devised which if successful will achieve all the political objectives of a limited war. In fact, in such conflicts there are often political aims that cannot be realized solely via victory on the battlefield. Not only are there inescapable limits on the utility of force as an instrument of policy, there can be unforeseen consequences of military victory and unexpected developments thereafter, as in the Gulf War, that handicap the ability of even sophisticated statesmen to convert military victory into full-blown political success.

In sum, although military success may be a necessary condition for achieving ambitious political war aims, it is seldom sufficient for doing so. Other variables and unpredictable developments often come into play in the complicated "end game" that determines the political outcome of a limited war such as that in the Persian Gulf. In this war, as in some others, the end of fighting begins a new phase in which pursuit of some of the political objectives of the war continues. In planning for such wars the critical question is how and to what extent the military strategy employed will, if it is successful, empower the victor to achieve all of the postwar political objectives.

The dilemma of converting battlefield success into full achievement of political war aims is a problem that frequently arises in war termination. It needs much more systematic comparative study than it has thus far received.

This brief account of flawed, ineffective strategies employed by the Bush administration to influence Iraq is, of course, not definitive, although it is quite consistent with available information. It points to deficient conceptualization and inadequate knowledge of strategies for resocialization of outlaw states and rogue leaders, appeasement, reassurance, and use of military force to achieve political war objectives. But, as noted earlier, since policy-relevant knowledge of these instruments did not exist, Bush administration officials had no other recourse but to operate on the basis of what proved to be inadequate conceptions of the strategies they attempted to employ. The purpose here is not to contribute to political criticism of the administration's policies toward Saddam Hussein. Rather, analytical evaluation of this experience has been provided in order to call attention to the types of knowledge needed for statecraft, to note that conceptualization and generic knowledge of these (and perhaps other) instruments of foreign policy remain surprisingly inadequate, and to urge historians and political scientists to accept as a challenge to scholarship the necessity to improve knowledge for statecraft. The chapters that follow illustrate how case studies can contribute to the knowledge base required for policy making.

Bibliographical Essay

For incisive discussions of the problem of using lessons of history, see Ernest R. May, *Lessons of the Past: The Use and Misuse of History in American Foreign Policy* (New York, 1973); Robert Jervis, *Perception and Misperception in International Politics* (Princeton, 1976), pp. 217–287; Richard E. Neustadt and Ernest R. May, *Thinking in Time: The Uses of History for Decision-Makers* (New York, 1986); and Yaacov Vertzberger, *The World in Their Minds* (Stanford, 1990).

Methods for converting "lessons of history" into a more comprehensive, differentiated theory and generic knowledge are outlined in Alexander L. George, "Case Studies and Theory Development: The Method of Structured, Focused Comparison," in *Diplomacy: New Approaches in History, Theory and Policy*, ed. Paul Gordon Lauren (New York, 1979), pp. 43–68. The case for collaboration between historians and political scientists in this endeavor is made in Gordon A. Craig, "The Historian and the Study of International Relations" (Presidential address to the American Historical Association, December 1982) *American Historical Review* 88, no. 1 (1983): 5–9.

The discussion of strategies the Bush administration pursued unsuccessfully toward Iraq draws from the fuller account in Alexander L. George, *Bridging the Gap: Theory and Practice of Foreign Policy* (Washington, D.C., 1993). For a general history of the Persian Gulf crisis, see Lawrence Freedman and Efraim Karsh, *The Gulf Conflict, 1990–1991* (Princeton, 1993). For a detailed, well-documented, and incisive critique of the Bush administration's policy toward Saddam Hussein prior to the war, see Bruce W. Jentleson, *With Friends Like These: Reagan, Bush, and Saddam, 1982–1990* (New York, 1994).

The quotation regarding the need to reconsider the possible utility of appeasement is from Evan Luard, "Conciliation and Deterrence: A Comparison of Political Strategies in the Interwar and Postwar Periods," *World Politics* (January 1967). Cautions against undiscriminating condemnation of appeasement are advanced also by Fred C. Iklé, *Every War Must End* (New York, 1971), p. 110; and J. L. Richardson, "New Perspectives on

Appeasement: Some Implications for International Relations,'' *World Politics* 40, no. 3 (1988): 312. See also Paul Kennedy, ''The Tradition of Appeasement in British Foreign Policy,'' *British Journal of International Studies* 2 (October 1976).

A comparative study of cases of appeasement is being undertaken by Stephen R. Rock, Vassar College. Drawing on his research in progress, Rock presented a paper, ''When Appeasement Worked: British Conciliation of the United States, 1895–1905,'' at the 1988 meeting of the Northeastern Political Science Association.

The best discussion of various reassurance strategies that may be adopted instead of or in conjunction with deterrence is Janice Gross Stein's ''Deterrence and Reassurance,'' in *Behavior, Society, and Nuclear War,* ed. Philip E. Tetlock et al. (New York, 1991), vol. 2, pp. 8–72. See also the earlier article by Richard Ned Lebow and Janice Gross Stein, ''Beyond Deterrence,'' *Journal of Social Issues* 43, no. 4 (1987): 5–71.

The quotation from White House spokesman Marlin Fitzwater appears in *Newsweek,* 22 April, 1991.

13

Negotiation

During the course of the last several centuries, both the international and domestic contexts of diplomacy have, in ways described in earlier chapters, changed dramatically, and technological advances in communications and transportation have altered its modalities. Even so, its chief instrument, negotiation, has essentially remained much the same. Indeed, by focusing on the fundamental characteristics of negotiation, we can identify the elements of both continuity and change in the efforts that states have made throughout the modern period to deal with conflicting interests and to promote their mutual interests.

Prerequisites for Negotiation

Fred C. Iklé has written that whatever the context or the substantive issue, "two elements must normally be present for negotiation to take place: there must be both common interests and issues of conflict. Without common interests there is nothing to negotiate for; without conflict there is nothing to negotiate about." This observation poses useful questions to ask in studying efforts to initiate negotiation, for it throws a sharp light upon a basic reason for success or failure. Even so, it should be noted that because of other considerations, governments sometimes enter into negotiations even when they are aware that there is no shared basis of interest. For example, a refusal to enter into negotiations sometimes may be politically damaging at home or present an image of inflexibility abroad that may harm relations with allies and neutrals. Then, too, even though the interested parties do not expect or want an agreement, they may nonetheless begin talks with the goal of gaining propaganda advantages at the expense of the opponent. Negotiations undertaken exclusively or largely for side effects of this kind have become more frequent with the increased importance of public opinion and mass media during the course of the diplomatic revolution. Finally, one or both sides may invite diplomatic exchanges simply in order to size up the opponent, to acquire information, to mislead and deceive him, or to "maintain contact" and use talk as a substitute for the possibility of violent action. Such reasons for negotiations, even when there is no expectation or desire for an agreement, may also be more common in the modern era than during the nineteenth century.

As these observations suggest, the objectives and goals of negotiation are by no means limited to seeking an agreement. Upon closer examination, therefore, the two prerequisites for negotiation emphasized by Iklé should be understood to apply to the initiation of serious negotiations aimed at achieving an agreement of some kind. It should also be noted that the two sides may not share the same view regarding the prospects of a negotiated agreement. Sometimes, and again perhaps this is more common in the modern era, when one side is more eager than the other to commence negotiations, its adversary may attempt to exact concessions as a payment for entering into negotiations.

Types of Agreements

Governments may seek different types of agreements via negotiations. Four kinds of agreements may be usefully distinguished since they reflect different ways in which states act to regulate their relations.

1. *Extension agreements* provide a formal ratification and continuation of existing arrangements. Examples are extensions of tariff agreements and renewal of overseas base rights.
2. *Normalization agreements* terminate an abnormal situation in relations between two or more parties. Diplomatic relations may be reestablished, trade wars ended, or a cease-fire put in effect.
3. *Redistribution agreements* benefit one side at the expense of the other. Examples are changes in territorial boundaries, in share of markets, in degree of political influence in third areas, and in financial contributions to bilateral or multilateral organizations.
4. *Innovation agreements* set up new arrangements or undertakings that benefit both parties (though not necessarily equally). They include the treaties that established the European Economic Community and the International Atomic Energy Agency; the Austrian State Treaty of 1955 that established an independent but neutral state in place of the four-power occupation; and the General Agreement on Tariffs and Trade (GATT) in 1947 that paved the way for tariff reductions and elimination of other barriers to trade.

The characteristics as well as the contexts of the negotiating process may differ depending on which type of agreement is being sought. When the parties are dealing with a number of outstanding issues, they may negotiate for several different types of agreements simultaneously.

Negotiation is essentially a process of communication and interaction that entails a number of tasks and purposes. These tasks are interrelated in practice but will be singled out for separate discussion here.

Procedural Arrangements and Agenda-Setting

Before substantive negotiations begin, and sometimes even before the sides commit themselves to enter into them, the actors must agree on a time, place, agenda, and other modalities such as conference arrangements and the diplomatic level (that is, foreign ministers, ambassadors, or lesser diplomatic officials) at which the discussions will be held. Any of these procedural matters may itself generate disagreement. Indeed, procedural wrangling may be an ominous sign of how far apart the two sides are on the substantive issues or reflect hostility and lack of trust. One side may also deliberately use procedural disagreements for tactical purposes—to achieve side effects such as propaganda advantages, to demonstrate toughness and resolve, to extract concessions, or to gain negotiating advantages. Procedural disagreement at the very outset of negotiations seems to have become much more common in the modern era. Certainly the tenacity with which one side or the other argues over seemingly minor procedural matters has taken on new dimensions in an age when passionate ideological and other differences have displaced the cultural homogeneity that facilitated diplomatic processes in the European system. In the Korean truce negotiations of 1951, the Vietnam peace talks, and the Geneva conference following the Arab-Israeli War of October 1973, agenda-setting and conference arrangements with respect to such trivial matters as the shape of the table and placement of the participants were the subject of prolonged and bitter wrangling. They were regarded as reflections of status and thus were of symbolic importance. With respect to the agenda itself, the two sides may disagree not only on what items and issues are to be discussed, but also on how these items are to be worded and in what order they will be taken up.

Acquisition and Exchange of Information

In the opening stages of a negotiation, or in "exploratory discussions," the two sides often seek to clarify the precise nature of their conflicting interests and the common concerns that have brought them to the negotiating table. The object at this stage may be to verify or correct initial beliefs regarding the prospects of an agreement. Is the common interest in reaching an agreement really strong enough, and are the conflicting interests not so intractable that there is a genuine possibility of working out a solution satisfactory to both sides?

In attempting to answer this question, each negotiator seeks from the other side a clear, authoritative, and reasonably specific statement of its demands. It is expected that, while each side will state its maximum terms for an agreement at the outset, at least some of these initial demands will be subject to modification during the course of persuasion and bargaining. At some point, one side may ask the other to give a general assurance that under certain conditions it will be prepared to moderate some of its demands.

Often, one side may seek to determine whether the other will negotiate in good faith, whether it is serious in attempting to explore the possibility of a mutually acceptable agreement, whether a relationship of trust can be established between the negotiators, and whether they can proceed to enter into serious and delicate negotiations on the basis of mutual confidence and what Iklé has called the "rules of accommodation." The answer to these questions is often elusive, and it may require considerable time and patience before both parties have satisfied themselves that it is prudent and timely to proceed to the next stages.

Ascertaining the Opponent's Resistance Point and Determining Whether There Exists a Settlement Range

Having ascertained the other side's maximum demands, each negotiator presses to find out its minimum objectives, that is, the least it is willing to settle for. Because this is presumably each side's irreducible goal in the negotiations, it is sometimes referred to as the *resistance point.*

Information about an opponent's resistance point is not always easily, quickly, or reliably obtained. Understandably, a negotiator may be reluctant to reveal his minimal demands prematurely. Since this constitutes valuable information to the other side, each would like to be assured that the opponent too is going to disclose his minimal demands. Very often neither side will move from its maximum demands to a complete disclosure of its minimum demands without satisfying itself that its opponent is ready to do the same. This emphasizes once again the importance of patience in negotiations until trust and a spirit of reciprocity can be established. Even so, negotiators may continue to conceal their true minimal demands, even while moderating their maximum demands. One must distinguish, therefore, between "declared" and "real" resistance points. In any case, at some stage one or both sides may conclude that it is fruitless to probe further in order to find out the opponent's real resistance point.

Figure 5

At this stage, having established what appear to be each other's resistance points, the two sides can identify how far apart they are from an agreement and assess the significance of the gap between their declared minimum demands. It is important here for each actor to judge whether somewhere between the two resistance points there is a settlement range, or one or more possible settlements which both sides might prefer to no agreement. This stage in the negotiations is depicted in Figure 5.

If the actors feel that the gap between the resistance points is too great and see no conceivable settlement, they may begin to feel it is useless to continue the negotiations. A stalemate develops in which further efforts may be made to clarify and alter each other's resistance points. As a result, the gap may be narrowed somewhat. If the possibility of a settlement through further negotiation is still not considered likely, the stalemate may continue. One or both sides may now utilize the negotiations for propaganda purposes or other side effects. Or they may agree to report back to their governments and ask for new instructions. Finally, they may agree to call off the negotiations temporarily or permanently; or one side may do so unilaterally. Sometimes one side (or both) will make minor concessions simply in order to keep the negotiations going or to get them started again.

Analyzing the Opponent's Resistance Point

Once a preliminary settlement range has emerged, each side seeks to find out more about the other side's resistance point. What set of interests, concerns, and attitudes lies behind the opponent's present resistance point? Information bearing on this question will help each actor find out whether there are ways of satisfying the opponent's essential demands without jeopardizing its own interests. Or such information may enable one to find ways of weakening or changing the other's minimal demands. At this stage in the negotiations, each side also wants to know how eager its opponent is for an agreement. Is the other side under some time constraint or domestic pressure to achieve resolution of the current issues?

Information that permits shrewd guesses or a better understanding of what lies behind the adversary's ostensible resistance point helps each side determine its combination of persuasion and bargaining.

Searching for a Referent or General
Principle That May Facilitate Agreement

When the issues in a dispute are complex, the parties to the negotiation may seek to bridge the gap between their resistance points in stages. One approach is to identify a referent or general principle that will provide a standard or framework that will assist in working out the specific details of a settlement. It may be difficult to choose the general principle, since one side may regard the proposed principle or referent as biasing the type of agreement that can be reached. Referents and principles that have proven useful in the past include the concepts of "power" and "balance of power" in determining territorial settlements and spheres of influence during the European era, "secure frontiers" in seeking political/territorial settlements at the end of many wars, and "parity" or "strategic equality" in arms control negotiations.

Persuasion and Bargaining

If the parties believe there is a potential agreement somewhere within the settlement range, they engage in persuasion and bargaining to move each other toward an agreement. "Persuasion" is usefully distinguished from "bargaining." In the former, efforts are made to get the other side to understand why your demands are so important to you and why you think its demands are excessive and difficult to accept. In arguing the merits of the case, one may appeal to reason and to emotion.

"Bargaining," on the other hand, is characterized by concessions, conditional offers, threats, and inducements. It may also include proposals for compromises, trades, and quid pro quos. Bargaining is generally facilitated if the two sides subscribe to similar rules of accommodation.

Agreement will be facilitated, too, if either side can strengthen the other's perception of their broader common interests, thus causing it to modify its minimum demands. This is sometimes attempted via the strategy of *linkage,* in which one side encourages the other to be more conciliatory by persuading it that, depending on how the current dispute is resolved, it stands to benefit or suffer in other issue areas.

Search for Creative Solutions

Negotiations that have reached a stalemate after the possibilities of persuasion and bargaining appear exhausted are sometimes unexpectedly successful because one side or a third party thinks of a quite novel way of resolving the disagreement. It may be possible for the parties to break the stalemate by enlarging the range and scope of issues brought into the negotiations. This may, at the extreme, extend to a review of their entire relationship. The actors may gain a new perspective on the matter under negotiation by undertaking a clarification or reorientation of their overall relations.

Bargaining Strategies

The parties to a negotiation in the modern era have often brought quite different diplomatic styles to bear. There was much less variance in the diplomatic styles and bargaining strategies employed by major powers in the European balance-of-power system. Diplomats in the classical era agreed upon and generally adhered to reasonably well-defined rules of accommodation. The diplomatic revolution has played havoc with the cultural homogeneity and consensus that facilitated negotiation in the nineteenth century and, in the modern era, the actors sometimes have different conceptions of negotiation. As noted below, diplomats representing totalitarian states often regard negotiation as another form of combat rather than as a vehicle for resolving or moderating conflicts of interest.

Two bargaining strategies may be identified: the *accommodative* and the *optimizing* approaches. Negotiators socialized in commercially oriented societies often pursue an accommodative approach to bargaining; that is, they do not ask for much more in a negotiation than they think is reasonable and likely to be acceptable. In contrast, negotiators socialized in revolutionary or totalitarian cultures often pursue an optimizing strategy, trying to achieve as much as possible in negotiation, not fearing to be unreasonable, combative, and abusive. Negotiators employing optimizing bargaining tactics are less likely to disclose their real resistance point and feel no obligation to reciprocate concessions.

Enforcement and Verification of Agreements

The question whether an agreement, if reached, will be honored by one's opponent is often of concern during the negotiations and may influence attitudes toward the shape of the agreement. That is, certain ways of resolving the issues may be perceived as less attractive, or even as unacceptable, because confidence is lacking in their enforceability. There are several dimensions to this problem that may be addressed during the course of the negotiations. First, the question often arises whether a contemplated agreement is "self-enforcing" or whether implementation will depend on the good faith of each side. Self-enforcing agreements are generally preferred (though not by states that do not want to be tied down to an unsatisfactory agreement); but it is often not possible to devise them. Particularly invidious are agreements that are asymmetrical in this respect, that is, when one side makes concessions that are irreversible, whereas its opponent's reciprocating concessions are such that it can take them back later on. A second, related question that plagues certain types of negotiation is whether violations of the agreement can be detected in a timely and unambiguous way. If this possibility is present, then one or both sides will attempt to contrive workable provisions for identifying and dealing with violations. Such provisions may be incorporated into the agreement. Agreement on enforcement provisions is less of a problem when the parties have unilateral means of monitoring them.

Multilateral Negotiations

The simple two-actor model presented thus far is greatly complicated, of course, when more than two parties engage in negotiations. Multilateral negotiations often did occur in the European system: witness the many conferences of the five great powers that constituted the concert of Europe. Multilateral negotiations of this kind were more complex and difficult than most bilateral negotiations, to be sure, but the challenge posed to diplomats was more manageable because the system was a relatively well-ordered one and because the European statesmen were culturally homogeneous. The absence of these conditions in the international system of the post-European era and other changes brought about by the diplomatic revolution have significantly altered the nature and difficulties of multilateral diplomacy in the modern era. This is strikingly evident in any number of post–World War I international conferences, beginning with the Paris Peace Conference that came at the end of that conflict. In contrast to their predecessors at Vienna, the leaders of the victorious powers came to Paris with quite different conceptions of the kind of international system that should be created, and the process of peacemaking was one of continual adaptation to these different objectives and priorities. They also discovered, as had their predecessors at Vienna, that their intention of making all the important decisions themselves was bitterly resented by the lesser powers and that concessions, in the form of a limited share in decision making, had to be made to them in order to alleviate that feeling. Finally, unlike the peacemakers at Vienna, they were continually subjected to the pressures of public opinion and domestic politics in their own countries. All of these constraints complicated their work and contributed to the unsatisfactory nature of the peace settlement of 1919.

These forces affected other large conferences in the interwar period—the disarmament conference of 1932 is a case in point—and they were present once more at the largest of the postwar meetings, the Conference on Security and Cooperation in Europe, which was held between 1973 and 1975.

The Conference on Security and Cooperation in Europe

No formal peace conference was held at the end of World War II as had been done in 1814–1815 and 1919. The closest approximation was the Conference on Security and Cooperation in Europe (CSCE).* By 1973, when it opened, considerable dissatisfaction had accumulated on all sides concerning the continued division of Europe and the dangerous tensions that had arisen during the course of the Cold War. Many of the representatives of the thirty-five states who gathered at Geneva in July 1973 wished to effect a change for the better, although there was no common agreement concerning what form that change should take.

Repeatedly during the Cold War, the Soviet Union had requested a European conference on security. Its early offers to participate in such a conference must certainly have been calculated merely to test Western solidarity. The demand that attendance be exclusively European and the timing of Soviet military and political offensives guaranteed that its requests would be rejected. In retrospect, however, it is evident that subsequent Soviet proposals became increasingly legitimate. By 1971, Willy Brandt, always interested in the opportunity for small steps toward more normalized East–West relations, was willing to co-sponsor the CSCE. The addition of this valuable spokesman in the West and increasing superpower interest in détente improved the prospects for the conference considerably. Unrealistic demands were dropped, agendas were proposed, and the initiation of CSCE was linked to progress in other talks on other issues. Gradually, opposition to CSCE gave way, and delegations were able to gather in Geneva to open negotiations. A serious handicap was the limited importance attached to the conference by the United States and the limited benefits American leadership expected from it. Pressure applied by European allies eventually achieved U.S. attendance, but American skepticism remained.

At Geneva, thirty-five states negotiated on the basis of multinational consultation and consensus. The conference adopted the remarkable rule, unthinkable at the time of the Congress of Vienna, that decisions would ultimately require unanimous approval of all states, large and small. And in contrast to the Paris Peace Conference, *all* of the thirty-five states participated in the actual

*The case study on the Conference on Security and Cooperation in Europe that appears below was prepared in its original form by Captain Alan Carver, U.S. Army.

negotiations. Various texts were submitted to small working committees in an effort to narrow differences. But texts continued to circulate to all participants until bracketed phrases were resolved to the satisfaction of all. This extraordinarily difficult and lengthy process was not confined to the conference alone. In the West, members of the European Economic Community occasionally discussed common positions and appointed spokesmen under their arrangements for political cooperation. Likewise, the members of NATO at the conference met periodically to prepare positions and select specific members to introduce proposals. The conference was also included on the agenda of the NATO council and was discussed at meetings attended by both the U.S. president and the secretary of state. The essentially solid front maintained by the members of the Warsaw Pact also suggests prior consultation. Nevertheless, neither the West nor the East was able to stifle all indication of disaffection and dissatisfaction with the positions adopted by the superpowers.

The negotiating positions of individual states were also subjected to diverse domestic influences and were not prepared by a single individual or governmental agency. All delegations with one exception arrived headed by diplomats of ambassadorial rank. The American delegation was initially headed by a senior foreign service officer, but in order to conform to the composition of the other missions, the State Department eventually replaced him with the U.S. ambassador to Czechoslovakia. He did not play a central role, however, in the formulation of the U.S. position, nor was the U.S. position prepared in Geneva by the delegation at all. Military confidence-building measures, an important agenda item, were discussed in Washington by representatives of the National Security Council staff, the Defense Department, and the State Department. Economic issues were discussed by representatives of the State Department, the Treasury, and the Commerce Department, and by special trade representatives. Other issues were generally dealt with by an inter-office committee within the State Department. Major positions were presented to the secretary of state for approval. Members of the delegation were occasionally replaced over the two-year period of general negotiations, and experts were frequently added to advise on specific issues. Congressmen and the undersecretary of state for European affairs made several visits to Geneva to attend conference deliberations. By 1975, the CSCE was being examined by several congressional subcommittees as well. The bureaucratic influences evident in the American CSCE process were remarkable for a nation that expressed little real interest or purpose at the conference, but they reveal the important changes in negotiations produced by technological advances and the increased complexity in international affairs and domestic politics.

Beyond vague notions of improved security and a desire for the continued progress of détente, the larger Western powers failed to bring a clear set of objectives to the conference. The Soviets, on the other hand, perceived the opportunity to achieve very specific and desirable ends in their interest. The conference offered them an opportunity to gain formal recognition of Eastern European borders and the acceptance of principles of sovereignty and nonintervention that would confirm Soviet influence in Eastern Europe and provide de facto recognition of the status quo. Many of these issues involved areas of dispute that had existed since the conclusion of World War II. The importance of these objectives led Brezhnev to stake his personal prestige on a rapid and favorable outcome. And, indeed, when the conference convened, it appeared that the Soviets were well-prepared to exercise an optimizing strategy and in an excellent position to deliver a diplomatic coup.

Several factors combined to rob the Soviets of a clearcut victory. The smaller countries attending the conference were able to gain much greater attention for human-rights issues than either of the two superpowers was willing to grant, the Soviet Union because of the potential for embarrassment and the United States because of the nebulous nature of the issue and the likelihood that it would jeopardize détente and prevent meaningful negotiations at Geneva. The tenacity of the human-rights advocates and the broad participation afforded all of the thirty-five delegations in attendance assured the inclusion of the human-rights issue on an equal basis with the other issues under negotiation. A second factor complicating the negotiations for the Soviets was the limited public interest in the conference in the West. In the United States, little attention was paid to CSCE by the media, the public, or Congress until 1975, after the negotiations were largely completed. Secretary of State Kissinger himself was skeptical of the potential benefits to be derived from the conference and preferred bilateral talks between the superpowers to the more difficult multilateral format of CSCE. Public opinion in Europe showed only slightly greater interest. The Soviet government had come to Geneva intent on concluding the process in time for a victory announcement at the Twenty-fifth Congress of the Communist party of the Soviet Union, and Brezhnev's prestige would suffer if a favorable conclusion was not brought about in time. Originally expected to be a short and uncomplicated conference dealing with security and economic issues, the CSCE proved to be a complex and difficult process. The important role of the smaller Western states and the elevation of the human-rights issue coupled with the self-imposed Soviet deadline ultimately worked to the advantage of the Western nations. However, the handicap of poor preparation and vague objectives played a large part in minimizing the Western countries' ability to make the most of their fortunate position.

CSCE was finally thrust into the limelight in the United States when plans were announced for a possible summit-level meeting in Helsinki for signing the accords. The press, Congress, and the public were caught by surprise at the new importance attached to the negotiations. A great deal of controversy was generated by belated efforts to discover the impact and scope of CSCE, and the

Ford administration sought to counter this by immoderate enthusiasm for what had been accomplished at Geneva. A spokesman for the White House said that the meeting would "codify East–West détente" and pointed out proudly that "the sheer size of the contemplated summit" would outstrip the Congress of Vienna and the Paris Peace Conference. "Maybe the pope himself would go to Helsinki," he said, adding that the meeting would be "a landmark event culminating nine years of East–West exchanges."

When the results of the security conference became clear, many Americans found these dithyrambs hard to justify. William Safire wrote in the *New York Times* before the end of the Helsinki meeting, "In case you hadn't heard, World War II will soon be coming to its official end. The Russians won." Former Undersecretary of State George Ball reviewed the terms of the agreement in *Newsweek* in an article entitled "Capitulation at Helsinki." Both writers, and many others, pointed out that the one clear and unambiguous result of CSCE was that the West explicitly accepted the new frontiers that the Russians had drawn all over Eastern Europe at the end of the war and thus implicitly accepted the ideological division of Europe. Article III of the agreement stated clearly that all signatory powers regarded each other's existing frontiers as inviolable. This gave the Soviets the formal recognition of their eastern gains that they had been seeking since 1945.

It was true that they did not get everything their own way. They had to accept the idea that, at least in theory, frontiers could be changed by peaceful agreement, which left the door open for German reunification. They had to agree that there would be no intervention in other countries' internal affairs, which would make it more difficult for them to act again as they had in Czechoslovakia in 1968. And they were forced, when Western delegations argued that Europe could never be normal unless people could travel where they wanted to, to accept some provisions, in the so-called Basket III clauses, about the movement of people and ideas, about family visits from East to West, marriages between citizens of different countries, and human rights in general. But these commitments, which represented the great victory of the smaller powers and the neutrals at Helsinki, were loosely drafted and in such general terms as—in Ball's words—"to portend only minuscule holes in the Iron Curtain." To Americans in particular, these Soviet concessions seemed an inadequate exchange for the gains they had registered.

The final act of CSCE was attacked also for the lack of adequate measures for enforcement. The conference had agreed upon periodic meetings of experts to consider alleged violations, but this arrangement—perhaps inevitably, considering the ambiguities and residual disagreements buried in the agreements— did not prove to be very satisfactory. The first review meeting, in Belgrade in 1977, resulted in a stalemate when the Soviet Union resisted an inquiry into its conformity with the standards of human rights required by the agreement. Similar difficulties developed at the second review meeting in Madrid in 1980–1981. This was disappointing, although it probably had a favorable spinoff effect for the West, inclining the neutral states, who have a strong commitment to the Helsinki Agreement and to human rights in general, to view Soviet professions more realistically than they have always done.

As the story of CSCE indicates, one consequence of the expanded membership of the diplomatic community has been a tendency on the part of the lesser states to demand not only representation but active participation and a voice in the settlement of international issues. The reliance by the superpowers on arsenals of sophisticated nuclear weapons that cannot rationally be employed to advance national interests has generally enhanced the relative importance of small nonnuclear nations whose power is derived from their inherent flexibility and combined capacity to influence the nature of superpower confrontation. Likewise, the increased influence of public opinion, bureaucratic practices, and domestic politics has made diplomacy more complex a process and less an art to be practiced by the individual statesman of great talent and personal influence.

A recent comparative study of ten major cases of multilateral negotiations in issue-areas of security, trade, and environmental problems adds to our understanding of the nature of this increasingly important dimension of international relations. The author, Fen Osler Hampson, finds that although multilateral diplomacy of the 1980s and 1990s shares some of the same characteristics of diplomacy in the previous era, it is complicated by ''(a) the larger number of states who participate in international negotiations as a result of decolonization and the formation of new states resulting from the break-up of the Soviet empire; and (b) the increasing complexity of the issues themselves such as in the areas of trade, environment, and even conventional arms control.'' Hampson also finds that such negotiations are increasingly affected by mobilized interest groups, including business, labor, nongovernmental organizations, and other actors, ''who see themselves as direct stakeholders and thus seek to affect outcomes by bringing pressure to bear on their national governments. Many of these groupings also have an international constituency . . . enabling them to mount effective campaigns at the national and international levels.''

In addition, international organizations created as a result of earlier negotiations become new actors in succeeding multilateral negotiations. ''The bureaucratic actors who staff international organizations have come to see themselves as having a direct stake in promoting the development and expansion of new international regimes associated with issue-areas falling under their mandate.'' Finally, Hampson concludes from his study of these recent cases that ''multilateral negotiation is, in essence, a coalition-building exercise involving states, non-state actors, and international organizations.'' This process, he finds, is essentially the same for multilateral negotiations in arms control, trade, and environment.

> The key players in this process are experts who define prenegotiation possibilities and the agenda for negotiations, coalitions of smaller states or lesser powers who sustain the momentum of negotiations and help devise bridging solutions to difficult problems, and officials in international agencies who use their positions to forge strategic alliances with their counterparts in national bureaucracies in an effort to move negotiations forward.

Several implications can be drawn from the changing character of negotiation. There is little prospect that the broadening trend in representation will recede. Bilateral negotiations will increasingly require ratification by the wider community of states if their effects on security are to be broadened and confirmed. Reliance on multinational consensual solutions will make the negotiation process difficult and results less definitive and binding. Coalitions will be less cohesive and less subject to superpower manipulation. These tendencies necessitate governing principles of restraint, mutual respect, and accommodation. When disaster can result as competing parties battle for mutually exclusive ends without restraint, each with moral justification, principles must operate to make resolution possible. Certainly, the resolution of the diverse interests brought about by the increased heterogeneity and expansion of the international community is the challenge of the diplomatic revolution of our time.

Bibliographical Essay

On negotiation in general, see the classic works of Wicquefort and Callières and the modern study by Harold Nicolson, all cited after chapter 1. The discussion of the simple two-actor model of negotiation draws on a number of sources, in particular Fred C. Iklé, *How Nations Negotiate* (New York, 1964). Among political scientists who have written extensively on negotiation is I. William Zartman; see, for example, *The 50% Solution* (New York, 1976), especially chap. 1, and, with respect to "referents" in negotiation, "Negotiation: Theory and Reality," *Journal of International Affairs* 29 (1975): 69–77. Important contributions to a general theory of negotiation, one not confined to diplomacy, have been made by many other writers, including those who have analyzed labor–management negotiations. See, for example, Richard E. Walton and Robert B. McKersie, *A Behavioral Theory of Labor Negotiations* (New York, 1965).

For a recent comprehensive assessment of the theory and practice of negotiation, see P. Terrence Hopmann, *Resolving International Conflicts: The Negotiation Process* (Columbia, S.C., 1994).

An important and comprehensive scholarly treatment from the broader perspective of bargaining strategy is provided in Glenn H. Synder and Paul Diesing, *Conflict Among Nations* (Princeton, 1977). Psychological dimensions are explored in Daniel Druckman, *Negotiations: Social Psychological Perspectives* (Beverly Hills, Calif., 1977). The perspective of decision analysis and game theory is reflected in Howard Raiffa, *The Art and Science of Negotiation* (Cambridge, Mass., 1982). Negotiation and bargaining are placed in the broader context of conflict resolution in Martin Patchen, *Resolving Disputes Between Nations: Coercion or Conciliation?* (Durham, N.C., 1988). A prescriptive theory of negotiations is presented in Roger Fisher and William Ury, *Getting to Yes: Negotiating Agreement Without Giving In* (Boston, 1981). Finally, deserving the serious attention of all students, is the seminal "Essay on Bargaining" by Thomas C. Schelling in his classic work, *The Strategy of Conflict* (Cambridge, Mass., 1960).

The best single factual and evaluative treatment of CSCE is provided by an American diplomat who participated in the negotiations, John J. Maresca, *To Helsinki: The Conference on Security and Cooperation in Europe, 1973–75* (Durham, N.C., 1985). A useful early treatment is provided by William I. Bacchus, "Multilateral Foreign Policy Making: The Conference on Security and Cooperation in Europe," in *The Politics of Policy Making in America,* ed. David A. Caputo (San Francisco, 1977). Important documentary materials are to be found in two sources: "Conference on Security and Cooperation in Europe," *Hearings before the Subcommittee on International Political and Military Affairs of the Senate Committee on Foreign Relations*, 94th Cong., 1st sess., 6 May 1975; and Igor I. Kavass, Jacqueline Paquin Gramer, and Mary Frances Dominick, eds., *Human Rights, European Politics, and the Helsinki Accord: The Documentary Evolution for the Conference on Security and Cooperation in Europe, 1973–75*, 6 vols. (Buffalo, N.Y., 1981).

The recent comparative study of multilateral negotiations quoted in the chapter is from Fen Osler Hampson with Michael Hart, *Multilateral Negotiations: Lessons from Arms Control, Trade, and the Environment* (Baltimore, 1994).

Note: The Expanding Field of Conflict Resolution: Theory and Practice

The past decade has seen an explosion of interest and activity in conflict resolution approaches that depart from the traditional model of formal negotiation between states. A variety of approaches and mechanisms for conflict avoidance, management, and resolution have been articulated and employed in different international and domestic conflict settings. Much of the activity has been undertaken by nongovernmental actors.

We have not attempted in this edition of *Force and Statecraft* to summarize this important development in the theory and practice of international relations. The vast literature on these activities focuses largely on descriptions of the approaches and techniques of conflict resolution advocated and employed by different practitioners and on the use of simulations and other devices for training persons to make use of them. There is as yet little by way of systematic research to evaluate the various techniques that would help identify conditions under which a particular approach is effective.

There evidently exists no national archive or center which maintains a continuing, up-to-date inventory of all such activities and the associated literature. A step in the direction is being taken by the new Center for Preventive Diplomacy at the Council on Foreign Relations. Useful information can be obtained from the United States Institute of Peace in Washington, D.C. Here only one or two sources can be provided for each of the major approaches.

On "Prenegotiation": Harold H. Saunders, "We Need a Larger Theory of Negotiation: The Importance of the Prenegotiating Phases," *Negotiation Journal* 3 (1985): 249–262.

On "Getting to the Table": Janice Gross Stein, ed., *Getting to the Table: The Process of International Prenegotiation* (Baltimore, 1989).

On "Track-Two Diplomacy": John W. McDonald and D. Bendahmane eds., *Conflict Resolution: Track-Two Diplomacy* (Washington, D.C., 1987).

On "Problem-Solving Workshops": Ronald Fisher, "Developing the Field of Interactive Conflict Resolution: Issues in Training, Funding and Institutionalization," *Political Psychology* 14, no. 1 (1993): 123–138.

On "Ripeness" and Mediation: I. W. Zartman, *Ripe for Resolution: Conflict and Intervention in Africa* (New York, 1985); and Stephen J. Stedman, *Peacemaking in Civil War: International Mediation in Zimbabwe, 1974–1980* (Boulder, Colo., 1991).

On "Preventive Diplomacy": Michael Lund, *Preventive Diplomacy and American Foreign Policy* (Washington, D.C., 1995).

14

Deterrence

Deterrence consists essentially of an effort by one actor to persuade an opponent not to take action of some kind against his interests by convincing the opponent that the costs and risks of doing so will outweigh what he hopes to gain thereby. In this simple and quite limited sense, deterrence rests upon the assumption of a "rational" opponent, that is, one who can be expected to calculate the utility of his alternative courses of action on the basis of available information. Logically speaking, the first step in formulating a deterrence policy is to weigh the *interests* of one's country that are engaged in the area that may be threatened by hostile action and to assess how important they are. The next step is to formulate and convey to the opponent a *commitment* to defend those interests. The deterring power backs its commitments by *threats* to respond if the opponent acts. Such threats must be both *credible* and *sufficiently potent* in the eyes of the opponent—that is, pose a level of costs and risks that he regards as of sufficient magnitude to overcome his motivation to challenge the defending power's position.

There are two interdependent dimensions of credibility. First, the deterring power must convey to the opponent that it has the *will and resolution* to defend the interests in question; second, it must possess *capabilities* for doing so that it regards—and persuades the opponent to regard—as appropriate and usable for the defense of those interests. These will have no persuasive force unless the deterring power has the ability to deal, by effective and appropriate measures, with the kinds of action that its opponent may take. American experience with the doctrine of massive retaliation is relevant here. In an effort to extend the threat of American strategic nuclear power, the Eisenhower administration in the early 1950s ominously warned it would "retaliate massively," not only against Soviet initiation of an all-out war, but also in a variety of possible lesser encroachments against free world countries. The credibility of massive retaliation for deterring Soviet or Chinese Communist initiation of lower-level conflicts declined, however, as the Soviets developed strategic nuclear capabilities of their own. Accordingly, the Kennedy administration and its successors moved to develop stronger conventional military capabilities that would be more appropriate and usable in limited encroachments of various kinds and hence would be more credible in deterring them. (For a more detailed analysis, see chapter 19.) Threats will lack credibility, of course, when a defending power lacks the capabilities needed for protecting an outpost. In these circumstances, the defending power can threaten to punish the aggressor in other ways, by broadening the arena of conflict or by engaging in retaliation or reprisal.

The study and practice of deterrence as a discrete foreign policy strategy did not become prominent until after World War II. Since then, the advent of nuclear weapons has elevated the role of deterrence strategy to a preeminent position in the study of international relations. It should not be assumed, however, that the concept of deterrence has forever languished in obscurity. Throughout history, city-states, kingdoms, empires, and nation-states have all sought to prevent or deter the actions of rivals which they found inimical to their best interests. Many of these past practitioners of deterrence understood quite clearly the requirements for a successful policy, and a study of their actions can reveal much about the nature of deterrence and its usefulness in the international arena. In the European balance-of-power system the great powers often sought to achieve deterrence of one another via alliances, but it must also be noted that formation of new alliances or invocation of existing ones was also used to support offensive foreign policy actions designed to change a status quo situation.

The historical cases chosen for analysis in this chapter offer three interesting and different views of deterrence in action.* All three cases, it will be noted, illustrate the fact that deterrence is rarely a strategy applied in isolation, but rather forms a part of a more comprehensive foreign policy approach that may involve other diplomatic strategies as well. In the first case, England was reasonably successful in its attempt to prevent a dangerous expansion of the terms of the Quadruple Alliance by the other European powers, while in the second, the Western Allies could not prevent Hitler from invading Poland. In the last case, the question of success or failure regarding the United States' commitment to Israel is not so easily answered, for the results are certainly mixed. There can be no doubt, however, that in each of the three cases, the international community lay poised on the brink of a major conflict which only a successful application of deterrence could avoid.

A number of factors complicate the use of deterrence strategy as an instru-

---

*The case studies in this chapter were prepared in their original form by Captain Richard J. Hoffman, U.S. Army. Helpful suggestions for the version of this chapter were made by Andrew Luks.

ment of foreign policy. This was always the case, but the diplomatic revolution introduced new complications, which will be evident as we move from our oldest case study to the most recent one.

France and the Congress System, 1816–1823

The peace of Europe in the post-Napoleonic period was to be secured by an alliance of the four victorious powers, Britain, Austria, Russia, and Prussia, in which each party pledged to act in concert with the others to prevent France from again seeking hegemony in Europe. This coalition, first formalized in the Treaty of Chaumont in March 1814, was confirmed as the Quadruple Alliance on 20 November 1815, after Napoleon's Waterloo campaign had reminded the Congress of Vienna members of the pressing need for a collective security agreement. As with the Chaumont agreement, the Quadruple Alliance was primarily aimed at restraining French aggression, but a provision was made for periodic meetings among the great powers "for the maintenance of the Peace of Europe."

The Quadruple Alliance was not the only accord concluded in Vienna in 1815. Another federation, called the Holy Alliance by its chief proponent, Alexander I of Russia, came into being as well. In this pact, the signatories agreed that the principles of Christianity should guide the conduct of nations in their international and domestic affairs. The exact purpose of the alliance never became clear, but its obscure wording later offered Austria's foreign minister, Prince Metternich, the possibility of constructing a conservative bulwark against any future revolutionary tide that might sweep through Europe, endangering its crowned heads. The British foreign secretary, Viscount Castlereagh, wisely refused to sign the document, and the Congress of Vienna concluded its work with the Second Peace of Paris, which established the shape of Europe in the years to come.

The next European congress convened at Aix-la-Chapelle in September 1818, and the principle topic on the agenda was the readmittance of France as the fifth great European power. This was readily accomplished, but Czar Alexander submitted a memorandum in which he proposed that the great European powers should confirm their adherence to the territorial settlement of Vienna and guarantee all legitimate regimes existing at that moment. Alexander's memorandum began a long series of confrontations between the czar and Castlereagh, in which the British foreign secretary strove successfully to prevent him from widening the specific principles of the Quadruple Alliance into a reactionary agreement on the order of the Holy Alliance. The confrontation culminated on 5 May 1820, on which date Castlereagh issued a famous memorandum to the powers of Europe stating Britain's unalterable opposition to any agreement involving the intervention of one state in another's internal affairs.

Unfortunately, Alexander found support for his cause growing as a wave of revolution swept Europe in 1820. The revolt of the Spanish army in January and the granting of a liberal constitution was followed by the assassination of the French king's nephew in February, an uprising in Naples in July, and another revolt in Portugal in August. As concern over these actions mounted, the powers, with the exception of Britain, met in Troppau in October and endorsed the principle of conservative intervention in the so-called Troppau Protocol. Later Russia, Prussia, and Austria met at Laibach to authorize Austria to intervene in Naples and restore the Bourbon dynasty, a task that was quickly accomplished. The next congress of Europe met at Vienna in October 1822 to consider the French government's proposal that it be allowed to intervene in Spain and restore the Bourbon monarchy there. The British, led after Castlereagh's death by George Canning, strongly opposed French intervention in Spanish affairs. Nevertheless, all of Canning's efforts, including numerous diplomatic notes and the withdrawal of his representative, the Duke of Wellington, were insufficient to deter the other powers from authorizing France to intervene. By April 1823, French armies were on the march for the first time since 1815, and within six months Ferdinand VII was back on the Spanish throne.

At this point, another issue arose to occupy the attention of the great powers. Spain's American colonies had taken the opportunity provided them by the revolt to declare their independence from the mother country. With his throne now restored, Ferdinand set about seeking assistance in recovering Spanish colonial possessions. He received support from a France interested in securing a share of the Latin American trade and a Russia anxious to partake in any action that might weaken Britain's position and strengthen its own. Canning, however, was fiercely determined to preserve Britain's newly developed economic ties with the former colonies and prevent any further expansion of the Holy Alliance. In a series of strongly worded memoranda, he exploited French indecision by affirming Spain's right to seek by its own efforts to recover its former colonies, but asserted that the British government would view with grave alarm the attempt of any other power to intervene in Latin America. He followed up these memoranda by a series of frank discussions in October 1823 with the French ambassador, Polignac, which won him a French promise of nonintervention in return for a vague statement of British interest in a conference on Spain's American problems. This was followed in December by the promulgation of the Monroe Doctrine, in which the United States, backed by the British Royal Navy, asserted its protectorate over the Western Hemisphere, thus effectively eliminating the threat of Spanish intervention. The combined effect of these two diplomatic maneuvers showed Europe that the power of the Holy Alliance stopped at the water's edge, and the crisis ended.

The Western Allies' Attempts to Deter the Attack on Poland, 1938–1939

The attempts of the Allies, Britain and France, to deter the German attack on Poland really began in March 1939 when, after German troops had occupied Prague in violation of the Munich Agreement, British Prime Minister Chamberlain realized that Hitler was not to be trusted and had to be opposed by threats of force. He was joined in this conviction by the French government, which after the Sudeten crisis was reduced to following Britain's lead in its foreign policy. Chamberlain wasted no time in attempting to build a new bulwark against German aggression in Central Europe. A mutual assistance pact was concluded with Turkey, and promises of support and protection were extended to Greece and Romania. By far the most important action taken was the pledge of support given Poland by Britain and France on 31 March 1939.

The question was now whether this would suffice to prevent Hitler from attacking Poland. Given the uncertain state of the Allied armed forces, and the difficulty they would have in rendering Poland timely military support regardless of their state of readiness, it became obvious that the Allies would require the support of the Soviet Union if they were to have any chance of preventing further aggression.

This idea proved to be easier to articulate than implement. To begin with, the Allies and the Soviet Union, although in general agreement that the course of German expansion must be contained, were of two minds when it came to implementation. The Allies, led by Chamberlain, were deeply suspicious of Russian motives, and only belatedly did they approach the Soviet Union in mid-April to inquire if the Soviet government might wish to extend a unilateral guarantee to the western frontiers of Poland and Romania. The Soviets declined the Allied offer, but inquired in turn about the possibility of a comprehensive alliance between themselves and the Western powers. In the Soviet view, a requirement for the success of such an alliance would be their ability to station troops in Poland and Romania to defend these countries in case of aggression. The Poles and the Romanians, being understandably wary of the Russians, would have nothing to do with this idea, and the matter stagnated until August 1939.

The Germans, however, had been far from quiet. On 28 April 1939, Hitler denounced the Nazi-Polish Nonaggression Pact of 1934 and the Anglo-German Naval Agreement of 1935. Later, in May 1939, Germany and Italy announced the signing of the Pact of Steel, a formal military alliance that seemingly indicated the commencement of hostilities in the near future. In point of fact, Hitler had decided to go to war over Poland, and he began urgently to seek a rapprochement with the Soviet Union in order to avoid a two-front war.

For their part, the Soviets, discouraged by the unresponsiveness of the Allies, had initiated conversations with the Germans in the spring of 1939. By way of warning to the Western powers, the Soviets replaced the pro-collective security foreign affairs commissar, Litvinow, with the staunch nationalist Molotow. Even as the Allies were seeking to respond to these moves, the Soviets agreed to open negotiations on a new economic pact with Germany, while at the same time inviting the Allies to send a military mission to Moscow to discuss the possibilities of defending Poland and the Baltic states. Having pitted the two opponents against each other in a race for Soviet favor, the Russians now waited for the outcome.

If they were in a race, the Allies were unaware of the necessity for speed. Their military mission, traveling by ship, took until 11 August to arrive in Moscow and, when informed by Marshal Voroshilow that the time had come for a military convention, the head of the British mission revealed that he had no power to conclude agreements. This performance contrasted unfavorably with that of the Germans, who were working at top speed to reach an accommodation. On 14 August, German foreign minister Ribbentrop proposed by wire that he fly to Moscow ''to lay the foundation for a final settlement of German-Russian relations.'' The Russians accepted the next day, and when Ribbentrop arrived in Moscow, the two parties concluded a pact by which they undertook to refrain both from aggression against each other and from participating in any grouping of powers aimed directly or indirectly against the other party. They undertook further to maintain contact for consultation and to settle disputes by ''friendly exchange of views'' and agreed that in the event of ''a territorial and political transformation'' in the territories belonging to the Baltic states, Polish territory west of a line formed by the Narev, Vistula, and San rivers should be regarded as falling within the German sphere of influence, as would Lithuania, while the rest of Poland plus Finland, Estonia and Latvia, and Bessarabia and Bukovina would be considered to be within the Soviet sphere of influence. (By a supplementary agreement of 28 September, it was decided that Lithuania would be added to the Soviet sphere and that there would be corrections in the German interest in the zonal frontiers.) The new partners announced the signing of the pact to a stunned world on 21 August 1939, the same day the British mission finally received its credentials.

With the signing of the Nazi-Soviet Pact, Hitler resolved to crush Poland without delay. Perhaps he felt that Britain and France would renege on their pledge and betray Poland, as they had the Czechs; but having prepared Germany for war, he had by now determined to continue his string of conquests by force of arms. Thus, even the resumption of peacetime conscription by Britain on 28 August failed to change his mind. On 1 September 1939, the German army, in response to a contrived border incident, commenced its well-planned invasion of Poland. Britain immediately informed the German government that it intended to honor its pledge to Poland unless the invasion was halted at once. Receiving no reply, the British government informed the Germans on 3 September that unless it was assured by 11:00 A.M. that all action would cease immediately and that the German forces would withdraw from Poland, a state of war would exist between Germany and Britain.

U.S. Deterrence Policy in the Middle East

The evolution of the United States security commitment to the state of Israel has been a slow, and some might say precarious, process since the United States supported the 1949 United Nations partition of Palestine and subsequently recognized the newly proclaimed state in May 1949. This action, taken by President Harry Truman against the counsel of some of his closest advisers, was the beginning of what was later to become a "moral" commitment by the United States to Israel's continued existence. The process was extensively aided by Zionist organizations within the United States and abroad. The government of the United States, however, was not blind to its very real strategic and economic interests in the Middle East among the Arab states. On the contrary, the "Arabists" of the State Department, led by Secretary George Marshall, pursued a determinedly even-handed policy in the Middle East despite strong Israeli pleas for economic and military assistance. This situation continued until the Suez crisis in 1956.

Egypt's President Gamal Abdel Nasser precipitated the crisis by nationalizing the Suez Canal in July 1956. The British, French, and Israeli governments, brought together in an alliance of convenience, resolved to rectify their common grievances against Egypt by force of arms. While the Israelis cleared the Sinai, a combined Anglo-French force attempted to seize the canal zone. Unfortunately for the allies, the United States, now led by President Dwight Eisenhower and Secretary of State John Foster Dulles, felt that their actions violated the 1947 UN mandate and joined with a majority of the United Nations in calling for an immediate withdrawal of all foreign forces from Egypt. Britain and France complied, but Israel, led by Prime Minister David Ben-Gurion, refused to withdraw Israeli forces unless guaranteed that Israel would have free passage through the Straits of Tiran and be free of terrorist attacks from the Gaza Strip. At this point, the United States stepped in to guarantee the placement of a UN force in the Gaza Strip and the Israeli right of passage in the straits. This guarantee constituted the first significant commitment by America to Israel and was "operationalized" on 20 February 1957 when President Eisenhower pledged in a public address that the United States recognized the concept of free right of passage in the Gulf of Aqaba and was prepared to exercise this right itself and with other nations.

After the Suez crisis, the United States attempted to return to an even-handed policy in the Middle East, but the growing belligerency of the Arab states and the increasing involvement of the Soviet Union in the region made this policy hard to maintain. The next test for the U.S. Mideast policy came in 1967 when Nasser, acting under pressure from the Arab League, took steps to test the credibility of the U.S. commitment and to demonstrate Egypt's support for the Palestinian cause.

On 14 May 1967, Nasser ordered the Egyptian army to occupy the Sinai Peninsula. When this move was unopposed by a U.S. administration deeply involved in Vietnam, Nasser was emboldened on 16 May to request that the UN security force be removed. To the surprise of everyone, including Nasser, Secretary General U Thant complied. At this point, President Lyndon Johnson, who for political and personal reasons stemming from the U.S. experience in Vietnam was strongly opposed to any unilateral American action in the Mideast, urged Premier Levi Eshkol of Israel and President Nasser to act with restraint. The United States then attempted to resolve the crisis in the UN, but Nasser took matters into his own hands on 22 May and closed the Straits of Tiran to Israeli shipping.

Johnson recognized that this last act was a true test of the commitment Eisenhower had made in 1957, but he was unable and unwilling to generate congressional support for unilateral action. Instead, it was decided that the situation could best be resolved through multilateral action by the UN Security Council. A proposal was made for a UN fleet to break the blockade, and Johnson asked the Israelis for time to put this proposal into effect. The Israelis at first agreed to wait two weeks before taking action but later felt compelled to launch a preemptive attack on Egypt, Jordan, and Syria on 5 June 1967. This initiated the so-called Six-Day War, in which the Israelis utterly defeated the Arab forces and occupied the Golan Heights, the West Bank of the Jordan River, and the Sinai.

Once hostilities commenced, U.S. policy shifted to attempting to obtain a UN-directed cease-fire. Significantly, however, Johnson extended the level of the U.S. commitment to Israel by intervening on its behalf to prevent the Soviet Union from coming to the aid of the Arabs. In this way, a U.S. strategic umbrella was raised over Israel, and America became actively committed to the principle of preventing gross Soviet interference in the Mideast. Interestingly enough, the Johnson administration further modified its Mideast position by not calling for an immediate withdrawal of Israeli forces from the occupied territories and by stepping up arms shipments to Israel.

This policy continued through the immediate postwar period, which saw the United States committed to maintaining Israeli military strength while at the same time supporting UN Resolution 242, which called for the eventual return of the occupied territories. The U.S.–Israeli bond was drawn even tighter by the Jordanian crisis of 1970, when the United States, now led by President Richard Nixon and his adviser Henry Kissinger, used Israel as a proxy in deterring the

Syrians from overthrowing King Hussein of Jordan. In American eyes, it now seemed that the best deterrent to another Mideast war was to maintain an Israel militarily strong enough to deter attack while the United States sought to establish a meaningful peace in the region and enlisted the aid of the Soviet Union in restraining its Arab clients.

This grand design, however, was to have unhappy consequences. The "no war-no peace" situation that followed the 1967 war proved to be incompatible with Arab pride and national interest. Following the inconclusive "war of attrition" in 1969–1970 and the so-called year of decision in 1971, Egypt's new President Sadat and Syria's Hafez Assad were anxious to break the deadlock. Both countries had been extensively resupplied with Soviet arms, and on 6 October 1973, Egypt and Syria attacked Israel on the Sinai and Golan fronts, respectively. The attack caught the Israelis unprepared, as a result both of U.S. pressure not to preempt as in 1967 and of the Israeli government's independent decision to avoid a costly early mobilization. In the ensuing fighting, the Israelis again prevailed, but not before they had suffered heavy casualties. The United States found itself once more intervening on Israel's behalf in order to prevent unilateral Soviet intervention and eventually had to undertake a major commitment to both Egypt and Israel in the hope of resolving the Arab-Israeli problem.

Analysis

Inherent in the calculus of deterrence lies the assumption of a rational opponent, one who can be deterred from a given course of action if the costs of pursuing it clearly outweigh the benefits to be gained thereby. While it is not the purpose here to explore all the ramifications of this assumption, it can be said that in making it, a grave and often fatal error may be committed. Not all actors in international politics calculate utility in making decisions in the same way. Differences in values, culture, attitudes toward risk-taking, and so on vary greatly. There is no substitute for knowledge of the adversary's mind-set and behavioral style, and this is often difficult to obtain or to apply correctly in assessing intentions or predicting responses.

The efforts of the Quadruple Alliance and the congress system were both almost brought to grief by the seemingly irrational desire of Czar Alexander II to suppress "liberal" regimes anywhere they might appear. Chamberlain's policy of appeasement rested upon an incorrect image of Hitler and foundered for the most part on the rocks of Hitler's insatiable demands. Even in 1967 and 1973, the Egyptian leaders Nasser and Anwar Sadat were forced to take risky, and by their opponents' calculations irrational, steps against Israel by pressures generated both domestically and in the Arab world at large.

Setting aside the rational-opponent assumption, the deterring power must consider the question of its own and its opponent's national interests in order to calculate the utility of the various policy options. It is often difficult to determine one's own national interests, let alone those of an opponent; but failure to do so can result in the disintegration of even the best deterrence strategy. This can be readily seen in the way in which the congress system sufficed to deter French aggression after 1815, as a result of both the solidarity of the Quadruple Alliance powers and the desire of France itself to renounce its hegemonic efforts, but started to show signs of strain as the divergent interests of the great powers began to manifest themselves on the Continent and in the New World. Likewise, the Allied desire to deter the German attack on Poland was hampered by the divergent interests of obtaining Russia's participation in the security agreement while limiting its penetration of Eastern Europe. Lastly, the United States has had great difficulty establishing the priority of its own interests in the Middle East among such conflicting goals as preserving the state of Israel, preventing Soviet penetration of the Arab world, and assuring itself and its allies of adequate supplies of Arab oil, all of which it seeks to accomplish in conjunction with or opposition to Arab, Israeli, and Soviet interests in the region.

Having successfully assessed its own and the other party's interests, the deterring power must now make an explicit or implicit commitment to defend the ally, territory, or interest its perceives as being threatened. This, too, is often not as simple a task as it might first appear. To be sure, in the first case, the commitment of the members of the Quadruple Alliance to prevent further French military action outside of France was clearly articulated from the start both in the terms of the alliance treaty and in the pledging of a specific quantity of troops in the event of a French violation. The commitment to prevent the intrusion of the Holy Alliance into South America was clearly stated both by Canning's actions and by those of the United States government, for example, the promulgation of the Monroe Doctrine.

By way of contrast, Canning's first attempts at preventing French intervention in Spain, and Chamberlain's attempt to pledge Allied support for Poland, although clearly articulated, suffered from other deficiencies which will be discussed later. The U.S. commitment to Israel, in contrast to both previous examples, evolved slowly between 1948 and 1973 in a series of ad-hoc operationalizations in which the United States sought to maintain its policy flexibility in the Middle East while the Israelis sought to obtain an ironclad guarantee of their security. The resulting ambiguous commitment did little to provide stability to the region or to relieve Israeli anxieties. As can be seen from the three cases studied, the articulation of a clear commitment is neither a simple nor a sufficient means of implementing a deterrence policy.

As discussed earlier in this chapter, the deterring power must back up its commitment with threats that are both credible and sufficiently potent in the eyes of the aggressor to prevent him from attempting the undesired course of action. The credibility of a threat is broken into two components, the first of which is the will and resolution of the deterring power to defend the interests in question. In the successful examples of deterrence among the case studies, it is evident that there exists a strong correlation between the demonstration of firm resolve and the success of the policy. When the Allied powers faced France in 1815, they were firmly opposed to allowing France to involve Europe in another set of wars, and they manifested this opposition in their use of occupying troops to enforce the terms of the peace. Likewise, Castlereagh and Canning both relied on European respect for British will and resolve in attempting to combat the ideological zeal of the czar. Presidents Johnson and Nixon clearly showed their determination in 1967 and 1973 to prevent any possibility of Soviet troop involvement in the Mideast, and they backed up their threats with visible force.

In contrast, in 1939 the will and resolve of the Allied powers was in considerable doubt as a result of the policy of appeasement that they had followed since 1937 and the lack of strong indication of Allied determination. Similarly, the lack of resolve on the part of both American administrations prior to the 1967 and 1973 Middle East wars reflected the deep internal divisions brought on by Vietnam and Watergate, respectively. More recently, the lack of will was painfully evident again in the Western powers failure to respond more energetically and forcefully in the face of "ethnic cleansing" in Bosnia.

But will and resolve are not sufficient to guarantee success. The deterring power must possess the other component of credibility, namely, the capability for inflicting damage on the opponent. In this regard, the members of the Quadruple Alliance were demonstrably capable of defeating France in the years after 1815 if they acted in concert. In the same vein, Britain was capable, by virtue of its naval superiority, of preventing any extension of the Holy Alliance to the New World. The United States also possessed sufficient capability to prevent unilateral Soviet involvement in the 1967 and 1973 Middle East wars.

Where capability fails, however, is in those instances where the force the deterring power possesses is either inappropriate or unusable in the given situation. All Britain's vaunted sea power could not prevent France from occupying Spain if the other great land powers approved of France's action. In the case of Poland in 1939, the Western Allies were, without the support of the Soviet Union, in no position to inflict unacceptable losses on Germany in the short run or to render timely assistance to their ally, Poland. Because of the distaste for foreign ground combat engendered by U.S. involvement in Vietnam, President Johnson found himself unable or unwilling to honor Eisenhower's 1956 commitment in reference to the Straits of Tiran; and President Nixon and Secretary Kissinger found that, much to their surprise, supplying arms to Israel was not a sufficient means of preventing an Arab attack. Thus, the question of a deterring power's capability can be seen as a key point in the development of a successful strategy.

In considering the second aspect of the threat, we must ask: Is it sufficiently potent to overcome the opponent's motivation to change the status quo? Here the level of the opponent's motivation is the key. The newly restored Bourbon monarchy in France was in no way inclined to start another series of disastrous wars in Europe after 1815, and thus it submitted willingly to the restrictions placed on it by the Quadruple Alliance in that year and by Britain alone in 1823. By the same token, the Soviet Union was not inclined to risk a nuclear confrontation with the United States as long as the existence of its client states in the Mideast was preserved and it was allowed an equal role in determining the outcome of any conflict.

On the other hand, it can be safely stated that Hitler had decided in 1939 to seek further solutions to his foreign policy problems by force of arms; as a result, the Allied threats were doomed to insufficiency without either Soviet assistance or a vastly expanded military establishment, which they did not possess. In 1967 and 1973, the costs of a war with a militarily powerful Israel and the enmity of the United States were insufficient to overcome pressures within the Arab camp on both Nasser and Sadat to take some drastic action to change the status quo. It can be seen, then, that a sufficiently potent deterring force must exist not only in reality but, more important, in the mind of the potential aggressor as well.

Having examined these three historical cases within the general framework of deterrence theory, it is now desirable to turn to some of the specific components of that theory which have not yet been mentioned. Earlier research on experience with deterrence strategy led to the formulation of four important propositions that have received additional support from the examination of the three cases discussed in this chapter.

The first proposition that deterrence theory stresses is that *deterrence is not simply a matter of announcing a commitment and backing it with threats.* The validity of a given commitment is directly related to its possessing a demonstrable or reasonable relationship to the maker's real national interests. This can be seen quite clearly in each of the three cases studied. Before the French invasion of Spain in April 1823, it was obvious to the other European powers that Britain opposed any action to suppress the Spanish revolt; but they were also aware that Britain's real interests lay elsewhere, in its international trade and in the maintenance of its naval supremacy. Thus, while the other powers sanctioned the invasion of Spain, they were unwilling to proceed from there with the reconquest of Portugal and the Spanish colonies, and thus to risk almost certain war with Britain. The Allied guarantee to Poland in 1939 suffered from a similar confusion of commitment and national interest. Hitler rationalized that

Poland was of little value to the Allies and that in the end they would abandon it, like Czechoslovakia, in the interest of encouraging German expansion eastward rather than westward against themselves. The same sort of problem occurred in 1973, when Sadat correctly deduced that the U.S. commitment to Israel did not extend to territory captured by the Israelis in the 1967 war and thus attempted to recover Arab morale and the Suez Canal by force of arms. Initially willing to leave the Israelis to their own resources, the United States was finally forced to act when the flow of Russian arms into Arab hands threatened to decide the issue in a manner extremely adverse to U.S. Mideast policy. Thus, it can be seen that a commitment must be validated by its relationship to an appropriate national interest.

The second observation to be made about deterrence is that *it is heavily context dependent.* That is to say, as a deterrence situation changes, so does the commitment/threat calculation. This phenomenon was present in both sides of the situation in 1939. As the Allies saw their appeasement plans shattered and their safeguards destroyed one after another by German actions after 1936, their level of commitment increased until, after Prague in 1939, it became apparent that Hitler would have to be stopped in Poland. Unfortunately, Hitler perceived the situation in exactly the opposite manner. He reasoned that Allied resolve had been steadily waning since his reoccupation of the Rhineland and had collapsed at Munich in 1938. He therefore felt that Poland was his for the taking, with only a small risk of a major war if he was quickly successful. In 1967, Johnson was painfully unable, because of Vietnam, to honor the commitment to Israel made by the Eisenhower administration in 1956–1957. The conditions of a possible U.S. unilateral action had been so drastically altered since that time that Israel was forced to resolve the situation itself and hope that the United States would support it ex post facto.

The very nature of this second characteristic of deterrence leads directly to the third proposition emphasized in deterrence theory. Since deterrence is heavily context dependent, *it is often difficult to design a strategy that will deter all options available to the dissatisfied power.* Thus, research on deterrence failures has indicated that states often have multiple options available for challenging a status quo situation and manage to find one with which to probe and exploit a loophole in the deterrence strategy aimed at them. When the Quadruple Alliance was formalized in 1815, it was intended to prevent a revolutionary France from upsetting the European status quo. Little did the signatories guess that by 1823 France would have become one of the most reactionary powers in Europe and would be desirous of invading Spain to suppress a liberal revolt. It is no wonder that the Quadruple Alliance had difficulty deciding on the proper course of action. Likewise, the Allied attempts to deter Germany from attacking Poland were based on the assumptions that Hitler did not want a general European war with the possibility of a hostile Soviet Union at his rear and that if war did come, Poland would be able to resist long enough for the French army to make itself felt. Hitler circumvented these problems by signing a previously inconceivable nonaggression pact with the Russians and by overrunning Poland in a matter of weeks, not months. Despite all its diplomatic efforts, the United States was unable to guarantee Israel's security from a variety of Arab threats ranging from economic blockade to terrorist attacks to full-scale offensives by conventional forces. It can thus be seen that in each of the three cases studied, the deterring powers found themselves forced to reevaluate their commitments as the dissatisfied powers altered their strategies in accordance with perceived weaknesses in these commitments.

Still another point emphasized by the theory is that *deterrence often fails in stages* rather than all at once. Each of the three cases illustrates this point. The difference of interests among the members of the Quadruple Alliance manifested itself slowly in the series of European conferences conducted after 1815. In 1939, the Allies had several clear warnings of the impending collapse of their position in Poland, namely, the change in Nazi rhetoric, the Pact of Steel between Germany and Italy, and the dismissal of Litvinow by the Russians. Nasser's step-by-step occupation of the Sinai in 1967 represents an almost classic example of a commitment failing in stages. At each stage, the United States proved powerless to honor its commitments, and Nasser became bolder with each success. Even in 1973, the evacuation of Russian noncombatants forty-eight hours prior to the Egyptian attack provided Israel and U.S. intelligence with a warning (though it was not recognized as such) of the invasion to follow. The usual deterrence commitment, then, does not collapse all at once like a house of cards, but rather weakens slowly like a dike being worn away by the sea. The key question is whether or not the deterring power has the perception, the will, or the capability to shore up its commitment before it is too late.

The three cases as well as many others that have been studied illustrate the final proposition emphasized in modern deterrence theory—that *deterrence is often at best a time-buying strategy*—and as such it is only one instrument of foreign policy and not a substitute for a creative approach that also relies on other means. The Allied powers in 1815 clearly recognized this fact when, at the Congress of Vienna, they allowed for the rapid rehabilitation of France in the international system and established their deterrence commitments accordingly. By reintegrating France and establishing the concert of Europe, the members of the Vienna Congress laid the groundwork for a system that prevented a major war in Europe until 1854. This was truly a successful application of the strategy of deterrence in conjunction with other diplomatic means.

The same cannot be said for the Versailles Conference that met after the First World War. In their efforts to deter Germany from further aggression and to isolate the Soviet Union in order to prevent the spread of communism, the Allied powers created two "pariah" nations that would later combine to thwart the deterrent provisions of the Versailles Treaty and eventually conclude the 1939 Nazi-Soviet Pact, which would make the Second World War virtually inevitable.

In the Mideast, the United States, as a result of two Arab–Israeli wars that led to superpower confrontations, finally realized the necessity of doing more in the region than supplying arms to Israel and countering Soviet actions with threats. The peace treaty between Egypt and Israel concluded under U.S. auspices at Camp David in 1978 marked a significant step toward a resolution of the Arab–Israeli conflict which, it was hoped, would eventually obviate the need for further U.S. deterrence commitments to Israel. However, these hopes were shattered by subsequent developments, in particular the Israeli invasion of Lebanon in 1982. Several efforts by the United States to revive and broaden the peace process proved to be abortive. Finally, in the closing days of his administration, President Reagan decided to initiate diplomatic contact with representatives of the Palestine Liberation Organization (PLO) in return for a statement by its leader, Yasir Arafat, acknowledging Israel's existence as a state. In the early days of his administration, President Bush initiated a policy of encouraging both sides to undertake small steps of a confidence-building nature that might pave the way for eventual negotiations. The peace process lagged, however, until the aftermath of the Cold War, and the Gulf War created new opportunities that led in 1993 to an agreement for partial Palestinian autonomy in Gaza and Jericho.

Bibliographical Essay

The general theory of deterrence on which this chapter draws is to be found in Alexander L. George and Richard Smoke, *Deterrence in American Foreign Policy: Theory and Practice* (New York, 1974). Some of the most useful discussions are Bernard Brodie, *Strategy in the Missile Age* (Princeton, 1959), chap. 9; Karl W. Deutsch, *The Analysis of International Relations,* 2d ed. (Englewood Cliffs, N.J., 1978), pp. 154–161; Robert Jervis, "Deterrence Theory Revisited," *World Politics* 31 (1979): 289–324; Stephen Maxwell, *Rationality in Deterrence,* Adelphi Paper no. 50 (London: International Institute for Strategic Studies, August 1968); Patrick M. Morgan, *Deterrence: A Conceptual Analysis* (Beverly Hills, Calif., 1977); John Raser, "Theories of Deterrence" [special issue], *Peace Research Reviews* 3 (1969); and Thomas C. Schelling, *The Strategy of Conflict* (Cambridge, Mass., 1960), especially chaps. 2, 3, 5, and 8.

How to conceptualize deterrence theory and how to evaluate the effectiveness of deterrence strategy continue to be subjects of lively controversy. Important recent contributions to this scholarly discussion include Richard Ned Lebow, *Between Peace and War: The Nature of International Crisis* (Baltimore, 1981); Robert Jervis, Richard Ned Lebow, and Janice Gross Stein, *Psychology and Deterrence* (Baltimore, 1985); Paul K. Huth and Bruce M. Russett, "What Makes Deterrence Work? Cases from 1900 to 1980," *World Politics* (July 1985); Paul K. Huth, *Extended Deterrence and the Prevention of War* (New Haven, 1986); Robert Jervis, "War and Misperception," *Journal of Interdis-*

ciplinary History 18, no. 4 (Spring 1988); Paul K. Huth and Bruce M. Russett, "Deterrence Failure and Crisis Escalation," *International Studies Quarterly* (March 1988); Jack Levy, "Quantitative Studies of Deterrence Success and Failure," in *Perspectives on Deterrence,* ed. Paul C. Stern, Robert Axelrod, Robert Jervis, and Roy Radner (New York, 1989); Richard Ned Lebow and Janice Gross Stein, "Deterrence: The Elusive Dependent Variable," *World Politics* 42, no. 3 (April 1990); Paul K. Huth and Bruce M. Russett, "Testing Deterrence Theory: Rigor Makes A Difference," *World Politics* 42, no. 4 (July 1990); and two lively symposia on deterrence in *Journal of Social Issues* 43, no. 4 (1988), and *World Politics* (January 1989).

Nuclear deterrence strategy has been the subject of numerous critical assessments, all of them hampered by lack of good data on the impact that nuclear threats have had on intended targets. A balanced, sophisticated analysis of available data for a variety of historical cases is provided by Richard K. Betts, *Nuclear Blackmail and Nuclear Balance* (Washington, D.C., 1987). That a compelling desire to avoid escalation to nuclear war has more influence on statesmen caught in crises than do nuclear threats or the nuclear balance is persuasively argued, without being oversimplified, by McGeorge Bundy, *Danger and Survival: Choices About the Bomb in the First Fifty Years* (New York, 1988).

In the 1980s a large number of well-informed analysts, Soviet as well as American, expressed grave concern that strategic nuclear deterrence, quite stable in peacetime, would prove to be highly unstable in the event of another major diplomatic crisis involving the United States and the Soviet Union and might accidentally lead to war. Their concern focused on developments in nuclear weapons, force deployments, warning and alert systems, and vulnerabilities in command and control systems. Among the contributions to this literature are John D. Steinbruner, "Launch Under Attack," *Scientific American,* January 1984; Paul Bracken, *The Command and Control of Nuclear Forces* (New Haven, 1983); Bruce G. Blair, *Strategic Command and Control: Redefining the Nuclear Threat* (Washington, D.C., 1985); Kurt Gottfried and Bruce G. Blair, eds., *Crisis Stability and Nuclear War* (New York, 1988); Ashton B. Carter, John D. Steinbruner, and Charles A. Zraket, eds., *Managing Nuclear Operations* (Washington, D.C., 1987); and Richard Ned Lebow, *Nuclear Crisis Management: A Dangerous Illusion* (Ithaca, N.Y., 1987).

15

Coercive Diplomacy

The strategy of coercive diplomacy (or *compellance,* as some prefer to call it) employs threats or limited force to persuade an opponent to call off or undo an encroachment—for example, to halt an invasion or give up territory that has been occupied. Coercive diplomacy therefore differs from the strategy of deterrence, discussed in the preceding chapter; whereas deterrence represents an effort to dissuade an opponent from undertaking an action that *has not yet been initiated,* coercive diplomacy attempts to reverse actions which *have already been undertaken* by the adversary.

Coercive diplomacy needs to be distinguished from pure coercion. It seeks to *persuade* the opponent to cease his aggression rather than bludgeon him into stopping. In contrast to the crude use of force to repel the opponent, coercive diplomacy emphasizes the use of threats and the exemplary use of limited force to persuade him to back down. The strategy of coercive diplomacy calls for using just enough force to demonstrate resolution to protect one's interests and to emphasize the credibility of one's determination to use more force if necessary. In coercive diplomacy, one gives the opponent an opportunity to stop or back off before employing force or escalating its use, as the British did in the early stages of the Falklands dispute in 1982. To this end, the employment of threats and of initially limited force is closely coordinated with appropriate communications to the opponent. Even more so than with deterrence strategy important signaling, bargaining, and negotiating dimensions are built into the strategy of coercive diplomacy.

Coercive diplomacy offers the possibility of achieving one's objective economically, with little bloodshed, fewer political and psychological costs, and often with much less risk of escalation than does traditional military strategy. For this reason, it is often a beguiling strategy. Leaders of militarily powerful countries—like Lyndon Johnson, for example, in his unsuccessful use of air power against Hanoi in 1965—are tempted to believe that they can, with little risk to themselves, intimidate weaker opponents to give up their gains and objectives. If the opponent refuses to be threatened and, in effect, calls the bluff of the coercing power, the latter must then decide whether to back off himself or to escalate the use of force.

It is important to identify the conditions necessary for successful employment of this strategy, since in their absence even a superpower can fail to intimidate a weak opponent and find itself drawn into a costly, prolonged conflict. Comparison of cases of successful coercive diplomacy (for example, the Cuban missile crisis) and unsuccessful ones (for example, the U.S. effort to coerce Japan prior to its attack on Pearl Harbor) has enabled researchers to identify a number of such conditions. Three in particular appear to be of critical importance: the coercing power must create in the opponent's mind a sense of urgency for compliance with its demand, a belief that the coercing power is more highly motivated to achieve its stated demand than the opponent is to oppose it, and a fear of unacceptable escalation if the demand is not accepted. We must recognize that what one demands of the opponent can affect the balance of motivation. If one demands a great deal, the opponent's motivation not to comply will likely be strengthened. But if the coercing power can carefully limit its demands to what is essential to itself without thereby engaging important interests of the opponent, then it is more likely to create an asymmetry of motivation that favors the success of the strategy.

The essentials and drawbacks of the strategy of coercive diplomacy have long been known, although its use in the European balance-of-power era was evidently not systematically articulated. Rather, it was part of the conventional wisdom of those who engaged in statecraft and diplomacy. Properly analyzed, however, older historical cases of coercive diplomacy can contribute to a more refined understanding of the uses and limitations of this strategy as an instrument of foreign policy.

Coercive diplomacy bears a close resemblance to the ultimata that were often employed in the conduct of European diplomacy. A full-blown ultimatum has three components: a specific, clear demand on the opponent; a time limit for compliance; and a threat of punishment for noncompliance which is both credible and sufficiently potent to impress upon the opponent that compliance is preferable. These three components are not always fully present in efforts at coercive diplomacy. The demand on the opponent, for example, may lack clarity or specificity. It may not be accompanied by a specific time limit for compliance, and the coercing power may fail to convey a sense of urgency. The threat of punishment for noncompliance may be ambiguous, of insufficient magnitude, or lacking in credibility. Generally speaking, dilution of any of these three components in the ultimatum may weaken its impact on the other actor's calculations and behavior.

There are several variants of coercive diplomacy. In addition to the full-ultimatum version of the strategy already mentioned, there is what has been called the "try-and-see" approach. In this variant of the strategy, only the first element of an ultimatum, a specific and clear demand, is conveyed, and the coercing power does not announce a time limit or attempt to create a strong sense of urgency for compliance. The try-and-see form is not uncommon; a coercing power often shies away from employing the ultimatum form for one reason or another. Instead, it takes one limited action, as the United States did in attempting to pressure Japan for several years before Pearl Harbor, and waits to see whether it will suffice to persuade the opponent before threatening or taking the next step. There are several variants of the try-and-see strategy. In some circumstances, as in two of the historical cases we shall examine later in this chapter, a gradual "turning of the screw" may be more appropriate than the ultimatum form.

Systematic study of cases of coercive diplomacy has shown that this strategy, perhaps even more so than deterrence strategy, is highly context-dependent. This means that the strategy must be tailored in a rather exacting way to fit the unique configuration of each situation. But the special configuration of a crisis in which coercive diplomacy may be employed is seldom clearly visible to the policy maker and, as a result, the strategy can easily fail. For this and other reasons, as our historical studies will suggest, efforts to engage in coercive diplomacy rest heavily upon skill at improvisation. The actor employing coercive diplomacy must continually evaluate the risks of what he is doing. He must slow the momentum of events as necessary in order to give the opponent time to digest the signals sent him. He has to choose and time his actions carefully to make them compatible with the opponent's ability to appraise the evolving situation and to respond appropriately, and he must always leave him with a way out of the crisis. As these remarks suggest, coercive diplomacy includes some of the important requirements of crisis management, a topic that will be taken up in the next chapter.

Generally speaking, the strategy of coercive diplomacy is in fact more difficult and problematical than is often thought to be the case. Leaders who consider using the strategy against opponents enroaching on their country's interests often erroneously assume that prevailing conditions favor its successful use, that the communication of their demands and threats will be clear and credible to the opponent, and that they are more highly motivated by what is at stake than the opponent. Practitioners of coercive diplomacy also often mistakenly rely solely on threats of punishment for noncompliance with their demands instead of offering incentives for compliance as well. They fail to recognize as clearly as President Kennedy did in the Cuban missile crisis that the objectives on behalf of which coercive diplomacy is exercised can sometimes be achieved only if one makes genuine, even substantial concessions. It will be recalled that Kennedy and Khrushchev did negotiate and agree upon a quid pro quo which ended the missile crisis, Khrushchev agreeing to remove the missiles and bombers in return for Kennedy's pledge not to invade Cuba. Coercive diplomacy, then, is best conceived as a flexible strategy in which what the stick cannot always achieve by itself one can possibly obtain by adding a carrot. Thus, as already noted, in contrast to pure coercion, coercive diplomacy typically requires negotiation, bargaining, and compromise.

To demonstrate coercive diplomacy in practice, three case studies will be briefly outlined and the causes of its successful or unsuccessful application evaluated. The first case, the American effort to coerce Japan between 1938 and 1941, illustrates how an overly ambitious use of the strategy boomeranged and led to the Japanese attack on Pearl Harbor. The second case documents and analyzes the successful use of coercive diplomacy by President Kennedy in the Cuban missile crisis of 1962 which enabled him to strike a deal with Nikita Khrushchev to remove his missiles from Cuba. The third case analyzes the failure of the very strong variant of the strategy President Bush employed to pressure Saddam Hussein to remove his troops from Kuwait in 1991. As these cases will show, coercive diplomacy strategy is highly context dependent; careful consideration must always be given to the circumstances, known and unknown to the actors involved, contributing to the course of events in each case. The warning suggested by these case studies is clear. Success in the application of coercive diplomacy is not easily achieved. Disaster is always a single bad decision away.

U.S. Policy Toward Japan, 1938–1941

Between 1938 and 1940, Japanese expansion into China proceeded in earnest and became increasingly worrisome to the United States. The United States responded first with a policy of deterrence to dissuade further Japanese advances. In time, however, Washington added a very strong variant of coercive diplomacy in an effort to reverse previous Japanese advances.

War in China represented a heavy commitment of men, resources, and prestige on the part of the Japanese. Their stated ambition was the creation of a "greater East Asia co-prosperity sphere." Aggressive and militaristic policies demonstrated a fundamental belief in Japanese destiny. U.S. interests in China were minor in comparison and lacked the driving force that characterized Japanese actions. Moreover, the ability of the American government to make strong signals of displeasure and warning to Japan was limited by domestic politics. And, in any case, the strength and credibility of objections to Japanese violations of certain treaties and international laws were severely diluted by American policies of isolationism and "correct" neutrality.

Despite these domestic constraints, the United States eventually responded to Japanese expansion with an embargo on certain military goods and a cancellation of credits in 1939. Later that year, the Japanese–American commercial treaty of 1911 was abrogated. These measures were meant to restrain Japan and moderate its policies in Asia. However, this policy of coercion through economic punishment was not precise and did not make clear to the Japanese what the next step might be. Cordell Hull, the American secretary of state, was reluctant to stop all trade with Japan in order to maintain leverage but would not specify how he expected to use this weapon in the future. Despite these early pressures, clear communication of a firm U.S. commitment to back rhetorical demands on Japan was lacking, and the Japanese leaders were entitled to believe that they were more strongly motivated to resist U.S. demands than U.S. leaders were to enforce them. The stake in the conflict of interests in Asia was clearly greater for Japan than for the United States. Minor efforts were made to avoid flagrant antagonism of the Americans, but the Japanese continued their policy of military expansion so that, by 1940, the Dutch East Indies and French Indochina were threatened.

The United States continued to send conflicting signals, containing elements of both a hard and a moderate line, for some time, reflecting a lack of consensus among policy makers in Washington. Meanwhile, economic sanctions were increased by selective embargo. By mid-1940, moderate voices in the U.S. government were largely silenced by a general dissatisfaction with the evident failure of limited measures. During that summer, more severe embargoes were imposed. Having been presented with few concrete demands, the Japanese were somewhat startled by the avalanche of new economic hardships that now faced them. Rather than make compliance more attractive, however, the new American policy of stepped-up pressures boomeranged, making the Japanese government only more determined to acquire secure and independent sources of raw materials and weakening the moderates within the Japanese cabinet. The new U.S. threat to escalate pressures confirmed Tokyo's worst fears about the future and prompted a faster pace of expansion. It seemed certain in Tokyo that the United States did not want war with Japan and would not easily be driven into one, especially as the war in Europe accelerated and turned against the Allies resisting Hitler. The embargo of needed materials was interpreted as a challenge, not a warning, a challenge that would not be backed up by the United States. The fact that Japan had imposed similar embargoes to protect its own warmaking potential was ignored, and hardliners in Tokyo denounced each new American restriction as unwarranted and a sign of bad faith.

On 27 September 1940, Japan joined the Tripartite Pact, allying itself with Germany and Italy and thereby conveying a counterwarning to the United States against further interference in Asia. Japan derived few concrete benefits from the alliance, but in the United States it fostered new anxieties, linking Japan with aggression elsewhere. Nevertheless, the American government was not prepared for direct confrontation with Japan and continued a policy of weak countermeasures and uncompromising demands. Negotiations proved fruitless, each power resolutely demanding total concession. A critical turning point that severely escalated the diplomatic confrontation occurred on 25 July 1941, when the United States imposed a total embargo on oil and froze Japanese assets in American banks. U.S. strength and resolve were on the increase, and the threat of escalation was now clear. In November, Japan was presented with demands that included withdrawal from all occupied territories, repudiation of the Tripartite Pact, and an end to expansion. Faced with visions of economic strangulation, Japan chose the alternative, war with the United States. Pearl Harbor was, in this sense, a rational response to the choice posed by the American ultimatum, for the alternative—acceptance of U.S. demands—was even more unpalatable than war with a stronger opponent, the outcome of which was uncertain.

The Japanese decision was not a hasty one, but evolved as a product of cabinet and domestic politics. By September 1941, plans for war had turned to rehearsals, and October was established as the time for decision. In mid-October, the Konoye cabinet fell, and General Tojo became prime minister. Although the deadline had been reached, the new government elected to continue to seek an alternative to what would certainly be a dangerous war. The tightening restrictions on Japan's oil supply, however, had imposed a time limit for adopting a military option. As supplies diminished, the chances that war could be sustained until independent sources were secured grew smaller. So far, Roosevelt had refused to make a firm commitment to respond to a Japanese attack on British and Dutch possessions in the Pacific, but the risk that such an attack would trigger U.S. military intervention seemed to require a preemptive attack on American means to do so. On 5 November, the new Japanese cabinet resolved to stake everything on their last set of proposals. Cordell Hull was presented with them on 20 November. Two days later, Admiral Yamamoto was directed to assemble the Japanese fleet on 3 December. The U.S. ultimatum on 26 November, demanding that Japan surrender its position of power in Asia after years of investing resources and prestige in a policy of expansion, made the outcome certain. On 1 December at 2:00 P.M. Tokyo time, the imperial council made the decision for war.

The American failure to clarify and, particularly, to limit policy objectives from the beginning enormously strengthened Japanese motivation not to comply. Unable to understand that Japan would not suddenly reverse long-held values and beliefs and agree under pressure to dismantle ten years of expansion, the U.S. government simply reinforced Japanese attitudes about the world. And by initiating a complete embargo of American oil, Washington in effect gave Japan an eighteen-month deadline for the achievement of petroleum self-sufficiency.

The few carrots offered by the United States to encourage compliance with its demands—most-favored-nation status and a mutual nonaggression treaty—did not affect Japan's motivation or its analysis of costs and benefits. The only Japanese counterproposal—an offer to withdraw from Indochina upon the conclusion of the war with China if the United States would support both a negotiated settlement that favored Japan and the restoration of full Japanese–American relations—was bluntly rejected in Washington, thereby preventing any chance of a compromise. The incorrect image of the Japanese position held by many top American decision makers prevented a more precise and calculated application of coercive diplomacy and doomed U.S. policy to failure. The situation developed its own dynamics beyond the control of either country, and war became inevitable.

The Cuban Missile Crisis

The Soviet deployment of medium-range ballistic missiles into Cuba during the late summer and early fall of 1962 triggered the most dangerous crisis of the Cold War. A peaceful outcome was possible because, instead of resorting to military action to destroy the missiles, President Kennedy decided to try the strategy of coercive diplomacy in an effort to induce Khrushchev to remove them. Although the naval blockade that the United States put into effect could prevent additional missiles and military equipment from reaching Cuba, it obviously could not remove the missiles that had already arrived and were being made operational. It was Kennedy's hope, however, that the blockade and preparations for a possible air strike or invasion of Cuba would demonstrate his resolution and exert enough pressure to induce Khrushchev to remove the missiles.

But would the Soviet leader challenge the naval blockade which he denounced as an "act of war"? Would Soviet vessels and submarines attempt to pass through the blockade line and, if so, might this lead to a shooting war on the high seas or escalation elsewhere? There was no assurance that coercive diplomacy was a viable strategy or that it could be applied without setting into motion developments that would lead to war.

Kennedy initially employed a relatively weak "try-and-see" approach. He deliberately slowed implementation of the blockade, subdividing it into a series of small steps. And although the coercive impact of the try-and-see strategy was strengthened because the blockade was accompanied by an ominous build-up of U.S. military forces, the president deliberately steered clear, during the first five days of the confrontation, of giving Khrushchev a time limit for compliance with his demand for removal of the missiles and backing it with an explicit threat of an air strike or invasion for noncompliance.

In employing coercive diplomacy the president had to engage in careful crisis management, hoping that Khrushchev would do the same so that they could together try to end the confrontation before it escalated to war. Indeed, the president carefully observed relevant crisis management principles, as is noted in chapter 16 on crisis management.

As for Khrushchev, even though he blustered and issued coercive threats of his own in an effort to undermine Kennedy's resolve, he nonetheless went to great lengths to avoid a clash at sea. Within hours after Kennedy announced the blockade on Monday evening, 22 October, and well before Washington became aware of it, Khrushchev directed Soviet vessels carrying missiles and other military equipment to Cuba to turn back immediately. Other Soviet vessels carrying nonmilitary cargo temporarily halted and later resumed movement toward the blockade line to test and, if possible, weaken Kennedy's resolution to implement it. In addition, the Soviet leader placed heavy reliance, but to no avail, on efforts to persuade the president and the world of the legitimacy of his military assistance to Cuba and his claim that the missiles were "defensive."

Thus, both Khrushchev and Kennedy behaved with sober prudence and reasonable skill to extricate themselves from the war-threatening crisis. The danger of escalation to war did indeed cast an ominous pall over crisis developments. But although both leaders attempted to gain advantage through crisis bargaining and although their behavior evoked concern that they might be about to embark on a dangerous game of chicken on the high seas, in fact neither Kennedy nor Khrushchev engaged in a reckless competition in risk-taking but acted cautiously to avoid escalation.

Once the danger of a clash on the high seas was safely managed, however, U.S. and Soviet cooperation in managing the crisis began to break down. On Saturday morning, 27 October, which was to become the last day of the confrontation, both leaders suddenly experienced disturbing new challenges to their ability to control escalation. A startling lack of synchronization in the interaction between the two sides emerged. The context and meaning of possibly critical moves and communications became confusing; deciphering the intentions and calculations behind specific moves of the opponent became difficult. Policy makers in Washington puzzled over the discrepancy between Khrushchev's personal and emotional private letter of Friday evening, in which he hinted at a deal for withdrawal of the missiles in return for a U.S. pledge of noninvasion of Cuba, and his more formal letter of Saturday morning that advanced the additional demand for removal of U.S. Jupiter missiles from Turkey. Other disturbing events occurred on Saturday. A U-2 spy plane was shot down over Cuba; two other U.S. reconnaissance aircraft were shot at by Cuban air defense forces as they swooped low over the missile sites; a U.S. reconnaissance plane wandered over Siberia; reports came in that Soviet consulate personnel were burning classified papers. Confused by these developments, U.S. policy makers anxiously speculated that the Kremlin was now taking a harder line and was determined to test U.S. resolution, that Khrushchev was no longer in charge, or that Moscow was trying to extract a higher price for removal of the missiles.

The president and his advisers worried that the downing of the U-2 portended a major escalation of the crisis. Kennedy momentarily withstood pressures within his advisory group to retaliate via an air strike against a Soviet surface-to-air missile site in Cuba. But it was clear that U-2 reconnaissance flights over Cuba would have to continue in order to monitor activity at the missile sites and that if another U-2 were shot down, a development which had to be expected, the president could not continue to hold off reprisal. What would happen thereafter, he feared, could lead to uncontrollable military escalation.

A new sense of urgency to end the crisis emerged since it could be only a matter of days before another U-2 was shot down. An immediate effort to end the crisis before it went out of control was deemed necessary. To this end the president was finally ready, indeed now felt compelled, to strengthen coercive pressure on Khrushchev. But at the same time Kennedy believed it was necessary to couple the additional pressure with concessions to make it easier for the Soviet leader to agree to remove the missiles.

Two important changes now took place in the president's strategy of coercive diplomacy. He finally converted his try-and-see approach into a virtual ultimatum. But at the same time he made the ultimatum part of a carrot-and-stick, adding concessions he had earlier refused to discuss. The president responded positively to the hint that Khrushchev had conveyed in his Friday letter that a U.S. pledge not to invade Cuba be given in return for removal of the missiles, and added to it a secret agreement to remove U.S. Jupiter missiles from Turkey. At the same time Kennedy conveyed the equivalent of an ultimatum by having his brother warn Soviet ambassador Dobrynin that the president had to have Khrushchev's acceptance of this offer within twenty-four hours because he would not be able to hold off taking stronger action much longer. The substance of this time-urgent ultimatum was conveyed in other ways as well; preparations for an invasion of Cuba had been completed on the same day, and Soviet and Cuban intelligence appear to have warned Moscow that American military action was imminent.

Disturbing developments of Saturday, 27 October, had a profoundly unsettling effect on Khrushchev as well, in particular the U-2 shooting, which Soviet commanders in Cuba undertook without an explicit order from Moscow to do so. Evidently Khrushchev, too, feared that the crisis was getting out of control and that American military action could be expected shortly. Within a few hours he accepted Kennedy's formula for settling the crisis.

The strategy of coercive diplomacy, therefore, eventually did work in this case. It worked because Kennedy limited his objective and the means he employed on its behalf. Whether it would have worked had Kennedy not made the concessions he did is arguable. Adherence to crisis management principles by both sides was of critical importance. Critical, too, was Kennedy's success in convincing Khrushchev that the United States was more highly motivated by what was at stake than the Soviet Union—that is, that it was more important to the United States to get the missiles out of Cuba than it was to the Soviet Union to keep them there—and that he had the resolution to achieve that objective.

A number of other factors also contributed to the peaceful resolution of this crisis. The image of thermonuclear war shared by the two leaders created powerful incentives on both sides to manage and terminate the crisis peacefully. Opportunities for avoiding escalation were available; they were highly valued and carefully cultivated by both leaders. The two leaders operated with sufficient understanding of the requirements of crisis management and with adequate skill to bring the confrontation to a close without being drawn into a war. However, several serious threats to effective crisis management did occur. Foremost among them were the downing of the U-2 and aggressive antisubmarine activities of the U.S. Navy, which pursued all five Soviet submarines in the area and forced them to surface, an activity that might have led to serious incidents between the forces. Under different circumstances either of these two developments might have triggered escalation to a war.

Finally, we must note that the images Kennedy and Khrushchev held of each other played an important role in the inception and resolution of the crisis. Just as Khrushchev's *defective* image of Kennedy—as a young, inexperienced leader who could be pushed around and who was too weak or too "rational" to risk war to get the missiles out—played a role in his decision to deploy the missiles, so did Kennedy's *correct* image of Khrushchev as a rational, intelligent man who would retreat if opposed resolutely and given sufficient time play a critical role in the president's choice of the strategy of coercive diplomacy and his determination to give it a chance to succeed.

One would like to believe that fateful questions of war and peace are not influenced by subjective, psychological variables of this kind. However, a full understanding of the missile crisis is not possible without taking into account the personalities of the two leaders and the personal aspects of their interaction.

The Persian Gulf Crisis

Following the unexpected and shocking Iraqi invasion and quick overrunning of Kuwait in early August 1990, President Bush was able to put together a multinational coalition of states that opposed Saddam Hussein's blatant aggression and to obtain a series of Security Council resolutions designed to force Iraq out of Kuwait.

At first, the U.S.-led coalition backed its demand that Iraqi forces get out of

Kuwait by imposing economic sanctions and by progressively tightening the embargo on Iraq's imports and exports. This is an example of the variant of coercive diplomacy that has been labeled a gradual turning of the screw. The threat of resorting to military force remained in the background.

It was understood from the beginning that economic sanctions, even though unusually tight in this case, would require considerable time to achieve maximum effectiveness and that it was uncertain whether and when they might induce Hussein to comply with the UN demands. Whether the embargo, if given more time, might have succeeded became a controversial, divisive issue in the United States after the administration moved in November to secure a new Security Council resolution authorizing the use of military force at some point after 15 January and began to sound out Congress on the possibility of a similar congressional resolution. Washington also announced that an additional 200,000 soldiers would be sent to the Gulf to create an offensive option.

This development marked a significant shift in coercive diplomacy from a gradual turning of the screw via sanctions to an ultimatum backed by the threat of force. There were several reasons for this move to the stronger form of coercive diplomacy, among them the difficulty of making reliable intelligence estimates of the effect sanctions would have on Iraq's economy, and the administration's fear that the international coalition might not hold together over the long period required for the embargo to have its full effect. Moreover, the rationale for shifting to the ultimatum was strongly supported by personality assessments of Saddam Hussein that encouraged the belief that only an ultimatum backed by the threat of war had a chance of impressing him with the need to back down.

However, not all U.S. policy makers were sanguine that coercive diplomacy would be successful. Besides, some members of the administration, including perhaps President Bush and his national security adviser, Brent Scowcroft, believed that success in persuading Saddam Hussein to withdraw from Kuwait would be an unsatisfactory outcome to the crisis: it would leave him in power, his military forces intact, and Iraq free to pursue its military programs for development of weapons of mass destruction. From this standpoint, the failure of coercive diplomacy was acceptable, if not preferred, since it would provide an opportunity to use military force to remove Saddam from power, destroy his military forces, and end Iraq's weapons development programs.

The ultimatum type of coercive strategy the administration employed against Saddam was a diplomatic version of the well-known game of chicken. The United States deliberately set itself on a collision course with Hussein and tried to convince him that it had thrown away its steering wheel; therefore, a "crash" (that is, war) could be avoided only if he got off the road. To this end the administration repeatedly emphasized that it was embarked on an irreversible course, that the large offensive force being created in the Gulf could not be sustained for a long period and would have to be used sometime before the Muslim holiday of Ramadan in mid-March and certainly before the onset of the hot summer weather in the Gulf. Coupled with this scenario, the Bush administration insisted that there would be no negotiations, no weakening of UN demands, and no "rewards for aggression."

It would appear, however, that the administration ignored the fact that *both* sides can play the game of diplomatic chicken. As the 15 January deadline set by the Security Council resolution approached, some members of the administration showed signs of increasing perplexity and frustration at indications that Hussein would not back down and instead seemed bent on calling its bluff. The administration also became aware that Hussein had options—for example, beginning a partial withdrawal from Kuwait and calling for negotiations linking total withdrawal with conditions of his own—and that, if he chose to exercise such options either before or just after 15 January, he might well succeed in eroding the coercive pressure of the ultimatum and push the crisis into prolonged negotiations. Although earlier the administration had indicated it would not be in a hurry to initiate war after the 15 January deadline, President Bush eventually decided to do so as soon as possible after 15 January because he was concerned that Saddam might at any moment take seemingly conciliatory actions in order to trap the allied coalition into negotiations. Some members of the press referred to this as the administration's "nightmare scenario."

Why, then, did coercive diplomacy not work and war become necessary? Why did Saddam persist in his confrontational course in the face of the overwhelming military forces arrayed against him? Was the profile of him on which the policy of coercive diplomacy had been based incorrect? Or had Saddam been insufficiently impressed with the credibility and potency of the threat of war? In other words, had he miscalculated? The latter explanation was favored by some of those in the administration who had subscribed earlier to the view that Saddam was capable of retreat in the face of a threat to his survival. One of these persons was Dennis Ross, head of policy planning in the State Department. A more complex explanation was offered by Jerrold M. Post, a psychiatrist for many years within the government who specialized in the psychology of political leaders. (See Bibliographical Essay at end of chapter.)

As was noted earlier in the chapter, coercive diplomacy is an attractive, indeed sometimes a beguiling, strategy because it offers strong powers the possibility of achieving their objectives without war. But coercive diplomacy typically assumes a type of simple, uncomplicated rationality on the part of the opponent. The assumption on which coercive diplomacy is based is that if the opponent is rational, he will surely see that it is in his interest to back down. This assumption oversimplifies the roots of motivation and the considerations that may influence leaders who are the targets of coercive diplomacy. The assumption of rationality does not suffice to make a confident prediction as to what an opponent will do when subjected, as Hussein was, to an ultimatum. In this situation, one does not have to be irrational to refuse to knuckle under in the face of the threat of war. The assumption of rationality on which the strategy of coercive diplomacy relies must somehow take into account psychological, cultural, and political variables that can affect the opponent's response to an ultimatum.

The Persian Gulf case illustrates, then, the importance of working with an accurate profile of the adversary. But, it also shows the difficulty of fine-tuning the strategy so as to activate precisely the desired response. Even when an insightful, sophisticated psychological profile of the adversary is available, supplemented by a knowledge of the adversary's political culture and political system, and used appropriately in policy-making, there can be no guarantee of success. The adversary's reluctance to undertake a humiliating, costly retreat (one of the risks of an ultimatum) can activate psychological tendencies on his part to look for indications that the threat is not credible or that the coercing state lacks the political will to engage in a costly war. Similarly, if the adversary is prone to wishful thinking, his estimate of the relative military strength of the two sides will be distorted. As cognitive psychology has repeatedly and persuasively emphasized, a person tends to give greater, often uncritical weight to new information that supports an existing policy or preference and tends to discount evidence that challenges his existing preconceptions. As a result, the adversary may make critical miscalculations that feed on his distaste for drawing the conclusion that it is really in his best interest to meet the demands made on him. Such miscalculations can be abetted if the adversary entertains, as Saddam evidently did, an image of the coercing state as lacking the political will to engage in a tough battle in which it would have to take heavy casualties.

The failure of coercive diplomacy in the Gulf crisis also calls attention to the impact the adversary's self-image can have on his calculations and judgment when he is forced to decide whether to meet the demands made on him. That Saddam entertained an inflated image of himself as a heroic leader destined to transform the Arab world was known to those who have studied him. What was not anticipated was that Saddam's self-image may have been so magnified by developments during the crisis that retreating became more difficult for him.

In sum, the lesson is that the outcome of coercive diplomacy may depend on psychological, cultural, and political variables operating on the adversary, which may be difficult to foresee and to deal with in a way that ensures the success of the strategy.

The Gulf crisis was a tough case for coercive diplomacy for a number of other reasons as well which will be discussed in the conclusion of this chapter, which contrasts the Gulf and Cuban missile cases.

A final comment on the experience with coercive diplomacy in the Gulf crisis seems appropriate. The administration's willingness to contemplate use of force was a factor from an early stage in the crisis, when President Bush stated that Iraqi occupation of Kuwait was unacceptable. Thereafter, American policy was driven as much by the objective of creating and maintaining an international coalition under the aegis of the UN Security Council as it was by the desire to persuade Saddam Hussein to withdraw from Kuwait. Although the strategy of coercive diplomacy may have had little chance of success, the attempt to employ it in the hope of avoiding war was necessary for building and maintaining international and domestic support for the objective of liberating Kuwait. Ironically, the failure of coercive diplomacy was necessary to gain support for war when war became the last resort.

Analysis

American policy toward Japan in the years before Pearl Harbor failed for the fundamental reason that the core values held by the Japanese were nonnegotiable, and American demands merely increased their intransigence. It is sometimes assumed that the strategy of coercive diplomacy is certain to succeed if only the demand one makes on the opponent is backed by an unmistakably credible threat of severe punishment. The case of U.S.–Japanese relations leading to Pearl Harbor reveals that this is a dangerously oversimplified assumption. In fact, the oil embargo Washington imposed in July 1941 was so credible and so potent that it quickly provoked Japanese leaders into making a very difficult and desperate decision to initiate war unless the United States appreciably softened its extreme demands that Japan get out of China and, in effect, give up its aspirations for regional hegemony in Southeast Asia.

In reflecting on the nature of Japanese imperialistic ambitions and America's emerging conception of its own global interests and its strategic conceptions, one might conclude that a war between the two countries was inevitable and that historical developments leading to Pearl Harbor merely determined the timing and circumstances of such a war. Some would even argue that, however costly the war with Japan proved to be, it was necessary in order to eliminate Japan as a militaristic, imperialistic power. We need not debate this proposition here in order to call attention to the narrower set of lessons this case provides regarding problems that the strategy of coercive diplomacy can encounter and the conditions under which, instead of providing a peaceful alternative, the strong ultimatum variant of the strategy can boomerang and provoke war. Besides, it should be noted that at the beginning of their prolonged diplomatic crisis and for some time thereafter, neither Japanese nor American leaders believed that their disagreement would or should lead to war. Developments in U.S.–Japanese relations between 1938 and 1941 are replete with instances of misperception and miscalculation, failure to convey clear commitment and to

Table 1. *Six Variables That Help Explain Success or Failure of Coercive Diplomacy*

Variables That Favor Success of Coercive Diplomacy	Cuban Missile Crisis	Gulf Crisis
Non-zero-sum view of the conflict	+	−
Overwhelmingly negative image of war	+	−
Carrot as well as stick	+	−
Asymmetry of motivation favoring state employing coercive diplomacy	+	−
Opponent's fear of unacceptable "punishment" for noncompliance	+	−
No significant misperceptions or miscalculations	+	−

+ = variable present; − = variable absent.

send consistent signals, and inability to understand each other's perspective. The result was that the dispute assumed an escalatory dynamic beyond the control of either side, and war became inevitable.

Conclusion

Table 1 lists a number of variables that favor the success of coercive diplomacy or, by their absence, militate against it.

In the Cuban missile crisis Kennedy and Khrushchev could cooperate to avoid war because neither leader believed that their disagreement approximated a zero-sum (unconditional) contest, and because their image of war, should it occur, was that of a nuclear catastrophe. In contrast, President Bush and Saddam Hussein tended to see their conflict in unconditional terms, and this tendency was reinforced by the highly invidious image each had of the other. Moreover, unlike Kennedy and Khrushchev, who were horrified by the possibility that, if mismanaged, the crisis could lead to thermonuclear war, Bush and Saddam held an image of the outcome, costs, and consequences of war that was not distasteful enough to motivate them to seek a compromise settlement. Incentives for cooperating to avoid war were lacking on both sides. Indeed, it is not far-fetched to characterize the Bush administration's policy as coercive diplomacy without fear of the consequences of failure.

In the Cuban crisis, moreover, Kennedy coupled his ultimatum with a substantial carrot: an agreement not to invade Cuba and a secret agreement to remove the U.S. Jupiter missiles from Turkey. In the Gulf crisis Bush relied solely on the "stick" and offered no carrot for a compromise settlement, insisting that there be no reward for aggression, although the ingredients for face saving were available to Saddam. In the Cuban crisis, in contrast to the Gulf crisis, neither side had any significant misperceptions or miscalculations during the crisis that might have led to war. In the Cuban crisis, again unlike the Gulf case, Kennedy operated with an image of Khrushchev as a leader who was capable of retreating, which he was able to capitalize on in orchestrating an effective carrot-and-stick variant of the ultimatum.

Two other psychological variables that appear to have been important in past cases of coercive diplomacy were not present in the Gulf crisis. First, Kennedy succeeded in impressing Khrushchev that getting the missiles out of Cuba was more important to the United States than keeping the missiles there was to the Soviet Union. Evidently Bush did not succeed, despite considerable efforts, in convincing Saddam that getting Iraqi forces out of Kuwait was more important to the United States than refusing to remove them under threat of war was to Iraq. Second, Kennedy created fear of unacceptable escalation of the crisis in Khrushchev's mind, but Bush did not succeed in creating fear of unacceptable punishment in Saddam's mind for noncompliance with the ultimatum.

More generally, these cases and other recent efforts to make use of coercive diplomacy reflect the impact of many of the features of the diplomatic revolution described in this book. Bureaucratic decision making and the influence of domestic politics have become even stronger constraints at times on the ability of statesmen to exercise prudent judgment. The inability of major powers and the United Nations to keep weaker states in check is being repeatedly demonstrated in the post–Cold War era. Deterrence and coercive diplomacy encounter special difficulties in the increasing number of ethnic conflicts, such as those resulting from the breakup of Yugoslavia and the Soviet Union.

It is clear that advances in communications technology and intelligence gathering have not reduced the problems that diplomacy must deal with. The media, whose role in foreign affairs has been much enhanced, often control the attention of statesmen, shape their agenda, and influence their priorities. Under new circumstances, as the Bosnian case demonstrates, the requirements for coercive diplomacy become more difficult to satisfy and the limits of the strategy more evident.

Bibliographical Essay

The general theory of coercive diplomacy presented in this chapter draws from the original formulation of it in Alexander L. George, David K. Hall, and William E. Simons, *The Limits of Coercive Diplomacy* (Boston, 1971). Three historical cases were analyzed in that publication: the Laos crisis of 1960–1961, the Cuban missile crisis of 1962, and the abortive effort to use U.S. air power to coerce North Vietnam in 1965. Subsequent publication included four additional cases: the Pearl Harbor case, the Reagan administration's coercive pressures against Nicaragua and Libya, and the Bush administration's use of coercive diplomacy against Saddam Hussein in the Persian Gulf crisis. The three earlier cases have been updated. For a brief treatment of the seven cases, see A. L.

George, *Forceful Persuasion* (Washington, D.C., 1991). A fuller analysis of the seven cases and a refinement of the theory of coercive diplomacy appear in A. L. George and W. E. Simons, eds., *The Limits of Coercive Diplomacy,* 2d ed. (Boulder, Colo., 1994).

Other useful discussions are available in Paul Gordon Lauren, "Ultimata and Coercive Diplomacy," *International Studies Quarterly* 16 (1972): 131–165, and "Theories of Bargaining with Threats of Force: Deterrence and Coercive Diplomacy," in *Diplomacy: New Approaches in History, Theory, and Policy,* ed. Paul Gordon Lauren (New York, 1979); Thomas C. Schelling, *Arms and Influence* (New Haven, 1966); Glenn H. Snyder, "Crisis Bargaining," in *International Crises: Insights from Behavioral Research,* ed. Charles F. Hermann (New York, 1972); Glenn H. Snyder and Paul Diesing, *Conflict Among Nations* (Princeton, 1977); Charles Lockhart, *Bargaining in International Conflicts* (New York, 1979); Russell J. Leng, "When Will They Ever Learn: Coercive Bargaining in Recurrent Crises," *Journal of Conflict Resolution* (September 1983); Richard Ned Lebow, *Between Peace and War* (Baltimore, 1981), chaps. 8–10; and John Philip Rogers, "The Crisis Bargaining Code Model: The Influence of Cognitive Beliefs and Processes on U.S. Policymaking During Crises" (Ph.D. diss., University of Texas, 1986).

For the Pearl Harbor case, Scott Sagan provides a penetrating, well-documented analysis of policy-making in Japan and the United States that was critically influenced by cabinet and bureaucratic politics. Sagan also analyzes the interaction between the two powers that led to the Japanese war decision. See his "From Deterrence to Coercion to War: The Road to Pearl Harbor," in *Limits of Coercive Diplomacy,* ed. George and Simons, pp. 57–90. This case also receives admirable treatment in the well-respected work by Herbert Feis, *The Road to Pearl Harbor: The Coming of the War Between the United States and Japan* (Princeton, 1950). While this book provides an excellent starting point, the serious reader might try Nobutaka Ike, ed., *Japan's Decision for War* (Stanford, Calif., 1967), or P. W. Schroeder, *The Axis Alliance and Japanese-American Relations* (Ithaca, N.Y., 1958). For those interested in the Japanese perspectives and bureaucratic decision making in the prewar years, R. J. C. Butow, *Tojo and the Coming of the War* (Princeton, 1961), is also recommended, although U.S. policy is treated in a more peripheral fashion than in the other works. All these books can direct the reader to more technical or primary sources on the subject.

The Cuban missile crisis has spawned a vast literature in the past thirty years with no end in sight as new data continue to emerge. Early accounts, written mostly by members of the Kennedy administration or based on information from American sources generally gave highly favorable accounts of the president's conduct of the crisis. They were paralleled, however, by highly critical accounts by a number of revisionist scholars and journalists. In time, more balanced accounts have been published, but disagreements over important aspects of the crisis persist.

Among the major recent accounts of the crisis are Raymond L. Garthoff, *Reflections on the Cuban Missile Crisis,* rev. ed. (Washington, D.C., 1989); McGeorge Bundy, *Danger and Survival* (New York, 1988); James G. Blight and David A. Welch, *On the Brink* (New York, 1989); Richard Ned Lebow and Janice Gross Stein, *We All Lost the Cold War* (Princeton, 1994); Michael R. Beschloss, *The Crisis Years: Kennedy and Khrushchev, 1960–1963* (New York, 1991); James A. Nathan, ed., *The Cuban Missile Crisis Reconsidered* (New York, 1992); and James G. Blight and David A. Welch, eds., *Cuba on the Brink: Americans and Soviets Reexamine the Cuban Missile Crisis* (New York, 1989).

Perhaps the best depiction of the intense pressures and stresses experienced by President Kennedy's advisers during the crisis is Robert Kennedy's posthumously published account, *Thirteen Days* (New York, 1969). Important materials furnished by Soviet sources are contained in the books by Blight and Welch, Lebow and Stein, and Garthoff.

A thoroughly researched study of the recent Persian Gulf crisis cannot be expected for some time. A great deal is known about U.S. policy in this case but there is only informed speculation about Saddam Hussein's beliefs, expectations, and the bases for his decisions.

The account of the Gulf crisis described here draws mostly from the analysis in A. L. George, *Bridging the Gap: Theory and Practice* (Washington, D.C., 1993), chap. 7. An insightful, broader analysis of the case is provided by Richard Herrmann, "Coercive Diplomacy and the Crisis Over Kuwait," in *Limits of Coercive Diplomacy*, ed. George and Simons, pp. 229–26, which contains references to most of the existing sources.

For Dennis Ross's postwar reflections on why the effort to coerce Saddam Hussein failed, see the interview with him by David Hoffman, *Washington Post,* 28 October 1991. Dr. Jerrold M. Post's influential, widely circulated profile of Saddam Hussein was later published as "Saddam Hussein of Iraq: A Political Psychological Profile," *Political Psychology* 12, no.2 (1991): 279–289. See also Post's postwar reflection on why Saddam Hussein did not back down in "Afterword," *Political Psychology* 12, no. 4 (1992): 723–725.

16

Crisis Management

The history of relations among states is studded with innumerable diplomatic confrontations, some that were resolved peacefully and others that ended in war. Crises are generated by conflicts of interest that erupt into war-threatening situations either through the deliberate action of the parties involved or through inadvertence. In the ensuing crisis, policy makers are called upon to make delicate diplomatic and military decisions under the pressure of time and events. Such decisions may result not merely in success or failure for the nations they represent, but in the preservation or destruction of the existing international order.

We are interested here particularly in the phenomenon of *inadvertent war,* defined as a war that neither side wants or expects at the outset of a diplomatic crisis but one that nonetheless occurs during the course of the development of the crisis. This definition serves as a starting point for comparative analysis of diplomatic crises, some of which led to inadvertent war and others which did not. How does one account for the differences in the outcomes of such diplomatic disputes? To what extent does the ability or failure of the adversaries to apply principles of crisis management explain whether crises of this kind end up in war? What are the "principles" of crisis management?

Crisis management, a familiar phenomenon during the European balance-of-power era, took on a new urgency in the age of thermonuclear weapons. Shortly after the harrowing experience of the Cuban missile crisis, Secretary of Defense Robert McNamara remarked soberly, "Today there is no longer any such thing as military strategy; there is only crisis management." This was, to be sure, an overstatement, but it emphasized the critical role of the managerial aspect of the unprecedented Soviet–American confrontation of 1962.

The necessity and the modalities of effective crisis management did not emerge for the first time during the Cuban crisis. The two superpowers had already acquired considerable experience in controlling and managing tense situations in Berlin. It is nevertheless essentially correct to say that before Cuba, there was little in the way of an explicit theory of crisis management to guide policy makers who wanted to protect the national interest without becoming involved in a war. Robert F. Kennedy has written that shortly before the discovery of the missile sites, his brother had read Barbara Tuchman's book *The Guns of August,* which tells how Europe stumbled into war in 1914. It is possible that this helped alert him to the kinds of mistakes that can be made by statesmen at moments of high crisis. But certainly there was no handbook of management techniques to help the president.

Inspired by the Cuban experience, scholars and policy researchers have now studied the tasks and requirements of crisis management in considerable detail. Both within the government and in research institutes, crises that have occurred since World War II have been examined with an eye to the light they might throw upon problems of information processing and decision making under crisis conditions, on the special requirements of command and control, on the means of coordinating diplomatic and military actions, and on the problems of communication with an opponent during crises and the advisable methods of maintaining it.

Not all of this work (some of which remains highly classified) need or can be summarized here. For our purposes, it is enough to identify the general tasks and requirements of crisis management that have been emphasized by those who have studied it. Analysis of a number of crises—some successfully managed, like the Cuban missile crisis, and others not, like the outbreak of World War I and the Chinese intervention into the Korean War in 1950—supports the proposition that it facilitates management of a crisis if one or both sides limit the *objectives* they pursue in the confrontation and/or the *means* they employ in pursuing them. But it must also be noted that limitation of objectives and means will not suffice for managing a crisis without war. These studies indicate that *both* sides must understand the following requirements of crisis management and be willing and able to act in accordance with them:

1. *Maintain top-level civilian control of military options.* Of surpassing importance for crisis management is top-level civilian control over the selection and timing of military actions. This requirement may extend even to control over specific tactical maneuvers and operations that might lead to an undesired clash with the opponent's forces.
2. *Create pauses in the tempo of military actions.* The momentum of military movements may have to be deliberately slowed down in order to provide enough time for the two sides to exchange diplomatic signals and communications, and to give each side adequate time to assess the situation, make decisions, and respond to proposals.

3. *Coordinate diplomatic and military moves.* Whatever military moves are undertaken must be carefully coordinated with political-diplomatic actions and communications as part of a carefully integrated strategy for terminating the crisis acceptably without war.

4. *Confine military moves to those that constitute clear demonstrations of one's resolve and are appropriate to one's limited crisis objectives.*

5. *Avoid military moves that give the opponent the impression that one is about to resort to large-scale warfare and, therefore, force him to consider preemption.*

6. *Choose diplomatic-military options that signal a desire to negotiate rather than to seek a military solution.*

7. *Select diplomatic-military options that leave the opponent a way out of the crisis that is compatible with his fundamental interests.*

Both Kennedy and Khrushchev displayed a keen awareness of these requirements and regulated their behavior in accordance with them in the Cuban missile crisis. But the principles have not always been well understood by policy makers in other crises. President Truman, for example, failed to observe them when he dealt with the intervention of Chinese Communist forces into the Korean War in November 1950. In any case, mere awareness of the requirements of crisis management by no means assures that they will be effectively implemented. Leaders of one or both sides may have imperfect control over their military forces. Military forces may have been designed and structured in ways that rob them of the flexibility needed in a crisis. Military doctrine governing use of forces may, as in the events leading to the outbreak of World War I, which will be discussed later in this chapter, deprive governments of the kinds of limited mobilization and deployment options required for careful management.

It must be recognized that crisis management requires novel concepts of planning, control, and conduct of military operations and that these requirements may strain the experience, imagination, and patience of military professionals. The seven requirements for crisis management noted above impose stringent constraints on the use of military force and can easily lead to serious tensions between the military and political leaders of a nation. It is not easy to adapt military capabilities to meet these exacting requirements unless weapons systems possess flexible characteristics and unless planners are ingenious in contriving somewhat novel uses of existing forces. Moreover, options that meet these criteria and are therefore considered "usable" by a president who wants to manage the crisis effectively tend to be quickly used up. If the Cuban blockade had failed, there were few remaining options that President Kennedy could have used without triggering war. Efforts by strategists and civilian leaders to transform force into a highly refined, discriminating instrument that will support an assertive foreign policy and also be appropriate for crisis management eventually break down if pushed too far.

In sum, effective adherence to the principles of crisis management requires, among other things, appropriate military capabilities, doctrines, and options, effective command and control from top-level authorities to tactical units, intimate interaction between civilian and military planners in order to design usable options compatible with crisis-management requirements, and skill and flexibility in adapting contingency plans to unexpected developments as a crisis unfolds.

Utilizing the seven requirements of successful crisis management, it is possible to compare the relative performance of policy makers in different crises and to come to a deeper understanding of the impact of the diplomatic revolution on the management of crises in general. The three cases chosen—the Crimean War, World War I, and the 1973 Arab-Israeli War—are particularly significant in that their outcomes reflect directly not only the international community's ability to resolve conflict short of general war, but the more far-reaching question regarding the preservation or dissolution of the then current international system.*

The Crimean War, 1854

The origins of the crisis precipitating the Crimean War lay in the slow disintegration of the Ottoman Empire and the destabilizing effect this process was to have on the concert of Europe system established in 1815. Four of the five European powers—England, France, Russia, and Austria—possessed some vested interest in the affairs of the sultan's domain, while the fifth, Prussia, remained an interested observer. The Russians, led by an active Czar Nicholas, had long-standing concerns in the region that brought them into conflict on religious grounds with the France of Napoleon III, and on economic ones with an England that had been left divided politically by the acrimonius debate over the Corn Laws in 1846. Austria, although always interested in its Balkan frontier, was in the process of recovery from the divisive effects of the 1848 revolution, and its young emperor, Franz Joseph, was reluctant to engage in foreign adventure without a sure guarantee of success.

The same could not be said for the newly proclaimed emperor of the French, Napoleon III. Anxious to improve France's reputation abroad and his own at home, Napoleon in early 1852 pressured the sultan into a series of concessions concerning the rights of Roman Catholic orders in the holy lands. These con-

*The case studies in this chapter were prepared in their original form by Captain Richard J. Hoffman, U.S. Army.

cessions seemed to conflict with earlier privileges granted Greek Orthodox holy orders in 1740, and the czar, as protector of the Greek Orthodox faith, felt compelled to act in their defense. His initial action was to dispatch an envoy, Prince Menshikow, to demand, as he did with some arrogance, that Turkey reverse its earlier decision and give formal recognition to Russia's right to protect Orthodox believers in the Ottoman Empire. As a result of Menshikow's blunt negotiations, a decree apportioning religious rights in the holy lands was published on 4 May 1853. Unsatisfied, the czar sent Russian troops to occupy the Danubian Principalities with the intention of holding these Turkish dependencies until his original demands were met.

In doing so, Nicholas acted in the belief that Austria and England would support him. Austria, as a result of indecision in the ruling council, remained neutral. England, ruled by a coalition cabinet, pursued two policies simultaneously. The pro-Russian faction, headed by Prime Minister Aberdeen, sustained Nicholas in his belief. Unfortunately, the anti-Russian faction, led by the popular home secretary, Lord Palmerston, and assisted by an independently minded ambassador to Turkey, Stratford Canning, did its best to stir up opposition to the Russian move both at home and at the court of the sultan.

As the governments of Europe sought a solution to the deepening crisis, a council of ambassadors convened in Vienna in July 1853. The result of these consultations was the "Vienna Note" of 28 July 1853, which held the promise of acceding to Russia's demands while preserving Turkish sovereignty. At this juncture, Ambassador Canning intervened to persuade the Turks to reject the note and assured them that, should the situation require it, England would support Turkey with force. The sultan's ministers then demanded that the Russians withdraw from the principalities and, receiving no answer, declared war in October.

The first major action of the Russo-Turkish War was a naval battle at Sinope in the Black Sea on 30 November 1853, in which the Russians destroyed the totally outdated Turkish fleet. At this point, the czar attempted to resume negotiations, but events began to pass beyond his control. At home in England, Palmerston was using the power of a jingoistic press to whip the British public into a war frenzy over the alleged "massacre" at Sinope. Meanwhile, Canning, acting on his own authority, concentrated the British and—with the French now following the British lead—French fleets near the Dardanelles to stiffen the Turks and provide the opportunity for intervention. Despite the efforts of Aberdeen, Palmerston's exertions had the desired effect, and the British cabinet was forced to authorize the deployment of the combined fleets into the Black Sea in January 1854.

Taking this action as a *casus belli,* Nicholas broke relations with Britain and France in February 1854. In return, the two powers demanded evacuation of the principalities. When the czar failed to respond, Britain and France began hostilities in March, thus opening the Crimean War.

World War I

Like the Crimean War, the origin of the final crisis of 1914 lies in the disintegration of the Ottoman Empire and the repercussions this had on the international situation. The Europe of 1914 was very different, however, from the one of 1854. By 1914, the European concert of five great powers established in 1815 had been replaced by a bipolar arrangement of alliances. The states of Germany, Austro-Hungary, and Italy were committed to the Triple Alliance, while those of Britain, France, and Russia composed the Triple Entente. These alliance systems had by 1914 divided Europe into two heavily armed camps, in which the actions of any member of an alliance involved, by custom or commitment, the national interests of the other members.

In this tense international situation, the unsettled affairs in the Balkans had remained a festering sore since the Bosnian crisis of 1908. The Austrians remained convinced of the need to crush Serbia at the earliest possible opportunity. For their part, the Serbs fostered dreams of a Serbian-led Slav national state, and the Russians sought to advance their traditional interests at the Straits of the Dardanelles.

When Austrian Crown Prince Ferdinand and his wife were assassinated by Serbian terrorists on 28 June 1914, the policy makers in Vienna decided to use the event as a pretext for a permanent resolution of the Serbian problem. Their next prime concern was to secure German support for the operation in order to counterbalance the threat of Russian intervention. This they received on 5 July 1914 when the German kaiser in effect issued a blank check to the Austrian emperor to resolve the matter as he saw fit, assuring him of Germany's support. The Austrian response was a harsh ultimatum that they issued to the shocked Serbs on 23 July. The terms were such that compliance would deprive Serbia of independence. Under Russian pressure to compromise, the Serbians composed a masterful reply that acceded to most of the Austrian demands save the virtual occupation of Serbia. Unsatisfied, the Austrians commenced their preparations and declared war on Serbia on 28 July 1914.

With the reality of a Balkan war established, the focus of events now shifted to attempts to localize the conflict short of a general European conflagration. Although most of the powers involved recognized a need to accomplish this task, their alliance systems, war plans, and generally inept political leadership balked their efforts. On 29 July, the Russians made the first major attempt at limitation when, in response to the Austrian move, they announced a partial mobilization aimed only at war with Austria, in the hopes of keeping Germany out of the conflict. Their hopes were ill-founded, however, for despite the misgivings of the kaiser and the chancellor, Bethmann Hollweg, Chief of the General Staff Moltke was already contemplating Germany's mobilization against both Russia and its principal continental ally, France. Since German plans for a two-front war envisaged an initial attack on France through Belgium and since Britain was committed to the defence of Belgian neutrality, the stage was set for a war of global proportions.

The kaiser and chancellor tried on 30 July to hold off the now escalating crisis, but even as Bethmann Hollweg sought to restrain the Austrians short of war, the Austrian chief of staff, Conrad von Hötzendorf, was receiving a telegram from Moltke urging him to mobilize the Austrian army at once. The Austrian government gave orders to that effect on 31 July, and the Russians, their attempt at partial mobilization a failure, responded with a full call-up against Germany and Austria. On 31 July, the German government sent an ultimatum to Russia, demanding that this be halted. When the czar failed to comply, Moltke ordered German mobilization on 1 August, with a formal declaration of war against Russia following on the same day. Dismissing the kaiser's attempt to limit German mobilization to the Russian front as an invitation to disaster, and in any case impossible, Moltke secured the dispatch of an ultimatum to France and a diplomatic note to Belgium demanding free passage for German troops. When these demands were refused, Germany declared war on both countries on 3 August 1914 and began to invade Belgium. The British, honoring their public commitment to preserve Belgian neutrality and their private agreements with France, declared war on Germany on 4 August. Thus, by 4 August 1914, all the major European powers, save Italy, which had declared itself neutral on the grounds that Austria and Germany had initiated the conflict, were locked into what was to be the most devastating war the world had yet seen.

The 1973 Arab-Israeli War

Although the 1967 Arab–Israeli conflict seemed to have resulted in a resounding Israeli victory, its conclusion resulted in bitter antagonisms that were later to burst forth in more violence. By 1973, the Egyptians and Syrians had little to show for their efforts since the self-proclaimed "year of decision" in 1971. Both Arab states had been substantially supplied with up-to-date Russian military equipment and resolved to break the existing stalemate by force of arms.

The other powers involved in this Middle East dispute were, of course, the two superpowers, the United States and the USSR. For its part, Russia at first attempted to restrain the Arab states from overt military action through diplomatic efforts and a slowdown in the delivery of arms; later, the Soviet leaders reluctantly dropped their opposition to Arab use of force. The United States, led by its ubiquitous secretary of state, Henry Kissinger, pursued a policy of ''no war-no peace'' with the hopes of eventually ejecting the Soviet Union from the Middle East and assuming the role of moderator in the Arab–Israeli conflict.

Nevertheless, the stalemate ended abruptly on 6 October 1973, when the armed forces of Syria and Egypt launched coordinated offensives on the Golan and Sinai fronts, respectively. The Israelis, although not taken totally by surprise, were heavily outnumbered as a result of an internal decision not to mobilize until attacked. Consequently, the Arab forces scored tactical successes on both fronts, with the Egyptians eventually forcing the abandonment of the Bar-Lev fortified line along the Suez Canal. By 7 October, the Israeli army had stopped the Syrian attack, and by 8 October, it began to counterattack on the Sinai front as well. These attacks were not initially successful, but the pressure generated on the Arab armies was so severe that they appealed to Moscow for aid.

Although the Russians were at first wary of the Arabs' decision to resort to force, the actions of their clients placed them in an unenviable position. To refuse the request for aid would jeopardize their entire position in the Middle East, while to grant it would risk the possible escalation of the conflict. In response to this problem, the Russians began a massive airlift of military supplies on 10 October and dispatched Premier Kosygin to Cairo on 16 October to observe the situation at first hand. By 18 October, it had become apparent that the course of the war was turning against the Egyptians, and Sadat authorized Kosygin to initiate a cease-fire in place on the Sinai front. On 20 October 1973, Secretary Kissinger visited Moscow at Brezhnev's request to negotiate a cease-fire. The result of that trip was UN Resolution 338, enacted on 22 October, calling for a cease-fire in place and the start of negotiations. On his return from Moscow, Kissinger stopped in Tel Aviv to apprise the Israelis of his actions and to ensure compliance with their part in the cease-fire. Dependent on the American airlift, which had begun on 14 October in response to the Soviet effort, the Israelis had little choice but to agree to the conditions of Resolution 338, and on 22 October it seemed that peace had been restored.

But the cease-fire of 22 October was not to last. It is difficult to determine who first violated it, but by 23 October the Russians were reporting Israeli violations as the Israeli army sought to continue its encirclement of the Egyptian Third Army east of Suez and the Egyptians fought to escape. At the superpowers' request, the UN Security Council met that night and passed Resolution 339, which confirmed 338 and authorized the dispatch of UN observers to the battlefield. Unfortunately, a new cease-fire agreed to on 24 October collapsed almost as soon as it was enacted, and Sadat sent a note to Brezhnev and Nixon asking for joint military enforcement of the UN cease-fire. At this point, the crisis passed into its most dangerous stage.

The Russians apparently wished to avoid direct intervention, but they were determined to make the U.S. have its client live up to the 22 October agreement. Accordingly, Russian airborne forces were put on alert for possible movement to the Middle East, and that evening Brezhnev sent Nixon a note suggesting joint intervention and threatening to act unilaterally if necessary.

The American response was swift and, as events were to prove, decisive. Six hours after receiving the Brezhnev note, Nixon dispatched a reply warning against unilateral intervention and stating that such an action would violate the U.S.-Soviet agreement on the prevention of nuclear war. To signal the seriousness of the situation, the president placed American military forces in a precautionary alert status known as DEFCON 3. At the same time, Secretary Kissinger was meeting with the Israeli ambassador and urging in the strongest possible language that Israel abide by the cease-fire of 22 October. Later that day, 25 October, the UN Security Council met to pass Resolution 340, which increased the size of the UN observer force and called for an immediate cease-fire with a return to the 22 October 1973 positions of the combatants. This time, under strong U.S. pressure, Israel complied, and the fighting stopped.

Freed from the need for intervention, the Russians contented themselves with sending seventy observers with the UN force and making public pronouncements about their peacemaking efforts. Satisfied that the UN and Israel had the situation well in hand, and that the USSR no longer seriously contemplated intervention, the United States relaxed its alert on 26 October, and the crisis ended.

Analysis

With the help of the seven requirements mentioned at the beginning of this chapter, we can now make some general comments about these cases and also about the way in which the diplomatic revolution that has been mentioned so frequently in these pages has affected the art of crisis management.

1. With regard to the maintenance of top-level civilian control over military options, there can be no doubt that the modern policy maker enjoys many technological advantages over his predecessor. Improvements in communications and transportation allow him to exert personal control over military forces stationed in practically any area of the globe. One has only to compare the relative inaccessibility of the crisis area in 1854 with Kissinger and Kosygin's ability to fly to the threatened region in a matter of hours to appreciate the handicap that Aberdeen had in controlling Ambassador Canning and his use of the fleet in the Crimean case. Additionally, rapid worldwide communications enable the top policy makers to be in instant contact with their military forces, even though they may be half a world away.

But the vast growth in the size and diversity of a modern world power's internal bureaucratic organization and the complexity of the international alliance structure have created new problems for the exercise of top-level civilian control. Here the problems experienced by the German chancellor prior to World War I in controlling his own military organization, Foreign Office, and principal ally give notice of the difficulty often experienced in coordinating the affairs of a modern nation-state. How much more difficult, then, the task of the superpowers in 1973, who had to control not only their own forces but those of their client states as well! Indeed, had the two superpowers been able to exert better control, the Egyptians and Syrians might not have started the war, and the Israelis might not have brought about the resulting nuclear confrontation.

2. With regard to the need to slow down the tempo of military action, crisis managers in the modern era are likely to encounter greater difficulties than did statesmen in the nineteenth and early twentieth centuries. With events driven at an even-faster pace by improvements in communication, transportation, and weapons technology, political leaders are under pressure to make critical decisions in shorter and shorter time intervals. This becomes evident when one compares the duration of the three crises above. The crisis leading up to the Crimean War lasted from 1852 until the outbreak of war in 1854, a period of two years. The crisis leading up to World War I was of little more than one month's duration. The critical period in the 1973 Arab-Israeli War lasted less than a week, with the principal action taking place in the course of forty-eight hours. It is difficult, indeed, to create pauses when the momentum of events is so pressing.

Moreover, the increasing impact of public opinion on decision making has complicated the policy maker's task of slowing down or "freezing" the crisis. In 1854, only the British government had to contend with a public opinion that seemed rabid for war. By 1914, despite the attempt of professional diplomats to ignore it, and their success in doing so in normal times, public opinion in time of crisis was apt to be whipped up by the sensational press, a phenomenon of significance in several European capitals in the last days before war broke out. So demanding has public sentiment become in the years since then that Secretary Kissinger's ability to restrain the Western press while the United States and the Soviet Union moved to resolve the Arab–Israeli conflict before it caused a general war was a remarkable performance.

3. The requirement for coordinating diplomatic and military moves in a crisis also encounters new difficulties under the impact of the diplomatic revolution. First, decisions that shape the capabilities and doctrines of modern military forces do not always take sufficiently into account the task of managing these forces in crises. Policy makers who possess forces only capable of being utilized in large-scale warfare are severely limited in their ability to coordinate military and diplomatic moves. In the World War I case, for example, the opposing sides possessed mass armies, inflexible plans for mobilization, and intricate war plans

which, if employed, necessitated the resort to full-scale military conflict. Thus, the attempts of Germany and Russia at coercive diplomacy became de facto declarations of war once mobilization was instituted. This situation contrasts unfavorably with events in the 1973 war, in which both the United States and the USSR were able to coordinate their diplomatic notes with selective alerts of portions of their armed forces.

The second problem for modern decision makers derives directly from the first. The very flexibility of modern military forces complicates their use. It is extremely difficult to predict how a given military move will be perceived by an opponent. For example, certain Soviet naval maneuvers during the 1973 crisis raised the question whether the Russians had the limited aim of backing up their client Egypt or intended to pose a threat to the U.S. Sixth Fleet in the Mediterranean. Likewise, would the deployment of U.S. carriers to the eastern Mediterranean be viewed as a tactical move to support Israel or a strategic one to position them to attack the USSR proper? Problems such as these repeatedly confront modern policy makers when they seek to coordinate diplomatic and military moves in the nuclear age.

Finally, with the substantial increase in the number of individuals and departments that participate in a modern government's foreign policy, special efforts must be made to coordinate diplomatic communications with overall policy and military actions. Ambassador Canning's handling of the Vienna Note is a minor example of the failure to do so when compared to the situation in 1914, when all sorts of people tied up the telegraph lines to Europe until no one knew who spoke for the German Empire or what its policy actually was. These examples contrast unfavorably with the 1973 crisis, in which communication was confined primarily to the five principals: Nixon, Kissinger, Brezhnev, Meir, and Sadat, with notably successful results.

4. The diplomatic revolution has both complicated and aided the ability of statesmen to confine military moves in a crisis to those that constitute clear demonstrations of their resolve and are appropriate to their limited objectives. As already noted, the scope and complexity of military action has increased greatly from the time of the Crimean War. In 1854, the British cabinet was unable to restrain Ambassador Canning from needlessly provoking the Russians with the British fleet. Prior to the First World War, civilian leaders found it difficult to prevent their military organizations from expanding a conflict through the use of force. The inability of Russia and Germany to force their professional military to modify their existing mobilization schedules and war plans to meet the current diplomatic situation illustrates how militarily expedient moves can have unintended consequences.

Fortunately, policy makers have benefited from technological change as well. During the Crimean War and World War I crises, the policy makers of the involved nations depended on the activities of their legations, intelligence networks, and the international press for information. All of these sources in turn depended upon transmission of the written word, and as such they were continuously subject to misinterpretation. By contrast, modern policy makers have at their disposal all the sophisticated intelligence means of the modern age. The advent of high-level reconnaissance aircraft and satellite photography gives the contemporary decision maker the ability to interpret his opponent's military moves for himself.

5. Advances in military technology have made it vastly more difficult to avoid military moves that give the opponent the impression that large-scale warfare is about to be initiated. The nature of modern warfare has been so altered that in many situations a great premium has been placed on the ability of a belligerent to launch a preventive strike, thus gaining a rapid, decisive victory while limiting its own losses by retaliation. The limited regular forces possessed by the belligerents in 1854 effectively precluded one power from overwhelming another preemptively. By 1914, however, the mass armies of the major powers made the delay of mobilization by even a single day an almost fatal mistake. It is no wonder then that when German Chief of Staff Moltke pressed the kaiser to order German mobilization in response to a similar Russian action, it was difficult for the kaiser to refuse.

In the contemporary nuclear environment, the situation is even graver. If a policy maker hesitates for even an hour when confronted with a nuclear threat, total destruction of his nation could result. It is thus not surprising that the tense diplomatic exchanges between Nixon and Brezhnev in 1973 were carefully worded to allow time for reflection. Neither Secretary Brezhnev nor President Nixon wanted to place his opponent in a position similar to that of the German kaiser and risk the nuclear exchange that might follow.

6. The very destructiveness of modern weaponry, with its capacity to annihilate not only military forces but civilization as well, has greatly strengthened policy makers' incentives to choose diplomatic-military options that will signal a desire to negotiate rather than to seek a military solution. Since the Second World War, the leaders of every major country have been acutely aware of the possible costs of seeking a military solution in a crisis. Because of this firm belief in the horrors of modern war, the contemporary policy maker is much less likely to indulge in the belligerent nationalism of Palmerston or fatalistically accept the inevitability of war, as civilian leaders did in 1914. The current generation of policy makers in the industrialized world is likely to explore every possible avenue of negotiation rather than resort to force. The problem is whether or not the next generation will hold the same views and, if so, will be able to restrain Third World leaders, like Sadat in 1973, who may feel compelled to utilize force to accomplish their goals.

7. As a result of the increase in the ideological nature of many international disputes, it has become more difficult to select diplomatic-military options that

leave an opponent a way out of the crisis compatible with his fundamental interests. The conflict between the interested parties in 1854 was only nominally over the question of the Christian minorities in the Ottoman Empire. The real reasons behind the crisis were those of classic power politics. By 1914, however, nationalism and imperialism had combined forces to add an extra dimension to the international situation. Ideology was notably present in the 1973 crisis, first as a function of the Arab–Israeli rivalry and ultimately as a sort of Islamic jihad against the developed world by means of the oil embargo. Separating the opponent's fundamental interests from his rhetoric is one of the truly difficult tasks facing modern foreign policy makers.

Fortunately, they will be greatly assisted in this task by the vast improvements already made in communications and transportation, which provide policy makers the luxury of face-to-face negotiations, and by improvements in the study of human crisis behavior. The importance of the ability of Secretary Kissinger to fly to Moscow in 1973 cannot be underestimated, but of even greater significance is the sober realization among policy makers in the thermonuclear age of the potential for misinterpretation in a crisis, and the need to eliminate it. Because of this, the disastrous misperceptions of a Palmerston, a Czar Nicholas, or a Bethmann Hollweg may be avoided in the future.

The results of this analysis show that the decision makers' decreasing capability to avoid escalation, coupled with an increasing limitation on their traditional means of control, brought disaster in two of the cases studied: the Crimean War and World War I. The successful example of crisis management in the 1973 Arab-Israeli War (and, earlier, in the Cuban missile crisis) clearly illustrates how decision makers must maximize their capabilities, as Kissinger, Nixon, and Brezhnev did by their personal visits and carefully phrased responses, while minimizing their limitations by controlling the media, their own forces, and those of client states.

Our analysis of these as well as other instances of inadvertent war indicates that not all diplomatic crises are equally manageable by leaders. In fact, some crises are peculiarly resistant to even the best efforts of statesmen to avoid war either because of the structure and dynamics of the international system, balance-of-power considerations, domestic and alliance constraints on the parties to the dispute, or because the interests of the two sides are so fundamentally antagonistic that they cannot be easily reconciled. An inadvertent war may occur because during the course of the crisis, one or the other side reaches the conclusion that initiation of war has become necessary in order to secure its objectives or to avoid an unacceptable diplomatic outcome, or because one or the other side decides to embrace more ambitious objectives than it entertained at the outset of the crisis and is willing to accept the risk of war or resort to force for this purpose.

It is important, therefore, not to permit our interest in improving crisis management to lead us to exaggerate its potential for avoiding war or to overstate the significance of inadequate crisis management as a causal factor explaining inadvertent war. Clearly a broader theoretical and policy framework is needed within which to evaluate the role that crisis management can play. Thus, three additional variables can be seen to operate in assessing the scope and efficacy of crisis management in different crises: (1) the *incentives* to avoid war; (2) the *opportunities* for constructive crisis management; and (3) the *level of skill and capabilities* for crisis management.

When incentives for avoiding war are very weak, opportunities for avoiding war are quite limited, or relevant skills are in short supply, then the likelihood of a crisis developing into inadvertent war is very high. The converse is also to be expected. Comparison of successes and failures to avoid inadvertent war indicates the relevance and impact of these three variables. The strength of incentives to avoid war can be particularly important. For in the absence of a pronounced desire to avoid war, as in the Crimean case (but not in the Cuban missile crisis in which both Kennedy and Khrushchev had strong incentives to avoid war), the actors are less likely to look for and utilize opportunities for crisis management and so their skills and capabilities are less likely to be called upon to the fullest extent. At the same time, an initially strong incentive to avoid war (as was generally experienced by Israeli leaders in the early stages of the 1967 crisis with Egypt) may erode as the crisis develops. And in any case, a clear disincentive for war, as experienced by U.S. policy makers in the confrontation with China over Korea in October–November 1950, by no means suffices to avoid a conflict when opportunities for crisis management are neglected and the actors are unskilled or insensitive to the modalities of crisis management.

One thing is clear from everything that has been said: if catastrophe is to be avoided, decision makers in a crisis must be capable of functioning at a very high level. The tragic consequences of carelessness and lack of reflection on the part of single individuals is apparent in all of the cases reviewed.

Bibliographical Essay

For a detailed analysis of the requirements, modalities, and problems of crisis management, see Alexander L. George, ed., *Avoiding War: Problems of Crisis Management* (Boulder, Colo., 1991). This book contains case studies of five inadvertent wars and compares them with three cases of diplomatic disputes which, with the aid of effective crisis management, were resolved without war. Included also is an analysis of the Arab-Israeli conflicts of 1967, 1969–1970, and 1973 which focuses on the greater complexity of crisis management created by involvement of the superpowers on behalf of their regional allies.

Important analyses of crisis management are found in a number of earlier studies, including Alexander L. George, David K. Hall, and William E. Simons, *The Limits of Coercive Diplomacy* (Boston, 1971); A. L. George, "Crisis Management: The Interaction of Political and Military Considerations," *Survival* (September–October 1984); Coral Bell, *The Conventions of Crisis: A Study in Diplomatic Management* (London, 1971); Ole R. Holsti, *Crisis, Escalation, War* (Montreal and London, 1972); Thomas W. Milburn, "The Management of Crises," in *International Crises: Insights from Behavioral Research,* ed. Charles F. Hermann (New York, 1972); Richard Smoke, *War: Controlling Escalation* (Cambridge, Mass., 1977); Phil Williams, *Crisis Management* (New York, 1976); Oran Young, *Politics of Force* (Princeton, 1968), chaps. 8, 9, 10, 13; Richard Smoke and William L. Ury, *Beyond the Hotline: Controlling a Nuclear Crisis* (Cambridge, Mass., 1984); Richard Ned Lebow, *Between Peace and War* (Baltimore, 1981), chaps. 1–4, 8–10; Scott D. Sagan, "Nuclear Alerts and Crisis Management," *International Security* (Spring 1985); Gilbert R. Winham, ed., *New Issues in International Crisis Management* (Boulder, Colo., 1988); and James G. Blight and David A. Welch, *On the Brink: Americans and Soviets Reexamine the Cuban Missile Crisis* (New York, 1989).

New primary materials and interpretations of the Cuban missile crisis and the 1973 Middle East war are provided in Richard Ned Lebow and Janice Gross Stein, *We All Lost the Cold War* (Princeton, 1994).

How the U.S. military command system controls naval operations in international crises is the subject of an unusually well-documented study by Joseph F. Bouchard, *Command in Crisis: Four Case Studies* (New York, 1991).

17

War Termination

Students of military strategy have not given much systematic attention to the problem of terminating wars, and military planners have also traditionally neglected this problem, concentrating upon how to start wars and fight them successfully rather than upon how to end them if things do not go according to plan. Japanese leaders, for example, developed an ingenious plan for a surprise attack upon Pearl Harbor but had no notion of how the resulting war with the United States might be concluded.

I

In considering this subject, one must distinguish between a mere cessation of hostilities and a peace agreement that attempts to resolve the conflicting aims over which the battle has been waged. Hostilities may end with a cease-fire or armistice that leaves the issues at stake unsettled and defers their consideration to a later peace conference. Indeed, an end to the fighting may be accompanied or followed by a variety of outcomes. The total military defeat of one side, which stands at one extreme, poses much simpler problems for the peacemakers than conflicts that grind to a military stalemate and can be settled only by negotiations.

Students of war termination have to distinguish also between various types of war, each of which poses somewhat different problems for termination. In total war, each side strives for complete victory, that is, the unconditional surrender of its opponent. Examples of total war include World War I, which did not start out as such but gradually became so, and World War II, which was more nearly a total war from the outset. In such conflicts, negotiation plays a lesser role in war termination than in wars fought for limited objectives with limited means. There are several types of limited war. In some, there is a rough symmetry of objectives, both sides viewing the conflict as limited, while in others the aims and stakes of the two sides are markedly different. Terminating a symmetrical limited war poses problems that differ significantly from those encountered in an asymmetrical conflict in which one side regards the stakes as being limited while its opponent views them as being virtually without limit.

Falling into the latter category are many wars between great and small states: for example, anticolonial and insurgency wars in which those on the weaker side fight for their independence and perceive their very existence to be at stake. In such contests, the leaders of the militarily weaker side can make virtually unlimited demands on their people. By waging a war of attrition against the great power and exacting prolonged and mounting sacrifices, the small state hopes to wear down popular support for the war in the stronger state and eventually to convince its people and leaders that the costs of continuing the war outweigh the objectives for which they have been fighting. A great power has other disadvantages in this type of war, for it has many other interests and commitments to meet which compete for scarce resources with the demands of the war. Although it possesses formidable military capabilities, it may find many of them inappropriate for the kind of warfare imposed on it by its weaker adversary. Also, it often happens that a great power is held by its own people, as well as by world opinion, to a higher standard than its weak adversary if it uses morally repugnant means of warfare. The war in Vietnam, which we will discuss in detail later in this chapter, is a prominent recent example of this type of asymmetrical conflict, but one can recall many other such wars, for example, the Boer War at the turn of the century and the French-Algerian War of the 1960s.

Generally speaking, the war objectives of both sides are more flexible in a symmetrical limited war than in total war, and it is easier for their governments and peoples to envisage compromise settlements. At the same time, however, initially limited low-level conflicts may escalate; both the objectives for which the war is being fought and the value placed on them may increase as the war progresses and, with this, escalation of means employed may follow.

II

Many different variables are capable of prolonging wars or speeding their termination. The number of these variables and the complexity of their interaction have increased as a result of the diplomatic revolution. A state's decision to continue or to terminate a war and its ability to do either may be affected by the personalities of its leaders, its political structure, the role of military leaders and their ability to influence the decision-making process, and the role of public opinion and organized interest groups.

In addition to these domestic factors that influence the willingness and ability of governmental leaders to terminate a military conflict, various aspects of the international system may also play a significant role. Local conflicts often have complex international dimensions that reduce a warring state's freedom of action and create dilemmas for its leaders. For example, a great power, like the United States in Vietnam, may remain in a local war longer than it would otherwise wish to because it feels obliged to maintain the credibility of its commitments elsewhere in the world and its general "reputation for resolve." But at the same time, a great power attempting to fight and win a limited war, like the United States in the Korean War, may be constrained by its other alliance commitments, which compete for its resources.

In many military conflicts, one or both combatants may be dependent on allies for material or diplomatic support, but their willingness to provide it often shifts during the course of the war. Weak states often require a secure sanctuary in a neighboring country in order to maintain a combat capability. The strong power may be reluctant to attack the sanctuary because of the political-diplomatic costs or the fear of a major escalation of the conflict. Considerations of this kind constrained the United States from bombing Manchuria during the Korean War after the Chinese Communists intervened. International organizations like the United Nations or regional organizations like the Organization of African Unity play a variety of roles in influencing war termination. The UN may legitimize one side's war objectives and bring pressure to bear on the other side to moderate its terms. It often brings pressure for a cease-fire on both sides and may attempt to formulate the terms of a compromise settlement.

The international dimension of war termination was of considerable importance, of course, in many conflicts fought in the era of the European balance-of-power system. With the developments associated with the diplomatic revolution, the structure and dynamics of international politics have become more complex. So far as termination of ongoing military contests is concerned, international pressures in the modern era operate in a multiplicity of ways, not always consistent with each other, to facilitate or prevent cessation of hostilities, and sometimes in both ways simultaneously.

Let us consider more systematically factors that hamper war termination. Once governments become involved in a war, they often find it much more difficult to back out of it than they had imagined, even if they keenly regret having entered it. Students of international relations have observed this phenomenon often enough to be able to identify some of the reasons for it. In certain conflicts, as in World War I, the leaders and peoples of the countries at war may continue to pour out blood and treasure because they are determined to achieve a settlement that will provide a more secure and peaceful world than existed before the fighting began. In this fashion, the objectives for which a war is fought—the so-called war aims of the belligerents—may differ from and go well beyond the causes of the war and the reasons for having entered it. The example of Woodrow Wilson comes to mind. Having tried to keep the United States out of World War I but being forced into it by the resumption of German submarine warfare, Wilson then embraced the ambitious objective of making the world "safe for democracy." But even before U.S. entry into the war, European leaders and peoples had set themselves far-reaching war aims. Unwilling to return to the uneasy balance-of-power situation that had existed in 1914, they sought to achieve through military victory a sufficient punishment and weakening of their opponents to make it impossible for them to fight another war in the future, and thereby to ensure a "lasting peace." A similar phenomenon occurred again during World War II.

In the classical European balance-of-power era, an enemy in today's war could become one's ally at some future point. Wars between the major powers were usually limited in their objectives and, if they ended with one side victorious, the loser paid, to be sure, but the victor did not usually seek to crush or fatally weaken his opponent. It was not unusual deliberately to limit one's gains from a victorious war, to grant generous terms in the interest of a "peace of reconciliation." As the roles of ideology, nationalism, and public opinion increased in international affairs, these factors encouraged a tendency to view the current enemy as the embodiment of evil rather than as a potential ally. Such psychological aspects operate to prolong wars and to hinder attempts at termination.

A related factor that often prolongs war is conveyed in the proposition that "sacrifice creates value." As the costs of the war mount, this fact itself often strengthens, at least initially, the determination of leaders and public alike to achieve the objectives for which the war is being fought. Such escalation of motivation may, in turn, lead to escalation of war objectives and/or the military means employed to gain them. As was true in World War I, leaders of the nation disposed to seek a compromise settlement may be constrained by the public's mood and its demand that the outcome of the war "justify" the enormous sacrifices already made. It may be some time before prolongation of the war and mounting sacrifices reverse the public's mood sufficiently to permit the opposite proposition—that it is time to "cut one's losses" and to "stop throwing good money after bad."

Another factor that prolongs some wars is the stubborn refusal of leaders who involved their country in a war that is proving to be increasingly disastrous to "admit" their mistake by seeking a way out. Their insistence on victory or "peace with honor" for the nation may be buttressed, often unconsciously, by personal and partisan motives. Whatever the explanation for the fact that leaders and governments become locked into a disastrous war, often the move to terminate the conflict can gain momentum only through a change in leadership, whether through orderly constitutional methods or extralegal means.

Entrance into a war usually alters the internal structure of power and influence within a government. As many observers have noted, with the onset of war, a country's military leaders and the governmental departments and industrial sectors most closely associated with the war effort move closer to the center of power. Fred Iklé writes:

> As "diplomacy breaks down" at the beginning of hostilities, the role of foreign ministries in dealing with the enemy is much diminished. Officials in the foreign ministries may still write background papers and plan for possible future peace settlements, but the influence that comes with day-to-day decisions is transferred to military staffs. At the very moment that the diplomats are being expelled from the enemy capitals, the military leaders come to command a vastly increased segment of national resources.

The heightened influence of military leaders during wartime sometimes gets completely out of hand, as in Japan during World War II, when military fanatics took ruthless action against leaders who favored a move toward peace. It would be erroneous to conclude, however, that military leaders are always less disposed to peace than other governmental officials. In many crises, military leaders have been more reluctant to resort to force than civilian leaders, and in some wars military leaders have taken the initiative for terminating hostilities.

The role of the military as it affects war termination, then, should not be oversimplified or distorted. It is misleading to speak of "the military" as if it constitutes a homogeneous actor; actually, there is considerable diversity of opinion and judgment within most military organizations. It stems not only from the differentiation of the armed forces into army, air, and naval services but also from functional roles and specializations held by the heads of the several services in the central governmental establishment and among the general staff or joint chiefs of staff and theater commanders. In the United States, with similar observations no doubt applying to other countries as well, there are three sources of wartime advice given by the military, each a little different from the other. The first comes from the commander of the theater in which the war is being fought. This usually stresses the importance of that particular theater and the need to support the effort there and indicates a belief in eventual success in that theater. It is often overly optimistic. The second comes from the heads of the individual services, who are normally located in the nation's capital. These officers tend to focus more on the role of their service in the war and in the postwar world, and they try to increase its budget and power in relation to the other services. The third is from the senior military advisers to the nation's leadership, often a number of military officers detached from their services to serve in a joint staff for planning purposes. These advisers tend to be closer to the overall political realities of the war and less influenced by parochial considerations. Because of its more objective view, this last group carries great weight in war-termination calculations.

Still another factor that works to prolong a war is the tendency of civilian and military leaders alike to postpone serious efforts to negotiate an end to the war until they have achieved an advantage on the battlefield. The commonsensical logic behind this preference is that a superior military position on the battlefield will yield additional diplomatic leverage at the negotiating table. Hence, the side that suffers a disadvantage in combat often prefers to postpone serious negotiations until it has corrected the military balance. What defeats this logic very often is that *both* sides operate with the same premise. When both sides take this approach to ending the conflict, as in World War I, they take turns escalating the war and seeking a battlefield success that will prove decisive or influential in obtaining a better negotiated settlement. The quest for a politically decisive military advantage often proves elusive, and the conflict is needlessly prolonged. Analysis of the Korean, Algerian, and Vietnam wars shows how efforts to employ additional increments of force as a means to induce the opponent to moderate his position in the negotiations did not succeed.

Wars are also often prolonged as a result of military estimates that prove too optimistic regarding the expected effectiveness of one's own military strategy and unrealistically downgrade the capabilities and will of the opponent.

What factors, then, set into motion and facilitate efforts to terminate a conflict? Generally speaking, a belligerent state will not consider ending the war unless it stands to realize at least the minimum—that is, the most important—goals for which it has been fighting. But it must also have the resources and the will to continue fighting for this minimally acceptable outcome. As the cost of the war increases, so may the disposition to question whether the minimal goal is worth the continued expenditure of precious resources. In other words, the attitude toward termination is in the end sensitive to the calculation of utility. As the expected costs and benefits of continuing are weighed, it may lead at some point to a policy reassessment and a modification of the minimal outcome one is willing to settle for. This process of reevaluation may actually take place on both sides and, in any case, it continues until the two sides agree that settling for less than they had hoped for is preferable to continuing hostilities.

Various factors may erode willingness to continue expenditure of resources on behalf of existing war objectives. The cost of the war may have severe economic consequences which, together with mounting casualties, weaken public support and generate domestic pressures for termination. World opinion may become increasingly critical toward one or both belligerents and bring strong diplomatic pressure on them to moderate their terms for a settlement. International developments may lead belligerent governments to reorder their foreign policy priorities and downgrade the importance heretofore assigned to the war.

New threats may emerge in the international arena that require a shift in allo-
cation of resources to the war effort. As a result, one or both sides may be
willing, or even eager, to initiate negotiations for ending the war.

III

Many of the observations regarding the nature and process of negotiation presented in chapter 12 are relevant here. But to an extent that is not usual in other
forms of negotiation, war termination typically involves not one but a number
of important issues on which the two sides disagree: for example, the timing
and other conditions of a cease-fire; the disposition of territories and the drawing
of boundaries; arrangements for exchange of prisoners and withdrawal of forces;
provisions for reparations; and the nature and composition of a regime.

Accordingly, the process of negotiation leads to the identification of the
resistance points of the two sides on each of these issues. Both actors engage
in persuasion and bargaining to narrow the gap between their positions not only
on an issue-by-issue basis but across issues in search of an overall agreement
acceptable to both sides. Persuasion makes use of carrot-and-stick tactics; bargaining employs concessions, conditional offers, quid pro quos, or stonewalling
tactics. Complex negotiations often take considerable time. Attempts to bridge
the resistance points may be initially successful on only one or two issues. At
a later stage in the negotiations, additional questions may be resolved. At still
a later stage, compromise may be achieved by linking two issues so that each
side trades its concessions on one for concessions by its opponent on another.

Complex, prolonged negotiations of this kind often characterize war termination. One can trace progress toward a final agreement by identifying a number
of different phases and turning points in the negotiations that follow on each
other. Figure 6 depicts a hypothetical negotiation of this kind. As shown there,
progress toward settlement of the different issues proceeds at an uneven pace.
Tentative agreement achieved on any single issue in one phase of the negotiations may be dissolved in a subsequent phase. During the course of the negotiations, new developments may take place on the battlefield or in domestic and
international arenas that lead to a reassessment of negotiating objectives and
tactics. During the process of persuasion and bargaining at the negotiating table,
each side may highlight those issues and aspects of issues that are particularly
important to it and on which it is least likely to compromise. Mutual adjustment
of concessions may then take place, with one side yielding more on one issue
and the other side more on another issue. Remaining differences may be com-
promised or made part of a package deal linking several issues in a quid pro
quo.

Finally, by analyzing the process of negotiations sequentially, we discover

Development of Negotiation of Multi-issued War Termination (Hypothetical Case)

Issues	Phase I	Phase II	Phase III
		New developments on battlefield and in domestic and international arenas; additional persuasion and bargaining	New developments on battlefield and in domestic and international arenas; additional persuasion and bargaining
#1	Resistance points far apart	→ Disagreement narrowed (Side B makes concessions to A)	→ Settled as part of quid pro quo with Issue #5
#2	Disagreement narrowed (mutual concessions by sides A and B)	→ no change	→ Compromise agreed to
#3	Tentative agreement reached	→ Side A withdraws support for tentative agreement	→ Settled (A and B compromise their remaining differences)
#4	Settled (Side A makes concessions to Side B)	→ no change	→ no change
#5	Resistance points far apart	→ Disagreement narrowed (major concession by A; minor concession by B)	→ Settled as part of quid pro quo with Issue #1

agreement to terminate the war

Figure 6

that it is often characterized by a series of stopping points at which negotiations are slowed down or temporarily adjourned while the two governments reassess their positions. A sequential analysis of the negotiations should, therefore, take note of new developments on the battlefield, in the domestic situations of the two sides, and in the international context that influence the negotiating goals of both actors.

Negotiations do not necessarily lead to symmetrical agreements. Both sides need not make roughly equal concessions or achieve a settlement which balances their competing interests. The bargaining power (a combination of capabilities and motivation) of the two sides may not be equal. And in any case, one side may negotiate more skillfully than the other. Even when one side is thoroughly defeated, as were Germany and Japan in World War II, it may still possess some residual bargaining power that it can utilize during the course of surrender negotiations in order to achieve somewhat better terms on matters it regards as of vital importance.

We should note, too, that peace negotiations may result in only a partial settlement of the issues at stake. The two sides may agree to terminate military hostilities without having reached an agreement on all of the issues in conflict. They may agree to take them up themselves at a later date, set up ad-hoc international commissions to deal with them, or use the auspices of existing international bodies.

Elements of a peace agreement often lack clarity, suffer from ambiguity, and permit of contradictory interpretations. Sometimes acceptance of such flaws may be necessary if any agreement at all is to be achieved. Some matters dealt with in the peace settlement, therefore, may in fact be in the nature of pseudo-agreements that merely paper over fundamental disagreement and pave the way for future conflict. Or enforcement provisions for key components of the agreement may be so inadequate as to create the likelihood that the settlement will crumble and perhaps entirely collapse at some later point.

Many of the factors that facilitate and impede the process of war termination and the negotiation of multiple issues can be seen in the process that ended the Vietnam War.

Vietnam: A Case Study of War Termination*

The Communist war against foreign domination in Indochina can really be said to have begun in 1930 with the founding of the Indochinese Communist party. From that date until the final collapse of resistance in South Vietnam in 1975, the party of Ho Chi Minh and his heirs never once wavered from its announced

*This case study was prepared in its original form by Major Clinton Anker III, U.S. Army.

goal of a unified, Communist Vietnam. It was less the appeal of Communist ideology per se than Ho's ability to blend it with powerful sentiments of nationalism and anticolonialism that enabled him and his people to fight three wars against, in turn, the Japanese, the French, and the Americans. In contrast to this simple, single-minded aim of the strongly motivated Vietminh, the Americans, like the Japanese and French before them, had other, competing interests that detracted from their efforts in Vietnam. Only this can explain how the Communists could prevail against one of the two world superpowers, the United States of America.

The gradual involvement of the United States in Vietnam originated during World War II when, ironically, the American Office of Strategic Services (OSS) (forerunner of the CIA) actually helped the Communists against the Japanese. Involvement didn't really take on ominous tones until the early 1950s, when the United States aided France against the Communists. This aid must be seen in the context of the Cold War mentality of this period, which created the conditions that ultimately resulted in over five hundred thousand American troops in Vietnam; later on, a change in the Cold War mentality significantly contributed to the final outcome. In 1949, China became a Communist state. In late 1950, Communist Chinese troops entered into prolonged combat with Americans in Korea. Chinese aid to the Vietnamese was increasing substantially after 1949, and there seemed little doubt that the Chinese were part of the Soviet Union's growing collection of puppet states. Beset in both Asia and Europe by Communist expansion, the United States adopted a policy of containment. When the French left Indochina in 1954, the United States stepped in to help the new nation of South Vietnam maintain its pro-Western independence, much as it had aided Greece after Britain withdrew in 1947.

Hoping for and expecting a political victory, the Communists in South Vietnam conducted a quiet, semilegal struggle to unify North and South. But the surprising success of South Vietnamese President Diem in consolidating his position in the South led to renewed warfare beginning in 1959. By 1965, this violence threatened to overthrow South Vietnam, and the United States began sending massive numbers of troops to bolster a faltering ally. To many, including a significant portion of American leaders, it seemed the proper thing to do. The United States had turned back the effort to spread communism by means of a conventional war in Korea, it had stared down the Soviet Union in a nuclear confrontation over missiles in Cuba, and a defeat of a Communist guerrilla army in Southeast Asia would seemingly close off the entire spectrum of violence through which communism could expand. As a world power and as the leader of the free world, the United States had a commitment to prevent Communist aggression wherever it occurred. Several successive administrations had pledged the United States to stand by South Vietnam, and its reputation for resolve and as a world power was seemingly at stake. What is more, under the proddings of President Kennedy, U.S. military forces had been nurturing an unconventional warfare capability, and Vietnam provided an occasion to use it. With a hubris born of repeated successes in the postwar world, with a Cold War mentality that saw communism encroaching everywhere, and with a typical disdain of Third World capabilities, the United States undertook to save South Vietnam. But beyond that vague goal, American leaders never did clearly define how the United States would do it, or what success would look like.

Nevertheless, things seemed to go well. By the end of 1967, American military leaders were confidently predicting victory, domestic opposition to the war was muted by its apparent success, and the rising costs of the war were hidden by President Johnson's decision to rely upon deficit spending. The Communist Tet Offensive in February 1968 once and for all shattered the illusions, and suddenly American leadership had to face a situation that could no longer be ignored. While the Tet Offensive ended in a shattering tactical defeat for the Vietcong and North Vietnamese, it was a strategic victory, for it had a tremendous psychological and political impact on American opinion. Hanoi had never really hoped to defeat the United States in a military confrontation; rather, the North Vietnamese leaders simply wanted to make the war so costly to the United States in manpower, money, and international prestige that it would finally decide that continuing the war was too expensive relative to the possible benefits. The Tet Offensive created a feeling of hopelessness and presented the specter of a long, drawn-out conflict with no end in sight for the American public. Support for the Johnson administration's Vietnam policies plummeted below 50 percent in public opinion polls for the first time since the war had heated up. Widespread vocal protests gained tremendous impetus now that the saving grace of "victory" in the struggle appeared to be a chimera. The media, already hostile to the war, became more and more virulent in opposition to its continuation. Many intellectuals from all walks of life joined the antiwar movement. And just as important, President Johnson's advisers now convinced him that a purely military solution to the insurgency was beyond reach. North Vietnam was more than willing to sustain the level of losses and suffer through the level of deprivation that could be imposed on it by U.S. military forces in South Vietnam and the bombing of the North.

As a result of the foregoing, Lyndon Johnson radically altered the U.S. strategy for the war. He now sought to deescalate American involvement and to seek a negotiated settlement. This, however, proved to be very difficult. Hanoi was under little time pressure, and the North Vietnamese exhibited a willingness to wait as long as necessary to achieve their unaltered goal of a unified Vietnam. Besides, they were past masters at using negotiations to secure victory when armed force had either failed or merely provided a basis for talks. Thus, when the two sides put forward their preconditions for negotiations, they were found to be mutually exclusive. The North Vietnamese did agree to bargain about negotiations in April 1968 after Johnson halted the bombing of the North, but apparently this was only a ploy to gain a respite from massive air attacks, and nothing of substance was really achieved.

But Johnson was a lame-duck president anyway. On 20 January 1969, Richard Nixon was inaugurated as president, bringing a whole new approach to the war. It was Nixon, and his foreign affairs adviser, Henry Kissinger, who would eventually end the war. As often happens, it took a change in leadership to create an effective change in policy.

Nixon's approach was a multifaceted strategy, each part designed to work on one aspect of the problem, and the whole designed to end U.S. involvement in Vietnam on the best terms possible. First, to help quiet antiwar sentiment at home, he announced that the United States would begin large withdrawals of troops and a process of reequipping and retraining the South Vietnamese army. This Vietnamization process, as it was called, was meant to result in the South Vietnamese assuming the main role in defending their country and significantly reduce American casualties, thereby, it was hoped, taking the war off the front page of newspapers. To put increased pressure on the North Vietnamese, Nixon drastically widened the war by increasing bombing in the North and by spreading the bombing and ground combat to Cambodia and Laos. Additionally, to bring international pressure to bear on Hanoi, Nixon and Kissinger attempted to link progress on improved relations with China and the Soviet Union to those nations' use of their influence to pressure Hanoi to stop the war. Finally, Kissinger opened secret negotiations with North Vietnamese representatives in an attempt to find a way out of the war.

What might have looked like a comprehensive U.S. strategy was in fact riddled with contradictions. While removing U.S. troops initially calmed the antiwar movement, the expansion of the bombing in the North and the moves into Cambodia and Laos had the opposite effect and caused antiwar protests to burst forth with renewed vigor. Not only did all the old arguments against the war resurface, but the moral question was given much greater play, with the United States cast in the role of an aggressor conducting an immoral war. While violations of morality occurred on both sides, America was unilaterally called to task in both the domestic and international press. Congressmen began to oppose the war in even greater numbers, and support for the administration, already weak in a Democratic-controlled Congress, diminished further. Inflation, the result of deficit spending to finance the war, was added to the list of evils charged to U.S. involvement in Vietnam. And allies were increasingly critical of U.S. involvement, since it made their relations with the USSR more difficult, created problems in their approaches to China, and, by weakening the dollar abroad, posed a growing threat to international monetary stability.

The increased pressure on North Vietnam caused by the bombing and the invasions of Laos and Cambodia did not change Hanoi's mind about the costversus-benefit calculations. Indeed, the beginning of U.S. withdrawal sent a clear message to Hanoi that American involvement was drawing down even if the tonnage of bombs was up. This simply reinforced Hanoi's belief that time was on its side.

The negotiations, too, proved initially to be futile. Kissinger wanted first and foremost to decouple the military and political issues, settling the military question first and then negotiating on the political future of South Vietnam. Hanoi, which had always considered the military aspect subordinate to its overriding political goals, would not even consider such a decoupling. After all, the North Vietnamese asked, what was the point of the war if not to decide the South's political future? In addition, the Communist negotiators put forth a tough demand for a Communist government in South Vietnam as one of their requirements for a settlement. By adhering stubbornly to this unrealistic requirement, they were able to extract concession after concession from the United States before finally conceding at the last minute in order to bring about a peace agreement that was in other respects highly favorable to them.

Finally, in the international arena, the Nixon and Kissinger attempt at linkage produced limited results. Because the Soviet Union and China each reciprocated Nixon's desire for closer ties, the diplomatic strategy of linkage at first allowed Nixon to expand the war without either of the Communist giants reacting violently and either killing the initiative for better relations or, as Johnson had feared, intervening militarily on Hanoi's behalf. It is also possible that the desire for détente with the United States may have led Soviet and Chinese leaders to exert some limited pressure on Hanoi to reach a settlement. But linkage and the desire for improved relations were double-edged. Nixon and Kissinger had always considered Vietnam as merely a sideshow in a much greater global policy. The endless prolongation of negotiations with Hanoi stood in the way of implementing their grand strategy and increased pressure on them to make damaging concessions in order to end the war, regardless of the ultimate consequences to South Vietnam.

The gradual withdrawal of U.S. forces from South Vietnam was originally linked to a demand for reduction in North Vietnamese activities in the South. Once it was implemented, however, Nixon could not respond to such activities without raising even greater opposition at home, and he thus lost the ability to extract reciprocal reductions from the North. Given this and increased congressional restrictions on U.S. air power in Indochina, the Saigon regime's only hope was to gain the ability to defend itself in the face of Northern aggression. The prospects for doing so did improve in some respects after the Tet Offensive, which shocked and galvanized many elements of the South Vietnamese leadership and population. In addition, progress was made in pacification programs in the South and in the restructuring of the South Vietnamese army; and land reform and a new security orientation were making significant inroads into Vietcong strength and the ability of the North Vietnamese army to operate at will. But a successful program of this type required time, and time was a commodity in very short supply in 1972, the decisive year of the war.

Negotiations up to early 1972 had really accomplished little and had hardly narrowed the bargaining gap at all. In April, the North Vietnamese launched a conventional invasion of South Vietnam, the so-called Easter Offensive. It was eventually stopped by May of that year through a combination of massive U.S. air strikes throughout Indochina and by the surprising toughness of the South Vietnamese army, which fought the Northern regulars to a stalemate at Au Loc, Kontum, and Quang Tri. As a result of the outcome of the offensive and the upcoming U.S. presidential elections, both sides now had an increased incentive to negotiate a settlement. Nixon was under renewed and increased pressure from both the public and Congress to stop the war. The massive U.S. air strikes had raised howls of opposition, and Congress was closer than ever to passing serious restrictive legislation concerning future U.S. actions in Indochina and the president's ability to wage war at all. With the election coming in November, Nixon felt a settlement in Vietnam would be a tremendous boost to his campaign. But this time Hanoi, too, wanted a settlement. North Vietnamese leaders feared that once reelected, Nixon might take a harder line. Moreover, they were surprised by the resilience of the South Vietnamese army. They recognized that given enough time, American supplies and assistance might help it to close the gap with North Vietnam and that eventually the South might be able to defend itself. Thus, it was prudent to get the United States out of Vietnam while the advantages for eventual victory still lay with the North.

Kissinger and the North Vietnamese negotiator, Le Duc Tho, made rapid progress in secret negotiations during the summer and early autumn of 1972. Both sides made concessions, although the American ones were more substantial than those of Hanoi. The United States agreed to withdraw all its forces without a concurrent withdrawal of North Vietnamese troops. In fact, the United States agreed to allow North Vietnamese troops to stay in South Vietnam, a significant and ultimately fatal concession. Additionally, America agreed to combine the military and political agreements into one document. In turn, Le Duc Tho agreed to drop Hanoi's demand for President Thieu's immediate removal as a precondition for a cease-fire. This had been, from the American negotiators' standpoint, the major stumbling block all along. Having achieved their immediate goal of a withdrawal of U.S. troops without having to abandon their own gains in the South, Hanoi felt a concession on Thieu an acceptable price to pay.

But peace was not yet at hand, for President Thieu exploded in opposition to what he considered a sellout by the United States. Not having been privy to the terms being discussed, Thieu was aghast at the U.S. position. His absolute refusal to consider the terms quashed any hope Nixon and Kissinger had of ending U.S. involvement before the November elections. In reaction to the U.S.

failure to ratify the accords, Hanoi reverted to an unacceptable, hard-line position on the political future of the South. For a moment, it looked as if the elusive peace had once again slipped out of U.S. hands.

Nixon and Kissinger, both tiring of the interminable problems of Vietnam and its effects on their cherished global policy, now decided to apply pressure on all fronts. For Thieu, the carrot and stick consisted of massive material aid to bolster the South Vietnamese army, a promise of massive U.S. air intervention if Hanoi violated the proposed accords, and, finally, a threat to conclude a unilateral treaty if Thieu balked. That was enough to secure Thieu's reluctant acquiescence. For Hanoi, a new massive bombing and mining campaign coupled with pressure applied through the Soviet Union and China served to break their hard-line attitude. The agreement finally signed in early 1973 was essentially similar to the aborted October 1972 accords; it included amorphous, predictably unworkable, provisions for implementation. But it ended the war for the United States.

As it turned out, the accords were a poor substitute for a genuine peace. None of the real issues in Indochina was resolved, and the enforcement machinery was virtually useless. Having secured a complete U.S. withdrawal, Hanoi waited two years to mount its massive conventional attack, which finally achieved the long-held, never-altered goal of a unified, Communist Vietnam. Time, and U.S. support, had run out for the Saigon regime.

Bibliographical Essay

The general analysis of war termination presented in the first part of the chapter draws upon the following sources: William T. R. Fox, ed., "How Wars End," *Annals of the American Academy of Political and Social Science* 392 (1970); Morton H. Halperin, "War Termination as a Problem in Civil—Military Relations," *Annals of the American Academy of Political and Social Science* 392 (1970): 86–95; Michael Handel, "The Study of War Termination," *Journal of Strategic Studies* 1 (1978): 51–75; Fred C. Iklé, *Every War Must End* (New York, 1971); Paul Kecskemeti, *Strategic Surrender* (Stanford, Calif., 1958), which is particularly good on the residual bargaining power of defeated nations; Robert Randle, *The Origins of Peace: A Study of Peacemaking and the Structure of Peace Settlements* (New York, 1973); Janice G. Stein, "War Termination and Conflict Reduction, or How Wars Should End," *Jerusalem Journal of International Relations* 1 (1975): 1–25; Major Clinton J. Ancker III, U.S. Army, "The Franco-Algerian War: A Study in War Termination" (Seminar paper, Political Science Department, Stanford University, 1979); and Helen Milner, "Case Studies in the Termination of Modern Limited Wars" (Senior honors thesis, Stanford University, 1980). More recent analytical studies include Leon V. Sigal, *Fighting to a Finish* (Ithaca, N.Y., 1988); Paul R. Pillar, *Negotiating Peace: War Termination as a Bargaining Process* (Princeton, 1983); Sydney D. Bailey, *How Wars End: The United Nations and the Termination of Armed Conflict, 1946–1964,* 2 vols. (Oxford, 1982); and David Wittman, "How A War Ends: A Rational Model Approach," *Journal of Conflict Resolution* (December 1979).

Books available on the war in Vietnam and especially on war termination suffer from two problems. First, almost nothing of any real substance has come out of Hanoi, the People's Republic of China, or the Soviet Union. What has appeared has been polemical in nature and so full of rhetoric that the serious scholar must dig long and hard to find relevant facts. Most of it consists merely of paeans of praise to the North Vietnamese army. Second, not enough time has yet elapsed since the crucial events. The controversy and emotionalism engendered by the war inevitably distort objectivity. In addition, the authors' desire to defend their war policy makes it necessary to deal cautiously with Henry Kissinger's *White House Years* (Boston, 1979) and Richard M. Nixon's *RN: The Memoirs of Richard Nixon* (New York, 1978), both of which, however, are indispensable sources. See also Henry A. Kissinger, *Diplomacy* (New York, 1994), and Francis L. Loewenheim, "Dean Rusk: The Diplomacy of Principle," in *The Diplomats, 1939–1979*, ed. Gordon A. Craig and Francis L. Loewenheim (Princeton, 1994).

Among the first attempts at a detached, scholarly look at Vietnam are Allan E. Goodman, *The Lost Peace* (Stanford, Calif., 1978); Leslie H. Gelb and Richard K. Betts, *The Irony of Vietnam: The System Worked* (Washington, D.C., 1979), which maintains that, far from being a failure of the American system, Vietnam was a good example of how it should work; and Peter Braestrup, *The Big Story* (New York, 1978), a critical look at media coverage of the war. Herbert Y. Schandler, *The Unmaking of a President: Lyndon B. Johnson and Vietnam* (Princeton, 1977), is a scholarly work that is indispensable for understanding factors contributing to Johnson's decision to deescalate the war and to seek a negotiated settlement. Particularly useful for understanding the U.S.–South Vietnam relationship during 1968–1973 as the United States sought to end its involvement are Nguyen Tien Hung and Jerrold L. Schechter, *The Palace File* (New York, 1986), and Wallace J. Thies, "Searching for Peace: Vietnam and the Question of How Wars End," *Polity* (Spring 1975). But see also the memoirs of Lyndon B. Johnson, *Vantage Point* (New York, 1971), particularly the invaluable index, which details the president's peace efforts.

The close relationship of President Nixon's gradual, phased withdrawal of U.S. troops from Vietnam to his concern over domestic political opposition to the war is the focus of the incisive study by Jane Holl, "From the Streets of Washington to the Roofs of Saigon: Domestic Politics and the Termination of the Vietnam War" (Ph.D. diss., Stanford University, 1989).

The special difficulties of terminating civil wars is the subject of the comparative study in Roy Licklider, ed., *Stopping the Killing: How Civil Wars End* (New York, 1993). An exemplary study of the efforts to end the civil war in Rhodesia and to bring about the transition to Zimbabwe is Stephen J. Stedman's *Peacemaking in Civil War: International Mediation in Zimbabwe, 1974–1980* (Boulder, Colo., 1991). See also the "Note: The Expanding Field of Conflict Resolution: Theory and Practice," in the Bibliographical Essay for chapter 13.

18

Détente

There has been little systematic study by historians and political scientists of the phenomenon of détente in interstate relations. In the modern era, even the meaning of the term has become opaque, and it is often misused by policy makers as well as by specialists in international relations and members of the general public. The reasons for this are instructive in themselves.

In the United States, the term *détente* came suddenly into vogue following the conclusion of the partial test ban treaty in the summer of 1963. After the brush with thermonuclear disaster in the Cuban missile crisis, Kennedy and Khrushchev attempted to place U.S.–Soviet relations on a new basis in order to alleviate the extreme distrust and conflict that had characterized the Cold War. With the signing of the partial test ban treaty, the first arms control agreement between the two nuclear superpowers, the term *détente* began to be employed by policy makers and commentators. The word was used, somewhat inconsistently, for a variety of purposes: to describe the emergence of a new atmosphere in U.S.–Soviet relations; to characterize the passing of the acute phase of the Cold War; to refer to a new but not too well-defined policy toward the Soviet Union; and to identify a more cooperative relationship with the Soviet Union that might be gradually achieved in the future.

The deep concern, often forcefully expressed, of those who continued to distrust the Soviet Union compounded confusion over the meaning of the term and its applicability to U.S.–Soviet relations. Many people felt that the signing of the test ban treaty did not signify any diminution of Russia's hostility toward the West or any modification of its long-range intentions. They argued that Soviet interest in détente was merely a tactical stratagem designed to lull the West into complacency. Disagreements quickly arose as to what détente did and did not mean, what it should and should not be allowed to become.

It is important to recognize that the problem of ascertaining the correct meaning of détente following the missile crisis was not solely semantical. It was not cleared up by consulting the dictionaries and learning that in the era of classical diplomacy, "détente" meant simply "a relaxation of tensions" in relations between two states whose policies had been previously characterized by considerable rivalry that posed the danger of war. The question remained as to what a "relaxation of tensions" meant in the era of the Cold War and what its implications should signify for future U.S.–Soviet relations.

Clarification of these questions will be facilitated if we recognize that détente was a different phenomenon in the context of the Cold War than it was in the nineteenth and early twentieth centuries. As we have seen, the old European system was a relatively well-ordered multipolar system in which the major actors were committed to the maintenance of a balance of power. Competition and rivalry among them were not unlimited; there was a great deal of cultural homogeneity among the ruling classes; ideological differences were not pronounced; and, finally, the conduct of foreign policy was left largely in the hands of professional diplomats. All these characteristics of the classical era of European diplomacy had long since given way; traces of them could scarcely be found in the period of the Cold War.

Given the striking differences between these two international systems, it is not surprising that efforts to transfer diplomatic concepts from one era to the other should generate confusion and malaise. Such concepts and practices had well-defined meanings and uses in the European system. Diplomats and statesmen of that period had developed a rich, differentiated, and relatively precise set of technical phrases that facilitated communication in the conduct of interstate relations. With the breakdown and transformation of the older system, however, the diplomatic vocabulary of the classical era was debased. Its terminology lost much of its precision and, in consequence, attempts to use the old concepts in contemporary foreign relations were apt to lead to confusion.

We can demonstrate this by recalling how precisely the language of the older diplomacy characterized the progressive stages of improvement that were possible in the relations of two states that were experiencing acute conflict in their policies. The process might begin with "détente" and possibly develop into "rapprochement"; this, in turn, could lead to "entente." Two further developments could then take place: one or both sides could engage in "appeasement" of the other and/or the two sides could form an "alliance." But this stage-by-stage improvement in relations could stop at any point. The specific meanings of these concepts and the relationships among them are depicted schematically in Figure 7.

The following example illustrates the utility of such precise terminology in aiding effective communication between diplomats. In the course of his mission to Berlin in February 1912, the British war minister, Lord Haldane, met with Jules Cambon, the French ambassador at Berlin, to explain to him the object

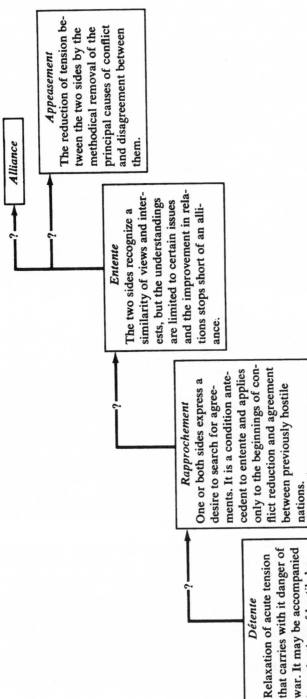

Alliance

Appeasement
The reduction of tension between the two sides by the methodical removal of the principal causes of conflict and disagreement between them.

Entente
The two sides recognize a similarity of views and interests, but the understandings are limited to certain issues and the improvement in relations stops short of an alliance.

Rapprochement
One or both sides express a desire to search for agreements. It is a condition antecedent to entente and applies only to the beginnings of conflict reduction and agreement between previously hostile nations.

Détente
Relaxation of acute tension that carries with it danger of war. It may be accompanied by reduction of hostile behavior but does not settle the prevailing disagreements or remove the underlying conflicts of interest.

The question marks indicate that the process of improvement in relations between the two states need not go beyond détente and could stop at any point.

Figure 7

and significance of the talks he was then having with the German chancellor, Bethmann Hollweg, about the possibility of an Anglo-German agreement to limit naval expenditures. Aware that such discussions were taking place and concerned lest they portend the loosening of England's relationship with France and Russia, Cambon met with Haldane at the British embassy and anxiously sought to be informed about the talks. Haldane later recorded in his diary that

> without telling him anything, I said emphatically that we were not going to be disloyal to France or Russia, that the Chancellor agreed that it would be dishonorable in us if we even talked of departing from the existing agreements, and that we believed a better state of public opinion between England and Germany would benefit France. With that he [Cambon] agreed. He suggested that my conversation had no other end than to create a *détente,* as distinguished from an *entente.* I said this was so as regards my conversation. I had not come there to draw up an agreement, or to do more than *tâter le terrain.* But that I hoped more than a détente would follow later on—if my very limited mission succeeded.

The concern for precision in the interest of avoiding misperception and distrust is further illustrated by Haldane's belief that it would be "a useful precaution" if he could see Cambon's telegraphed report of their conversation to the French premier, Raymond Poincaré, before it was sent to Paris. Cambon agreed, and upon reading it Haldane concurred with the way in which the French ambassador described the distinction he had made between "détente" and "entente."

The relevance of these conceptual distinctions to the conduct of foreign policy in the European system can be further illustrated by tracing their application to the gradual improvement in relations between England and France beginning in 1898.

Anglo-French Entente, 1898–1904

In that year, the protracted antagonism between Great Britain and France in the colonial area came to a head when the French government, seeking to force the British to terminate the occupation of Egypt that they had begun in 1882 and to conclude a settlement that would recognize French interests, sent troops commanded by Colonel Marchand from West Africa to the upper Nile. Here, at a place called Fashoda, the French were met by a stronger British force commanded by General Kitchener, and the danger of an incident that might trigger a European war became obvious. This had a sobering effect upon the French government, distracted by the domestic agitations caused by the Dreyfus affair, with naval forces only half those of Britain, with its only ally too deeply involved in the Far East to be able to give it effective support, and with no expectation of assistance from the Triple Alliance powers, who were not displeased with the possibility of an Anglo-French conflict. The French foreign minister, Théophile Delcassé, a nationalist who believed that the lost provinces of Alsace and Lorraine might be worth a war but that Egypt certainly was not, temporized and, when the British showed no inclination to make concessions, he capitulated in November 1898 by ordering Marchand to withdraw.

Even before the crisis, Delcassé had been telling the British ambassador that he desired a rapprochement with Great Britain, and in a letter to his wife in October he wrote, ''I hope it has been realized that the desire for an agreement with England, very freely expressed by me since I became Foreign Minister, came not from a feeling of weakness but from a general conception of policy.'' The French withdrawal from Fashoda both facilitated and impeded progress toward his goal. It significantly lowered tension and diminished the possibility of war and thus, in a real sense, represented a détente in the relations of the two powers, while at the same time leaving a heritage of bitterness in France and, in some quarters, a desire for revenge. For some time after Fashoda, circumstances were not propitious for an improvement in Anglo-French relations. The British were still giving serious consideration to the possibility and advantages of an alliance with Germany, which Colonial Secretary Joseph Chamberlain believed would provide an effective defense against the expansionist tendencies of France's ally Russia in China.

Détente was nevertheless gradually transformed into rapprochement within the next three years. During the Boer War, the British became aware of the disadvantages of what they had called ''splendid isolation,'' for they were never entirely sure that they might not have to cope with the intervention of one or more of the continental powers. They were particularly suspicious of the German government, for it proved to be an unreliable partner in the Far East, made no attempt to temper the strident pro-Boer sentiment of the press, and, in 1900, pushed through the Reichstag a supplementary naval bill that marked the beginning of Grand Admiral Tirpitz's campaign to build a battle fleet big enough to threaten British security in the North Sea. The British did not react immediately by turning to the French. Their most urgent concern, aside from the war, was Russian policy in China, and to counter this they finally abandoned their isolationist policy, concluding an alliance with Japan in 1902.

But this step had sensible reverberations in Paris. The French government had long been as concerned about Russia's Far Eastern policy as the British (in 1898, Delcassé had said to the British ambassador, ''I would rather have England for our ally than that other''), and now the Anglo-Japanese alliance opened up the prospect of a war in the Far East between the new partners and Russia, in which France would be called upon to make good its treaty with the latter. This Delcassé wished to avoid at all costs, and he saw a rapprochement with the British as the best way of doing so. Indeed, as he saw it, an Anglo-French agreement might facilitate a general settlement in the Far East by providing the basis for an accommodation between Japan and Russia. The French foreign minister therefore made soundings in London, which met a cordial response, for British disillusionment with the Germans was now complete. Even Joseph Chamberlain, the most ardent of the advocates of the German connection, was enthusiastic about a settlement with France.

The progress from this initial rapprochement to entente was, if not quick, deliberate. The first approaches were given more weight by an exchange of official visits, King Edward VII making an unprecedented but highly successful trip to Paris in May 1903 and President Loubet returning the compliment by going to London in July. Meanwhile, the diplomats began to deal with the hard issues that had troubled the relationship since 1882. These involved disputes over sovereignty, economic interest, and boundaries in Newfoundland, Siam, and West Africa, which were settled with no great difficulty, and the thornier problem of Egypt. The words *Fashoda* and *Marchand* were still capable of arousing patriotic indignation in France, but on the whole the French had no expectation of regaining their pre-1882 position there and were intent upon receiving an equivalence in the area of their greatest current interest, Morocco.

With a disregard for the interests of the native populations that would seem outrageous today, the French government recognized the British protectorate at Cairo and declared that it would not obstruct British work in Egypt by calling for a time limit to the British occupation. On their part, the British recognized Morocco as a French sphere of influence, adding that it was for France alone to provide order in that enormously rich area and to suggest reforms to its sultan. In secret articles, they agreed further that they would not object to action that the French might consider appropriate in the case of a collapse of the sultan's authority, provided that whatever became of Morocco, the Atlantic coastline should, for obvious reasons, go not to France but to Spain.

The broader significance of the Entente Cordiale that resulted from these agreements was that it marked the beginning of Anglo-French collaboration in other quarters and the first step toward the alliance between the two Western powers in World War I. It was not transformed into a formal alliance earlier largely because of the traditional British reluctance to make commitments for contingencies that had not yet arisen. Even so, in the decade before the war it more and more acquired the normal characteristics of an alliance. After the Moroccan crisis of 1905, in which the Germans sought to drive the new friends apart by menaces, the two governments instituted military staff talks which, in a professedly theoretical and nonbinding manner, discussed joint operations in time of war. In the wake of the second Moroccan crisis of 1911 and in response to Germany's rapid naval buildup, the British government not only authorized a continuation of the staff talks but also assured the French that "if either

Government had grave reason to expect an unprovoked attack by a third Power, it should immediately discuss with the other whether both Governments should act together.'' This action was taken in order to persuade the French to move their Atlantic fleet to the Mediterranean so as to protect British interests while the Royal Navy was being concentrated in home waters.

As this account indicates, the process of moving successively from détente to rapprochement to entente and then to appeasement or alliance or both was in this case very deliberate. Moreover, entering into a détente did not carry with it any commitment or assurance that the two sides would move on to a further improvement of their relations. What is more, statesmen in the classical European era proceeded cautiously at every stage, assessing carefully the hoped-for benefits and possible risks of moving to the next phase. Whereas diplomats in the European state system understood well the prudential need for taking careful soundings and preparing the diplomatic ground as well as public opinion before engaging in appeasement or entering into an alliance with a former adversary, this practice was not always followed when the impact of the diplomatic revolution had altered statecraft and had introduced new imperatives and constraints into the conduct of foreign policy.

British Appeasement Policy

The policy of appeasement followed by the National government in Great Britain during the prime ministership of Neville Chamberlain, for example, was based upon an earnest desire to create the conditions for European peace and stability, but it was vitiated by Chamberlain's impatience and his contempt for the cautionary expedients of traditional diplomacy. While between 1933 and 1937, the British Foreign Office had sought, however imperfectly, to establish the bona fides of the dictators and to determine whether there were common interests and values that would serve as a basis for cooperation with them before undertaking a systematic removal of specific causes of conflict, Chamberlain saw no point in these preliminaries and soon got rid of those people, like Eden and Vansittart, who insisted on them. With the general support of a Parliament and a public opinion that wanted no repetition of the 1914 war, he heedlessly plunged ahead to what should have been the final stage of a laborious process, on the mistaken assumption that Hitler and Mussolini shared his objectives and that a demonstration of his readiness to satisfy their demands would bring him the peace that he desired. All that it brought him, of course, was new and more outrageous demands, which in the end had to be resisted by force. As an example of how not to conduct a policy of détente, the appeasement policy of 1937–1939 is not likely to be easily surpassed.

The Soviet–American Détente

These comments on the diplomatic practices of the past provide a basis for a comparison with developments in the Cold War in the period after the Cuban missile crisis. It has already been noted that the ensuing relaxation of tension in U.S.–Soviet relations, which some referred to as a détente, was a significantly different phenomenon than its counterpart during the era of the European balance-of-power system. In that earlier context, substantial improvements were possible in the relations between the major powers. Adversaries could become allies; reversal of alliances was not uncommon. What is more, such pronounced shifts could take place and were expected to take place as part of the practices required to regulate and maintain the multipolar European system. This stands in sharp contrast with the bipolar Cold War system, which was characterized by acute hostility bordering on a zero-sum conflict. While détente→rapprochement→entente→appeasement→ alliance were *system-maintaining* processes in the European system, this degree of improvement in U.S.–Soviet relations could take place only as part of a gradual replacement of the Cold War system by one based on a much more cooperative relation between the two superpowers.

Therefore, when a relaxation of tension took place in U.S.–Soviet relations, the question was whether this signaled the beginnings of the gradual displacement of the Cold War system with some other kind of international system (and, if so, what), or whether détente was either only a quite limited modification of the Cold War system or a temporary respite from the acute hostility of the Cold War. Accordingly, it is not surprising that following the partial test ban treaty in the summer of 1963, skeptics questioned both the desirability and feasibility of the apparent relaxation of tensions. Was détente a purely tactical maneuver, an instrument of Soviet Cold War strategy into which the Russians entered to gain time to improve their position and to disarm the West psychologically? Could Soviet leaders be trusted? Would not a relaxation of tensions and the apparent reduction of Soviet hostility create a widespread and dangerous euphoria in the West and lead to a lowering of its guard and a weakening of its defense? Would not détente between the United States and the Soviet Union have adverse effects on our allies in Europe and elsewhere, weakening the free world alliance system and reducing its alertness to the further spread of communism?

Thus, within the framework of the Cold War system, it was much more critical and difficult to judge the opponent's *motivation* for wanting a relaxation of tensions. Similarly, the possibly adverse *consequences* of permitting a relaxation of tensions were a more pressing concern than in the older European system.

Interestingly enough, uneasy questions of this kind arose not only in the United States but to some extent within the Soviet Union as well. Soviet leaders were obliged to assure those skeptical of détente in their own country that they were not lowering their guard, would not neglect Soviet military defenses, were not naively trusting American leaders, were not betraying Marxist ideology and Socialist aspirations. Both American and, to a lesser extent, Soviet leaders faced the difficult task of obtaining domestic political legitimacy for their efforts to move away from the acute Cold War era to a less dangerous form of competition. The roles of ideology, public opinion, domestic constraints, and other features of the diplomatic revolution particularly complicated the efforts of American leaders to move beyond a mere relaxation of tensions toward a more significant restructuring of and improvement in relations with the Soviet Union.

With the passage of time, particularly in the Nixon administration, the search for an improvement in U.S.–Soviet relations went well beyond a relaxation of tensions. As noted in chapter 10, Nixon and Kissinger announced that it was their goal to develop a new ''constructive'' relationship with the Soviet Union that would constitute the foundation for a new international system to replace the Cold War. Nonetheless, it is significant that they continued to use the term *détente* to characterize this more ambitious long-range policy objective. Nixon and Kissinger spoke of maintaining and furthering the ''détente process,'' while in fact the state of Soviet–American relations moved from ''détente'' to ''rapprochement'' to partial ''appeasement.'' The term *détente* was stretched to encompass most of the discrete stages in the gradual improvement of relations between previously hostile states. One can, of course, understand Kissinger's reluctance to employ the term *appeasement* to describe his policies and activities, since it had acquired a highly negative and emotional connotation for the American public as a result of the disastrous effort to appease Hitler in the 1930s. But he was unable to dispel the unhappy association, and it haunted the Ford administration when the American public, as we have seen above, turned against the détente policy and forced its abandonment.

The effort to replace the Cold War with détente was by no means monopolized by American and Soviet leaders. During the early sixties, President Charles de Gaulle had unilaterally taken steps to bring France into closer relations with the Soviet Union; and, before the end of that decade, the West German government was moving cautiously to normalize and develop its relations with the USSR, the Eastern European states, and the German Democratic Republic. The lead was taken by Willy Brandt, first as foreign minister in the government of the Great Coalition headed by Kurt Georg Kiesinger, and later as chancellor of the SPD/FDP coalition that emerged after the elections of 1969.

The motivation and general course of Brandt's *Ostpolitik* have been touched on-already in chapter 10, but it is worthwhile dwelling here upon the diplomatic technique of what was a remarkably skillful performance, undertaken in a complex international environment and under difficult domestic political conditions. It was all the more difficult because the procedures that Brandt followed were closer to nineteenth-century practice than more recent experiments in détente diplomacy.

Brandt's Ostpolitik

It should be noted at the outset that Brandt had a clear notion not only of the changes that he wished to effect but also of the difficulties that lay in his path. His initiative was based on a shrewd assessment of potential risks and gains and of how to utilize leverage to maneuver around obstacles. Since his *Ostpolitik* willingly embraced the possibility of major concessions to the Soviet Union and the East German regime, it certainly contained elements of what we would regard as appeasement; but Brandt orchestrated the complex process of détente to ensure that he gained important benefits in return, not only for West Germany but for Europe as a whole. He established diplomatic relations with Rumania and Yugoslavia and increased economic and cultural ties with other states in Eastern Europe. In 1970, he worked out a major deal with the Soviet Union, exchanging German-made pipe for Soviet natural gas. He dangled the possibility of favorable credit and commercial arrangements before the economically depressed Eastern European governments.

Unlike Chamberlain in his dealings with Hitler, Brandt did not rush the détente process in order to move as quickly as possible into appeasement. The British prime minister had been so certain of the ultimate success of appeasement that he engaged in a gigantic gamble, without assessing what would happen if his calculations proved to be in error and without having a prepared fallback position. In contrast, Brandt made a realistic calculation of the complexity and dangers of the course upon which he was embarking and devised a strategy and tactics that took them into account. Failure of *Ostpolitik* at any point might, to be sure, have led to the chancellor's political demise, but it would not have constituted a catastrophic setback either for West Germany or for NATO. Brandt minimized the risks by moving one step at a time and then waiting until the situation ripened before moving ahead again. He never forgot that he could negotiate successfully with the Soviet Union and its allies only if he operated from a position of strength based upon his NATO connection. Nevertheless, he did not allow the initiatives that he wished to take to be paralyzed by the sometimes lukewarm support of the United States.

At the same time, Brandt's freedom of maneuver was always severely constrained by divided opinion at home. *Ostpolitik,* therefore, inevitably required a strategy in which diplomatic moves were carefully controlled and timed to solidify domestic support or to neutralize political opposition. Indeed, some of the chancellor's initiatives toward the East were shrewdly calculated to weaken opposition at home.

A good illustration of this is the way in which he dramatized his policy at the outset, by means of his unprecedented trip to Erfurt in East Germany in March 1970, an action that was strongly reminiscent of the visit that King Edward VII made to Paris as part of the preparation for the Anglo-French entente of 1904. In his first policy statement after becoming chancellor, Brandt had announced in October 1969 that he intended to seek conversations with both the Soviet and Polish governments, and almost immediately he sent Egon Bahr to Moscow to sound out Andrei Gromyko on the possibility of a normalization of relations. Simultaneously, Georg von Duckwitz, state secretary in the Foreign Office in Bonn, began similar talks with the Poles. The approach to the German Democratic Republic Brandt reserved for himself, doubtless because of the intensity of his feelings concerning the necessity of restoring contact between Germans who had been brutally separated by the results of the Cold War. On 22 January 1970, he wrote to the chairman of the Council of Ministers in the German Democratic Republic, Willi Stoph, and suggested a personal meeting to discuss "practical questions . . . that could alleviate the life of people in divided Germany." After some diplomatic sparring, in which Stoph sought to make the talks conditional upon preliminary concessions by the Federal Republic, he received a favorable reply, possibly because of Soviet pressure on East Berlin. On 19 March, a day that seemed to many European observers to mark a decisive change in the direction of Central European politics, Brandt arrived in Erfurt.

The chancellor did not expect to register a great success at this meeting or at its sequel in Kassel in West Germany. The Erfurt trip was planned for its impact upon public opinion on both sides of the common frontier. Aside from that, Brandt's goal had been to take the initiative in a way that, if it accomplished nothing else, would neutralize negative East German influence in Moscow while the Bahr–Gromyko talks were proceeding, while at the same time letting Eastern European governments see that there were areas of policy in which the Federal Republic was able and willing to conclude bilateral agreements. Without in any way loosening his ties with the West, Brandt was making it known that the *Bundesrepublik* was prepared to follow an independent line in the interest of general appeasement.

This had positive results. In August 1970, the Moscow talks ended successfully with the signature of a Soviet–West German treaty that provided for the pacific resolution of all disputes between the signatories and recognized the existing frontiers between the two Germanies and between Germany and Poland, while not excluding the possibility of German reunification "in free self-determination." (This treaty was a way station in the progress of the Soviet Union toward the more comprehensive border clauses negotiated at the Conference on Security and Cooperation in Europe and embodied in the Helsinki Agreement of 1975.) Four months later, a similar treaty normalized relations between the Federal Republic and Poland, stipulating the recognition by the former of the inviolability of Poland's frontiers, including the Oder-Neisse line, which Western governments had long insisted was a merely provisional border.

What were the benefits derived by West Germany and the West in general? Brandt wanted to extract from the Soviets and the East Germans an agreement that would guarantee the independent status of West Berlin and access to it by the Western powers. He assured this by indicating to the Soviets that he would not submit the Moscow Treaty to the German parliament for ratification until a satisfactory agreement on Berlin was negotiated by the four occupying powers. This was accomplished in due course, and the Berlin Agreement was signed by the powers in September 1971. Under pressure from the Soviets, the East German government, which had been reluctant to respond positively to Brandt's earlier overtures, now worked out agreements with the Federal Republic governing access to West Berlin and transit between the two parts of the city. The Moscow Treaty was then ratified by the Bundestag in May 1972. Six months later, after numerous meetings between officials of the Federal and Democratic republics, relations between the two Germanies were finally normalized by the so-called Basic Treaty, in which each agreed to respect the other's territorial integrity and to renounce the use of force in settling disputes, while also promising collaboration on practical and humane questions. In 1973, both governments applied, and were accepted, for membership in the United Nations.

With Brandt's fight to win parliamentary ratification of his work, in which he succeeded by defeating a vote of no confidence in April 1972 and, five months later, by forcing new parliamentary elections, we need not concern ourselves here. This is true also of the long-term results of *Ostpolitik,* which have been discussed in chapter 10. On the other hand, it is worth emphasizing that the manner in which Brandt and Bahr pursued their diplomatic goals illustrates some of the prerequisites for effective use of the détente strategy. Among them, of course, is the importance of skillful political leadership that understands the multiple risks of embarking on such a course. The contrast between Brandt and Chamberlain was in this respect, as we have noted, striking. *Ostpolitik* is also a useful reminder that, while the sequence détente→rapprochement→entente→appeasement cannot be pursued in today's world in precisely the same manner as it was in the European balance-of-power system, the older historical experience with this process retains relevance and value. Although the Cold War provided an entirely different context for the pursuit of détente/appeasement, this strategy remained potentially viable if employed with due caution and with sensitivity to the greater complexity of the situation and the nature of the risks involved. Indeed, the careful, step-by-step way in which Brandt pursued *Ostpolitik* bears important similarities with the measured management of the détente process by English and French statesmen at the turn of the century.

Bibliographical Essay

There has been relatively little systematic comparative analysis of the phenomenon of détente by historians and political scientists. One such study is being undertaken by Sean Lynn-Jones. Two useful discussions are Evan Luard, "Conciliation and Deterrence," *World Politics* 19 (1967): 167–189, and John Herz, "The Relevancy and Irrelevancy of Appeasement," *Social Research* 31 (1964): 296–320. See also Kal Holsti, *International Politics* (Englewood Cliffs, N.J., 1972).

The historical shift from adversarial to peaceful policies in state relations is analyzed by John Mueller in *Retreat from Doomsday: The Obsolescence of Major War* (New York, 1989) and by Stephen Ray Rock in *Why Peace Breaks Out: Great Powers Rapprochement in Historical Perspective* (Chapel Hill, N.C., 1989). The historical shift from territorial expansion to trade as the key to international position, wealth, and power is the subject of Richard Rosecrance, *The Rise of the Trading State* (New York, 1986).

On the Anglo-French entente of 1904, see especially Christopher Andrew, *Théophile Delcassé and the Making of the Entente Cordiale* (New York, 1968); G. P. Gooch, *Before the War: Studies in Diplomacy*, vol. 1 (London, 1936); Zara S. Steiner, *The Foreign Office and Foreign Policy, 1898–1914* (Cambridge, 1965); and Paul Kennedy, *The Rise of Anglo-German Antagonism, 1860–1914* (London, 1980). The Haldane quotation is from his diary of his Berlin visit. See G. P. Gooch and H. W. Temperley, eds., *British Documents on the Origins of the War* (London, 1930ff.), vol. 6, no. 506, p. 681. We are indebted to David Jex for calling this to our attention.

For Chamberlain's appeasement policy, see Bibliographical Essay to chapter 7.

For Brandt's views on the development of *Ostpolitik,* see Willy Brandt, *Begegnungen und Einsichten: Die Jahre 1960–1975* (Hamburg, 1976). Other useful sources include Karl Birnbaum, *East and West Germany* (Lexington, Mass., 1973); Michael Freund, *From Cold War to Ostpolitik* (London, 1972); William E. Griffith, *The Ostpolitik of the Federal Republic of Germany* (Cambridge, Mass., 1978); Peter Merkl, *German Foreign Policies, West and East* (Santa Barbara, Calif., 1974); Roger Tilford, *The Ostpolitik and Political Change in Germany* (Lexington, Mass., 1975); Lawrence Whetten, *Germany's Ostpolitik* (London, 1971); Philip Windsor, *Germany and the Management of Detente* (New York, 1971); and Christian Hacke, *Weltmacht wider Willen: Die Aussenpolitik der Bundesrepublik Deutschland,* rev. ed. (Frankfurt-am-Main, 1993). See also the Bibliographical Essay for chapter 10.

19

The Role of Force in Diplomacy: A Continuing Dilemma for U.S. Foreign Policy

The proposition that force and threats of force are at times a necessary instrument of diplomacy and have a role to play in foreign policy is part of the conventional wisdom of statecraft. And it is true that history supports the view that efforts to deal with interstate conflicts of interest solely by means of rational persuasion and peaceful diplomacy do not always succeed and may result in substantial damage to one's national interests. On the other hand, one can also find in history many cases in which threats of force or the actual use of force were often not only ineffective but seriously aggravated disputes between states or even triggered wars that might otherwise have been avoided.

Given that historical experience supports both the necessity as well as the risks of resorting to force and threats of force we are left with a central, difficult question in the theory and practice of foreign policy: Under what conditions and how can military force and threats of force be used effectively to accomplish different types of foreign policy objectives at an acceptable level of cost and risk?

This has sharply divided American strategic thinkers; it has been a focal point in many controversies over foreign policy since the early days of the Cold War. More recently, in 1992 and 1993, as the debate whether the United States should intervene in the Bosnian crisis and, if so, how and on behalf of what objectives, demonstrated that this question continues to pose acute dilemmas for American policy in the post–Cold War era as well. This issue and the controversy surrounding it was exacerbated in the early autumn of 1993 when U.S. military forces suffered casualties in Somalia, a development that led to efforts to redefine and restrict U.S. participation in UN peacekeeping efforts. Thus, although the geopolitical and strategic context has changed dramatically, the dilemma remains as to what role force and threats of force can be expected to play in a variety of novel settings.

This issue is of central importance in that it undergirds strategies of deterrence and coercive diplomacy that are often employed in dealing with conflicts of interest with other states. Efforts to deter adversaries from serious encroachments on one's interests and those of friendly states often require an ability to make threats that are sufficiently credible and potent enough to dissuade the adversary. This is especially true when sanctions and other nonviolent measures are expected to be or prove to be an ineffective backup to diplomacy. Not only deterrence strategy but coercive diplomacy as well often depends on an ability to generate credible threats to use force if necessary. As the Bosnian case strikingly demonstrates, however, threats appropriate to a situation are not easily generated. In this case, as in earlier crises, ample military capabilities are available but for various reasons are not usable. When policy makers are confronted by a low-level military conflict they may face the difficult choice between escalating to higher levels of violence or backing down if they lack appropriate and usable military options.

"Massive Retaliation" and Its Critics

American strategic thinking and war planning during the early period of the Cold War operated on the assumption that any military engagement with Soviet forces would likely be the trigger for World War III. Accordingly, to prevent such a development it appeared necessary to deter any Soviet military initiatives, however limited their scope, by threatening that the United States response might entail general nuclear war. However, when the Soviet Union began to acquire nuclear weapons of its own, policy planners in the Truman administration saw the need to focus on strengthening conventional capabilities in order to shore up deterrence and have the option of dealing with lesser conflicts without having to resort to nuclear weapons. On the other hand, the Eisenhower administration did not find this an attractive option. When John Foster Dulles, newly designated to be Eisenhower's secretary of state, announced in January 1954 that "massive retaliation" would be the new administration's policy, he seemed to imply that the United States would respond to low-level aggression against U.S. allies with a strategic nuclear attack against the homeland of the aggressor—whether it be the Soviet Union or the People's Republic of China. The possibility that the United States might convert local wars into a general nuclear war alarmed U.S. and allied opinion, and this in turn led Dulles into a series of efforts to clarify his meaning in a more specific and moderate direction. He was not entirely successful in this respect, and indeed could not afford to be. For massive retaliation was primarily a declaratory policy intended to deter various kinds of aggression against members of the free world. Dulles and Eisenhower used the threat of massive retaliation as a means of warning a would-be Soviet or Chinese

Communist aggressor that the United States would not allow it the choice of conditions for combat. Rather, as Dulles put it, the United States would respond "at places and with means of our own choosing."

Massive retaliation, therefore, threatened substantial escalation of any conflict imposed on the United States or its allies. The administration made such threats during several crises. But, in fact, a striking divergence occurred between the slogan of massive retaliation and the Eisenhower administration's actual behavior in dealing with conflicts in Third World areas. When war threatened over Indochina, Lebanon, the offshore islands of Quemoy and Matsu, and Berlin, the Eisenhower administration either refrained from action or desperately sought the conventional forces with which to manage the situation.

Criticisms of massive retaliation by defense intellectuals and members of the opposition party mounted during the Eisenhower era. Massive retaliation and its cornerstone, U.S. strategic superiority, they pointed out, had not prevented the occurrence of many limited conflicts. Deterrence of lesser conflicts had failed and would fail again in the future because the threat of massive retaliation was simply not a credible response to low-level aggression, particularly in conflicts in which Soviet forces were not involved. Massive retaliation would become even less credible in the future as the Soviet Union acquired larger strategic nuclear forces of its own. Moreover, critics argued that for various reasons the United States could not rely on the Eisenhower administration's proposed use of so-called tactical nuclear weapons. Therefore, most critics of massive retaliation and Eisenhower's overall defense doctrine concluded that to deter and deal with lower-level threats to the security of free world allies, the United States would need much stronger conventional war forces.

For all these reasons the major thrust of Kennedy's defense policies was the acquisition of a fuller array of military capabilities that would provide a larger, more diversified set of military options along the entire spectrum of violence. This was expected to make possible many more discriminating and effective uses of force and, accordingly, also provide a stronger backup for U.S. diplomacy and a basis for more effective deterrence of limited aggression. Soon after entering the presidency Kennedy announced a new doctrine of "flexible, controlled response" to guide his administration's defense policies. Response to attacks against any part of the free world, he said, would be "suitable, selective" as well as "swift and effective." The president also stated general guidelines for the design and use of military force: "Our weapons systems must be *usable* in a manner permitting *deliberation* and *discrimination* as to timing, scope, and targets in *response to civilian authority*" (italics added).

Thus, the Kennedy administration attempted to develop a concept of controlled use of force appropriate to particular situations that would enable it to employ force and threats of force as a highly refined instrument of diplomacy. It was expected that force and threats of force would continue to be necessary even in an increasingly dangerous world in which both superpowers possessed large strategic nuclear arsenals; therefore, the new administration intended to give greater emphasis than before to ensuring controlled, discriminating use of force.

In time, however, the Kennedy administration's defense doctrine gave new impetus to a controversy over strategy that had emerged during and after the Korean War. Two quite different "lessons" had been drawn from that war that reflected sharp disagreement over the way in which the Truman administration conducted the war and dissatisfaction with its outcome. It may be recalled that after the Chinese communists entered the war in late November 1950 and imposed upon General MacArthur's forces what has been called "the longest retreat" in American military history, President Truman decided to abandon the ambitious objective he had been pursuing since the late summer of unifying the two Korean states by force of arms. Instead, Truman now limited the American objective to maintaining South Korea's independence and imposed important limits on military strategy and tactics in order to avoid the possibility of triggering escalation to a larger war that might lead to World War III. It was for this reason that Truman rejected General MacArthur's proposal that the war be expanded against the Chinese mainland in order to achieve a military victory, and when the general argued this case publicly, he was relieved of his command.

The "Never-Again" and "Limited War" Schools

General MacArthur's argument that there is no substitute for victory and that the U.S. military should not be forced to fight with one arm tied behind its back was not forgotten. After the war many military and civilian strategists argued that the United States should never again fight a similar limited, inconclusive war. Either it should stay out of such conflicts altogether or, if it intervened, it should use whatever military force might be required to win a decisive military victory.

Those who subscribed to this lesson of the Korean War quickly came to be known as the *Never-Again* School. The strategic doctrine they advocated regarding American military intervention was appropriately labeled *all-or-nothing*—that is, either the United States should be prepared to do everything necessary to win or it should not intervene at all.

A quite different lesson from the Korean War experience was drawn by other foreign policy specialists. They argued that in the age of thermonuclear weapons the United States might well have to fight limited wars again. One had to expect other regional conflicts would occur in which the United States felt obliged to intervene because important interests were at stake. If, as in Korea, there was a risk that these new regional conflicts could escalate to high levels of warfare which we wanted to avoid, then the United States would most likely have to limit its objectives and the military means it employed. Quite appropriately, those who drew this particular lesson from the Korean War came to be known as adherents of the *Limited War* School.

The disagreement over strategy between adherents of the Never-Again and the Limited War viewpoints was not resolved after the Korean War. These contending views had an impact on American policymaking in subsequent crises.

The Never-Again philosophy played a quite important role in keeping the Eisenhower administration from intervening in the Indochina crisis of 1954. The prolonged and costly French colonial war in Indochina seemed to be ending in defeat when the French army was surrounded by Vietminh forces at Dienbienphu. Everyone in the Eisenhower administration agreed that the loss of Indochina to the Communists would severely damage U.S. interests. They regarded it of the utmost importance to contain the spread of Chinese Communist influence in Asia. Eisenhower himself had coined the phrase "row of dominoes" to highlight concern that the loss of any country, however geographically remote, to communism would trigger further setbacks in adjacent countries. As the French defeat drew closer, some of Eisenhower's advisers favored air strikes to relieve French forces surrounded at Dienbienphu. The leading spokesman of the Never-Again School, General Mathew Ridgway, was Army Chief of Staff at the time. President Eisenhower himself held views that echoed the all-or-nothing thinking of the Never-Again School. Ridgway and Eisenhower believed that before intervening with air power, which could not be militarily decisive, a careful calculation should be made of the additional forces—ground forces—that would be necessary to defeat the communists in Indochina. Their sober calculation indicated that the United States could probably "win" such a war but that to do so would take an even larger military effort than had been expended in the Korean War. Sobered by this hard-boiled cost-benefit analysis, Eisenhower rejected military intervention altogether and decided to try to deal with the consequences of the now certain French defeat through diplomacy.

In the Offshore Islands crisis off mainland China in 1958, when a Chinese Communist invasion of the island of Quemoy seemed possible, the Joint Chiefs of Staff, reflecting the all-or-nothing point of view, requested President Eisenhower to predelegate to them the authority to use tactical nuclear weapons if they judged it necessary to use them to defeat an invasion. Eisenhower refused to do so this time, reflecting a view associated with Limited War thinking. He believed, just as Truman had in the Korean War, that the president himself must retain tight control over military options that could trigger unwanted escalation of a limited conflict. What this case illustrates, therefore, is not only the tension between the two strategic concepts but the fact that when confronted by the possibility of unwanted escalation of a local crisis even a president who sympathizes with the Never-Again philosophy will recognize the need to keep a limited conflict limited and forgo all-out use of force to gain a military victory. Which of the two strategic philosophies dominated, therefore, was sensitive to the special character of each crisis.

Several years later in the Laos crisis of 1961–1962, the all-or-nothing preference of the Never-Again School was present in the sweeping war plan prepared by Joint Chiefs of Staff that included possible use of nuclear weapons in response to President Kennedy's request for military options in case his diplomatic efforts to secure the neutralization of Laos failed and Communist forces continued to advance on the battlefield. It is not the case that U.S. military leaders were interested to fight a war over Laos; rather, they wanted to make the point that if we did intervene on a small scale to begin with, the war might escalate into a direct clash with Communist China and, then, in order not to lose or fight an inconclusive war as in Korea, it might be necessary to resort to nuclear weapons.

The Impact of Vietnam

Let us turn now to developments in U.S. policy toward Vietnam from 1961, when Kennedy became president, to 1965 when Johnson sent American combat forces into Vietnam. One of the puzzles which historians have not yet adequately clarified is the marked decline during this period of the influence of Never-Again thinking in American policy making. Neither the new civilian leaders nor the new military chiefs who came into office with President Kennedy subscribed to the all-or-nothing position of the old Never-Againers. Instead, Kennedy gave high priority to developing a strong counterinsurgency capability and tried to use it to help the South Vietnam government in Saigon to cope with the increasingly strong effort to overthrow it by the Communist-oriented Vietminh insurgents. Before his first year in office was over Kennedy had sent U.S. military advisers into South Vietnam. But although he was to increase the number of military advisers and indirect military assistance, Kennedy was assassinated before *he* had to face the critical decision whether to send U.S. combat forces or to accept the defeat of the Saigon government. His successor in the presidency, however, was confronted with this choice and, encouraged by all but one of his advisers, George Ball, Johnson crossed the threshold and began direct military intervention.

As events unfolded and more and more forces were sent to Vietnam, it became clear that Johnson had been prepared to do a great deal militarily to prevent the overrunning of South Vietnam. But from the beginning he was deeply worried that the Indochina conflict might escalate uncontrolably, draw us into another major war with China, and also force the Soviet Union into substantial involvement in support of North Vietnam. To avoid unwanted escalation, just as Truman had done in the Korean War, Johnson imposed important limits on the objectives and scope of the U.S. military effort. He ruled out an invasion of North Vietnam, limited the targets of air attacks on North Vietnam, refused to declare a national emergency and request Congress to authorize call-up of the military reserves. In consequence, U.S. strategic options for fighting the war were limited. For various reasons the seemingly attractive strategy of using major U.S. ground forces to seal off the borders between South Vietnam and North Vietnam and Laos and thereby put a stop to infiltration of large-scale North Vietnamese army units and supplies was rejected. Also rejected was another strategic option: the defense "enclave" strategy to protect major cities and ports in the South. The only remaining strategic option was the questionable and increasingly costly one of fighting a prolonged war of attrition to grind down the North Vietnamese armed forces, a contest in which we expected to prevail. However, in March 1968, after the Tet offensive, when Johnson's council of wise men told him that the war had reached the point at which it no longer made sense to increase U.S. forces and that he should move toward ending it, the president followed their advice.

After assuming the presidency in 1969, Richard Nixon introduced his "Vietnamization" policy of gradually withdrawing U.S. ground forces while beefing up the capability of the South Vietnam armed forces, and trying at the same time to negotiate an acceptable settlement of the war with Hanoi. Nixon's policy was a partial, limited success. He succeeded in ending the war in a way that secured his limited objective (which he and Kissinger never openly acknowledged) of obtaining a "decent interval" of time between the withdrawal of U.S. forces and the likely overrunning of South Vietnam by North Vietnamese forces. In fact, this outcome was virtually inevitable because to end the war Nixon and Kissinger had to make important concessions in the negotiations with Hanoi that left South Vietnam highly vulnerable whenever Hanoi should decide to resume the fighting.

If the Never-Again philosophy had become too impotent to be able to prevent U.S. military involvement in Vietnam in 1965, the unsatisfactory outcome of that war triggered a very strong revival of the all-or-nothing approach to military intervention that had been emphasized by the Never-Again School. This was coupled with severe criticism of the constraints that Johnson had imposed on military strategy and on the conduct of military operations which, it was argued, had prevented the United States from winning the war. It must be said that those who advanced these criticisms of Johnson's conduct of the war ignored the reasons, already noted, that led him to judge such constraints to be necessary. But the fact remains that instead of allowing the military chiefs to develop and apply a strategy that they thought might produce a quick decisive victory, Johnson had engaged in "micromanagement" of military operations and slow, piecemeal military pressure—a policy of "gradualism" that ran counter to professional military doctrine for war-fighting. These specific criticisms of Johnson's conduct of the war generated a strong revival and elaboration of the Never-Again approach in the post-Vietnam era. The new version of that doctrine came to dominate U.S. strategic thinking and was used to discredit the rationale of the Limited War approach. Those who continued to have misgivings over the all-or-nothing aspect of the post-Vietnam doctrine had a hard time gaining a hearing.

The Weinberger–Shultz Debate

Nowhere was this more evident than in the head-on clash during the first Reagan administration between Secretary of Defense Caspar Weinberger and Secretary of State George Shultz. Their debate, at times impassioned if not also acrimonious, was triggered by a number of difficult and controversial decisions the Reagan administration had to make concerning whether American military forces should intervene in some way in the civil war in El Salvador, whether direct U.S. military action of some kind should be threatened against the Sandinista regime in Nicaragua, what role U.S. forces should play in protecting neutral shipping in the Persian Gulf during the Iran–Iraq war, and finally the pros and cons of placing U.S. forces into Lebanon in 1982, an intervention which ended in the disastrous loss of the lives of 241 Marines when terrorists bombed the Marine barracks in Beirut in October 1983.

In addition to disagreeing on specific policies, Weinberger and Shultz cast their views in general philosophical-strategic terms. Secretary of Defense Weinberger, deeply influenced by the disaster of the Vietnam War and strongly supported by the Joint Chiefs of Staff, argued against direct participation of U.S. military forces in Third World conflicts. To intervene in such conflicts, he argued, could once again as in Vietnam draw us into prolonged, increasingly costly, and increasingly unpopular wars of attrition that might end inconclusively or in defeat. If we took the first small step of military intervention we might find ourselves, once again, as in Vietnam, on a "slippery slope" that would eventually lead to a large-scale involvement of U.S. forces and prestige.

Weinberger and the military chiefs recognized that important U.S. interests were often at stake in such Third World conflicts, but they argued that we should limit ourselves to giving economic aid, military supplies and advice, and making greater use of covert operations. Beyond indirect assistance of this kind, we should rely on diplomacy to protect our interests.

To this Shultz objected, arguing that diplomacy and force could not be completely separated. Diplomatic efforts not backed by credible threats of force and, when necessary, with limited use of force would often prove ineffectual, resulting in damage to U.S. interests. The views attributed here to Shultz should not be misunderstood; he was not stating or supporting the extreme position of hawks who argue for much more ambitious uses of military force. Rather, Shultz was articulating the traditional, conventional view that a great power with global interests must back its diplomacy from time to time with credible threats of force and be willing to use military force on occasion if threats did not suffice. In effect, Shultz was saying to Weinberger, how can I as secretary of state protect and advance American interests if my diplomatic efforts lack teeth?

Shultz went public with his views in a major address on April 3, 1984. He insisted: "Power and diplomacy always go together. . . . Certainly power must always be guided by purpose, but the hard reality is that diplomacy not backed by strength is ineffectual. . . . Power and diplomacy are not distinctive alternatives. They must go together, or we will accomplish very little in the world."

In his speech, Shultz did not reject the "lessons" of Vietnam to which Weinberger, the military chiefs, and many others have subscribed, but he observed that situations do arise when a "discrete assertion of power" will be needed to support our limited objectives.

This speech and another one Shultz made several months later (October 25, 1984) provoked Secretary of Defense Weinberger to rebut Shultz publicly. In a carefully crafted address to the National Press Club in Washington (November 28, 1984) Weinberger presented his own philosophy on the role of force. In this speech, which he titled "The Uses of Military Power," Weinberger listed what he called "six major tests" that should be made in judging whether the United States should employ its own military forces in Third World conflicts. (He later stated these same preconditions for use of force in an article in the journal of *Foreign Affairs,* spring 1986.)

Four of Weinberger's preconditions are of particular interest in that they have dominated American strategy ever since. (Each of his four conditions will be listed here with an indication how it differs from Shultz's position.) First, Weinberger insisted, the United States should use force *only* when its truly *vital interests* were at stake. Shultz, on the other hand, felt this condition was too restrictive. He argued that the United States had many important interests which, though less than "vital," had also to be protected and that these interests could not often be safeguarded unless our diplomatic efforts were backed by military power.

The second precondition Weinberger laid down reflected the all-or-nothing maxim and was equally restrictive: "Should the United States decide to commit its forces to combat, we must commit them in sufficient numbers . . . to win. If we are unwilling to commit the forces or resources to achieve our objectives, or if the objective is not important enough so that we must achieve it, [then] we should not commit our forces." In other words, the United States government should not intervene unless it was prepared to do everything necessary to win a quick, decisive military victory.

Shultz did not lack sympathy with this view but he took the position that the vast majority of foreign policy conflicts with which the United States must deal are cases which, unlike World War II, "fall short of an all-out national commitment." In this vein Shultz went on to argue that when confronted by lesser challenges the lesson of Vietnam that Weinberger emphasized could not be rigidly employed. Shultz argued as follows:

> The need to avoid no-win situations cannot mean that we turn automatically away from hard-to-win situations that call for prudent involvement. These [cases] will always involve risks; we will not always have the luxury to choose the most advantageous circumstances.

Weinberger's third precondition for the use of force was that U.S. military forces should not be committed to combat unless they were given "clearly defined political and military objectives"—a condition that, according to many critics of the conduct of the Vietnam War, was not present in that war and contributed to failure there. Shultz, again not entirely unsympathetic, pointed out that there were many murky, complicated crises in which Weinberger's third precondition could not be easily met. When U.S. interests were sufficiently at stake we would have to adapt military power to the situation as best we could. Our political objectives would have to have priority over establishing clear-cut military objectives, and we would have to accept political constraints on employment of military force that deviated from military doctrine on how to use military power most effectively.

Another of Weinberger's preconditions, again drawn from the Vietnam experience, referred to the importance of domestic political support. Notice the form in which Weinberger stated this caveat: "Before the United States commits combat forces abroad, the U.S. government should have reasonable assurance of the support of the American people and their elected representatives in Congress." Shultz certainly understood the importance of domestic political support for use of American forces abroad, but he could not accept Weinberger's extreme and unqualified position on the matter. Rather, the secretary of state argued, decisions to use force in defense of American interests "cannot be tied to opinion polls." And, in a further barbed reply to his cabinet colleague, Shultz reminded him that "a president who has the courage to lead will *win* public support if he acts wisely and effectively." (Weinberger's other two preconditions were that the use of U.S. forces for combat should be undertaken only as a last resort after exhausting other means for safeguarding our vital interests; and the relationship between objectives and means should be continually reassessed and adjusted as necessary.)

Although it was the criticism of Vietnam by U.S. military leaders that provided the impetus for a revival of Never-Again thinking, their views were strongly supported by many civilian leaders and strategists. The sweeping rejection of the Limited War concept put those, like Shultz in his debate with Weinberger, who tried to make the minimal case for the need to back diplomacy occasionally with threats of force or limited military actions, on the defensive. In fact, those who rejected Vietnam did not limit the lessons they drew and the prescriptions for the future to questions of military strategy. Not only did they revive the basic all-or-nothing maxim of the old Never-Again School; they broadened it into the assertion of a comprehensive national strategy which held that henceforth any contemplated use of force on behalf of foreign policy should be rejected unless it adhered to sound military doctrine for war-fighting and military victory.

Thus, the post-Vietnam doctrine called into question, tacitly rather than explicitly, Clausewitz's famous maxim that war is a continuation of politics by other means and that political considerations necessarily take precedence over military logic. Rather, the new doctrine argued, use of force in support of foreign policy must give way, if necessary, to military requirements for the effective, efficient use of force.

Tests and Challenges to the Post-Vietnam Strategic Doctrine

There was to be no significant challenge to the new political-military doctrine until the Bosnian war. The imperatives of the new way of thinking about the restricted role of force had been reinforced by the disastrous intervention in Lebanon which led to the bombing of the Marine barracks in Beirut in 1982. Successful U.S. military action that followed in Grenada and Panama was held to demonstrate the wisdom of the new doctrine's requirement for use of overwhelming force to achieve a decisive outcome quickly and cheaply. The Bush administration's response to Iraq's aggression against Kuwait was not only entirely consistent with the new doctrine; it constituted a textbook illustration of the wisdom of committing overwhelming military force and using it in accord with sound military doctrine that military leaders were allowed to implement without micromanagement of military operations by political leaders and without undue political constraints.

In the case of Somalia, U.S. military leaders initially hesitated to send forces to ensure delivery and distribution of food and medical supplies. Their hesitation was overcome by strictly delimiting the objective to the humanitarian task of eliminating starvation, by employing large enough forces to accomplish that mission, and by establishing in advance the terms for quick withdrawal of most

U.S. forces and turning over to the United Nations responsibility for disarming Somali clans and reconstructing state structures.

In this way the Bush administration hoped that U.S. forces could intervene effectively on behalf of the humanitarian objective without risk of being drawn into a "quagmire." The strategy for doing so reflected key principles of the post-Vietnam doctrine of getting in with ample force, achieving the military objective quickly, and getting out once it was accomplished. However, critics of Bush's policy of limited humanitarian intervention warned that withdrawal of U.S. forces without adequate disarmanment of the forces of rival Somali "war lords," who could be expected to lie low while U.S. forces were present, would lead to a resumption of violence thereafter in a struggle for power. Among those who voiced these concerns was UN Secretary General Boutros-Ghali, but he failed in his effort to obtain a broadened commitment from the Bush administration to participate in the necessary effort to secure substantial disarmament of the forces of the rival Somali clans. In effect, one can criticize the Bush administration for making a questionable effort to separate the achievement of humanitarian objectives from the other problems that had to be dealt with in order to obtain the secure environment needed for establishing a stable political structure in the country. Soon after the departure of the bulk of U.S. forces, the UN command in Somali found itself unable to make progress in encouraging political reconciliation in the country and increasingly at odds with the strongly armed forces of the Somali factional leader General Mohammed Farah Aidid in Mogadishu, the Somali capital. American forces were drawn into the UN effort to neutralize Aidid's forces and to capture him, a decision by the Clinton administration that subsequently received strong criticism at home. The result, a small but politically significant number of American military casualties, led in October to a major debate as to whether U.S. forces should remain in Somalia.

The domestic controversy over these developments forced President Clinton to delimit the U.S. military role in Somalia and to set a six-month limit for withdrawal of U.S. forces. In addition, controversy generated by the setback in Somalia reinforced the already strong inhibition against any U.S. military involvement in Bosnia, even as part of UN peacekeeping forces. The unsettling experience in Somalia also led the Clinton administration to raise questions openly about the wisdom of UN intervention in so many unstable crisis situations.

Although the threat of violence to U.S. forces in Somalia was so low as to make limited intervention initially acceptable, heavy casualties were deemed possible should U.S. military forces intervene in Bosnia. From the beginning of the Bosnian crisis the post-Vietnam doctrine played a significant role in discouraging U.S. military involvement. Neither the Bush nor the Clinton administration found it easy to identify usable military options, acceptable to domestic and international opinion, for dampening the conflict in ways that would avoid a long-term, costly involvement. The dilemma regarding the use of force was identified very clearly by a *New York Times* journalist:

> From the Pentagon's vantage point, the Balkan war was not an inviting conflict. In Panama and again in the Persian Gulf, the Pentagon demonstrated that its vision of warfare is a short violent conflict in which the United States brings overwhelming force to bear and then quickly withdraws, leaving the local inhabitants to sort things out for themselves. Anything short of that tends to be seen as a quagmire in which each small step deepens the military's involvement and raises the prospect of defeat. It is a dichotomy born out of the military's bitter experience in Vietnam and Lebanon . . . the plans that Western powers are developing for possible military intervention [in Bosnia] are shaped more by the desire to avoid being entangled in the region's blood feuds than to put an end to fighting.

The new Clinton administration seemed more disposed than its predecessor to use force, but its threat of doing so was limited to use of air power and excluded use of ground combat forces. Unilateral military action by the United States was excluded and the Clinton administration had great difficulty obtaining substantial support from Western allies; indeed, it did not appear to press them very hard. In fact, although not excluding use of force in Bosnia, Secretary of State Warren Christopher echoed some of the criteria for use of force that Weinberger had earlier laid down. Appearing before the Senate Appropriations Committee on 27 April 1993 Christopher stated that any use of force would have to meet "four strict tests: the goal must be stated clearly to the American people, there must be a strong likelihood of success, there must be an 'exit strategy' and the action must win sustained public support."

As the Bosnian tragedy dragged on and the Western powers delayed taking military action, numerous voices including those of George Shultz and Margaret Thatcher criticized the unwillingness to use force. The post-Vietnam doctrine, they felt, was dangerously inadequate if used as a guideline for policy in any and all circumstances. Critics complained that the administration and its Western allies "have allowed themselves to be paralyzed by the all-or-nothing school of military thinking."

Another critic argued that a "discriminate use of force would . . . be a good precedent. If the only time the United States is going to use force is on the huge scale of Desert Storm, the post–Cold War world is going to see few Saddam-like invasions but much more 'ethnic cleansing'."

Unable or unwilling to make threats of force that were sufficiently credible and potent, Washington's efforts to use deterrence strategy to deter aggression in the Balkans and to employ coercive diplomacy to persuade the Serbs and Croats to undo or at least halt their actions against the Bosnian Muslims proved largely ineffectual. Within the United States itself, the Bosnian experience revived the tension between the maxims of the Never-Again philosophy and those of the Limited War School, but this challenge to the post-Vietnam doctrine did not succeed in altering policy. In the end, as of the time of this writing, the most the Clinton administration was able to commit itself to was to provide a substantial U.S. force to help implement a genuine agreement among the Serbs, Croats, and Muslims to end the war. And even this ''commitment'' was qualified by attaching important conditions.

American leaders will have to develop concepts and general guidance for dealing more effectively with the dilemmas we have noted regarding the role of force and threats of force in post–Cold War diplomacy. It has been suggested, for example, that in Bosnia-type situations threats of force and, if necessary, limited force may be applied effectively only on behalf of setting clear limits to intolerable behavior. It is questioned whether current U.S. strategic doctrine that counsels the use of force only in the service of vital interests, and only as a last resort, serves American diplomacy well in all instances. Whereas no single one of the many individual conflicts throughout the world threatens vital U.S. national interests, taken together they threaten the stability of the international system and, it is argued, the United States has no alternative but to consider what it can and is willing to do, together with others, to limit this threat.

In the current international environment there will continue to be occasions where threats of force will not be sufficiently credible or potent enough to deter resorting to war or to reverse such behavior. This was certainly the case in Bosnia; however, that case also indicates that threats of force and exemplary use of limited force can still be used at least to set limits on unacceptable behavior. This limited objective can be accomplished by drawing clear lines as to what responsible members of the international community will not tolerate.

Presidential directive PDD-25, issued in May 1994, lays down very stringent conditions for U.S. participation in UN peacekeeping, peacemaking, and humanitarian operations in an effort to avoid the worst outcomes of U.S. involvement. However, the directive gives little attention to what might be done to achieve better outcomes when preventive diplomacy fails and major violence occurs within or between states. More attention needs to be given to ways of achieving modest, but still useful objectives in such conflicts. Again Bosnia provides a useful example. Thus, when members of the international community made specific, quite limited demands on the Bosnian Serbs, demonstrated unity in their determination, and generated credible threats of force, the Serbs substantially adhered to the lines that were drawn. These limited successes of coercive diplomacy occurred when the West demanded that Sarajevo airport be opened for delivery of humanitarian supplies, when it called for a ''No-Fly Zone'' over Bosnia, when air drops of supplies were initiated, and when ultimata were issued regarding Sarajevo and safe havens.

These were indeed modest, yet useful successes. However, the ''lesson'' of the Bosnian experience thus far is that threats of force were credible and potent enough *only* when issued on behalf of quite limited demands. Efforts to employ coercive diplomacy on behalf of more ambitious objectives were quite unsuccessful.

This may be the most that was possible in Bosnia because, as was noted in chapter 11, opportunities for timely preventive diplomacy at an early stage in the breakup of Yugoslavia were passed over. The broader, more fundamental lesson of Bosnia is, therefore, not that the international community did eventually establish that limited force is a legitimate policy instrument under such circumstances but, rather, that it is imperative to improve the international community's ability to engage in *timely* preventive diplomacy.

If the restrictive guidelines set forth in presidential directive PDD-25 are taken literally, the result would be to exclude participation of American military forces in most situations requiring peacekeeping, peacemaking, and even intervention for humanitarian purposes in unstable, chaotic situations. However, PDD-25 did not prevent President Clinton in the autumn of 1994 from enlisting Security Council support and then ordering U.S. military forces into Haiti to restore democracy and return President Aristide to power. When Washington's ultimation to the Haitian military junta to step aside failed, the president felt obliged to order American military forces to intervene. They were on their way to Haiti when literally a last-minute diplomatic mission by former President Jimmy Carter, General Colin Powell, and Senator Sam Nunn succeeded in arranging a peaceful military occupation of the country. Noteworthy in this case is that the president acted without seeking a congressional mandate; in fact, it seemed likely that if Clinton had waited another day or two before sending U.S. forces into Haiti, Congress would have voted to appose U.S. military intervention. As of this writing the occupation of Haiti has been remarkably peaceful with the loss of life of only one American soldier, and the withdrawal of most U.S. forces has begun. Successful use of military force, however, is not likely to moderate the strong opposition to U.S. involvement in peacemaking, peacekeeping, or humanitarian intervention when there is concern for loss of American lives and fear of prolonged involvement.

In conclusion, this brief history of U.S. efforts to consider when and how force can be used as an instrument of foreign policy indicates a continuing struggle between political and military dimensions of the problem. There is a fundamental conceptual tension between the logic of war as a political act and the "logic of the instrument" of war itself that argues for using ample force to destroy or render impotent an enemy's forces. The possibility that the all-or-nothing maxim and related criteria may inhibit a necessary use of force or threats of force when important interests are at stake must be considered. However, to act imprudently on this belief is fraught with risks for any state, especially one that is so greatly influenced by domestic opinion, and when, in addition, Washington feels it necessary not to act alone but as part of a multilateral coalition.

The role of force in diplomacy will continue to pose a difficult dilemma for American foreign policy. The fundamental tension between relevant political and military considerations permits no easy and definitive resolution. Policy makers can expect to be confronted repeatedly with challenging crises and difficult choices.

Bibliographical Essay

The first part of this chapter draws on Alexander L. George, David K. Hall, and William E. Simons, *The Limits of Coercive Diplomacy* (Boston, 1971), chap. 1. An incisive, detailed analysis of the major themes of this chapter is provided by Christopher Gacek, *The Logic of Force: The Dilemma of Limited War in American Policy* (New York, 1994). Richard N. Haass, *Intervention: The Use of American Military Force in the Post–Cold War World* (Washington, D.C., 1994), provides an incisive, well-documented analysis of the dilemmas the United States has faced in deciding whether, when, how, and why to intervene abroad.

A standard discussion of the rationale for the Limited War School is contained in Robert E. Osgood, *Limited War: The Challenge to American Strategy* (Chicago, 1957). An early account of the Never-Again School appears in Joseph Kraft, *Profiles in Power* (New York, 1966), chap. 14.

Clausewitz's concept of the dual nature of war, summarized in Gacek's book, is also discussed by Michael Howard, *Clausewitz* (Oxford, 1983), chaps. 2–4; and by Peter Paret, "Clausewitz," in *Makers of Modern Strategy from Machiavelli to the Nuclear Age,* ed. Peter Paret (Princeton, 1986).

The "debate" between Weinberger and Shultz is reflected in Caspar W. Weinberger, "U.S. Defense Strategy," *Foreign Affairs* 64 (Spring 1986), and George P. Schultz, address to New York Synagogue, 25 October 1984 (*Department of State Bulletin,* 1984) and address at Yeshiva University, 9 December 1984 (*Department of State Bulletin,* February 1985).

Of the many critical assessments of U.S. strategy in the Vietnam War, particularly influential was Harry G. Summers, Jr., *On Strategy: A Critical Analysis of the Vietnam War* (Washington, D.C., 1981). A useful general survey is Russell F. Weigley, *The American Way of War: A History of United States Military Strategy and Policy* (Bloomington, Ind., 1973).

For a critical analysis of President Bush's humanitarian intervention in Somalia see, for example, Sidney Blumenthal, "Why Are We in Somalia?" *New Yorker,* 25 October 1993. For newspaper comments cited in this chapter on Clinton's Bosnian dilemma, see Michael Gordon, "Limits of U.S. Role: White House Is Seeking to Minimize Any Use of Military in Balkan Conflict," *New York Times,* 11 August 1992; Elaine Sciolino, "Christopher Explains Conditions for Use of Force in Bosnia," *New York Times,* 28 April 1993; and Paul A. Gigot, "Foreign-Policy President Finally Acts on Yugoslavia," *Wall Street Journal,* 7 August 1992.

Jane Holl offers suggestions for rethinking the current U.S. doctrine regarding use of force in diplomacy in "We the People Here Don't Want No War: Executive Branch

Perspectives on the Use of Force'' (Paper presented at the Aspin Conference, August 1994).

For presidential directive PDD-25, "The Clinton Administration's Policy on Reforming Multilateral Peace Operations," see Department of State publication 10161, May 1994.

In recent years, numerous writers and observers have urged greater emphasis on preventive diplomacy as an alternative to international interventions after armed conflict has erupted. An excellent treatment of the subject is provided by Australian Foreign Minister Gareth Evans in *Cooperating for Peace: The Global Agenda for the 1990's and Beyond* (St. Leonards, Australia, 1993).

20

Problems of Ethical and Moral Restraints on the Use of Force in Foreign Policy

The question of the role that moral and ethical principles can, or should, play in the conduct of foreign relations has engaged the attention of philosophers for centuries and, in modern times, has preoccupied the thoughts of statesmen like Bismarck, whose sense of responsibility to his office was rooted in the Lutheran doctrine of the calling, and Gladstone, who strove prayerfully to make his foreign policy conform to Christian principles. That moral principles do have a part to play in foreign affairs is easy enough to demonstrate. In an interesting book on American foreign policy, Robert W. McElroy has described three recent instances in which the U.S. government has given moral principle priority over state interest: the decision to supply massive famine relief to Russia in 1921, at a time when it was in the American interest to weaken the Soviet government; President Richard Nixon's announcement in November 1969, against the advice of the Joint Chiefs of Staff, that the United States would destroy its stockpiles of biological weapons, pledge not to initiate the use of chemical weapons in warfare, and begin negotiations to ratify the Geneva Protocol of 1925, which forbade the first use of such weapons in combat; and the decision of President Gerald Ford in 1975, again against the opposition of the Joint Chiefs, to turn the Panama Canal over to Panama, a decision confirmed by his successor.

In each case, the governmental action represented a surrender to a widely accepted norm of international behavior: in the first case, the principle that national governments have a duty to help other countries that have been devastated by disaster; in the second, the widespread opinion, around the world and in the United States, that the use of biological and chemical weapons was abhorrent; and, in the third, the strong sentiment in the wake of the Second World War against the territorial domination of one country by another. That the existence of such international norms did not assure their primacy over the demands of national policy was, however, abundantly clear: McElroy points out that the ancient principle of noncombatant immunity in time of war—the long-accepted view, which had its origins in Greek and Roman times and was made explicit in the Hague Convention of 1907 and the Hague Rules of Air Warfare in 1922—that attack or bombardment, by whatever means, upon undefended places was prohibited—failed to prevent the Allied destruction in February 1945 of the city of Dresden, which was clearly undefended but nevertheless played some part in a transportation system that the Allies wished to dislocate in the interests of shortening the war.

The Dresden case demonstrates the ambiguities involved in all attempts to follow a strictly moral line in foreign policy, even when there exist long-standing and widely recognized international norms of behavior. It is this ambiguity that explains why the role that moral and ethical principles should play in the conduct of international affairs has not been resolved even on the theoretical level.

The problem is often put in the form of a question: Does the end justify the means? This is the way in which many people address such policy questions as: Was President Truman morally justified in using the atomic bomb against Japan? Was President Kennedy morally justified in approving the Bay of Pigs invasion of Cuba and, later, in risking a thermonuclear war by attempting to coerce Khrushchev into removing the missiles from Cuba? Was Nixon justified in using covert methods to try to prevent the election of a Socialist, Allende, in Chile and, afterward, to bring about the downfall of Allende's Socialist government? Similarly, was the Soviet Union justified in using its army to put down the Hungarian revolution in 1956 and to intervene in Czechoslovakia in 1968 and Afghanistan in 1979? There are, unfortunately, many other American and Soviet foreign policy actions about which the same question can be raised. But this question can also be raised about the foreign policies of other governments. For example, during the early part of World War II, the Swedish government, having adopted a policy of neutrality, felt it prudent to stop Norwegians being hunted by the Nazis who had occupied their country from escaping into Sweden. While recognizing the policy dilemma created for Sweden, many observers questioned the morality of its decision. As this example suggests, the morality of foreign policy can be questioned not only when a state takes actions that conflict with ethical principles but also when it fails to take actions to further a moral objective. Thus, many persons thought that President Eisenhower was morally delinquent when he refused in October 1956 to give strong support and military assistance to the Hungarians who had overthrown their Communist regime, thereby allowing their revolution to be crushed by the Soviet army. And, to cite a more recent example, many persons believe that the U.S. government is morally delinquent because it has not intervened more energetically to prevent the bloodshed and the starvation in Ruwanda.

I

As noted earlier, there is a long history of controversy over the question whether and how moral principles should apply in foreign policy. Three schools of thought may be identified, each of which takes a different position on the issue "Does the end justify the means?" There is, first, the *amoral* point of view, a designation that can be given to all those who believe that the question of morality applies only to the ends or goals of foreign policy, not to the selection of means to achieve those ends. This position is taken by adherents of an extreme *Realpolitik* approach to world politics as well as by a variety of political activists—whether ideological fanatics like Hitler and the old Bolsheviks or extreme nationalists and terrorists. They argue in effect that since the objectives they pursue are morally justified, that's all that matters. *Any* means to an end is then justified, with one caveat, to be sure, and that is that the means chosen should be effective. For the amoralists, then, the criterion to be applied in choosing methods is not their morality but rather their efficiency. They are interested only in whether the means chosen will be effective in promoting the moral objective.

It should be noted, however, that those who subscribe to the amoral position do not always feel free to choose morally questionable means. Sometimes they feel obliged to respect the moral standards of others, for they realize that to be completely ruthless can create strong opposition and set back their cause. Amoralists, therefore, may restrain themselves from taking certain actions, but they do so out of prudence and coldly calculated self-interest, not because they have moral scruples of their own.

The *perfectionist* approach to the question "Does the end justify the means?" is another familiar position. The perfectionist argues that no matter how noble and virtuous the end, it *never* justifies the use of means that violate moral/ethical standards. The moral perfectionists and the amoralists, therefore, stand at opposite ends of the spectrum. Perhaps the best example of a thoroughgoing moral perfectionist is the pacifist-one who excludes the use of military force and violence in all circumstances, even in self-defense. For the genuine, full-blown pacifist not even circumstances in which the physical survival of the nation is at stake can justify a resort to violence in self-defense. However, we must not assume that pacifists are cowards. Faced with aggression against his own country, a pacifist may rely on *nonviolent* techniques of passive resistance to frustrate the aggressor. A courageous pacifist may be willing to risk his own life in passive-resistance efforts.

Similar to the pacifists in some respects are those persons in the United States and elsewhere who some years ago used to criticize Cold War policies on the grounds that they plunged the world into crises, such as the Berlin crisis of 1948 and the Cuban missile crisis, which raised the danger of a thermonuclear war. These critics were not pro-Communist or pro-Soviet; they did not favor the spread of communism throughout the world. Rather, they felt that reliance on deterrence and military threats to defend against the spread of communism was immoral and unacceptable. Many of them, like the pacifists, were willing to pay a stiff price in order to avoid the danger of World War III. They recognized that if American leaders followed their advice and did not use force and threats of force to deter communism, then communism would inevitably spread. But they took the position that such an outcome, however distasteful, was preferable to a thermonuclear holocaust, and this position they expressed in the colorful phrase "Better Red than dead." This slogan was quite popular thirty years ago among some members of the peace movement and those who favored unilateral disarmament by the United States.

Even if one disagrees with pacifists and those who argued "Better Red than dead," one can respect them for their willingness to face up to the logical and political consequences of their beliefs. Of quite a different stripe, on the other hand, are other perfectionists, often referred to as *moralizers,* who avoid dealing with the question of the costs (to others as well as to themselves) if their moralistic views on foreign policy are actually adopted. Moralists of this kind are often accused by their critics of wanting to retain the comforts of a good conscience for themselves in matters of foreign policy without being prepared to pay the price. Moralists often are more concerned with the symbolic aspects of foreign policy than its actual substance. They frequently appear to be less concerned with influencing foreign policy than with registering virtuous attitudes.

There are other interesting aspects of the perfectionist position which deserve some attention. Some perfectionists have argued that states should behave in accord with the same high standards of morality that apply to individual persons in a well-ordered community. They recognize that states and their rulers do not behave according to these standards; but they believe that they *ought* to do so and that it is the task of enlightened leaders to create an international system in which they will. A well-known exponent of this view was Woodrow Wilson. As Wilson phrased it in his message to Congress in 1917 declaring war on Germany: "We are at the beginning of an age in which it will be insisted that the same standards of conduct and responsibility for wrong done shall be observed among nations and their governments that are observed among the individual citizens of civilized states."

Various objections have been raised against this kind of perfectionist view, not all of which can be taken up here. One of the criticisms is that states are different from individuals and that therefore moral standards that can be appropriately held up to guide and judge the behavior of individual persons in a well-ordered community cannot apply to states that are trying to provide for their security in an anarchic international system. Elaborating on this, some writers (for example, E. H. Carr, in *The Twenty Years' Crisis*) say that moral standards can take precedence only in a well-developed, well-ordered international community, one in which people agree that the good of the whole community must take precedence over the good of the parts. Viewed from this standpoint, it is obvious that loyalty and adherence to a world community are not yet powerful enough to override what individual states consider to be their "vital national interest."

Another familiar criticism of the perfectionists is that their emphasis on morality easily leads to a self-righteous moralism in foreign policy. Such a criticism was leveled against John Foster Dulles, Eisenhower's secretary of state. Dulles and moralists of his kind, it was charged, are dangerous people to have in charge of foreign policy because they tend to convert conflicts of interest among states into conflicts between "good" and "evil." This kind of moralization of foreign policy can have catastrophic consequences. The more passionately a moralist leader believes he is right in a dispute with another state, the more likely he is to reject compromise and accommodation and strive instead to secure a complete victory over the opponent on behalf of his moral principles. Thus, it is possible that a moralistic approach in foreign policy, if carried to an extreme, can end up in fanaticism, which in turn can lead to catastrophic results. This type of concern was registered by Hans Morgenthau, a leading proponent of the "realist" approach to international affairs, when he wrote: "We cannot conclude [merely] from the good intentions of a statesman that his foreign policies will be either morally praise-worthy or politically successful. . . . How often have statesmen been motivated by a desire to improve the world, and ended by making it worse?"

So much for the perfectionist answer to the question "Does the end justify the means?" This formulation of the problem is rejected by a third school of thought, the *nonperfectionists,* for whom Arnold Wolfers was a leading spokesman. For the nonperfectionists, there is no simple, unequivocal answer to the question as there is for the amoralists and the perfectionists. Nonperfectionists insist that this question has to be reformulated in a significantly different way, as follows: "Under *what* conditions do *which* ends justify *what* means?" And as their reformulation of the question implies, the nonperfectionists believe that whether morally questionable means are justified cannot be answered abstractly but depends on the specific circumstances of the situation as well as on the character of the objectives the policy maker pursues in that situation.

Because nonperfectionists stress the critical importance of the circumstances of each case, they are often said to take a *contextualist* approach to the problem. That is to say, the nonperfectionists employ *situational ethics,* not absolutist ethical standards.

Who, then, subscribes to the nonperfectionist view, a view that takes issue with both the amoralists and the moral absolutists? It may come as a surprise to learn that the original *Realpolitik* and "realist" approach to international politics subscribed not to the amoral position but to this contextualist view of the role of moral principles in the conduct of foreign policy. The realist approach, identified in modern times with the writings of Hans Morgenthau, goes back at least as far as Machiavelli. It is important to recall that the Florentine thinker, although he often sounded as if he adhered to the amoral position, was in fact a contextualist of the nonperfectionist stripe. It is true that many realists have misread Machiavelli's *The Prince* as saying that "the end justifies the means" and that international politics being what it is—a kind of "dog-eat-dog" contest—one has to take a cynical, amoral stance toward the problem of selecting means to pursue foreign policy objectives. Those who oversimplify Machiavelli's position in this way may be referred to as the *vulgar realists*— "vulgar" because they have misunderstood and distorted his realist approach to international politics. Actually, as Kenneth Waltz and Michael Walzer have emphasized, Machiavelli attached important qualifications to his advice to the ruler. Thus, Machiavelli says that *not all ends,* but only some ends, justify morally dubious means; they must be constructive, beneficent ends.

An even more important qualification is Machiavelli's additional caveat that whether unsavory, morally questionable means are justified depends upon what he calls "the necessity of the case"—that is, whether in a given situation there are no alternative modes of action that promise success in achieving the constructive end. The realist position on this issue has been developed further by academic theorists such as Morgenthau and Wolfers who defend the original realist position and distinguish it from the oversimplified, distorted views of the vulgar realists.

The amoralist and the perfectionist positions can be implemented much more easily than the situational ethics which are supposed to guide the realists. Thus, the perfectionist operates with a flat prohibition against using morally dubious methods even on behalf of the most virtuous ends. The amoralist's rule of action is exactly the opposite and almost as easy to apply: any means, however immoral, is acceptable so long as it promises success and is efficient. In contrast, it is impossible to convert the nonperfectionist point of view into simple rules of action that give explicit and clear-cut guidance to the decision maker. Since so much depends on the specific circumstances of the case, nonperfectionists can formulate only very general guidelines for decision making. Four such guidelines have been spelled out by Arnold Wolfers, and in listing them now it will become obvious why they are best regarded as general guidelines rather than specific rules for correct behavior.

The first is that the objective of a foreign policy action must be genuinely constructive and praiseworthy if the decision maker is even to consider choosing morally dubious methods on its behalf. Some would say that, if this guideline is taken seriously by the policy maker, then he would use force only to defend the truly "vital interests" of the nation.

The second is that morally dubious means should not be employed when less dubious means that may achieve the same objective are available.

Third, a statesman should choose that course of action which, in the given circumstances, promises to cause the least destruction of things of value.

Finally, the statesman who attempts to apply situational ethics in making difficult decisions of this kind should be constrained in the choice of means— particularly when military force is employed—by what theologians have referred to as the "principle of proportionality." This is an enjoinder to the effect that the dubious means employed must at least have a rational relationship to the ends pursued. In practice, this requires the statesman to avoid profligate use of force that will inflict more loss of life and more damage than is necessary or congruent with what is at stake. It will be recalled that American war policies in Vietnam were severely criticized, even among those who were not totally opposed to U.S. objectives, on the grounds that they grossly violated the principle of proportionality. The military means employed by U.S. forces and the enormous destruction they wrought were felt to be out of any conceivable proportion to the American interests involved.

II

What is the practical utility of the four guidelines offered by nonperfectionists for dealing with moral dilemmas arising from the use of force as an instrument of foreign policy? They are relevant and better than no guidance at all as to how situational ethics apply in practice, but nonetheless it must be recognized that their vagueness permits considerable subjectivity and elasticity in the way in which they are likely to be employed. The guidelines may have some useful effect, particularly where policy makers are not unduly pressed, but there is no guarantee whatsoever that they will force even those decision makers who subscribe to them to give conscientious attention and adequate weight to moral considerations in determining their foreign policies and actions.

Most policy makers and their advisers in a country like the United States probably regard themselves as practitioners of the nonperfectionist approach. But they generally apply it in very subjective, loose, and highly inconsistent ways, and they do so not only because these guidelines are so vague but because other pressures on policy making are often so much stronger than the force of moral considerations. The decision maker is under pressure to protect and advance his country's position in world affairs, even when vital national interests are not at stake; he is under pressure to achieve results and to be successful in foreign affairs; and he is usually concerned also to protect his personal political interests and those of his party, and to win elections. Considerations of this kind tend to have greater importance for most policy makers than what may seem to them to be an overly squeamish concern with the morality of the means employed. It is all too easy for decision makers to justify their resort to morally questionable means, to engage in self-deception, and to offer convenient rationalizations as to the necessity to do so.

Certainly it is the case that so long as more stringent guidelines for employing situational ethics are lacking, the policy maker can easily end by believing that results are more important than the moral purity of his actions. When hard-pressed by the exigencies and political controversies that surround his performance, the statesman tends to fall back to a last line of defense, arguing that the ultimate justification for what he has done is whether it turns out to be successful. Leaders of many different persuasions have at least one thing in common: they prefer to be judged by "history" when their compatriots render harsh judgments. Unfortunately, ample precedents—some of them highly respectable—are available to be called upon by leaders caught in such circumstances. It was, after all, Abraham Lincoln who on one occasion responded to criticism by stating that "if the end brings me out all right, what is said against me won't amount to anything. If the end brings me out wrong, ten angels swearing I was right would make no difference." This may be a good political argument—certainly it appealed to President Nixon, who quoted Lincoln to justify his highly controversial invasion of Cambodia, and to Bert Lance, director of the Office of Management and Budget in the Carter administration, who also quoted Lincoln when defending his unusual financial transactions before a Senate committee—but it remains a questionable approach to political morality.

Given the limitations of the nonperfectionist approach and the fact that nonetheless many statesmen will continue to make use of it, it is perhaps appropriate to end with a good word for the moral perfectionists—those persons who have an irrepressible tendency to express moral condemnation of this, that, and almost every aspect of foreign policy. While their preachments are often irritating and naively impractical, we should still appreciate the contribution they make to public debates about foreign policy. For their criticisms are a valuable reminder that foreign policy is often imperfect from a moral standpoint, and they provide a useful safeguard against the tendency of practical men to engage in moral self-deception. It is often forgotten that Machiavelli, even while advising the prince that circumstances would force him to use morally questionable means on behalf of worthwhile goals, also remarked that it was important that the prince should know that he was doing so and that he should suffer a bad conscience so that moral values would at least survive their violation.

Bibliographical Essay

The role of ethics and morality in international relations is closely related to that of religion and law. Among the most important recent books on these subjects are Robert W. McElroy, *Morality and American Foreign Policy: The Role of Ethics in International Affairs* (Princeton, 1992), whose case studies have been drawn upon in the text; Douglas Johnston and Cynthia Simpson, eds., *Religion: The Missing Dimension of Statecraft* (New York, 1994), a collection of case studies of largely successful interventions by religious groups and leaders in critical situations; David A. Welch, *Justice and the Genesis of War* (New York, 1993); and Geoffrey Best, *War and Law Since 1945* (Oxford, 1994), an impressive study of what might be called humanitarian law and its attempts to restrain excesses of violence.

The older literature is still relevant to contemporary problems. See particularly Arnold Wolfers's essay "Statemanship and Moral Choice," in his book *Discord and Collaboration* (Baltimore, 1962), and Michael Walzer "Political Action: The Problem of Dirty Hands," *Philosophy and Public Affairs* 2 (1973): 160–180. See also Kenneth Waltz, *Man, the State and War* (New York, 1954), pp. 210–217; Hans Morgenthau, *Politics Among Nations,* 4th ed. (New York, 1967), chap. 1; Michael Walzer, *Just and Unjust Wars* (New York, 1977); Stanley Hoffmann, *Duties Beyond Borders: On the Limits and Possibilities of Ethical International Politics* (Syracuse, 1981); and Sissela Bok, *Lying: Moral Choice in Public and Private Life* (New York, 1979).

Useful essays expressing various points of view appear in Ernest W. Lefever, ed., *Ethics and World Politics* (Baltimore, 1972), and Kenneth Thompson, ed., *Moral Dimensions of American Foreign Policy* (New Brunswick, N.J., 1984). The problem is viewed from the standpoint of political theory in Charles Beitz, *Political Theory and International Relations* (Princeton, 1979). The question of the morality of nuclear weapons is the subject of intensive debate; for the effort of a leading specialist on national security to deal with the issue, see Joseph S. Nye, Jr., *Nuclear Ethics* (New York, 1986), which also contains a useful bibliography.

Epilogue
Some Reflections on the
Diplomatic Revolution

This book has dealt with the attempts made by Western governments since the emergence of the modern state in the seventeenth century to limit and control interstate violence by devising viable international systems. The most effective of their experiments was the European balance-of-power system in the first half of the nineteenth century. Some of its forms and principles still influence contemporary international affairs, although the system as such was undermined and effectively destroyed by complex political, economic, military, and ideological developments in the late nineteenth and twentieth centuries—a "diplomatic revolution" that destroyed its homogeneity and effectiveness. Since World War I, statesmen have endeavored to devise a new international system that would no longer be confined to Europe. Their failure to do so was perhaps the most important cause of World War II.

The relative success of the European balance-of-power system was due to its decentralized and self-regulating nature, which assumed that all of the major actors (normally five in number) had equal responsibility for maintaining it. All of the great powers understood that they were essential players in the system, and that, while rivalry and competition among them was legitimate, it was their prime responsibility to limit and manage such friction in the interest of preserving the system and the independent existence of its members. The accepted conditions for the maintenance and viability of the system may be defined as follows:

1. The collaboration of all (at that time five) great powers, and the recognition that they should be roughly equal in power;
2. Agreement on simple criteria of state power;
3. The execution and administration of foreign policy by professional diplomats;

4. The determination of foreign policy solely by considerations of national interest and security;

5. Agreement that war was an extension of politics and hence a legitimate instrument of foreign policy but subject to limitation and control by the Concert of Europe, that is, the great powers speaking in behalf of the national community;

6. Willingness on the part of all great powers to employ diplomatic means and, if necessary, force of arms against any of their number who sought hegemony or preponderance, thus threatening to undermine or subvert the balance of power; and

7. Cultural homogeneity, manifested in the language and values of the ruling classes and the diplomatic establishment.

The diplomatic revolution eroded both the conditions and the norms that supported the classical European system. Developments in technology and science revolutionized transportation, communications, and the art of warfare; the emergence of mass political parties and of special interest groups rendered domestic peace more precarious and made it more difficult for governments to pursue coherent and consistent policies as in the past; and the rise of new ideologies and extreme forms of nationalism tended to increase international friction and dispute. As the international community became more conflict prone, the homogeneity of the diplomatic community deteriorated. As the new technologies of war became more difficult to control, diplomats and statesmen lost faith in the norms, procedures, and modalities that had maintained the flexibility and viability of the balance-of-power system in the past. Increasingly also foreign affairs fell into the hands of popularly elected heads of state who were more sensitive to the currents of domestic politics and public opinion.

The drastic impact of this diplomatic revolution on the classical European system is summarized in Table 2.

World War I marked the final collapse of the old system, which had been deteriorating ever since 1890. After the end of that dreadful conflict, strenuous efforts were made to construct a new international system (chapters 4 and 7), but these failed, and the failure contributed to the coming of World War II and, shortly after the ending of hostilities in 1945, the inception of the Cold War. In a curious way this essentially ideological conflict produced its own primitive international system, largely, we must suppose, because of the enormity of the nuclear threat. In any event, during the Cold War, certain restraints and norms emerged in the evolution of Western–Soviet relations that were generally adhered to, introducing a modicum of order, predictability, and stability. In chapter 9, this Cold War system is described as possessing three features of older systems: a tacit agreement on fundamental aims, a bipolar structure, and some important rules or norms. Despite the conflict-laden atmosphere of the

Table 2. *The Impact of the Diplomatic Revolution on the Classical European International System*

Critical System Variables	Classical System: Conditions for Maintenance and Performance	Breakdown of Classical System Due to New Developments
1. Structure and configuration of power	Multipolar (at least 5 major powers)	Increasing rigidities of alliance systems in pre-WWI gradually transform system into a virtual bipolar system
2. Basis of a state's power	Criteria of power were simple and stable enough to permit reasonably accurate estimates that could serve as basis for policy for a period of time	Rendered complex and unstable by revolution in military and other technology
3. Control of state policy	By statesmen and skilled professional diplomats free to make policy changes with secrecy and dispatch	Increasing diplomatic role of state leaders; demands for "democratic control"; influence of organized interests; role of public opinion
4. Criteria for conduct of interstate relations, formation of alliances, rearrangements of state boundaries	Power calculations alone; no ideological or nationalist constraints on boundary drawing or on formation or reversibility of alliances	Reduced flexibility due to rise of nationalism and ideological passion
5. Image of war	War seen as imaginable, controllable, usable—that is, serious enough to stimulate preventive measures, but mild enough to enable statesmen to invoke threat and/or occasional resort to force	Unprecedented destructive military capabilities; increased attractiveness of offensive strategy and premium on first strike; strains on capability for crisis management
6. Nature of permissible/feasible war objectives	Objectives limited through self-restraint derived from commitment to preserve system, and as result of undeveloped military technology	Military capabilities make possible more ambitious objectives
7. Leverage for achieving balance/equilibrium	Reversal of alliances; also, one major actor should be able to play role of "holder of balance," if necessary	Diplomatic flexibility reduced by fear of internal political instability; all major actors committed to rival coalitions, seemingly balanced

Cold War, the minimal agreement on aims, structure, norms, and procedures enabled the West and the Soviet Union to act with appropriate prudence to regulate their rivalry and temper their mutual distrust sufficiently to avoid a third world war.

The close brush with thermonuclear disaster during the Cuban missile crisis of 1962 catalyzed the beginnings of a joint search for a new international system that might end the Cold War or at least modify it in ways that would reduce the potential for disaster. In the period of détente (chapter 10), the Western powers and the Soviet Union wrestled with the difficulty of reaching agreement on the meaning of détente and how it would affect their continued rivalry and the extent of their cooperation. The unexpected dissolution of the Soviet empire and the subsequent breakup of the Soviet Union ended the debate, while at the same time confronting all governments with new challenges, as well as new opportunities for working toward the construction of some kind of a new international system.

How is one to characterize the present condition of the international system, and is it possible to project its possible development? Any attempt to answer these questions should begin perhaps with the observation that the new multipolarity that has emerged with the end of the Cold War is as strikingly different from the multipolarity of the European system after 1815 as the bipolarity of the Cold War was different from the bipolarity of the years 1907–1914. The contemporary manifestation of multipolarity is a much more asymmetrical structure than the earlier one, with only one superpower and many states of lesser though substantial strength and resources, some older ones and some newer, such as Germany, Japan, India, and Brazil. As a result—to take only one example of the resulting anomalies—the structure of the Security Council of the United Nations, in which permanent membership and the power of veto are given to the United States, Russia, Great Britain, France, and China, no longer reflects the power realities within the international community and, therefore, some appropriate restructuring of that body will, sooner or later, be necessary.

World Economy and World Society

In addition to these changes in relative power distribution among states, major economic and cultural developments are having an impact on international society. As Carl Kaysen recently noted, "the rapidity and scope of transformation in the world scene over the past seven or eight years [since the end of the Cold Warcb; is unparalleled." The breakup of the Soviet empire was followed almost immediately by the collapse of the Soviet Union itself. Other dramatic changes include the spread of democratic, quasi-democratic, and "populist" government.

One speaks now of the "globalization" of the world economy, a development stimulated and made possible by the continuing technological revolution in transportation and communication. The world economy, as Kaysen notes, has become much more compact and no country of importance remains untouched by and uninvolved in it. "One consequence of these changes . . . is the relative decline of North America and Western Europe in the world economic balance and the relative increase in the weight of newly-industrialized, but still not rich, countries, especially in East Asia." Another consequence is the diminished scope of state sovereignty. "In economic matters, there are many areas in which states are powerless to achieve their goals by acting alone."

Alongside this development of a world economy, Kaysen notes, is the development of a world society. Noteworthy and novel is the remarkable worldwide mobility of business elites, governmental elites, academic elites, elites of sports and of popular as well as high cultures. Another enormously significant element in the creation of world society is the much-heralded globalization of news via CNN and other channels. As a result, "awareness of distant events is no longer confined to the very small and sophisticated audiences."

Last, but not least, in the emerging world society are nongovernmental organizations (NGOs) which continue to grow in number, scope, and influence. Many of these NGOs have worldwide objectives and seek a variety of goals ranging from humanitarian objectives to environmental protection.

Together, these newly important elements, Kaysen observes, "contribute to the creation of a new kind of international society and the inter-penetration of national and international politics."

Conflict Management and Conflict Resolution in the Post–Cold War Era

Conflict management and resolution have long been a concern of statesmen in the history of diplomacy. Indeed, in the European balance-of-power system statesmen had at their disposal a variety of techniques for regulating and moderating their rivalry. Some of these techniques can perhaps be adapted to contemporary problems if the different contexts in which they arise are understood. Concern with conflict management and resolution is especially urgent now because rapid changes in the international arena have spawned new and often unanticipated conflicts. Many of these conflicts arise from multiethnic tensions and historic antipathies and have erupted in geographic areas where wars would have been unthinkable a few years ago. Fewer of them are inspired, as in the recent past, by an ideological struggle between capitalist and communist states.

*Intra*state conflicts now vastly outnumber the more conventional *inter*state type of conflict. Moreover, the dynamics of many of these conflicts do not follow the old rules, and knowledge from past experience may not be easily or fully transferable.

There is increasing recognition that ways must be found to deal with and head off simmering intra- and interstate conflicts *before* they erupt into large-scale violence after which it becomes much more difficult for members of the international community to muster the political will and resources needed for effective peacemaking. The importance of "preventive diplomacy," recognized and practiced by statesmen in the classical European system, has been rediscovered. There is much talk inside and outside the United Nations and indeed increasingly in Washington of the need for "early warning" of such conflicts and, in response to it, for prompt and effective measures to contain them at an early stage. Accompanying the renewed interest in preventive diplomacy is the effort to understand better, in order to make better use of, confidence-building measures, mediation, "Track-Two" diplomacy by nongovernmental actors, peacekeeping, and peacemaking.

Complex Interdependence: Implications for the International System

Today's world is influenced to a greater extent than ever before by complex forms of interdependence between states and people, particularly in the economic sphere, but also extending increasingly into life-essential ecological and biospheric systems. Perhaps no single event brought home the grim lesson of interdependence more forcefully than the disaster of the Chernobyl nuclear power reactor in the Ukraine, the dangerous fall-out from which extended into many states in Europe.

The growth of interdependence provides incentives for cooperation among states and, at least potentially, imposes constraints on some of the traditional forms of competition and rivalry. Interdependence is forcing important modifications of traditional "realist" premises regarding the essential characteristics of international systems and politics. Thus, the long-standing assumption that states are the dominant actors in world politics has been challenged by the growth in numbers and strength of nongovernmental actors such as multinational firms engaging in international transactions more or less independently of governments. The related realist assumption that states act as coherent units in international relations is also being substantially modified in view of the fact that subunits of different national governments tend increasingly to interact directly with each other on specific matters engaging their specialized responsibilities, sometimes with little direction or control by their own governmental leaders. This was true, for example, of aspects of the development of relations between the two Germanies in the years prior to German reunification.

Also called into question is the long-standing realist belief that the "high politics" of military security dominates the "low politics" of economic and social concerns. Nonmilitary issues—for example, international monetary policies, problems of trade, and commodity prices—have assumed vastly greater importance in interstate relations to the point that the hierarchy of issues for a country's foreign policy is not always dominated by questions of national security defined in military terms.

The traditional realist assumption that force is a usable and effective instrument of foreign policy also needs considerable qualification, especially as regards the major powers. There is increasing evidence of the declining efficiency of military power and threats of force as a means for settling conflicts between superpowers, and not merely because nuclear weapons have limited use for everyday diplomacy. The great powers in turn, feel new constraints against the use of force as an instrument of policy against lesser powers. Middle-rank and "weak" states, however, with increasingly easy access to sophisticated conventional weapons, continue to make considerable—some would say growing—use of military force in efforts to achieve their foreign policy objectives.

As the relevance and utility of force as a means of settling conflicts of interest decline, the distribution of nonmilitary forms of power and influence among states within specific issue areas becomes important. In other words, military power is less fungible across different issues than it used to be. Attempts by strong states to employ their military superiority as leverage to obtain better outcomes in specialized nonmilitary issue areas such as fisheries and prices for oil or coffee are less effective and are less often resorted to.

All this will doubtless influence the future structure of the international system and will encourage the creation of new modalities for managing the overlapping interests of its members. Progress in structuring and managing relations among states often proceeds in an ad hoc, issue-specific way. Some problems of mutual interest have been dealt with by setting up formal international organizations, for example, the World Health Organization, the International Postal Union, and the International Atomic Agency. In addition, states directly interested in a particular problem adopt a variety of looser, less formalized arrangements. Such arrangements—or *regimes,* as they are often called—typically include a set of procedures and substantive rules worked out by the interested parties for regulating their relationship in a given issue area. Since World War II, specific regimes have been developed to guide states and nongovernmental actors in a wide variety of issue areas, including aid to less developed countries; environmental protection; fisheries conservation; regulation of multinational corporations; international meteorological coordination; food, shipping, telecommunications, and monetary policy; and, of course, regulation of trade. Regimes vary in the formality, comprehensiveness, scope, and effectiveness of the arrangements made.

The increasing use by states of regimes to structure and order their relations is one of the most interesting and hopeful developments in contemporary world politics. While the creation of a viable world government continues to be infeasible, regimes can provide some of the functions of world government. In creating a regime, the interested parties in effect are exercising a *legislative* function. Regimes are a partial substitute for a central world government, which, were it to exist, would be expected to legislate and administer such arrangements for dealing with specific problems.

We can hope that with the proliferation of regimes and a continuation of the trend toward complex interdependence, the world can move toward a more comprehensive structure that will cut across the major groupings of states and subsystems and will eventually provide some kind of more closely knit international community. We can also hope that if such a development gathers momentum, the network of constructive relationships into which states are drawn and the mutual benefits they derive from their participation will dampen the potential for conflict in those of their competitive relationships that remain inadequately managed.

While this encouraging prospect has some basis in identifiable trends and untapped opportunities present in the world today, further progress in this direction will be at best slow and uncertain. Movement toward a more viable, stable, and peaceful world order is certain to proceed quite unevenly within and among the various regional groupings of developed and underdeveloped states, for conflicts of interest not only run across regional lines—in the form, for example, of "North-South" disputes over financial and material resources or contests between the oil-producing lands of the Middle East and their Western customers—but also affect intraregional relations, causing differences between European Union members on agricultural policy, dividing Arab states with respect to their attitude toward Israel, and causing rivalries and clashes between states in Africa or in South and Southeast Asia. The world system will continue to be plagued by dangerous crises, war, and threats of war. Weaker states and their peoples may become increasingly marginalized, left to their own devices by more capable states who find themselves unable or unwilling to commit the resources needed to prevent large-scale human and social catastrophes in lesser developed countries. As pessimistic commentators have warned, the world may become divided into a zone of relative peace, order, and economic sufficiency and a zone of chaos, violence, and starvation. If this bleak prospect materializes, one can hardly speak any longer of a single international system. The threat and the challenge is an immense one. The outcome cannot be confidently predicted.

Bibliographic Essay

The discussion of the emergence of a world economy and a world society draws from Carl Kaysen's "War, Peace and Politics: The U.S. and the New World Order," Working Paper no. 7, Center for International Relations, University of California, Los Angeles, February 1994. Many authors and commentators have written on emerging international patterns. See, for example, Seyom Brown, *New Forces, Old Forces, and the Future of World Politics* (Boston, 1988), and James Rosenau, *Turbulence in World Politics* (Princeton, 1990).

On the loss of American ascendancy within the international economy, the work of Robert Gilpin, *The Political Economy of International Relations* (Princeton, 1988) is important. See also Paul Kennedy, *The Rise and Fall of the Great Powers: Economic Change and Military Conflict From 1500 to 2000* (New York, 1987), pt. 7, and Robert O. Keohane, *After Hegemony* (Princeton, 1984).

The conflict avoidance and conflict management practices employed by statesmen in the European system are incisively described and illustrated by Paul Gordon Lauren, "Crisis Prevention in Nineteenth-Century Diplomacy," in *Managing U.S.–Soviet Rivalry: Problems of Crisis Prevention*, ed. Alexander L. George (Boulder, Colo., 1983). An early, influential analysis of the emergent phenomenon of complex interdependence was provided by Robert O. Keohane and Joseph S. Nye, *Power and Interdependence: World Politics in Transition* (Boston, 1977).

Index

Meetings, conferences, and treaties are indexed by keyword (i.e., Utrecht, Treaty of). Information on Germany is indexed under "Germany" for prepartition years, under "Germany, East" and "Germany, West" from partition to 1990, and under "Germany, unified" thereafter. References to figures are given in italics.